Army Regulars on the Western Frontier, 1848–1861

Army Regulars on the Western Frontier 1848–1861

DURWOOD BALL

University of Oklahoma Press : Norman

Library of Congress Cataloging-in-Publication Data

Ball, Durwood, 1960–

Army regulars on the western frontier, 1848–1861 / Durwood Ball.

p. cm.

Includes bibliographical references (p.) and index.

ISBN 0–8061–3312–0

1. West (U.S.)—History, Military—19th century. 2. United States. Army—History—19th century. 3. United States—Military policy—19th century. 4. Frontier and pioneer life—West (U.S.) 5. West (U.S.)—Race relations. 6. Indians of North America—Government relations—1789–1869. 7. Indians of North America—West (U.S.)—History—19th century. 8. Civil-military relations—West (U.S.)—History—19th century. 9. Violence—West (U.S.)—History—19th century. I. Title.

F593 .B18 2001

355′.00978′09034—dc21 00-047669

CIP

The paper in this book meets the guidelines for permanence and durability of the Committee on Production Guidelines for Book Longevity of the Council on Library Resources, Inc. ∞

Manufactured in the U.S.A.

1 2 3 4 5 6 7 8 9 10

For Mom, Dad, and Kristina

CONTENTS

ILLUSTRATIONS

FIGURES

following page 106

MAPS

TABLE

PREFACE

AT LAS VEGAS, New Mexico, 1st Lt. Henry B. Judd of the Third Artillery coldly received forty Jicarilla Apaches on 16 August 1849 and refused to trade with them for "powder and ball." He believed that these Indians had "falsely treated for peace at Taos" the previous year and invested Mora, Barclay Fort, and other settlements along the eastern frontier afterward. After dismissing them, the lieutenant decided to "seize" them and ordered 2nd Lt. Ambrose E. Burnside's company to "procede" to the Apaches' camp ten miles to the south.[1]

When Judd, Burnside, and the regulars rode in, the Apaches were in the saddle to meet them. Under Judd's instruction, the local prefect rode forward into their leveled lances, muskets, and bows and vainly harangued the Apaches to forego the lethal consequences of flight or resistance. As the prefect trotted back, Burnside deployed his regulars, probably men of the Third Artillery astride horses, into line and advanced to within "short range," but the Jicarillas turned to flee.

Burnside halted his line, and the Jicarillas suddenly wheeled to deliver "a flight of missiles from their bows and rifles." The twenty-five-year-old second lieutenant ordered a "charge as skirmishers," and the regulars drew sabers and swept forward. Slowed by "hills" and "ravines," some Apaches turned to fight "hand to hand." Over some nine miles, the regulars cut them down. Judd figured that only "8 to 10" escaped and added, "Many of the dead remain in the ravines where they were sabred." The only federal casualties were wounds to Burnside and a sergeant.[2]

Saber charges were the exception in nineteenth-century frontier combat, but armed force, actual and threatened, was commonplace in the interwar American West, the unincorporated frontier beyond the Missouri River and western Missouri, Arkansas, and Louisiana between the Mexican-American and Civil Wars. At the end of the conflict with Mexico, the army undertook an old mission on frontiers new to the United States: occupying territory; suppressing American Indian resistance; keeping the peace among feuding Indians, Hispanos, and Anglos; and consolidating United States sovereignty regionwide. As regular troops fanned out across the American West in 1848 and 1849, the diverse inhabitants intensified their competition for natural resources, political autonomy, and cultural survival. Their contests often erupted in violence that sucked the army into riot duty and bloody war.

This book examines the full continuum of martial force in the American West. The United States government called the post–Mexican-American War army a "peace establishment," treated its regulars as a federal police force, and labeled the army's frontier mission *constabulary duty*, which benignly meant keeping order and enforcing law. However, in the antebellum West, the army's field duty was rarely peaceful, generally dangerous, and often violent. Whether "chastising" Indians, quelling civil unrest, or ejecting trespassers, regular troops represented the militant will of the United States government and inflicted or threatened violence to coerce frontier peoples. The deployment of the standing army implied the anticipation of armed resistance that would overwhelm unescorted civilian law-enforcement officers but that federal regulars—professional men of violence—would overcome.

Frontier military historians have generally treated armed war and civil interventions as unrelated missions.[3] However, the Indian wars, political riots, and frontier lawlessness were threats to United States internal security, and the deployment of regular troops implied the breakdown of political negotiation or civil law and the anticipation of extraordinary armed violence. When waging war on indigenous peoples or suppressing public riot, the object was to establish United States sovereignty and force obedience to federal law. In the American West, the regular army was a federal agency deployed to assist the incorporation of frontier peoples, lands, and resources into the cultural, political, and economic system of the United States.

Federal regulars inflicted state-sanctioned violence inequitably in the American West. Citizenship, overlaid with race, was their measuring stick. American Indians enjoyed neither citizenship nor political rights, and United

States law protected them indifferently from Euroamerican assault. Anglo Americans incompletely accepted the citizenship of Hispanos living in the Mexican Cession. After the passage of the Compromise of 1850, Congress formally declared neither war on Indians, Mormons, Hispanos, or Anglos nor martial law in their homelands, territories, or states, but under executive order regulars waged war routinely on American Indians and sporadically on Hispanos and intervened repeatedly against social rebels, political dissidents, and armed brigands of all ethnicities.

Race, culture, and law protected white settlers. The U.S. Army—comprised exclusively of free white men when they enlisted or were commissioned in the service—envisioned itself as the sharp edge of Manifest Destiny, the Anglo-Saxon mission, divinely inspired, to spread Euroamerican civilization over North America. The officer corps hoped for an honorable conquest but assumed that the white race was destined to settle and develop the continent. Under the command of white officers, federal troops might police but would never interdict the frontier onslaught. In national mythology, the professional standing army occupied no firm place, and the U.S. Congress still distrusted the regular establishment. Martial violence against Anglo citizens would have destroyed what little credibility and toleration the army enjoyed. The president could and did deploy the federal military to maintain domestic order, but the Constitution made clear that the primary role of national military forces was to defend the United States against foreign enemies. Waging war on whites was generally forbidden.

Throughout the interwar period, churning through the East, the politics of slavery spilled into the new states and territories of the American West and helped trigger civil riot and mayhem on the frontier. Like federal executives before them, interwar presidents Zachary Taylor, Millard Fillmore, Franklin Pierce, and James Buchanan deployed their regulars as a heavily armed constabulary to contain or quell political unrest and social upheaval. The politics of slavery did not dictate federal action in the American West, but every interwar president figured sectional party politics into his legal response to frontier disorder, and the growing crisis shadowed all frontier commanders who deployed regular troops against civil lawlessness.[4]

Interwar civil constabulary duty in the West politically destabilized the regular army. As the slavery controversy stressed the Union, it also weakened the morale and cohesion of the officer corps. Frontier soldiering was lonely, aggravating, and punishing in good times; it became embarrassing and sometimes unbearable in the sectional cauldron. The effects of sectional politics in the field often humiliated professional soldiers and weakened their bond to the army, president, and Union. In the antebellum army, professionalism did not always translate into Union loyalty. Forging the two as one would require four years of Civil War bloodletting.

Federal regulars—commissioned officers and enlisted men—were remarkable soldiers in an extraordinary geographical, political, and human environment, the interwar American West. During thirteen turbulent years, they were both unwitting victims and conscientious agents of national policies and party politics that ultimately cleaved the United States in two in 1861. Although well underway by the Mexican-American War, the professionalization of the officer corps had not completely dampened political tempers during the interwar years. Despite their protestations of surprise and dismay at the sectional schism, commissioned officers harbored charged and violent political opinions, which they disguised as sentimental sectional loyalties in post–Civil War memoirs and reminiscences. In a way that no other history of the antebellum military does, *Army Regulars* traces the sharp edge of slavery politics slicing its way through the interwar regular army. Most of that story unfolded in the trans-Mississippi West.[5]

The temporal shutter of this study opens at the end of Mexican-American War and closes during the early months of the Civil War. The narrative eye follows the regular army as it explores, polices, and wages war in the United States's vast new western domain. The analytical focus frames the dynamics between soldiers, region, violence, and politics. During the interwar years, all four actively shaped the army's frontier experience.

I have divided the historical narrative into three parts. After the Prologue, Part One explores the army's perceptions, strategy, and tactics in its conflicts with the American Indians and the institutional army—the enlisted ranks, the officer corps, and army and sectional politics—prior to the secession crisis. Part Two traces the army's constabulary mission on the international borders of the Pacific Ocean and the Rio Grande. Part Three recounts the civil interventions during the Mormon Rebellion and Bleeding Kansas, ending with the breakup of the army and the Union in the early days of Southern secession and the Civil War. The Conclusion wraps up the story of the interwar regular army.

ACKNOWLEDGMENTS

I wish to thank numerous individuals, organizations, and institutions for their assistance during the long march toward this book. Paul Andrew Hutton has been my faithful professor, advisor, and friend throughout this project. He encouraged me to tackle the sweeping history of the interwar army at the dissertation stage, and I have never regretted the challenge. His letters of recommendation helped me secure research funding from the University of New Mexico Department of History and the Huntington Library. Paul's superb historical writing on the frontier army, particularly *Phil Sheridan and His Army*, has inspired the research and writing in *Army Regulars*. Completing this history would have been impossible without his unfailing support and constant encouragement.

I also wish to thank Richard N. Ellis, now professor of history at Fort Lewis College in Durango, Colorado, for introducing me to frontier military history. At the University of New Mexico, he guided the research and writing of my master's thesis on the military intervention in Bleeding Kansas. His own research on the frontier army has influenced a subsequent generation to ask new questions of the military experience in the American West. I hope that this book is worthy of following in his footsteps.

It has been a delight to work with the staff at the University of Oklahoma Press. Director John Drayton encouraged me to submit the manuscript; Randy Lewis saw it through peer review; and Jean Hurtado advised and encouraged me during the last stages of review and revision. Kevin Brock heroically copyedited the final manuscript and saved me from committing embarrassing errors to print. Glenda Madden and the Sales and Marketing Department have been wonderful to work with in publicizing and selling the book. I deeply appreciate everyone's hard work at the press during all stages of the publication process.

Several other individuals also invested their time in *Army Regulars*. Kristina E. Kachele designed the elegant interior and classic exterior. Thom Ross painted the delightful and striking cover illustration. Deborah Reade transformed my raw cartographical data into the four lovely maps illustrating the military geography of the West. I deeply appreciate their individual contributions, which add immeasurable value to the book.

Many other present and former faculty in the University of New Mexico Department of History shepherded my own development into a historian. In addition to Richard N. Ellis, Gerald Nash and Peter Kolchin oversaw my master's thesis on army intervention in Kansas Territory during the 1850s. Melvin Yazawa and Margaret Connell-Szasz graciously served on my dissertation committee. I also studied with or assisted other historians: Richard Etulain, Jane Slaughter, the late Howard Rabinowitz, Ferenc Szasz, Noel Pugach, Charles McClellan, Robert Kern, and William Roberts. Three different chairs in the department of history aided my academic career: Janet Roebuck, Jonathan Porter, and Richard Robbins. The department subvented my course of study and granted me the Dorothy Woodward Memorial Fellowship, which funded a year of dissertation research and writing.

The Henry E. Huntington Library brought me to San Marino, California, in summer 1989. My sincere appreciation goes to Dr. Martin Ridge, the director of research at the time. He is a gentleman, scholar, and friend in the profoundest sense. The many western and Civil War historians at the Huntington were a delight to engage: John Reid, William Deverell, David Gutierrez, Ann Hyde, and many others. I would like to single out two Huntington scholars in particular: the late Wilbur Jacobs became a good friend and inspired tennis partner, and Charles Royster, professor of history at Louisiana State University, initiated me to the rich history of the American Civil War.

The University of New Mexico Library has aided my research in innumerable ways. The staff of Interlibrary Loan tracked down many rare books and articles for me. The archivists at the Center for Southwest Research weekly retrieved paper collections, microfilm, and books. My sincere thanks goes to Ann Massman, Nancy Brown, Stella Desarego, and Teresa Marquez. The personnel in Government Information have graciously retrieved volume after volume of the Congressional Serial Set during my decade and a half of research on this project.

The staffs at the Library of Congress and National Archives in Washington, D.C., assisted with numerous documents and record collections. I wish to thank Michael Musick in the Military Records Division at the archives. His staff is the hardest working outfit in the federal government. At the National Archives branch in Chicago, Scott Forsythe generously shared his expertise in frontier military history.

The University of New Mexico Press has been a rich and rewarding source of personal support and professional development. Director Beth Hadas hired me as a student editorial assistant in summer 1987 and later promoted me to acquisitions editor. Over the past decade, former and current staff members encouraged me to pursue my passion for editing and writing. I would particularly like to thank Associate Director David Holtby, who enthusiastically served on my dissertation committee, mentored me in academic editing, and has supported my research and writing. His friendship has been one of the most rewarding in my life.

Nancy Coggeshall, former exhibit and advertising manager at the press, got after me to finish the dissertation and the book from the time we first met in 1990. No one loves the American West more than she does, and her daily embrace of life is an ongoing inspiration.

Many friends and colleagues have warmly and patiently weathered this long writing campaign. I never could have undertaken and completed this book without their encouragement and support: Claudia Clopton, Katherine Carley, Lenny Barnette, Michael Stanfield, Maria Montoya, Jim Brannen, Kevin Fernlund, Charles Rankin, Bart Barbour, Jennifer Wiley, Liping Zhu, Melissa Bokovoy, Jane Slaughter, David Farber, Beth Bailey, Sam Truett, Tim Moy, Rebecca Ullrich, Virginia Scharff, Peter Swift, Jack Wilson, Bruce Dinges, Jonathan Abrams, Fred and Joanne Chreist, and others.

As an editor, I have made professional contacts who have become good friends. Jerry Thompson, dean of humanities at Texas A&M International, has shared his research on Insp. Gen. Joseph K. F. Mansfield and Maj. Samuel Peter Heintzelman. Historian Mark Gardner has enthusiastically loaned me photographs and illustrations from his personal collection. I have enjoyed many long conversations with Louis Kraft and Fred Chiaventone on frontier military history and with Louis Hieb on western history.

A portion of chapter 5 of this book first appeared as an article in volume 28 of *Military History of the West* in fall 1998. I wish to extend my thanks to Richard Lowe, the journal's editor, who granted me permissoin to incorporate that material on the army in California. Likewise, a dollop of material in chapter 2 regulars waging war from Fort Craig, New Mexico—originally appeared in an article published in volume 73 of the *New Mexico Historical Review*.

Finally I wish to thank my family for its years of unwavering support and encouragement. My grandparents, Trafton and Beulah Mae Ball and Marion and Vera Lusk, have been a source of inspiration and fortitude. My only regret is that I did not complete this book before my Grandmother Lusk passed away. I can never thank Aunt Juanita Hamilton for her many years of encouragement. I would also like to thank Danny, Jan, Margo, Carolyn, Tommy, Brenda, Lisa, Mindy, and Mikki. To my newest family—Karen, Joe, and Terri—I extend my love and thanks. Howard Kachele, thank you for raising a beautiful daughter and letting her marry me.

Mom, Dad, and Kristina, there are no words to express the profound depth of my love and gratitude. Whatever strengths grace this book issue from your love, patience, and encouragement. Above and beyond the call, you soldiered with me through this project from dissertation to book. Thank you.

INTRODUCTION

ORGANIZE, DEPLOY, & MULTIPLY

IN late 1857 Secretary of War John B. Floyd pessimistically wrote, "If there is a higher duty than another devolved upon a well regulated government, it is to afford perfect protection to its citizens against outrages and personal violence; yet this great obligation is not performed by the government of the United States." With insufficient army manpower and budgets, the administration of Pres. James P. Buchanan had to stamp out political rebellion in Utah and Kansas, along with Indian uprisings in Texas, New Mexico, Oregon, Washington, and the Great Plains. Floyd's office learned weekly of some "Indian massacre" or other "outrage," but such heinous acts generally went "unpunished" from "the want of troops" or "their remoteness from the scenes of slaughter." On behalf of the Buchanan administration, the secretary of war pleaded to Congress for an increase of the U.S. Army by "five" full regiments.[1]

An imperial ambition of the United States in the 1850s was incorporating western lands and peoples into the nation. The American people believed that this continental expansion, Manifest Destiny, was God's will for Anglo-Saxon civilization.[2] In the new western territories, regional assimilation depended on the uninterrupted flow of people, money, and resources between the settlements of western Missouri, the Pacific Coast, and southern Texas, and the lightly populated frontiers of the interior West. Any disruption or blockade of principal roads by Indians, rebels, or outlaws would jeopardize the cultivation of the Euroamerican civilization in the West. The U.S. Army was the primary federal agency charged with sweeping roads and protecting settlements, but

Congress undermined its mission by strangling army personnel, materiel, and coffers.

The addition of Texas, New Mexico, California, and Oregon to the United States spurred few in Congress to enlarge the army. At the close of the Mexican-American War, lawmakers disbanded the volunteer regiments and legislated the regular army to prewar levels, a mere 9,852 commissioned officers and enlisted men. However, over the next thirteen years, civil riot and Indian wars forced Congress nearly to double the number of federal troops. Members authorized the president to enlarge companies serving on the frontier to 74 privates, raising army numbers—on paper—to 12,972 officers and men in 1850 and to 13,821 in 1853. The addition of four new regiments—two cavalry and two infantry—in 1855 boosted the legal aggregate to 17,867. However, Congress struck down the Buchanan administration's bid to create five new regiments in 1858 amid the Utah Expedition. At its peak on the eve of the Civil War, the legal size of the regular army stood at 18,615 officers and men, still too few to fulfill its frontier constabulary mission.[3]

Dominating military operations in the American West were the regular army's three principal combat arms—mounted troops, infantry, and artillery (see table 1). By 1855 the regimental breakdown of the army was the following: First and Second Regiments of Dragoons, Regiment of Mounted Riflemen, First and Second Regiments of Cavalry, First through Fourth Regiments of Artillery, and First through Tenth Regiments of Infantry. Congress legislated regimental strength as follows: Ten companies of fifty men each comprised a regiment of dragoons; ten companies of fifty men each, a regiment of cavalry; ten companies of sixty-four men each, a regiment of mounted rifles; twelve companies of forty-two men each, a regiment of artillery; and ten companies of forty-two men each, a regiment of infantry.[4]

In the interwar and post–Civil War American West, mounted troops—dragoons, mounted riflemen, and cavalry—became the dominant combat arm. In late 1850 Maj. Gen. Winfield Scott, commanding general of the army, explained, "The great extent of our frontiers, and the peculiar character of the service devolving on the troops, render it indispensable that the *cavalry* element should enter largely into the composition of the army." During the early years of the nation, the American people and the army had resisted the establishment of regular dragoon or cavalry regiments, which they associated with unrepublican European aristocracy, but in the West, foot soldiers were less mobile and lethal than cavalry in warfare with American Indian warriors mounted on fleet horses. Scott lobbied for two additional regiments of horse troops, which Secretary of War Jefferson Davis secured four years later.[5]

The mounted regiments bore different names and practiced eccentric regimental traditions, but almost no tactical or operational differences distinguished them in the western field. Throughout the West, each unit operated as heavily armed light cavalry from fixed stations. Dragoons, riflemen, and cavalry carried the Colt's revolver by mid-decade and rifled carbines by the Civil War. For the remainder of the nineteenth century, the horse soldiers bore the brunt of warfare with the Indians in the American West, while infantry and artillery troops tended and maintained the forts, outposts, and other fixed stations.[6]

In all combat arms, recruiting officers were unable to fill companies to legal capacity, and death, disease, and desertion reduced the ranks each year by one-quarter to one-third. The army's actual strength stood at 7,974 in 1849; 10,417 in 1853; 10,745 in 1854; 15,752 in 1855; and 16,006 in 1860. While the federal government manned its coastal and harbor fortifications largely with artillery troops, it posted three-quarters of the regulars to frontiers in the trans-Mississippi West. This tiny regular-army establishment explored, policed, and defended the vast interwar frontier.[7]

At the outbreak of the Mexican-American War, the United States military frontier was poised on the edge of the prairie West (see map 1). By 1846 the federal government had relocated nearly all Indian tribes east of the Mississippi River to reservations in Indian Territory, Iowa, and Wisconsin, creating what policymakers called the "Permanent Indian Frontier." With the administration of federal Indian policy in hands of the War Department before the Mexican-American War, the army enforced the Indian Intercourse Acts from its many frontier posts scattered from Fort Jesup in western Louisiana, to Fort Leavenworth on the right bank of the lower Missouri River, and Fort Snelling on the right bank of the upper Mississippi River.[8]

The annexation of Texas and Oregon and the conquest of New Mexico and California added 1.2 million square miles of new territory to the United States. In addition to fortifications on the Atlantic and Gulf coasts and on the border with Canada, the army had to occupy and police three major sections of the trans-Mississippi West: the prairies and plains; the Great Basin, Colorado Plateau, and Far Southwest; and the Pacific Coast and Northwest. The new defensive mission staggered the War Department. In 1857 Secretary of War Floyd graphically described the vast region: "From our western frontier of settlements [Missouri] to those of northern Oregon the distance is about 1,800 miles: from the same frontier to the settlements of California, *via* Salt Lake, is 1,800 miles; from the frontier of Arkansas, at Fort Smith, by Albuquerque or Santa Fe, to Fort Tejon, is about 1,700 miles; and from San Antonio, by El Paso, to San Diego, near the borders of the white settlements, is 1,400 miles; constituting an aggregate line of 6,700 miles which ought to be occupied, and which

Table of Organization
United States Army
Authorized Strength, 1855

	Commissioned Officers	Non-commissioned Officers	Privates	Total
General Officers	4			4
General Staff				
Adjutant General's Department	14			11[a]
Inspector General General's Department	2			2
Judge Advocate of the Army	1			0
Quartermaster's Department	37			31
Commissary General's Department	12			10
Medical Department	95			95
Pay Department	28			28
Corps of Engineers	43	22[b]	78[c]	143
Corps of Topographical Engineers	36			36
Ordnance Department	36	67[d]	250	353
Miliary Storekeepers				17
Line Regiments				
First and Second Regiments of Dragoons	70[e]	230[f]	1,000	1,300
Regiment of Mounted Riflemen	36	125	640	801
First and Second Regiments of Calvalry	70	230	1,000	1,300
First through Tenth Regiments of Infantry	340[g]	1,040[h]	4,200	5,580
First through Fourth Regiments of Artillery	208[i]	584[j]	2,192[k]	2,984
Total	1,032[l]	2,298	9,360	12,695[m]
Aggregate		12,690[n]		

Table of Organization
United States Army
Authorized Strength, 1855 *(continued)*

Sources:

This table of line and staff is taken from "Organization of the Army under the act of March 3, 1855" in Heitman, *Register*, 2:596–97. The layout of the table reflects the chart in Adj. Gen. Roger Jones to Sec. of War Charles M. Conrad, 28 November 1849, in RSW, SED 1, serial 549, 179.

[a]The general staff filled some of its slots with officers from line regiments. In this case, 3 assistant adjutant generals, 6 assistant quartermasters, and 2 commissaries of subsistence haled from the line and were counted in their regiment's total. A twelfth staff officer, the judge advocate, was commissioned in the Ordnance Department. These 12 officers are subtracted from the total of staff officers to avoid counting them twice.

[b]This noncommissioned total includes two musicians.

[c]The 100 noncommissioned officers and privates in the Corps of Engineers belonged to the Company of Engineer Soldiers, a combat engineering unit of "sappers, miners, and pontoniers" headquartered at the United States Military Academy. They were an elite unit in the enlisted corps.

[d]The number of ordnance sergeants could vary from year to year. According to law, each military post was entitled to one ordnance sergeant. In 1855 the total was 67.

[e]The officers for each mounted regiment were: 1 colonel, 1 lieutenant colonel, 2 majors, 10 captains, 10 first lieutenants, 10 second lieutenants, and 1 adjutant.

[f]The noncommissioned aggregate for mounted regiments also includes buglers and farrier-blacksmiths. The noncommissioned officers for each were: 1 regimental sergeant, 1 quartermaster sergeant, 1 chief musician, 2 chief buglers, 40 sergeants, 40 corporals, 20 buglers, and 10 farrier-blacksmiths. Congress legislated farrier-blacksmiths at 20 in the Regiment of Mounted Riflemen.

[g]The officers of an infantry regiment were: 1 colonel, 1 lieutenant colonel, 2 majors, 10 captains, 10 lieutenants, and 10 second lieutenants.

[h]The noncommissioned aggregate for infantry regiments includes musicians. The regimental noncommissioned officers were: 1 sergeant major, 1 quartermaster sergeant, 2 chief musicians, 40 sergeants, 40 corporals, and 20 musicians.

[i]The regimental officers of an artillery regiment were: 1 colonel, 1 lieutenant colonel, 2 majors, 12 captains, 24 first lieutenants, and 12 second lieutenants.

[j]The noncommissioned aggregate for artillery regiments includes musicians and artificers. The regimental noncommissioned officers were: 1 sergeant major, 1 quartermaster sergeant, 48 sergeants, 48 corporals, 24 musicians, and 24 artificers.

[k]The standard legal strength of an artillery company was forty-two privates. However, on 17 June 1850 Congress allowed the president to designate, in all four artillery regiments, two companies as light artillery, each with a compliment of sixty-four privates. These units were sent to the frontier, where they generally served as infantry. The aggregate of artillery privates, 2,192, incorporates the eight enlarged artillery companies.

[l]The total of commissioned officers does not include brevet second lieutenants, of which each company was allowed one and at this time totalled 199; the number fluctuated yearly.

[m]This sum contains twelve fewer staff officers but seventeen more military storekeepers than the sum of the first three columns (12,690).

[n]The act of 17 June 1850 empowered the president to raise the troop strength of mounted, infantry, and artillery companies serving on the frontier to 74 privates. In 1855 the commander-in-chief designated 181 companies elegible for the increase, thus raising the legal enlisted strength to 16,822 and the legal aggregate to 17,862 officers and enlisted men. If all 198 line companies were enlarged, the enlisted total would have been 17,278 and the legal aggregate 18,318 officers and enlisted men.

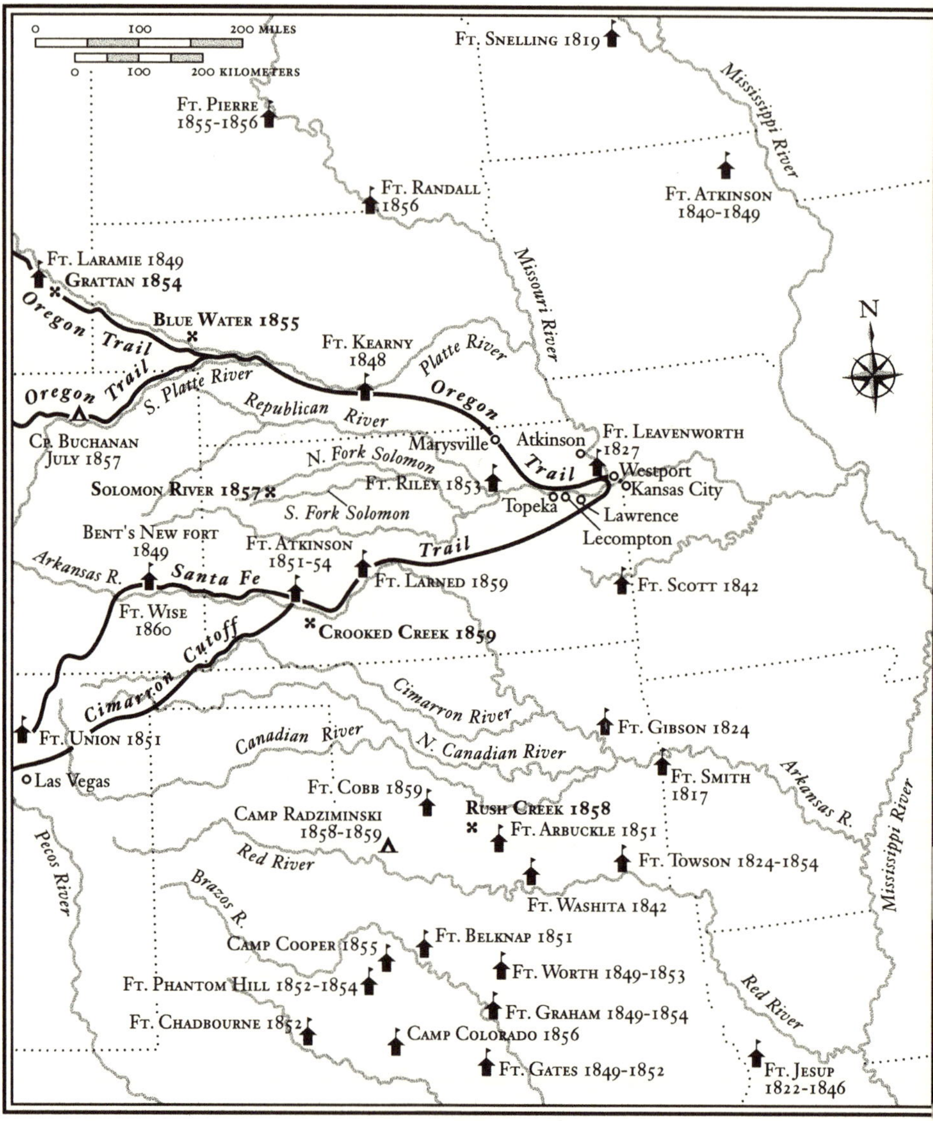

1. The Prairies and Plains

we pretend, in some sort, to keep open and defend." The frontier West was generally desert country that forced settlements into the river valleys and whose enormous spatial dimensions swallowed the manpower, materiel, and money of the tiny regular army.[9]

The U.S. Congress called the post–Mexican-American War army a peacetime establishment, but Maj. Gen. Winfield Scott, commanding general of the army, protested that his army was no *"peace establishment."* By late 1849 regular troops were at war with Indians "in Florida, Texas, New Mexico, California, and between the basin of the Mississippi and Rocky mountains." A few years later, conflicts would also explode in Oregon and Washington Territories. In 1853, sizing up hostilities in New Mexico, Col. Joseph K. F. Mansfield, the army's inspector general, opined, "All posts through an Indian country should be placed on, or near the great thoroughfares where aid and protection can be had by the traveler in case of necessity."[10]

Indeed, the military geography of the American West generally conformed to road networks and settlement lines. Dispersed in small posts along overland trails and near frontier communities, federal troops afforded emigrants, merchants, and settlers some protection from raids by Indians and outlaws, reminding forgetful settlers—sometimes at bayonet's point—of United States sovereignty in the far-away West. Points of embarkation to the military frontier were regional quartermaster depots: Forts Leavenworth and Smith in the East; Indianola, Fort Brown, and San Antonio in the South; and the Mission of San Diego, Benicia Barracks, and Fort Vancouver in the West. From these logistical centers, army units and quartermaster trains accessed overland trails plunging into the heart of the western frontier (see map 1).[11]

Established 460 miles above St. Louis on the right bank of the Missouri River in 1827, Fort Leavenworth was the military gateway to the American West. According to Lt. Orlando B. Willcox, Leavenworth in 1850 was an "extensive" post "situated in a handsome, uneven country." Outlining the parade ground were "two or three fine buildings," barracks and offices, and "large trees." Near the river wharf, a large warehouse received thousands of tons of quartermaster, subsistence, and ordnance supplies. Nearly all officers and enlisted men destined for western stations by overland routes marched from Fort Leavenworth over two principal roads, the California-Oregon Trail and the Santa Fe Trail.[12]

Along the former route on the banks of the Platte and North Platte Rivers stood Forts Kearny and Laramie, respectively 304 and 637 miles northwest of Fort Leavenworth (see maps 1, 3, 4). Built by mountain man Jim Bridger in 1842, Fort Bridger lay some 398 miles beyond Laramie, but west of Laramie the only consequential army post was Fort Dalles, erected on the left bank of the Columbia River 870 miles west of Fort Bridger on the trail's northern branch in Oregon Territory. In 1860 the army erected Fort Churchill on the Carson River in the eastern Great Basin to protect emigrant and commercial trains on the California branch from hard-pressed Paiutes. The Great Basin's other major post was Camp Floyd, established west of Utah Lake in 1858 to watch rebellious Mormons in the Great Salt Lake Valley.[13]

The second major road federal troops utilized from Fort Leavenworth was the Santa Fe Trail (see map 1). Since its inauguration in 1822, this overland highway carried primarily mercantile traffic of the lucrative Santa Fe trade between western Missouri and northern New Mexico. The trail coursed southwest across the central and southern plains through the homelands of the Osages, Cheyennes, Kiowas, Comanches, Apaches, and Arapahos. Forts Atkinson and Larned protected the main road down to the Cimarron Cutoff, while Fort Wise was built on the northern branch near Bent's New Fort in 1860. The termini of the Santa Fe Trail were Fort Union and Santa Fe, New Mexico, respectively 728 and 821 miles from Fort Leavenworth.[14]

South of Santa Fe, the road—now the Chihuahua Trail—followed the old Spanish Camino Real, paralleling the Rio Grande to Fort Bliss in El Paso, Texas, 327 miles below (see map 4). The route, passing from high-plains grassland desert to the blistering Chihuahuan Desert, was exposed to attacks by Comanches, Kiowas, Eastern and Western Apaches, and Navajos. A network of garrisons from Fort Marcy in Santa Fe to Fort Craig below Socorro to Fort Fillmore at Mesilla protected this road, the safety of which was critical to merchants traveling between Santa Fe and Chihuahua City, Mexico. An especially hazardous stretch was the Jornada del Muerto (Journey of the Dead), a ninety-mile waterless desert between Forts Craig and Fillmore.[15]

At Mesilla, New Mexico, thousands of emigrants bound for California turned west to trace the Gila Trail 683 miles to California. During the Mexican-American War, the Army of the West and the Mormon Battalion blazed and marked roads over the Chihuahuan Desert, Gila Mountains, Sonoran and Mojave Deserts, and Sierra Nevada to San Diego and Los Angeles, California (see map 4). Established 25 miles east of Tubac on the Mormon Road, Fort Buchanan defended travelers against the Western Apaches, while far to the northwest, Fort Yuma, some 500 miles west of Mesilla, watched over the critical ferry crossing at the junction of the Gila and Colorado Rivers. Another 272 miles—90 over the Mojave Desert—brought the weary traveler into San Diego.[16]

In the Department of Texas, the army delivered troops, dependents, and supplies directly onto the Gulf Coast beaches at Corpus Christi, Indianola, and Point Isabel, or Brazos Santiago. South Texas was yellow fever country, which ravaged soldiers, wives, and children. The spouse of a mounted rifleman, Lydia Spencer Lane recalled, "There was no escape, no running away from it, nothing to do but land, take the risk, and trust in Providence." From the coast, the defensive network reached northwest to Fort Bliss near El Paso in the Department of New Mexico and northeast to Fort Smith, Arkansas, in the Department of the West (see map 2). Departmental commanders designed this system to screen settlements in south and central Texas and to block Indian raids—principally Comanches, Kiowas, and Apaches—from United States soil to northern Mexico, a legal obligation in the Treaty of Guadalupe Hidalgo. In north Texas, Forts Worth and Belknap and Camp Cooper defined the northern perimeter.[17]

Texas was a huge, rugged military jurisdiction. Having seen much of central and northwest Texas, Mrs. Lane described the state as "desolate, dreary country, where nothing lived but Indians, snakes, and other venomous reptiles," but 1st Lt. Parmenas T. Turnley, who escorted quartermaster trains to El Paso, remembered the Texas landscape as a patchwork of bone-dry deserts, verdant river valleys, and dewy grasslands. From Indianola on the Texas coast, San Antonio—departmental headquarters—lay 125 miles away; El Paso, 803 miles; and Fort Worth, 420 miles. A string of posts lined the 678-mile-long San Antonio–El Paso Road, which lacked water along some stretches (see map 2). The picket line on the United States–Mexico frontier stretched from Fort Brown in the south to Fort Clark in the center to Fort Bliss in the northwest—836 miles of chaparral, desert, and mountains.[18]

Two thousand miles to the northwest of San Antonio, San Francisco, California, was the major Pacific port city, but Benicia Barracks was the principal army depot in the Pacific region. The site lay at the head of Suisun Bay, thirty miles northeast over the water from San Francisco and some fifteen miles downstream from rivers draining interior California (see map 3). The Benicia reservation included troop barracks; quartermaster, commissary, and subsistence depots; and an ordnance depot and armory. Unimpressed with the grounds and facilities in 1852, 2nd Lt. George Crook later wrote: "The roads and walks all around the town and barracks were one mud hole. It was nothing unusual to see the tops of boots sticking out of the mud in the streets." Despite the quagmire, the Benicia depots received military stores shipped from the East Coast around South America. Transported either around Cape Horn or across the Isthmus of Panama, troops bound for Pacific Coast stations usually stopped briefly at Benicia.[19]

When supplies and troops landed, the quartermaster transshipped them to interior California posts, San Diego, or Fort Vancouver. Army stations on the gold-rush watersheds included Fort Miller on the San Joaquin, Fort Reading on the Sacramento, and Fort Crook on the Pit Rivers. The Benicia quartermaster also forwarded supplies to coastal garrisons at Monterey, Fort Bragg, Fort Humboldt, and the Presidio of San Francisco. Military stores also sailed by steamer south around Baja California and north up the Gulf of California and Colorado River to Fort Yuma. Five hundred miles south of Benicia, the quartermaster and commissary subdepot at San Diego served troops at the Mission of San Diego a few miles away, Fort Tejon 197 miles north, Fort Mojave 325 miles to the northeast, and Fort Yuma 272 miles east.[20]

Far up the coast in the Pacific Northwest, regular troops under Capt. John S. Hathaway first occupied Astoria at the mouth of the Columbia River but soon relocated 124 miles upriver to Fort Vancouver, a Hudson's Bay Company fur-trade outpost (see map 3). Upon the detachment's arrival, Lt. Theodore Talbot wrote: "The Fort is situated in an extensive level plain . . . along the north bank of the River. It consists of a high quadrangular stockade with bastions, surrounding the numerous warehouses, shops, and dwelling houses of the Company and its officers. In its vicinity is a Catholic Chapel and a village of 40 or 50 houses occupied by servants of the company." In 1849 Hathaway's detachment built two barracks nearby and first called the location Columbia Barracks. Four years later the army formally named the station Fort Vancouver.[21]

In 1849 Oregon Territory was the forlorn far edge of the military frontier. Inflation, isolation, and civil-military squabbling soon soured the army on Oregon. Disgusted with Oregonians, First Lieutenant Talbot labeled them "illiterate mobocrats." To the north in what became Washington Territory in 1853, federal troops built Forts Steilacoom at the head of Puget Sound in 1849, Townsend at the sound's entrance in 1856, and Bellingham on the coast just south of the Canadian border in 1856. One hundred miles northeast of Fort Vancouver, regular troops established Fort Simcoe in the Simcoe Valley during the Yakama War in 1856, and two hundred miles farther Fort Coleville protected gold prospectors in the Coleville River country and supplied the Northwest Boundary Commission. Directly east of Fort Vancouver were Fort Dalles at the end of the Oregon Trail and Fort Walla Walla in the Walla Walla Valley.[22]

A third defensive axis ran southwestward from Fort Vancouver into Oregon Territory. Constructed in the wake of the Rogue River War, three posts—Forts Yamhill, Hoskins, and Umpqua—guarded Indians restricted to the Grand Ronde and Siletz Agencies, and helped police the Willamette River Valley, whose fertile soil was a magnet for Euroamerican farmers. In southern Oregon the army built Fort Lane on the Rogue River to police the Rogue

River Agency. A little to the northwest, Fort Orford watched over the head of Trichenor Bay until the army left in 1856.[23]

The army districted the military frontier in response to the western geography and redrew boundaries to meet local exigencies. At the close of the war with Mexico, the Department of War partitioned the nation's military geography into a total of eleven numbered military departments divided among the Eastern, Western, and Pacific Divisions. The boundary separating the Eastern and Western Divisions ran from Fond du Lac, Lake Superior, to Cape Sable, Florida. Excluding Georgia and Indiana, the Western Division, generally headquartered at New Orleans, included all the territory west of the Fond du Lac–Cape Sable line and embraced the northern and central plains, Texas and New Mexico, and the central and northern Rockies. It was subdivided into Military Departments Five, Six, Seven, Eight, and Nine. Usually commanded from San Francisco or Benicia Barracks, the Pacific Division—Military Departments Ten and Eleven—encompassed California, Oregon, and a piece of the Great Basin. Departmental commanders reported to their divisional commanders, who in turn answered to the adjutant general and general-in-chief.[24]

In a move toward efficiency, the War Department reorganized the military West in 1853. General Order No. 25 swept away the divisions and created departments directly under the adjutant general and general-in-chief: Pacific, New Mexico, Texas, West, and East. In 1858 the army carved the Department of Oregon from the Pacific and added the Department of Utah in the Great Basin. From 1858 to 1859 the Department of the Platte stood guard over the Oregon Trail in Nebraska Territory. For administrative convenience, departments were often subdivided into districts, each with its own commander. This new structure eliminated the divisional bureaucracy, allowing departmental commanders to report problems and negotiate solutions directly with Washington.[25]

Departmental commanders in the American West had to defend huge territories and wage war on Indians with remarkably few troops at their disposal. In 1849, with regulars redeployed to the frontiers, the Sixth and Seventh Military Departments were comprised of the woodland and plains country lying between Texas and Canada and drained by the upper Mississippi, Missouri, Platte, Arkansas, and Red Rivers, but the combined departmental strengths equaled only 1,337 troops dispersed among eleven posts. This region was home to the Woodland and Plains Sioux, the Northern and Southern Cheyennes, Arapahos, Pawnees, Osages, and other indigenous peoples. Kiowas and Comanches intermittently warred with the Cherokees,

Choctaws, Chickasaws, Creeks, and Seminoles relocated to Indian Territory west of Fort Smith. Departments Six and Seven became the Department of the West in 1853, although the Department of Texas took over Fort Smith and the posts in Indian Territory south and west of the Arkansas River in August 1859. At the end of 1860, the Department of the West, embracing this same region, had increased to 2,808 officers and men at eleven posts.[26]

In 1849, commanding from San Antonio, Brig. Gen. George M. Brooke of the Eighth Military Department defended the state of Texas excepting El Paso. His troops, a mere 1,205 officers and men, were distributed among thirteen posts from Fort Worth in the northeast to Fort Duncan in the far southwest and skirmished with Comanches, Kiowas, Apaches, Wacos, and other native tribes. By late 1860 the Department of Texas had absorbed Fort Smith and Indian Territory and now boasted 2,949 regulars in eighteen stations.[27] With too few regulars at hand, Indians could transit at will the yawning gaps between the Rio Grande picket posts to raid the ranches and settlements of northern Mexico.

To the northwest, Maj. John Munroe, commanding the Ninth Military Department, was responsible for New Mexico Territory and the plains, deserts, canyons, and mountains stretching from Texas in the east to California in the West. The Rios Pecos, Grande, Gila, and Colorado defined Munroe's military jurisdiction, but his troops had little presence outside the Rio Grande Valley. In 1849, 885 officers and men battled Comanches, Kiowas, Apaches, Utes, and Navajos from six or seven static posts generally lining the Rio Grande, the region's hydraulic lifeline, from Taos to El Paso. At the outbreak of the Civil War, only 3,104 officers and men at twelve posts defended the tumultuous Department of New Mexico, now adding Confederate Texans to their list of frontier military threats.[28]

To the west in California, forty-niners rushing to the gold fields severely stressed military and law enforcement institutions on the Pacific Coast. In the entire Pacific Division—the Tenth (California) and Eleventh (Oregon Territory) Military Departments—Col. Persifor F. Smith had only 1,371 officers and men. In California, Col. Bennet Riley deployed 676 regulars to seven posts from Sonoma in the north to San Diego in the south. The early years of placer mining focused on the drainages of the Sacramento and San Joaquin Rivers. However, gold fever triggered desertions from Riley's command and forced him to spread three companies between two posts in placer country and station the majority of his regulars at posts such as Monterey and San Diego, far away from the diggings.[29]

The reorganization of 1853 merged California and Oregon into a single department encompassing all territory west of the Rocky Mountains, excluding Utah Territory east of 117 degrees west longitude and New Mexico Territory east of 110 degrees west longitude. Five years later the Department of War divided the Pacific Coast between the Departments of California and Oregon. Headquartered at either San Francisco or Benicia Barracks, the California command also took in Oregon's Rogue River and Umpqua districts. When the South seceded in early 1861, Col. Albert S. Johnston had charge of 1,218 officers and men at thirteen posts.[30]

Headquartered at Fort Vancouver, the Eleventh Military Department, Oregon Territory, contended with friction between Anglo farmers and some miners in addition to American Indians. Euroamericans especially coveted the fertile river valleys such as the Rogue and Umpqua draining west into the Pacific and the Willamette rolling north to the Columbia. In early 1850 the department under Lt. Col. William W. Loring had 695 regulars, mostly mounted riflemen who had marched over the Oregon-California Trail from Fort Leavenworth but whose riotous behavior was alienating the Oregonians.[31]

Beginning in 1853 Oregon Territory north of the Columbia River became a new political jurisdiction, Washington Territory, and the Eleventh Military Department was abolished. All troops and posts in the Tenth and Eleventh fell under the Department of the Pacific until, five years later, the War Department created the Department of Oregon and gave the command to Brig. Gen. William S. Harney. The aim of the new department, now independent of California, was to provide Harney a free hand to crush Indian resistance in the Pacific Northwest, but he was removed in fall 1860 and the War Department again folded Oregon and California into the Department of the Pacific. As secession got underway in early 1861, the Oregon district contained 2,236 regulars at ten posts. When Sumner took command of the Department of the Pacific in April 1861, his command contained 3,484 officers and men at twenty-three stations.[32]

The western military frontier was a severe challenge to army planners, commanders, and units. The topography, distances, and cultures taxed the regulars' resources and tested their adaptability. In Mexico they had won the battles to add the Far West to the United States, but a long series of brutal wars and police actions lay ahead to incorporate fully its peoples and resources into the expanding nation. When the staff and line took their posts in the American West in 1848 and 1849, they had limited knowledge of surviving, operating, and thriving in the region. The interwar years would be a rigorous and arduous learning experience for the officers and enlisted men of the U.S. Army.

Army Regulars on the Western Frontier

PROLOGUE

THE Senate ratification of the Treaty of Guadalupe Hidalgo on 10 March 1848 ended the Mexican-American War and lit the fuse to the Civil War. As victorious United States troops, professional and volunteer, retired from central and northern Mexico, the regulars slowly began garrisoning the new American West from Missouri to the Pacific Coast and from Texas to the northern plains. The West seemed geographically remote from Washington, D.C., but North-South wrangling over slavery in the new western territories reached baldly into the army's occupation duty in far-away New Mexico and California, territory ceded by Mexico to the United States.

After the official United States–Mexico exchange of ratified treaties on 30 May 1848, Congressional lawmakers deadlocked over the extension of southern slavery into the territories of the Mexican Cession. In mid-August 1848 three slave-state senators defected from southern ranks to legislate a free-soil Oregon Territory. The emotional debate vexed Pres. James K. Polk of Tennessee, who grudgingly signed the Oregon Bill into law. Southern slavery and westward expansion, he argued, appeared on separate political pages altogether, and human bondage would never flourish in Oregon, California, or New Mexico. However, the specter of the Wilmot Proviso—which would bar slavery from the territories won or acquired from Mexico—panicked southern lawmakers. Led by radical slavocrats such as Andrew P. Butler of South Carolina, the South demanded its Constitutional right to bring all property, human chattel included, into the American West. Closer to home, Dixie politicians feared that a free New Mexico and California would irretrievably tip the balance of power in Congress against the southern states.[1]

Congress was still deadlocked over slavery in New Mexico and California when Whig president Zachary "Old Rough and Ready" Taylor took office in March 1849. He had conquered and occupied northeastern Mexico during the war, and having been a regular-army officer for forty years, he took the national view of political affairs. Although he owned some 140 slaves, Taylor was cool toward all self-righteous sectional radicals generally and yapping southern slavocrats specifically. Stunning both Whigs and Democrats in the South, the old soldier favored in principle a free-soil California and New Mexico. Time and again, he reiterated that the Wilmot debate was eating up good will and recklessly endangering the Union: slaves and slavery would never prosper in parsimonious western deserts. The howling South should take heed.[2]

President Taylor went on the political offensive. His worry was that the gut-wrenching debate over slavery might explode the Union, to which he had devoted his adult life. His plan was to flank and encircle the Congressional radicals by handing Congress a *fait accompli*, New Mexico and California statehood. That would silence the free-soil bellyachers and southern peacocks.[3]

In the meantime the U.S. Army took over the military governments of New Mexico and California and awaited the resolution of the national political process. Until Congress organized territories or granted statehood, the departmental commander doubled as military governor, ruled over the Mexican alcalde system, and enforced Mexican laws that were commensurate with the U.S. Constitution. However, while languishing under military government, the people of the Mexican Cession lacked any binding legislative process to address immediate military, social, political, or economic problems in their locales or regions.[4]

On 11 October 1848 Maj. John M. Washington assumed the command of the Ninth Military Department, the territory of New Mexico, in Santa Fe. His command of three First Dragoon companies, one Second Dragoon company, and an artillery battery had marched overland across rolling parched deserts from Monterrey, Nuevo León, Mexico. Major-Governor Washington stationed dragoons at Taos, Santa Fe, Albuquerque, Socorro, Tomé, and Doña Ana. In civil affairs, he enforced the policies of his predecessors, kept political supremacy in military hands, and awaited revised instructions from the president or legislative action from Congress. Like Col. Richard B. Mason governing occupied California, he advised authorities in Washington, D.C., to institute civilian government as soon as possible.[5]

A fifty-three-year-old artilleryman from Virginia, the doe-eyed Washington inherited a tumultuous territory. Two-hundred-year-old wars between Indians—Navajos, Apaches, Utes, Comanches, and Kiowas—and New Mexicans wracked the settlements and Indian homelands. Conquered Hispanos and victorious Anglos deeply resented one another, and their mutual animosity sometimes erupted in street violence in the major towns. Residents, both Anglo and Hispano, clamored for an end to the military government—army tyranny they called it—that had ruled them since Brig. Gen. Stephen W. Kearny occupied Santa Fe in August 1846 and imposed the Kearny Code a month later. From his headquarters in Santa Fe, Major Washington saw no end to New Mexico's problems.[6]

Even the politics of slavery vexed New Mexico and the military government. The major's jurisdiction was now the eye of a political storm boiling up in the United States Congress. Shortly before Washington arrived in Santa Fe, Antonio J. Martinéz, James Quinn, Donaciano Vigil, and others petitioned Congress to establish a civilian government, forbid slavery in the territory, and reject Texas's claim to the eastern half of New Mexico. Southern lawmakers deeply resented the proceedings of these "Mexicans," and Price's government and the Polk administration simply ignored the New Mexico convention and petition.[7]

While Major Washington led an armed expedition westward to Navajo country during late summer 1849, the interim departmental commander, First Dragoon major Benjamin "Old Brilliant" Beall, endorsed the assembly of a new convention by the American party in Santa Fe. After debating New Mexico's civil dilemmas, the representatives requested a civilian territorial government and elected Hugh N. Smith to represent New Mexico in Congress. Under the advice of Sen. Thomas H. Benton of Missouri, the American party studiously ignored slavery and the Texas boundary claim. When Smith reached Washington, D.C., however, Congress refused to recognize and seat him. After returning to Santa Fe with a Navajo treaty, an angry Major Washington disavowed the convention proceedings and probably chewed out the red-faced Beall.[8]

Now battling Congress over the disposition of the Mexican Cession, Taylor dispatched Mexican-American War comrade Maj. John Munroe to relieve Washington in Santa Fe. Graduating from West Point in 1816, Munroe had served in the artillery throughout his career. His distinguished service under Taylor from Palo Alto to Buena Vista and his identification with the Whig party probably explained his appointment to the Ninth Military Department. A delightful raconteur, the eccentric Munroe constantly entertained young officers with comical ribald stories. His curious work ethic was always to complete his paperwork in the morning and lounge and drink during the afternoon. Never would he command, his idle boast went, where it snowed in either May or November. It did both in Santa Fe.[9]

Unpredictable inclement weather was the least of Munroe's challenges. With the Treaty of Guadalupe Hidalgo signed, Texas pressed its claim to eastern New Mexico as far as the Rio Grande. Acquiescing to the Lone Star State, the Polk administration had instructed Major Washington to interfere with Texas agents "in no manner whatever" and "to lend aid on proper occasions in sustaining" them. As the new chief executive, General Taylor was equally emphatic: The Texas claim was incredible and ludicrous! Congress alone should settle the boundary dispute. Modifying Polk's instructions, the Taylor administration told New Mexico's commanding officer to avoid "conflict with the authorities so constituted" by Texas. In Taylor's mind, the clamoring in Texas was the passing of a lot of wind, no more.[10]

The Texas governor defied Taylor's prediction, dispatching Commissioner Robert S. Neighbors to define counties and establish county governments in eastern New Mexico. On 23 February 1850, from Franklin, Texas, Neighbors asked for Major Munroe's "friendly cooperation." Delighting New Mexicans, the firm but polite military governor lent Neighbors no assistance. Probably in the morning, Munroe wrote his field officers, "You will observe a rigid non-interference with him [Neighbors] in the exercise of his functions."[11]

"Non-interference" meant noncooperation. New Mexico had been ripped from Mexico; New Mexicans had been stripped of their Mexican citizenship. They promised to throw back, by force of arms, any Texas border that rolled westward into the streets of Santa Fe. Outraged by Texan political conceit, President Taylor threw his administration behind New Mexico's cause, and the sympathetic Major Munroe gave New Mexicans behind-the-scenes aid.[12]

Launching his statehood campaigns only a month into his presidency, Taylor dispatched James S. Calhoun to New Mexico and Thomas B. King to California in spring 1849. As the superintendent of Indian affairs in New Mexico, however, Calhoun encountered institutional prejudice from the army and failed to garner Munroe's cooperation. In November 1849 Taylor ordered Maj. George A. McCall, a close friend and regular-army officer, to New Mexico. (Taylor rewarded McCall with a promotion to colonel and a berth in the Inspector General's Office on 10 June 1850.) McCall's mission was to advise the army "to advance" all movements for statehood in New Mexico and to defend its borders against all Texas aggression. Traveling via New Orleans and San Antonio, Major McCall reached Santa Fe after dark on 11 March 1850. To a confidential correspondent he wrote, "The evening of my arrival

. . . I opened to some of the leading men the object of my mission, and enlisted them in the cause I desired to advance."[13]

Despite a case of neuralgia, the forty-one-year-old McCall opened negotiations between the two major political factions in New Mexico: the territorial party, led by Judge Jaob Houghton, and the statehood party, led by former Missouri volunteer Richard Weightman. The statehood party accused the army of unabashed tyranny, and Weightman complained that Major Munroe's regime rewarded the territorial-party cabal with political offices and quartermaster contracts. A formal territorial system promised New Mexico more of the same, while statehood would break the army's grip on New Mexico affairs and return political and economic power to towns and counties. Many Nuevomexicanos, represented by outspoken Padre Antonio J. Martinéz of Taos, supported the Weightman faction. The self-rule of statehood would grant Nuevomexicanos the political and legal weapons to defend better their way of life from Anglo assault.[14]

Much to the chagrin of Commissioner Neighbors, McCall's mediation bore fruit. While operating in Santa Fe during spring 1850, Neighbors lodged protests against broadsides calling for a public meeting on New Mexico statehood, but Munroe turned a deaf ear. Indeed, organizers petitioned Major Munroe for a state constitutional convention. In elections ordered for 6 May 1850, the territorial faction won a majority of the convention seats, but McCall counseled Houghton's followers that New Mexico territorialism was dead in the Taylor administration. Both parties united behind a free-state constitution and publicly defied Texas's claim to eastern New Mexico.[15]

In the elections for state officials, the statehood party won the Hispano vote and defeated the territorialists. New Mexicans elected Henry Connelly governor and Manuel Alvaréz lieutenant governor. The legislature selected Richard Weightman and Francis Cunningham senators and submitted the statehood petition to Congress. In Connelly's absence Alvaréz tried to implement the new state government, but unlike Col. Bennet Riley in California, Munroe kept civil power in his hands and ordered Alvaréz to desist until Congress acted on New Mexico's petition. Momentarily, New Mexico had two governments.[16]

Texas was all aflutter with outrage and indignation, and Texas governor Peter H. Bell vigorously disputed the New Mexico statehood movement. To fortify Lone Star honor, Texas lawmakers passed legislation to raise three thousand state troops and squash the "rebellion" in New Mexico. From Louisiana to Virginia, governors, legislatures, and newspapers accused Taylor of selling out Texas and the South, but the president scoffed at their posturing. He reminded everyone that New Mexico was a United States territorial possession and that his constitutional duty was to defend it against all aggression, foreign and domestic.[17]

President Taylor was not trifling with Texas and its southern allies. In mid-June 1850 he summoned Second Dragoon lieutenant Alfred M. Pleasonton to his office. At the time, the young lieutenant, who had fought under Taylor at Palo Alto and Resaca de la Palma, was only a few days short of traveling to New Mexico. Taylor had a message for Major Munroe: The Ninth Military Department would repulse any invasion by Texas volunteers, and, if Munroe's command needed reinforcements, the president would personally lead them to New Mexico and, his sword in hand, order volleys fired into the Texas ranks. The old soldier grimly told Pleasonton: "I will be there before those people [Texans] shall go into that country or have a foot of that territory. The whole business is infamous, and must be put down." Although Secretary of War George W. Crawford, a South Carolinian, refused to sign the resistance order, "Old Rough and Ready" Taylor said he would.[18]

Taylor never rode out to New Mexico; he tragically died of cholera morbus, or intestinal dysfunction, on 9 July. His successor, Millard Fillmore, cut and signed Munroe's orders, which reached Ninth Military Department Headquarters on 29 August 1850. The prospect of engaging Munroe's reinforced army, which included combat-seasoned regulars, cooled the Lone Star spirit. Swallowing their bluster, the Texans agreed to let Congress draw the disputed boundary.[19]

A thousand miles away in California, the U.S. Army also aided California statehood even before Taylor's orders arrived. In April 1849 the president dispatched Whig representative Thomas Butler King, a Georgia slaveholder, to the Pacific Coast. King's instructions were to consult with California leaders about the "measures best calculated" to achieve statehood, and Secretary of War Crawford advised Persifor F. Smith, colonel of the Regiment of Mounted Riflemen and commander of the Pacific Division, to "aid and assist" King. Headquartered at Monterey, the quiet and able Smith was eager to extract his little army from the daily embarrassments of California civil government. He gladly laid his services at King's feet and instructed Lt. Col. Bennet Riley, military governor of California and commander of the Tenth Military Department, to call a state constitutional convention.[20]

King's mission delighted Riley. Born to Catholic parents in Maryland in 1787, Riley was a cobbler when he volunteered for service in the War of 1812. Afterward he served on the trans-Appalachian frontier, north and south, and on the Santa Fe Trail. A junior officer recalled that Riley had "lost a part of his palate" and told hoary stories of frontier soldiering in a "remarkable" voice. In the late war, his brigade of regulars had whipped the Mexicans in battles from Vera Cruz to Mexico City. Enforcing Mexican law in California while Congress tittled and prattled over slavery disgusted and frustrated him.[21]

Riley had relieved Col. Richard B. Mason on 13 April 1849. At the time, the gold rush was turning California topsy-turvy. With hundreds more arriving daily, the thousands of miners working the northern diggings were violent, chaotic, and genocidal. Daily desertions to the gold fields were rapidly diminishing the ranks of Riley's regulars—only eight companies of infantry, two of artillery, and two of dragoons. Strung out between San Diego and San Francisco, his tiny military constabulary was powerless to prevent the slaughter of California Indians and suppress the mayhem in the unpoliced gold camps. He worried daily that these clashes, if unchecked, might escalate into full-scale war. In Riley's opinion elected representatives alone could bring law and order to California.[22]

The advice of Riley's predecessor, Col. Richard B. Mason, was to summon an unmandated state constitutional convention and let Californians govern themselves. The territory's human depravity and social convulsions readily impressed themselves on Riley, and he quickly concluded to hand power to a de facto civilian government. On 1 June 1849 Riley learned officially that Congress had failed again to organize the territories of California and New Mexico, their civil governments included. Forty-eight hours later he issued his "Proclamation to the People of California," one day before King's arrival. His declaration called for the election of civil officers to the de facto government and of statewide representatives to frame "State government" or "territorial organization," either of which would be submitted to Congress. Colonel Smith encouraged Riley's course.[23]

The Taylor administration also fell in behind Riley, who ordered elections for 1 August. Thomas O. Larkin, Mariano G. Vallejo, William Gwinn, Wilson E. Shannon, John A. Sutter, and Lilburn W. Boggs were a few of the delegates chosen to represent their districts at the California constitutional convention. Two army officers, Henry W. Halleck and Cave J. Couts, were also elected to the body.[24]

The representatives convened at Colton Hall in Monterey on 1 September. Observing the proceedings from the gallery were John C. and Jessie Benton Frémont. Another witness was Lt. William T. Sherman, Colonel Smith's representative. According to Sherman, his commander, a resident of Louisiana, neither discussed the issue of slavery nor tried to influence the convention debates. Stranded in Monterey during the proceedings, Capt. Robert S. Garnett drafted the Great Seal of California. His sketch included "a view of the Sierra Nevada in the distance, a sheaf of wheat, a bear, . . . a grape vine in the foreground, and the motto 'Eureka.'"[25]

Colonel Riley declared that if the state constitution were ratified, he would, "with pleasure, surrender his powers." An independent party nominated him for governor, but the old warrior declined. On 13 November 1849 the people went to the polls in drenching rain, voted in a free-state constitution, and elected Peter A. Burnet governor and John McDougal lieutenant governor. Speaking on behalf of President Taylor, Secretary of War Crawford sanctioned the statehood process and Riley's course of action. As the colonel-governor promised, he relinquished all civil power to the elected officials on 20 December 1849. De facto civil government was in operation, and Riley, Smith, and the army were delighted.[26]

After months of vitriolic wrangling and backroom maneuvering, Congressional lawmakers, led by Sen. Stephen A. Douglas and encouraged by President Fillmore, passed a series of bills that threw sops to pro- and antislavery radicals and organized the territories of the Mexican Cession. Known as the Compromise of 1850, the historic legislation abolished the slave trade in Washington, D.C., and toughened fugitive-slave laws. Both New Mexico and Utah officially became territories. Congress increased the size of Texas by thirty-three thousand square miles, but New Mexico retained nearly all of its preconquest territory. In addition, gold-rush California won its statehood bid.[27]

The compromise was a weak salve slapped on deep political gashes. Northern and southern radicals had driven the slavery wedge deeply into the public consciousness and the American West. Professional soldiers stationed across the interwar frontier would joust with the agents of political sectionalism for the next eleven years while they waged war on American Indians, policed the reservations and settlements, and suppressed civil unrest. The sectional conflict would profoundly shape the army's frontier mission and eventually unravel the officer corps.

I

Defense, War, & Politics

1

AMBIVALENT DUTY

Soldiers, Indians, and Frontiersmen

ENFORCING United States Indian policy was a primary mission of the frontier army. Regular troops assisted the Bureau of Indian Affairs (BIA) with executing the Indian Intercourse Acts and policing federal Indian reservations. By the end of the Mexican-American War, the federal government had already relocated thousands of eastern Indians to treaty lands from Wisconsin to Indian Territory and would begin to confine western Indians over the next thirteen years. Federal policy was to negotiate the opening of Indian land to Euroamerican settlement and to protect indigenous peoples in tribal homelands or on legal reservations. However well intentioned, this strategy routinely broke down, resulting in frontier warfare. Whether victims or aggressors, Indian tribes who went to war were counterattacked by the regular army.

An eyewitness to the destructive clash of cultures on the frontier, the officer corps acknowledged that covetous Anglo frontiersmen triggered most of the wars with western Indians, but as agents of the United States, regular officers were not neutral enforcers of federal Indian policy. Ultimately shared by the officer corps, the goals of the federal government for the western Indians overcame any personal reservations against the immoral and un-Christian treatment of indigenous people. Subscribing to Anglo racial attitudes, they concluded that American Indians had to make way for the march of Euroamerican civilization.

In late 1848 Secretary of the Treasury Robert J. Walker urged Congress to create a new cabinet-level post to oversee the internal welfare and development of the nation, particularly in the wake of national expansion into the Far West. Legislators responded by authorizing the new Department of the Interior in early 1849, giving it authority over the General Land Office, Patent Office, Pension Office, and Bureau of Indian Affairs.[1] The transfer of the BIA aroused heated debate in Congress. Since the creation of the federal government in 1789, the Department of War had administered Indian affairs, and warfare had constituted the primary intercourse between whites and Indians. Indian-white relations at the end of the Mexican-American War, however, seemed uncommonly peaceful and stable, and federal policymakers concluded that a pacific civilian agency would better serve the Indians and nation.

Although the BIA had flourished under the War Department since 1824, it had reported to a civilian cabinet officer—the secretary of war—and its commissioner and field officers were civilian. Only in rare cases did army officers serve the bureau. Housed in the new Interior Department, the BIA simply reported to a different cabinet officer and conducted its business as usual. Overwhelmed by extraordinary demands in the western acquisitions, Secretary of War William Conrad did not strenuously object to the transfer.[2]

The peaceful frontier, more chimera than reality, was short-lived. Columns of white emigrants were slicing through the Permanent Indian Frontier, the trans-Mississippi West to which the United States had relocated trans-Appalachian Indians in the 1830s and 1840s. When Pres. James Monroe and Pres. John Quincy Adams inaugurated the policy in the 1820s, they and Congressional lawmakers assumed that Anglo civilization would never break the climatic barrier of the Great American Desert, the semiarid prairies and arid plains where, unmolested by white frontiersmen, the Indians would practice their traditional ways of life.[3]

The trickle of emigration to the Oregon Country in the early 1840s became a flood during and after the Mexican-American War. On foot, horseback, and wagon, thousands of settlers streamed to the new western territories over the Santa Fe and Oregon-California Trails each year. By the mid-1850s they had killed off most of the wild game and their livestock had eaten up much of the grass along the overland routes. The westward migration pooled in the settlements of Utah, Oregon, California, New Mexico, and Texas. As frontiersmen poured into the trans-Mississippi West, the pools became ponds and then lakes, submerging more and more Indian land under farms, ranches, and towns. At the end of the interwar period, the Permanent Indian Frontier was a patchwork of tribal islands besieged by ever-expanding settlement.[4]

National leaders never entertained blocking the march of American civilization into the West. To the contrary, the federal government facilitated emigration, settlement, and development. Americans were pursuing their destiny to conquer, settle, and exploit North America. That nation-making process added up to progress, and "uncivilized" Indians had several choices: adapt to the change, move out of the way, or die in war.[5]

Although United States policy ultimately devastated American Indian societies, policymakers still nourished some humane obligation toward them. According to public rhetoric, the historical role of the United States was to bring the fruits of Anglo democracy and Christian civilization to all people in the world, Indians included. When the Americans created their republic in 1789, they intended their government to conduct a new Indian policy founded on the principles of law and justice, unlike their iron-fisted European rivals. In the best of all possible worlds, the protections of the law applied equally to settlers and Indians, but the American frontier often lay beyond the law, and what law there was shielded indigenous peoples imperfectly or not at all. Without federal protection, policymakers knew and feared, American Indians faced extermination.

The reservation policy was the "alternative to extinction." The idea was to extinguish Indian claims to contested land through treaties, relocate threatened tribes to treaty reservations, teach the Indians ranching and farming, and assimilate them into the national citizenry. During the transition, American Indian cultures would probably die out but Indian bloodlines would survive. All armed Indian resistance would be met with war, for the American people would settle and exploit their country.[6]

To clear the roads to the Pacific Coast, the federal government began negotiating rights of way with Indian tribes in the early 1850s. On the Great Plains, United States commissioners treated with ten thousand Sioux, Cheyennes, Crows, Arapahos, and other plains tribes at Fort Laramie on the North Platte River in 1851. Federal agents David D. Mitchell and Thomas "Broken Hand" Fitzpatrick drew boundaries between the tribes, whose own traditional wars equally threatened traffic on the Oregon-California Trail. The Indians agreed to permit roads and military posts in their territory and compensate emigrants for property losses at the hands of errant warriors. The United States promised to defend the Indians from marauding whites and pay them annuities for fifty years. Two years later at Fort Atkinson on the Santa Fe Trail, Fitzpatrick met with Comanches, Kiowas, and Plains Apaches. The treaty terms were similar to those signed at Fort Laramie. In addition, obligated by the Treaty of Guadalupe Hidalgo, the United States extracted a hollow promise from the southern plains tribes not to raid settlements in northern Mexico.[7]

In New Mexico Territory, the United States tried to control the Navajos, Utes, and southwestern Apaches, who raided settlements in the Rio Grande Valley and who suffered raids by Hispanos, Anglos, and Pueblo Indians. In summer 1855 Gov. David Meriwether treated with Apaches, Navajos, and Utes in separate talks. In return for government annuities, these tribes agreed to surrender specific territorial land claims, give up their nomadic or seminomadic way of life, settle on federal reservations, and raise crops and livestock like civilized farmers.[8]

During the 1850s federal authorities in California scrambled to develop a workable reservation system. Driving into the western slope of the Sierra Nevada range, gold-rush miners slaughtered tiny bands of California Indians at a horrifying rate. In 1851 federal commissioners negotiated treaties with 139 groups and set aside a twelve-thousand-acre reservation, but the California delegation successfully pressured the U.S. Senate to reject the treaties. By 1858 only a few thousand Indians inhabited some three thousand acres of infertile land. When the Civil War broke out, the Indian population stood at 35,000 souls, down from 150,000 in 1845.[9]

Indian affairs in Oregon and Washington Territories were equally grim. Anglo farmers coveted the fertile lands west of the Cascade Mountains and harbored no compassion for their Indian neighbors. In 1855 tempers flared into the bloody Rogue River War near the California border. When regulars and volunteers defeated the Rogue River tribes a year later, the federal government banished Oregon Indians to Coastal Range reservations. To the north in Washington Territory, the Yakama Indians rose up against the Anglo invasion in 1856. Most of their Indian neighbors in the Columbia Basin joined them. Two years later in the summer of 1858, regulars under Col. George Wright brutally squashed the uprising at the Battles of Four Lakes and Spokane Plain. By decade's end the federal government had relocated the Oregon and Washington Indians onto eight reservations.[10]

The U.S. Army was unhappy with the transfer of the BIA to the Department of the Interior. Regular officers served the bureau only occasionally in the first half of the nineteenth century, but when the bureau resided in the Department of War, professional soldiers believed that they exercised some direct influence over its policies and operations. With the bureau lodged in the Department of the Interior, it now seemed beyond the reach of army counsel. Political patrons almost entirely, BIA field agents were frequently unfamiliar with Indian peoples and cultures and often incompetently administered their agencies and reservations. Across the American West, BIA corruption and graft were endemic. To regular army officers, the many political hacks in the federal Indian service dishonored their government, harmed their Indian charges, and slowed the civilizing process.

The interwar frontier was a civil-military gray zone, neither entirely at peace nor at war. The federal government tried to administer the West as a pacific civilian outpost but exerted little control over frontier anarchy. Recalling gold-rush California in the 1850s, Lt. George Crook of the Fourth Infantry wrote, "Greed was almost unrestrained, and from the nature of our government there was little or no law that these people were bound to respect." Frontier warfare seemed inevitable.[11]

To the U.S. Army, the West was a military theater in which the conditions of war generally prevailed. Throughout the region Anglos, Hispanos, and Indians resorted to armed force to dispossess the other and settle old scores. Under such belligerence, the army wanted military agendas given the highest priority. Speaking for many fellow officers, Lt. William W. Averell of the Mounted Riflemen wrote, "It must be understood that amid the clashing and warring elements of savagery that were ever ready to rend each other, to maintain any sort of security for life, property and commerce, it was supreme necessity that the army should dominate with undisputed sway, without reference to a feeble civil authority which was generally remote, sometimes unfriendly and always slow."[12] During the 1850s, despite the regularity of violence, the president never put any part of the American West directly under martial law.

The federal government subordinated the military to civilian authority, even in times of frontier warfare. In theory, regular troops could not pursue Indian depredators until the local federal Indian agent investigated and confirmed the report of violence and requested military intervention. In the field, however, post commanders checked most any credible civilian report. Although the policy of civil confirmation sometimes frustrated field commanders, it helped protect Indians from unwarranted army attack. Across the West, frontiersmen precipitated wars to wrest land from indigenous tribes. Under these circumstances, army officers had to assess cautiously any claim of Indian depredations.[13]

The status of Indian tribes as friendly or hostile could change weekly, blurring civil and military jurisdictions further. Within the same tribe, one band might be at war with settlers, while another might be at peace. Factions within bands might take different sides, complicating the job of the civilian agents and placing entire tribal populations at risk. In such situations, civilian agents and army officers often disagreed over with whom the United States was at war and whom they ought to punish for the bloodshed. Once war did break out, the army ascended to the lion's share of power in the affected district until it restored peace.[14]

The army officer's general contempt for frontiersmen complicated his working relationship with civilian authorities. On all frontiers, officers were struck by the basic disregard for human life—Indian life in particular—and decency among settlers of all ethnicities. Stationed at Fort Duncan in Eagle Pass, Texas, Lt. Richard Johnson wrote: "People are ignorant, destitute of any refinement, and have no respect for law and order. . . . I can safely say that someone was murdered in Eagle Pass or its vicinity every day in the year." Although the Texas Rangers enjoyed a giant reputation in their state, the regular army thought their legendary status was unmerited chest thumping. Army surgeon Albert J. Meyer described the Texas ranger as "an animal," a "lazy ruffianly scoundrel." The ranger's beloved state was "a country where little is known of, less cared for, the laws of God or man."[15]

The bloodthirstiness of the California frontiersmen appalled army officers. Prospectors and farmers showed no human compassion for besieged Indians, whose way of life the gold rush shattered. While searching for remnants of a hostile band on Yager Creek near Fort Humboldt, Lt. Aaron Hardcastle wrote, "For the past two years it has been the custom of the boys, says Wasgott-the-Guide, to shoot indians on sight, and he himself seems to convey the impression that he is one of the Boys." In late July 1852, Col. Ethan A. Hitchcock and Capt. Edward D. Townsend, headquartered in San Francisco, visited a cultivated Methodist minister, who turned the talk toward Indian affairs. His solution to the indigenous obstacle was to plant a smallpox epidemic among the Indians. After all, the clergyman noted, Indian "extermination" was part of God's design for the United States. Hitchcock, a humanitarian and reformer of national reputation, let the minister know that he and Townsend embraced no part of his unconscionable scheme. The two officers knew, however, that frontiersmen generally shared the preacher's genocidal sentiment.[16]

With a few exceptions, army officers sought an honorable solution to Indian-white friction. Like most federal policymakers, professional soldiers advocated Indian assimilation. In their opinion, progress was inevitable, and under the pressure of Anglo farms and towns, "primitive" indigenous peoples would fade away. However, army officers wanted that end to come through peaceful diplomacy and education, not through war.

Capt. Randolph B. Marcy, an infantry officer on the southern plains, argued that the United States, a great political democracy of a Christian people, was obligated to absorb Indians into American civilization. Introducing the

Indians to the "light of Christianity" and the "art" of farming would prepare them to take responsible roles in Anglo society. Lieutenant Johnson opined that federal reservations were expedient to politicians but unjust to the Indians: reservations encouraged "indolence and laziness of the hunter's life." A good Jeffersonian, Johnson encouraged Congress to grant each Indian family a "home" and "tract of land." Only farming would lift tribes from the poverty and ignorance to enjoy the fruits of Anglo-American civilization.[17]

Most army officers were no more anthropologically sophisticated about Indian cultures than the American citizenry was, but they were better informed about the desperate plight of indigenous peoples. Commissioned officers across the West agreed that impatient, grasping settlers sparked most of the so-called Indian wars. From Fort Randall in Nebraska Territory, Capt. Thomas W. Sweeny wrote, "All our *Indian wars*, with very few exceptions, are brought on either by our *frontier settlers* . . . or the traders in the Indian Country, who as a class, are an unmitigated set of *scoundrels.*" In March 1856 former regular William T. Sherman, then a banker in San Francisco, advised his brother, Congressman John Sherman, not to "meddle" in the Pacific Northwest Indian wars, explaining, "These wars are doubtless provoked by the indiscriminate robbery of the Indians, who, driven from the valleys, find no alternative but to steal and kill."[18]

The regular army was the martial van of Anglo progress, but professional soldiers were nonetheless ashamed of the dispossession and murder of the American Indians. When Captain Townsend assisted with the Cherokee Removal in 1838, he condemned the systematic plundering of the Cherokees by the Georgia volunteers. Of the experience he wrote, "Who can blame these poor creatures for fighting rather than remove from a country which but a small number agreed to sell?" Commanding the removal operation, Maj. Gen. Winfield Scott stung from pangs of guilt over the welfare of displaced Cherokees. While Capt. Ulysses S. Grant served at Columbia Barracks in Oregon Territory, he wrote his wife, Julia, "It is really my opinion that the whole race would be harmless and peaceable if they were not put upon by the whites." Officers believed that so-called "civilized" peoples ought to treat Indians, an inferior culture, with justice and humanity.[19]

When frontiersmen wanted to punish, remove, or destroy Indian peoples, they summoned the regular army. Whether their cause was just mattered little to Euroamerican settlers, but it mattered a great deal to the officer corps. Lieutenant Hardcastle expressed the army's ideal role during Indian-white conflict: "Army Officers should act as arbiters first and only punish the guilty afterwards." The Indians seemed to understand, Hardcastle elaborated, that the army, unlike the civilian volunteers, did not randomly slaughter their people and that officers exercised some judgment and compassion in Indian-white affairs. The Indians could trust few whites, but placing some faith in the army, they discussed their peoples' problems with the professional soldiers. Maybe Indians saw the U.S. Army, like themselves, as a society apart from the Euroamericans.[20]

One officer, Lt. Col. Edwin V. "Bull" Sumner of the First Dragoons, adamantly refused to join the civilian wars on the Indians. During thirty-two years of federal army service, this hard-boiled dragoon had seen settlers of all stripes stir up as much trouble as the Indians did on frontiers from New York to New Mexico, and he disliked both sides in equal portions. Assigned to command the Ninth Military Department, or New Mexico, in April 1851, he was ordered to whip the Navajos, Apaches, and Utes if they needed "severe chastisement," recast the "whole system of defense," and "reduce" the department's gargantuan quartermaster and subsistence "expenditures." One hundred percent a professional soldier, the Massachusetts-born Sumner threw himself into his command with Puritanical devotion.[21]

Lieutenant Colonel Sumner quickly shook up the Ninth Military Department. On 19 July he pulled into Santa Fe, "that sink of vice and extravagance," which he already knew from his service in Kearny's Army of the West during the late war. To check the settlements' "vicious" influences on his troops, he immediately ordered most of the Fort Marcy garrison to his new headquarters at Fort Union, twenty-one miles northeast of Las Vegas, and removed others from "Rayado, Albuquerque, Ciboleta, Secorro, Doña Ana, San Elizario, and El Paso" to the frontiers. Impatient to punish Indians, Sumner personally led "four companies of horse[,] one of Artillery, and two of Infantry" from Santo Domingo west toward Navajo country on 17 August. Bull Sumner intended to make a lasting impression on New Mexico Territory.[22]

However, within a month his zealousness had cultivated an enemy in James S. Calhoun, governor and ex officio superintendent of Indian affairs. Sumner's predecessor, Maj. John Munroe, had already taxed the governor's patience, but the new commander's cantankerousness escalated Calhoun's frustration and anxiety to alpine heights. Haunted by visions of territorial apocalypse, Calhoun feared a Pueblo and Hispano revolt joined by hundreds of grousing, disorderly teamsters, muleskinners, and drovers laid off by Sumner. The desperate governor requested army transportation and escorts for his field agents as well as guns and ammunition for the civilian militia, but with twisted logic, the hoary dragoon refused the governor's requisitions and entreaties. During Sumner's absence, Calhoun inveighed against the "want of military cooperation," Indian depredations in Sumner's rear, and the impotence of his own office.[23]

Frontier experience and institutional jealousy informed Sumner's professional discourtesies. The life-long federal servant in him despised the patronage hacks who all too frequently disgraced frontier federal offices while the professional soldier scoffed at civilian militias that killed Indians for personal gain. New Mexico's Indian wars especially rankled the methodical soldier. On 20 November 1851 Sumner wrote Adj. Gen. Roger Jones: "This predatory war has been carried on for two hundred years, between the Mexicans & Indians, quite time enough to prove, that unless some change is made the war will be interminable. They steal women and children, and Cattle from each other, and in fact carry on the war, in all respects, like two indian nations." Arming the militia would only fan the flames of Nuevomexicano-Indian vengeance.[24]

For all his froth and vinegar, Sumner was profoundly exasperated by the military challenges of the Ninth Military Department. In fall 1851 he was outraged when a Hispano gambler "killed two Apaches and dangerously wounded a third during a game" in San Antonio. Local authorities arrested but then freed the murderer. On scouts after Indians, the high desert reduced his big, beautiful dragoon mounts to hobbled, starved, and gasping nags. A proud and prickly regular, he admitted that his Navajo expedition had struck no crushing blows. His column penetrated Cañon de Chelly in fall 1851, but after only eleven miles he ordered its withdrawal, a painful sacrifice to military prudence. However, Sumner did leave behind Fort Defiance, whose troops would claw at the Navajos for the next twelve years.[25]

Sumner's command only got worse. By spring 1852 stress and scurvy were killing the fifty-year-old Calhoun. An empty territorial treasury forced his release of prisoners from the Santa Fe jail, and his civil officers were generally demoralized and impotent. Calhoun's territorial secretary—his legal successor—had left for the East. Fear of a bloody rebellion tortured Calhoun's weakened mind, and he claimed that agents from Mexico were trying to rally the "wild Indians" and disaffected Hispanos in Texas and New Mexico to drive out the Americans. Headquartered at Albuquerque, the ever-vigorous Sumner thought the conspiracy reports fantastic and incredible, but at Calhoun's behest, he transferred his offices to Santa Fe on 15 April and put regulars on the streets to restore confidence and order. In his sickbed at the Palace of the Governors on the Plaza, Calhoun could rest a little easier.[26]

Even more astonishing was that the governor relinquished his civil office to Bull Sumner. Three weeks into April, the governor and commander issued a joint proclamation: should Calhoun leave for the states, Sumner would "take charge of the Executive Office" until a successor arrived. Calhoun believed that Sumner alone had the power and means to keep the peace in New

Mexico. On 6 May, accompanied by his son-in-law, his private secretary, an Indian agent, and five Pueblos, the dying Calhoun pulled out of Santa Fe for Missouri, hauling his own coffin. The new commander-governor took pity enough to outfit Calhoun with "two wall tents, two water tanks, and second hand harness for 8 mules," but still obedient to his "existing orders," withheld "subsistence stores" and "corn." Probably with some pleasure, Calhoun took all "the Indian funds," leaving Sumner to buy territorial peace with army money. Somewhere near Missouri, Calhoun died and was interred at Independence.[27]

Sumner hated New Mexico—the people, culture, government, economy, environment, everything—and urged United States abandonment of the territory. In his sneering eyes, civil territorialism had utterly "failed": Nuevomexicanos were ignorant, promiscuous, and lazy; the soil killed crops; and "government money" was the only territorial "resource." Bull Sumner's advice was to withdraw the army, leave behind arms and ammunition, and let the Hispanos govern themselves and fight Indians in their time-honored way. They would be much happier, and the American people a little richer. On 10 September 1852 he gladly transferred the executive office to Gov. William Carr Lane and returned to fighting Indians and harassing lieutenants and captains.[28]

Bullied enough by Sumner, New Mexicans returned his spite. Published in the *Annual Report of the Secretary of War* at year's end, Sumner's official counsel infuriated New Mexicans, Anglo and Hispano. From the beginning, the soldier had punished the territory for his predecessors' "sins," and his penurious policies had pitched the territorial economy into deep depression. Fed up with his scorn, a newspaper editor in Santa Fe dubbed the frontier dragoon, "THE BIG BUG OF ALBUQUERQUE." Relieved of command on 1 July 1853, the fractious officer went east, studied military systems in Europe, and returned to the colonelcy of the First Cavalry. New Mexicans cheered his departure, and Sumner never looked back.[29]

Despite his impolitic command, credible arguments, applicable throughout the West, underlay some of Sumner's policies. If the United States government ever hoped to treat American Indians justly, it had to interdict the settlers' slaughter and enslavement of the indigenous inhabitants of the region. "Chastising" rampaging Anglo or Hispano frontiersmen with regular troops, however, would have ended any professional military career and sparked civil and criminal prosecutions of the officers involved. Frontier juries rarely convicted settlers of crimes against Indians, but frontier courts often decided in favor of civil plaintiffs who sued army officers for "false" arrest or illegal harassment. American society damned the army for acting against white settlers in support of the Indians; history has damned professional soldiers for failing to intervene vigorously on their behalf. The regulars' mission was hopeless, their legacy mixed.

Professional soldiers chose to obey their president right or wrong. When officers received the secretary of war's order to lead their troops to war on American Indians, they faithfully, if sometimes grudgingly, executed the mission. The pious Colonel Hitchcock wrote, "It is a hard case for troops to know the whites are in the wrong, and yet be compelled to *punish* the Indians if they attempt to defend themselves." Professional soldiers were taught to aid the weak and protect the defenseless; they were also indoctrinated to heed their president, no matter how misinformed or wrong. In the case of unjust wars, officers nearly always fell back on their constitutional obligations.[30]

Regulars often sympathized with American Indians, but officers fundamentally believed in the superiority of Anglo civilization. They were concerned less with the Indians' right to pursue their traditional way of life than with their speedy and just assimilation, which would release the army from frontier constabulary duty to prepare for wars with civilized enemies. To military observers, Indian society and culture would inevitably give way to farms, towns, and industries. However, the unsanctioned assaults of citizen militias inflicted irreparable damage to Indian trust and confidence in the federal government, stiffened indigenous resistance, and slowed the civilizing process. So long as Indians freely lived on land coveted by Euroamericans, the frontier unrest would tie down the regulars.

In addition to constitutional obligations and racial attitudes, military glory compelled the officer corps to tamp down moral outrage and wage war on the Indians. In the nineteenth-century army, promotion was by seniority alone, and combat—even against an uncivilized foe—was one of the few avenues to military distinction, particularly brevet promotion, open to the average line officer (see chapter 4). Professional soldiers agreed that most indigenous tribes would surrender their homeland only with a fight, some military coercion was inevitable, and war was a natural recourse in the settlement of the North American continent. When a war with Indians came, regular officers often set aside their moral reservations, embraced the opportunity with enthusiasm, and waged war with brutality.

2

ALL FRONT, NO REAR

Soldiers, Desert, and War

IN the nineteenth century, the American people treated federal regulars as more a police force than a standing army. The army staff and line advocated the deployment of seasonal campaigns from large regimental garrisons at the frontier's edge or in Indian homelands, but the federal government and its constituencies demanded the defense of the West from tiny static posts in the heart of the frontier. Stationed on territorial, racial, and cultural borders, regulars were indeed a federal constabulary mediating between settlers and Indians, but when racial tensions erupted into armed conflict, the army went to war only against the indigenous peoples.

Frontier warfare was partisan warfare, the fluid technique of the guerrilla and counterguerrilla. On both sides surprise, savagery, and terror were all-too-common methods, and killing was swift and indiscriminate. In the regular army no doctrine guided the conduct of war against American Indians in the West, and neither officers nor recruits received systematic training to conduct war on Indians. However, as military policymakers debated strategy to defend frontier settlements and overland trails, regulars in the field improvised small-unit tactics adapted to the realities of western deployment, logistics, environment, and culture. In a short time, tactics coalesced around horses and modern small arms, which gave regular troops mobility over large areas and lethal killing power against superior numbers. Small units such as squadrons and companies subsisted more readily than brigades without cumbersome supply trains in the western deserts and mountains. Across the West, post commanders deployed "scouts" of dragoons, mounted riflemen, and cavalry to trail and hunt indigenous raiding or war parties and destroy them upon contact. Field experience and skilled leadership made the scout a successful, if not decisive, field tactic.

In the trans-Mississippi West, there were no distinct lines of battle, only massive spaces and rugged topography. A veteran of campaigns in Washington Territory, Capt. Erasmus Keyes wrote, "In a campaign against Indians, the front is all around, and the rear is nowhere." To men schooled in nineteenth-century codes of manhood, frontier warfare lacked the honor of pitched battles between professional armies. To fight American Indians, officers and men searched for and invaded their villages; attacked men, women, and children; and burned their homes, belongings, and stores. Doggedly pursuing bands into fatigue and starvation was a common practice of seasoned campaigners. In this kind of warfare, psychological victories were more decisive than battlefield victories.[1]

No matter how many posts the U.S. Army constructed, regular troops could never adequately defend the trans-Mississippi West. The vast distances, constant relocation of the frontier, and shortages of troops, supplies, and transportation hampered unit deployment. The United States government and its constituency often labeled the army a failed protector. William P. Floyd, a civilian on the topographical Whipple Expedition in New Mexico, accused the army of bleeding the federal government "most lavishly." As regulars campaigned against the Navajos in 1859, he wrote: "Congress had better disband the army. . . . The life of no citizen is protected by the army and the death of none has been avenged by it[.]"[2] Floyd, like many civilians in the East and West, wanted the Indian wars turned over to volunteers—the nightmare of professionals like Edwin V. Sumner and Ethan A. Hitchcock. Local militia had concrete stakes—homes, families, farms, and businesses—in their conflict's outcome, and vengeance would come easily to them.

The army labored under a number of handicaps in the frontier West. One was a shortage of officers serving on the line. In 1853 and 1854, as Insp. Gen. Joseph K. F. Mansfield toured the New Mexico and Pacific Coast military frontiers, he reported "too few officers" on duty with their companies. Inspecting the post at Los Lunas, New Mexico, he found only one commissioned officer, Capt. Richard S. Ewell, "present for duty." The aggregate force of Ewell's Company G, First Dragoons, was eighty-four. However, one of Ewell's officers was on detached service as regimental quartermaster, while another had never joined the unit. In New Mexico eleven companies had only one officer present. In four of those instances, the commanding officer, like Ewell, was simultaneously commander, quartermaster, and commissary.[3]

According to Mansfield the military instruction of enlisted men suffered when officers were absent. During his Pacific Coast inspection, he observed expert line evolutions by the men at Forts Humboldt and Jones, but their skirmishing drills were unspectacular. Too few units, Mansfield lamented, enjoyed routine "target practice." Bayonet drill received no attention. (Troops on the western frontier were rarely compelled to fix bayonets and charge an enemy. No rank of American Indians was reckless enough to let regular troops close with bayonets.) Overburdened with staff and command duties, few officers could give sufficient attention to military drill, but their extraordinary devotion had kept frontier units reasonably fit and sober.[4]

On remote frontiers both officers and enlisted men had to be more than combat soldiers. Poorly funded by Congress, the Department of War lacked the budget to hire large crews of civilian employees to service frontier military stations. When the army erected a post, it often used the officers and men who would afterward man it. A cheap pool of labor, enlisted men earned extra pay "as carpenters, wheelwrights, blacksmiths, stonemasons, saddlers, clerks, teamsters, and woodcutters." Befitting their military rank and social station, commissioned officers supervised the work.

To construction and maintenance the army added farming and gardening. Most companies raised garden vegetables to supplement their diet of army rations, but in the early 1850s, the Fillmore administration ordered a post-farm program to eliminate the cost of shipping vegetables and other perishable foods from eastern depots. Poor growing conditions, ignorance of farming, and the absence of troops on campaign doomed the plan. Critical of the post farms, Mansfield wrote: "All military instructions, drills, and expeditions after an enemy will become onerous and distasteful and neglected, in view of the all absorbing love of gain. If a command is to be marched, it cannot be done till the crops are gathered and the spoils divided." The army's mission was not "to make farmers" but create soldiers.[5]

When new soldiers reached their frontier stations, their military training was often inadequate. After inducting recruits, the army shipped them to training schools—infantry to Governor's Island, New York; artillery to Newport Barracks, Kentucky; and mounted troops to Carlisle Barracks, Pennsylvania, or Jefferson Barracks, Missouri. Drill instructors introduced the novice soldiers to the rigors of military life, discipline, and drill, putting them through the paces of squad, company, battalion, and regimental exercises. The demand for replacements in frontier regiments, however, often prematurely stole recruits away from basic training, sometimes even before they learned to fire their weapons. Along the Santa Fe Trail in summer 1855, a fire swept through the camp of recruits destined for New Mexico. Some rifles discharged, others simply burned. When officers and men examined the weapons, they "found that 140 of them out of 325 had been loaded with the Ball first." According to Charles Whilden, a civilian clerk, these recruits were "mostly dutchmen," many of whom probably understood English imperfectly.[6]

To rectify such deficiencies, frontier commanders tried to institute training regimens for their troops. Sgt. Percival G. Lowe recalled that during the fall of 1851 and through the following winter at Fort Leavenworth, the First Dragoons devoted one hour to mounted drill before noon and one hour to foot drill in the afternoon. All men performed the "evolutions, saber exercises and pistol practice" at all gaits. Weather permitting, the dragoons never missed a session, except foot drill on Saturday. The officers inspected their men on horseback on Sunday morning. In case of snow or rain, the dragoons "drilled on foot in quarters."[7]

Lt. William W. Averell ardently trained Company F of the Mounted Riflemen. En route to the West, he was impressed by the intensive drilling and training of the newly formed Second Cavalry, "nearly a thousand mounted men," at Jefferson Barracks in fall 1855. At Fort Craig, New Mexico, Averell routinely put Company F through "drill and target practice." His men exercised both on horseback and foot. Anticipating their deployment against Indians, he developed "a special drill for Indian fighting." Marching in a column of twos, his company could deploy in sets of four "one hundred yards in any direction" in less than sixty seconds. Across the frontier, however, fatigue duty and campaigning cut into the regulars' instruction.[8]

Basic training tactically prepared recruits to fight conventional European armies, not western Indians. Several experienced officers suggested that the army train soldiers to campaign in the desert and fight Indians. The frontier hunter was their model. "Hunting parties," not fatigue details, Asst. Surgeon Rodney Glisan advised, ought to command the frontier soldier's time. He wrote, "Hunting is the handmaid of war." In his eyes, chasing Indians was similar to stalking wild game. Immigrant recruits would especially benefit from practice at tracking and shooting.[9]

Capt. Randolph Marcy, a western veteran, agreed with Glisan. During the frontier period, dress parades and guard mountings composed most of the recruit's military training. Heavily armed "well-disciplined hunters" made the best Indian-fighting unit, Marcy argued. The army ought to add hunting, or "field-sports," to its training regimen. While learning to shoot straight the recruit would adapt to wilderness hardships, develop physical stamina, and learn to track and bivouac. Such training and skills would aid the soldier in "border warfare." During the interwar period, the enlisted man was generally encouraged to hunt in his spare time, and Sgt. Eugene Bandel recalled that the army was not "stingy" with ammunition. In fact, at Jefferson Barracks the young German trooper fired off "seventy-five cartridges in one day alone," largely at "the wild pigeons."[10]

Throughout the 1850s, army commanders disagreed over what constituted the most efficient and effective military defense system for the West. In any scheme, the army had to deal with several constants: enormous distances, slow and tenuous supply lines, a tiny regular army, disorderly frontiersmen, and skillful, stubborn, and elusive Indians. Throughout the nation's frontier period, the fundamental defensive unit was the static, or fixed, post, which one or two companies usually garrisoned. Breaking up regiments, the policy scattered company-sized units throughout the vast western expanse. Secretary of War Jefferson Davis admonished Congress that dismembering regiments was "injurious to the discipline, instruction and efficiency of the troops." Colonels in the field rarely united their regiments in exercises or campaigns.[11]

Supplying fixed posts was a financial embarrassment to the cost-conscious Congress and army. After the Mexican-American War, the military frontier relocated from the Mississippi River Valley, intersected by navigable rivers, to the American West, accessed by poor, undeveloped roads and trails. In 1850 Secretary of War Charles Conrad graphically wrote, "They [posts] are either on the Pacific coast, on the route to Oregon, or far in the interior of Texas and New Mexico, remote from navigable streams and from the States where enlistments were made and whence all supplies are drawn." Consequently, the army supplied its dozens of posts by costly wagon freighters from supply depots at Fort Leavenworth in Kansas, Fort Union in New Mexico, San Antonio in Texas, Benicia Barracks in California, and Fort Vancouver in the Pacific Northwest. The federal government shipped supplies and stores to the latter two either around the South American cape or across the Isthmus of Panama.[12]

Costs skyrocketed. After 1848 federal regulars redeployed to new stations across the western frontier. In 1849 Q.M. Gen. Thomas S. Jesup reported that his department hired 658 wagons, 2,440 mules, 374 horses, and 2,794 oxen to transport supplies and property for troops marching overland to Oregon and New Mexico and 220 wagons, 750 horses and mules, and 1,000 oxen for troops marching overland to El Paso. Contracts for transportation to Santa Fe, Fort Kearny, and Fort Laramie cost $133,000 alone. In the fiscal year ending 30 June 1860, the outlay for transportation in the Department of New Mexico was $80,000. The most graphic and shocking figures, undoubtedly generated by Jesup, appeared in Secretary of War Conrad's annual report in 1850. Previous to the war with Mexico, in the fiscal year 1 July 1843–30 June 1844, total Quartermaster Department expenditures were $870,999.73. After the conflict, in the fiscal year ending 30 June 1850, they had nearly quintupled to $4,295,298.60. Conrad's successor, Jefferson Davis, believed that the expense of the post system far outweighed its public utility.[13]

To reduce army expenditures, secretaries of war and Quartermaster General Jesup advocated transportation improvements, frontier settlement, and economic development in the American West. In 1849 Jesup urged congressional appropriations to improve Gulf Coast harbors, the lower Rio Grande, and the Trinity, Colorado, and Red Rivers in Texas; to clear the Missouri and upper Mississippi Rivers for navigation; and to explore and survey the shortest and most direct routes between frontier posts. The quartermaster general concluded, "I recommend these improvements as military works of more importance in defence of the country . . . than the best system of fortifications that could be adopted." Instead of purchasing supplies from merchants in the East, contracting with local grain, vegetable, and meat providers would cut supply expenditures and encourage settlement, ranching, and farming in the American West. To that end in 1850, Secretary of War Conrad requested the expansion of the army's cavalry in order to sweep the West of the Indians.[14]

The primary alternative to the static post was the roving column, a system proposed by Col. Stephen W. Kearny of the First Dragoons in 1845. During the summer of that year, he had led a brigade of infantry, dragoons, and artillery up the Oregon-California Trail to the head of South Pass. His column snaked through the plains country of the Northern Cheyennes and Plains Sioux. Kearny believed that the martial cavalcade of blue-clad troops mounted on tall strong horses and armed with glistening sabers, pistols, muskets, and howitzers had impressed the natives of United States military might. For a few years at least, Kearny anticipated no Sioux or Cheyenne attacks on emigrants and merchants plying the Oregon-California Trail.[15]

Upon his return to Fort Leavenworth in fall 1845, Kearny opposed establishing a regular-army post on the North Platte River near Fort Laramie, then an old fur-trade outpost that served the northern Rockies. Hundreds of miles from the nearest military depot, the new installation would have no water access and cost an Astorian fortune to supply. Wanting to keep the First Dragoons as intact as possible, Kearny suggested an alternative, the roving column. Every two or three years from large garrisons on the prairie's edge, the U.S. Army ought to deploy a major "military expedition" into Indian homelands to awe their "occupants." In the event of war, such columns of horse also could steal quickly into Indian country to punish the inhabitants. Supply by rail or river would be simple and economical.[16]

Throughout the 1850s civilian and military leaders echoed Kearny's roving column. In 1851 Maj. Gen. Winfield Scott urged the withdrawal of garrisons from Forts Atkinson, Kearny, and Laramie, all of which were located hundreds of miles west of Fort Leavenworth. Instead, each summer the army ought to dispatch two or three dragoon or mounted rifle companies to roam the plains all the way to the Rocky Mountains. In Scott's opinion, mobile columns of troops fit enough to track and attack war parties and villages at a moment's notice would cow the "wild Indians" into keeping the peace.[17]

To Lt. Col. Edwin V. Sumner in New Mexico Territory, keeping horses and men fit in the western deserts and mountains was the nub of the challenge. After his frustrating Navajo campaign in 1851 he concluded, "It is impossible *to make long marches* with Cavalry, *on grass alone.*" A year later from Fort Massachusetts, Sgt. Frank Clarke succinctly described the dragoon field kit and daily horse ration: "[W]e carry a rifle, a heavy single barrelled dragoon Pistol, one of Colts Revolving Pistols (6 shooters), & a heavy Dragoon Sabre. The weight of a man & kit upon a horse will average 350 pounds. Our forage Ration is very small considering it being but 12 pounds of Hay & 8 pounds of Corn, or 12 pounds of Oats, per diem, barely sufficient to keep a horse alive much more in condition. On a Summer Scout the horses having nothing but Grass." Western deserts and mountains offered little grass and almost no grain, and eastern-bred dragoon horses required a lot of both. Upon reaching their campaign destinations, they were often too "broken down" to overtake fresh, desert-adapted Indian ponies.[18]

Mulling over these handicaps, Sumner offered the beginnings of a solution. Urging the withdrawal of most cavalry from New Mexico, he recommended campaigning with infantry but attaching small specialized units of "*very select horse*" to the column. This mounted strike force—almost a special forces unit—would be highly trained and heavily armed, and its horses would be well maintained. Leading their animals on long marches, the cavalrymen would mount up and give chase at the critical moment. Sumner concluded, "A small body of this kind would be worth ten times their number of ordinary men on broken down horses."[19]

Indeed, men on foot could travel farther than horses in the desert. Apaches in flight were known to hike seventy-five miles a day. The dismounted soldier or warrior could also cross the country with greater stealth. If on a horse-stealing expedition, Apaches and Navajos often struck out for the settlements on foot and returned on their enemies' horses. Should regular troops have done the same? Although infantrymen might display greater stamina than dragoon horses, they still had to steal into Indian homelands quickly and quietly and catch stationary targets—unsuspecting villages or camps—completely by surprise. Mounted units were still necessary to pursue horse-borne Indians. Usually guarding military posts, frontier infantrymen never got the training and experience to conduct the mission Sumner envisioned. Dragoons, mounted riflemen, and cavalry remained the basic combat arm on the interwar frontier.

During the Franklin Pierce administration, Secretary of War Davis recommended a variation on the roving column. He opined that the weakly manned fixed post invited Indian "aggression" and envisioned large garrisons erected in Indian homelands and holding neighboring Indians in the army's grip. Battalion- and regimental-sized units in these installations would promote the troops' "instruction and discipline, . . . efficiency and usefulness" and would cause "a material diminution of expense." The army had already begun to experiment with the large garrison and roving columns at Fort Defiance, which Lieutenant Colonel Sumner planted on the doorstep to Navajo country in New Mexico Territory in 1851. With five companies garrisoning Defiance, Sumner wrote, "If this post does not put a stop to the Navajo depredations, nothing will do it but their entire extermination." However, Fort Defiance was expensive to supply, and its troops inflicted limited immediate casualties on the Navajos.[20]

Frontier politics mitigated the application of the roving column. Consolidating small garrisons into larger ones would have raised a storm of protest in areas stripped of regulars. Throughout the nineteenth century, frontiersmen complained that static-post systems were a porous defense at best, but with regulars nearby, settlers felt a little more secure nonetheless. In addition, military posts of all sizes were economic boons to nearby communities. In the West's boom-and-bust economy, no settlement wanted to loose the reliable income from army contracts and business.

The roving column was a flawed concept anyway. Mobile battalions would surprise their adversaries on occasion, but the Indians would have dodged the large columns just as often. Those "fine" American horses that Kearny boasted of grew weak on the plains and prairie grasses and broke down under hard desert service. Brigade-sized garrisons and columns satisfied the army's love of showy pageantry but would have provided an inadequate frontier defense.

The problem was not that the static-post system was a flawed defensive strategy but that the army was too small to man it adequately. By 1850 American settlement had demolished the Permanent Indian Frontier envisioned by policymakers before the Mexican-American War. Sometime during the 1850s, all regions in the West experienced a war between settlers and American Indians. Although the static-post system was unsatisfactory to civilians and soldiers, it was politically feasible to officials in Washington, D.C., and acceptable to state and territorial authorities. Pressured by their constituencies, politicians demanded that the posts remain dispersed over the frontier. The lonely army station, a cluster of nondescript buildings enclosing a dusty parade ground, remained a fixture in the American West for the next half-century.

Despite complaints from the American West, regular troops operating from fixed posts were far more lethal and effective than frontiersmen credited them. At their best, they were the "well-disciplined hunters" that Captain Marcy desired. For four decades regulars waged a low-intensity war that punished American Indians for raiding homesteads and settlements. Frontier-army warfare was no Napoleonic campaign but a form of war, however imperfect, well adapted to the wide-open West and the elusive Indian adversary. The variables that worked for the army and against the Indians were time and resources. Constantly deploying company-sized scouts and seasonal brigade-sized expeditions, the army chipped away at the edges of American Indian societies until they crumbled by century's end.

Soon after his experiences in the Spokane Expedition in 1858, Lt. Lawrence Kip of the Third Artillery wrote, "An Indian war is a chapter of accidents." As enemies on the field of battle, Indian warriors defied all categories of western military science, and a lot of dumb luck was necessary to corner them. Captain Marcy rued, "Their tactics are such as to render the old system almost wholly impotent." The application of military science as it was taught at West Point was a futile exercise. The best of the professional soldiers adapted to the West and Indians.[21]

For the frontier commander, the arena of war was an entire region of deserts and mountains. His Indian foes rarely closed on his troops or allowed his men to get very near. Sergeant Lowe, however, reassured his readers that Indian warriors were no "cowards." To the contrary, armed with bows and arrows they were keenly aware of their technological deficiencies and "skirmished for the advantage." Their guerrilla-warfare tactics—sudden ambush and lightning attack—were skillfully tailored to western terrain.[22] Unable to defeat the army on its terms, American Indians forced regulars to conform to their way of war.

The basic frontier field operation was the squadron or company scout. Riding out from a fixed post, the detachment generally had one of two missions (though sometimes both): to pursue a specific enemy or to patrol a well-defined territory. While on patrol, a detachment often struck the trail of a raiding or war party and literally hunted the warriors. The detachment's luck, the commander's skill, and the unit's field experience combined to dictate success or failure. The random method, physical exhaustion, revolving pistol, and emotional frustration combined to make the scout an especially violent offensive-defensive tactic of warfare.

Although the army launched scouts from garrisons throughout the American West, it deployed more of them on the southern plains and in the

Southwest than anywhere else. Feeling the pressure of American expansion yet attracted by the spoils—horses, cattle, and sheep—of weakly defended settlements, the Comanches, Kiowas, Apaches, Navajos, and Utes were locked in a brutal war with frontier regulars in Texas and New Mexico throughout the interwar decade. Hampered by limited manpower, federal troops deployed the scout, usually a mounted force, as its principal tactical field unit.

Begun by the Spanish and Mexicans, carried on by the Anglo Texans, and assumed by the United States, the war on the Comanches, Kiowas, and Apaches in Texas was "one of extermination," in the words of Asst. Surgeon Albert J. Meyer. Briefly applied by Col. William S. Harney in the early 1850s, the strategy adopted by Col. Albert S. Johnston and Brig. Gen. David E. Twiggs was to take the war directly to Indian country in all four seasons, putting the warriors on the defensive. Determined to blunt Comanche raiding, Johnston ordered his Second Cavalry to prosecute the most destructive war possible and to treat all Comanche people "with rigorous hostility."[23]

The warfare in Texas was punishing and lethal. On 14 February 1856 a company of Second Cavalry under Capt. James Oakes struck out from Fort Mason, near the confluence of Comanche Creek and the Llano River, after a party of Waco Indians (see map 2). After eight days of hard trailing to the south, Oakes's troopers caught and routed the party, "killing and wounding several warriors and capturing their animals and other property." Two soldiers received serious arrow wounds. Overtaken by cold, damp weather, Oakes's men lived on two days' rations, what game animals they could kill, and the flesh of broken-down horses until they reached their post. In fall 1857, commanding the Second Cavalry in Colonel Johnston's absence, Lt. Col. Robert E. Lee recounted four separate scouts during which cavalry detachments tracked down war parties, killed fifteen Comanches and Apaches, and wounded others. Lee reported, "So you see the Regt. . . . is constantly inflicting more or less punishment on the disturbers of the frontier."[24]

The bloodiest of the fall scouts was Lt. John B. Hood's operation to the headwaters of Devil's River. On 5 July 1857, with an Indian guide and a compass, he led twenty-five Second Cavalry from Fort Mason toward the Concho River and, on day ten, struck the trail of fifteen to twenty warriors heading for Mexico. Four days onto the Staked Plains, trail sign showed that the war party had enlarged to fifty warriors. At the headwaters of the Devil's River, Hood's detachment, now reduced to seventeen men, came upon the Indians arrayed on a distant hill.

Lured by a white flag, the regulars warily approached, but warriors sprang up from concealment and opened fire, the muzzles of their small arms setting fire to the dry brush. Other warriors charged. Hood's men blazed away with carbines and pistols, often at point-blank range. Cracking their shields over the cavalry mounts' foreheads, the warriors forced the troopers to fall back but suddenly halted their attack and set up a mournful howling. The two sides disengaged. While the war party, probably Comanche and Lipan Apache, lost nine or ten men, Hood's detachment suffered two men killed and four wounded.[25]

Grisly warfare was not restricted to Texas; New Mexico was equally bloody. Fort Craig south of Socorro in the Rio Grande Valley was in the middle of a war between frontier settlers—Anglo and Hispano—and Apache, Navajo, and Comanche Indians (see map 4). On 22 July 1857 Capt. Andrew Porter of the Mounted Riflemen, commanding the post, detached 1st Sgt. Hugh McQuaide and seven men from Company F to investigate a report of Indians below the post. A twenty-seven-year-old Irishman and former silk-cord dresser, McQuaide had joined the regiment in 1851, learned and perfected his frontier soldiering on the Texas frontier, and developed into an outstanding combat leader. His tenacity and skill earned the respect of both commissioned and noncommissioned officers who served with him.[26]

In the evening of 22 July 1857, Sergeant McQuaide led his squadron southward from Fort Craig, struck the trail of four Indians fifteen miles below the post, and ordered his men to encamp. The next morning McQuaide and his men crossed to the east bank of the Rio Grande, followed the trail of the Indians, and soon discovered several "Mexicans killed and scalped." After burying the victims, the squadron pursued and overtook "7000 head" of stolen sheep, but the Indians, detecting the pursuit, fled across the river.

McQuaide now tracked the warriors. Three were mounted, one was on foot. Recrossing to the western bank of the Rio Grande, McQuaide and his squadron trailed the Indians' "zig-zag course for 25 or 30 miles" to the west toward the Mogollon Mountains and then to the northwest toward either the Magdalena or the San Mateo Mountains. After resting his men and horses at a waterless camp, he resumed the pursuit at 12:30 A.M. and reached the western entrance of a pass at daybreak. He rested his men and horses at a waterhole for an hour and then led them through.

After emerging onto the eastern slope, McQuaide tracked the Indians to the northeast. At 3:00 P.M. he and the squadron rode upon an Indian mount killed not more than thirty minutes earlier. Ten miles later they discovered another abandoned horse. By sunset all four of the Indians had dispersed on foot into the mountains behind San Antonio. McQuaide concluded that further pursuit was hopeless and encamped his men for the night. The detachment returned to Fort Craig the following day. He had led the squadron on a scout of one hundred and sixty miles.[27]

Although McQuaide failed to strike the Indians, he demonstrated the perseverance and knowledge that successful frontier warfare demanded. He knew the locations of water and grass, the endurance and breaking point of his men and horses, and the practices of Indian warriors in flight. He drew on his experiences in Texas and New Mexico and on those of other officers stationed at Fort Craig. The leader of a scout or reconnaissance often kept field notes of distance, direction, and terrain, and he carefully recorded the location, abundance, quality, and seasonality of water and grass. Such information often became a part of the permanent post record. If a scout commander was unfamiliar with the Fort Craig sector, he could usually requisition or hire a civilian guide to lead his troops.[28]

In addition to Mescalero and Gila Apaches, troops at Fort Craig fought the Navajos, who also raided the middle Rio Grande. During the second half of 1858, regular troops from Fort Defiance wreaked havoc on the Navajos, forcing them to sue for peace at year's end. Although quiet throughout most of 1859, the Indians made a "general descent" on the Rio Grande settlements below Albuquerque in early 1860 and stole vast herds of livestock. As they drove the animals down the east bank of the river toward crossings below Fort Craig, Capt. Andrew Porter, commanding the post, dispatched squadrons to punish the Navajos.[29]

The Mounted Riflemen at Fort Craig mauled the Navajos. On 7 February 1860 Sergeant McQuaide and fifteen men of Company F trailed stolen stock from the northern mouth of the Jornada del Muerto westward and northwestward, overtook the Navajos at the head of Cañon Alamosa, killed one warrior in the attack, and recovered twelve hundred sheep. On the same day, Captain Porter and twenty-five Mounted Riflemen rushed to cut off the retreat of a Navajo raiding party west of Fort Craig. The following day, unaware of the riflemen's proximity, forty Navajos drove four hundred sheep and a few beeves in full view of Porter's camp "on a wooded knoll at the base" of the Lucera Mountains. The captain quietly but quickly ordered his men to mount up. Their pistols blazing, the soldiers charged into the Navajos. In a running fight covering eighteen miles, Porter's men either killed or wounded sixteen warriors and recovered the stock.[30]

On 8 February Capt. George McLane and forty-one Mounted Riflemen surprised a party of approximately seventy Navajos driving a large herd of sheep and cattle through Cañon del Muerto below Fort Craig. McLane sent Lieutenant Cressey and a squadron after fifteen mounted Navajos who fled back up the canyon. As forty-five warriors detached themselves from driving the herd and lodged themselves on a hillside, McLane halted his column, ordered his men to dismount, and flung them against the Navajos. In a fifteen-minute close combat, some hand-to-hand, his men killed thirteen warriors and drove the others over the hill. At the river crossing, a corporal's detail of ten men, concealed in the brush and trees, ambushed approximately ten Navajos driving the herd, killing two and recovering one thousand sheep and forty-five cattle. In all that day, McLane's Mounted Riflemen recovered five thousand sheep and a hundred cattle.[31]

During the first two weeks of February 1860, three of five scouting missions from Fort Craig struck heavy blows. After he assessed the performance of his command and the "additional information" that poured into Fort Craig, an ecstatic Porter reported, "Those Indians killed by different detachments could not fall short of forty."[32] His final tally for Navajo casualties was probably high, but his command's success demonstrated that ably led field units, girded by grit and determination and blessed with a little luck, could levy a heavy toll on American Indians in war.

In the interwar American West, the combination of static post and roving column was reasonably well adapted to national politics and western conditions. No session of Congress would raise and field a professional army large enough to defeat the Indians within ten or fifteen years. Nor would the army, for ethical and professional reasons, cooperate with frontier volunteers to bring the wars against the Indians to a speedy end. Too weak to overwhelm the Indians and politicians, the regular army learned to survive and fight in the American West.

Army officers disliked the isolated small commands of the static-post system, but the company-sized scouting operations made some sense in the American West. Good water and nutritious grass were often scarce in the region during much of the year. The desert could support small squadrons better than large brigades. Against mounted Indian warriors, the scouting detachment was more highly mobile and flexible than the battalion-sized expedition, which was often burdened with a wagon or mule train. When officers and men were field conditioned, battle hardened, and heavily armed, they comprised a formidable, destructive combat force. Their greatest handicap was the army's small numbers of officers and men, too few to cover the West adequately and break Indian resistance quickly.

The ignorance of the army high command handicapped regular troops in the field. In the United States, military policymakers and thinkers never recognized frontier constabulary duty as a legitimate mission of a professional standing army, and frontier warfare, neither a western science nor civilized art, was bloodthirsty savagery driven by instinct and whim. Their object was to prepare the regular army for wars against civilized—particularly European—

armies. When officers and enlisted men assumed their duty station on the western frontiers, they were woefully ill prepared to police racial unrest and fight Indians. Soldiers—officers and enlisted men alike—learned frontier campaigning and fighting from their experienced comrades and while in the field. Indeed, from regiment to regiment, the best units absorbed the lessons of western defense and warfare, developed into superb frontier combat units, and used surprise, geography, climate, horses, and technology to their advantage.

3

CHASTISE THEM

Campaigns, Combat, and Killing

FEDERAL Indian policy directly informed the army's summer campaigns. Throughout the American West, regular troops delivered state-sanctioned violence to execute United States law and policy. The mission was either to punish and terrorize Indian depredators, drive specific tribes onto legal reservations, or force Indians to the treaty table. Race, environment, technology, profession, and fear aggravated the pitch of violence on the frontier battlefield.

In every western department, several hundred regular troops crossed difficult terrain, searched for Indians, and struck devastating blows. The success of these "scouts in force" was tied directly to the commanding officer, who personally led the brigade into the field and into combat. These ambitious men linked the destiny of their civilization, their nation, their race, their regiment, and themselves to their victories in battle with the Indians. In the frontier army, professional soldiers earned distinction through exploration or combat, and the majority of officers embraced combat opportunities, for battlefield glory might later translate into professional advancement.

Frontier campaigns were a battery of physical punishments and natural hazards. The best commanders skillfully managed their men and animals to minimize their loss to exposure, exhaustion, and accident. Successful combat officers utilized environment, technology, surprise, and aggression to terrorize, destroy, and defeat their Indian enemy. This is best demonstrated by looking at the campaigns of four commanders: Col. Edwin V. Sumner, Col. William S. Harney, Capt. Earl Van Dorn, and Col. George Wright.

Inspired by the promise of western adventure, seventeen-year-old Robert M. Peck abandoned his printer's apprenticeship in Covington, Kentucky, and enlisted in the U.S. Army's First Cavalry Regiment. Assigned to Company E, he trained and drilled at Jefferson Barracks, Missouri, during the winter of 1856–57. When the Missouri River ice broke, he and other recruits steamed upstream to Fort Leavenworth, Kansas, headquarters of the First Cavalry.[1]

Private Peck landed in the middle of the biggest cavalry campaign of the 1857 season. Fed up with white intruders in their central plains homeland, the Cheyennes had skirmished with traffic on the Platte River Road the previous year. In August a retaliatory scout of First Cavalry had killed six Cheyennes on Grand Island in the Platte River. The Cheyennes responded by assaulting an emigrant camp, killing two men and an infant and abducting the mother.[2] Full-scale war was engaged.

Private Peck and Company E would ride with Edwin V. Sumner, recently promoted colonel of the First Cavalry, to hunt and punish the Cheyennes. That spring of 1857 General-in-Chief Winfield Scott ordered Colonel Sumner into the central plains either to treat with or chastise the Cheyennes. Enthralled with combat, Sumner was for fighting. Enlisted men like Private Peck "idolized" their colonel, emulated his "dash and aggressiveness," and proudly rode behind him.[3]

The Cheyenne Expedition proceeded toward Indian country in two separate battalions. Exiting Fort Leavenworth on 18 May, Peck's Company E was one of four First Cavalry companies that marched down the Santa Fe Trail toward the upper Arkansas River under Maj. John Sedgwick. His instructions were to hold no "intercourse" with the Cheyennes along the route until Sumner's arrival. The colonel explained, "We do not go upon the plains this year to coax Indians but to teach them that their depredations must cease at once, and forever."[4]

Peck never imagined his first combat would be with *Bison bison*, the North American buffalo. As the column approached the Big Bend of the Arkansas, a massive herd thundered out of the north toward Sedgwick's strung-out cavalry and wagon train. As an artilleryman, the major was brevetted twice for bravery in the Mexican-American War, but he froze before the shaggy, brown tidal wave some two miles out, churning and spilling toward his command.[5]

Peck's captain, Samuel D. Sturgis, had survived these stampedes before. Gingerly taking over, he ordered the wagons circled, teams, cattle, and horses corralled, and the regulars deployed into a wedge. At Sturgis's command the troopers poured on a "withering fire" to part the squalling brown flood. A solid half-hour and several thousand rounds later, the bison sea had passed. Resuming command, the grateful Sedgwick led his battalion along the

Arkansas to Fountain que Bouille Creek near the Rockies, where the column turned north. On 3 July his troops came to a rest on the banks of the South Platte River to await Sumner's column.[6]

As Col. William S. Harney scrambled to organize the Utah Expedition, his professional rival, Colonel Sumner, led two companies of First Cavalry from Fort Leavenworth on 20 May. At Fort Kearny Sumner hired Pawnee scouts and attached two Second Dragoon companies to his force. Taking the Platte River Road, his battalion pulled into Fort Laramie on 22 June. Five days later, leaving behind the dragoons but augmented by three companies of Sixth Infantry, his column struck out southward, rendezvoused with Sedgwick's command, and established Camp Buchanan a few miles west of Kiowa Creek on the South Platte River (see map 1).[7]

Sumner's plan was to cut loose from his wagon train and march southeastward toward the Republican River, the heart of the Cheyenne homeland. In bivouac at Camp Buchanan, Private Peck and his comrades prepared horses and tack, mules and packs, and kits and weapons for Sumner's bold strike. The colonel's scout in force included six companies of First Cavalry, three of Sixth Infantry, four prairie howitzers and crews, Delaware and Pawnee scouts, and a mule train, remuda, and beef herd. To preserve their horses, the cavalrymen stripped to their clothes, "saddle-blankets," and weapons. Sumner's headquarters and the hospital carried one "rainfly" each. The mule train packed ammunition and twenty days' rations. Casting off from the wagons, the Cheyenne Expedition snaked eastward along the South Platte River on 13 July.[8]

"Bull" Sumner intended to dog the Cheyennes into battle, all summer long if necessary. Four days later his expedition, three columns arrayed "en echelon," left behind the South Platte drainage and coursed southeast toward the Republican River. According to Private Peck, the short-grass plains country was "somewhat broken" and almost entirely "treeless." The scouts screened the advance and flanks at a distance of ten to twelve miles. Their information was that a large Cheyenne village had stood on Beaver Creek as late as May. The hunt was fatiguing and tedious until, three weeks into July, the regulars crossed the south fork of the Republican. Pursuing a wide, fresh trail, they passed through the sites of three abandoned villages and one sun-dance village before encamping at Bow Creek between the North and South Forks of the Solomon River on 28 July.[9] The following day, still tracking southeastward, the Cheyenne Expedition entered the south fork drainage. Late that morning one of the trackers bumped into Cheyenne scouts, who slowly retreated toward the east.

Anxious to hit the Cheyennes before they fled, Sumner immediately readied his First Cavalry to give chase. Private Peck recalled, "At the command, we dismounted, tightened up saddle-girths, and examined arms and equipments to see that everything was in fighting order." Next, sitting astride his cavalry mount, the "white-headed, white-bearded" Sumner harangued everyone to obey orders, pull "together," and proclaimed, "We can whip the whole tribe." Today, the men and officers would learn whether his epithet "Bull" connoted his booming parade-ground voice, thick forehead, or fighting temper.[10]

Sumner had no clear idea of how many Cheyennes awaited the First Cavalry in the Solomon River Valley, but he probably figured that his regulars' discipline and firepower would offset any Cheyenne numerical advantage. Glory and/or death came to the frontier soldier who struck quickly and hard, and Bull Sumner had come to fight. He put in motion his six companies of cavalry followed by the artillery and the mule train. A few minutes later, Sumner's bugler sounded "Trot." The infantry dropped behind, and the howitzers soon sank in a streambed. The First Cavalry and the pack train jogged onward.[11]

Sumner's column descended from the "upland prairie" to the "Solomon River bottom." A few men short of three hundred, the regulars moved eastward along the north bank in three parallel columns but crossed in single file a narrow spit between a rocky point and the river. It was now approximately 1:00 P.M. At the far end of a broad plain extending two and one-half miles and crowned with a few cottonwoods, a small army of Cheyenne Indians mounted up, spread across the valley in a rough line, and loped toward the regulars. Through their field glasses, Sumner and his officers realized that the Cheyennes had suckered the blue coats onto ground of their own choosing. The colonel grimly bellowed, "Front into the line!" His right sat on the river, his left grazed the bluff. By God, he had his fight.[12]

Going into battle without the infantry "seemed a little reckless" to Peck and his comrades, but Colonel Sumner, a thirty-eight-year veteran, cautiously approached the Cheyennes. Painted and dressed for war, they eerily warbled death songs and gesticulated with shields, spears, bows, muskets, rifles, and pistols. To the astonished Peck they seemed nine hundred to a thousand strong, but Sumner's more sober calculation was approximately three hundred. Nearly ten years before, at Molino del Rey in central Mexico, with shells falling and exploding all around, his battalion of 270 regular dragoons had held at bay four thousand of the finest Mexican cavalry. Bull Sumner would not balk at fighting fifteen score Cheyennes.[13]

Riding at point, he ordered the march and then the trot. Nervously clutching their carbines and rifles, the regulars quietly swept forward in a solid line toward the commoting Cheyennes. Without halting, Sumner's wing companies momentarily detached to drive in enemy flankers while the center, silent and tense, trotted onward. When within rifle range, chief scout Fall Leaf "dashed out" front to fire his weapon. Several Cheyenne rounds chased him back. Swelled with pleasure, Sumner declared to the young officer riding next to him, "Bear witness, Lieutenant Stanley, that an Indian fired the first shot."[14]

Sumner's calculations were a mystery to everyone. First Cavalry firepower was formidable and lethal. From company to company, the regiment carried the most modern small arms: Springfield rifled carbines, Merrill breech-loading carbines, and Springfield pistol carbines. The First's sidearm was the Colt's Navy revolver, and everyone had the saber. Recruited and organized in 1855, the First Cavalry had suppressed political riot and guerrilla atrocities—hardly combat training—in Bleeding Kansas during most of 1856. The Cheyenne Expedition was the regiment's first large-scale Indian campaign; the Solomon River fight its baptism of fire. Bull Sumner, the men agreed, was a fighting cavalryman. Behind him, the line kept moving in formation over the plain.[15]

Officers and men expected to stagger the Cheyennes with volleys of small-arms fire. At a hundred yards and closing, however, Colonel Sumner—the "old man" to his men and an old "fogey" to some junior officers—suddenly roared, "Sling—carbine!" followed by "Gallop—march!" A short moment later he bellowed, "Draw—sabre! . . . Charge!" The order irritated his officers; the ring and flash of sharpened steel startled the Cheyennes. Their long, beautiful bonnets trailing behind, war leaders darted up and down the line and exhorted their warriors "to fight manfully." However, their prepared "battle medicine" only protected them from bullets, not sabers. The edged steel bearing down on them—terrifying for both attacker and defender—completely rattled the Indians.[16]

As the regulars closed, they "set up a terrific yell," and the warriors, formidable though they were, jerked around their horses and bolted for the river and plains with the regulars in hot pursuit. Undoubtedly one of the oldest warriors on the field that day, Sumner probably knew that taking life does not come naturally to humans, that the saber charge would likely unnerve the Cheyennes, and that the real killing on a battlefield only begins when the enemy's back is turned. At a full gallop, the First Cavalry pursued its victims, cutting down nine warriors in the chase and wounding many more before the bugler sounded recall at 3:00 P.M.[17]

First Lt. J. E. B Stuart later disparaged the saber charge as a "dernier ressort." He had wanted to wade into Cheyenne ranks and blaze away with pistols—maybe Stuart was that rare human, the natural-born killer. Ironically, during the frantic pursuit he rode down and nearly decapitated a warrior with a single saber blow, saving the life of Lieutenant Stanley. Wounded by a pistol ball in the chest, the gallant Stuart finished the Cheyenne Expedition in a "mule litter."[18]

In a tactical sense, however, Stuart was correct: small-arms fire would have produced more Cheyenne casualties. The Indian ponies were fresh and fleet, while the cavalry mounts, working since early morning, were too worn out to overtake many of them. Private Peck recalled that most Cheyenne dead—nine known—were unhorsed by river quicksands and ridden down on the far slope.

The day's most dramatic combat pitted Pvt. Rollin M. Taylor against a lone Cheyenne warrior. After getting over the river, Taylor spotted and chased the man, but his horse pitched him and the cavalryman lost his pistol. Wheeling around, the warrior fired arrows, one splitting Taylor's scalp. The soldier counter-attacked with his saber and, after several desperate minutes, spiked the blade clean through the man. Taylor sat down on his victim in exhaustion, relief, and grief. The dying warrior looked him in the eye and signed to ask whether Taylor would take his scalp. The soldier assured him that he would not, and the smiling warrior died. True to his word, Taylor drove off a Pawnee scout scavenging for scalp trophies afterward.[19]

On 31 July, leaving two dead and eight wounded men with an infantry detachment, Sumner launched the pursuit. A few miles into the march, Fall Leaf's scouts reported a Cheyenne village lying only fifteen miles to the south. A chagrined Sumner reported, "There were one hundred and seventy-one lodges standing, and about as many more that had been hastily taken down." Private Peck later inventoried the Cheyenne property hastily abandoned: "buffalo robes, blankets, skins of many kinds, dressed, half-dressed, and undressed, bead-worked leggings and moccasins." Some warriors even departed without their "scalp strings." Clothed in rags and tatters, Sumner's troops outfitted themselves in Cheyenne "leggings and moccasins" and augmented their meager beef ration with "dried buffalo meat packed up in parfleche cases." Everything else was destroyed on huge bonfires.[20]

For Private Peck and his comrades, the next twenty-three days were hungry, hot, dusty, and miserable. Each man subsisted on three-quarters of a pound of beef per day, and scurvy began to appear in the ranks. The farther south the regulars pursued, the fainter the Cheyenne trail became. On 8 August, when the Cheyenne Expedition landed on the north bank of the Arkansas near deserted Fort Atkinson, neither Sumner nor his troops held out much hope of tearing into the Cheyennes one last time. However, with the "elite" of his cavalry, Bull stormed up the road to Bent's Fort and confiscated federal annuity goods, especially guns and ammunition, due the Cheyennes. By 2 September his command had returned as far east as Walnut Creek, where

Captain Ketchum had established a camp to await resupply from Forts Riley or Leavenworth. Here, the Cheyenne Expedition came to an end.[21]

To Sumner's disbelief, General-in-Chief Scott broke up the campaign. With the Cheyennes ever more hostile, the expedition's work, the colonel believed, was still "unfinished," but what most incensed him was Scott's order to redeploy four companies of First Cavalry and two of Sixth Infantry overland to support Harney's Utah Expedition. According to Private Peck, the day Sedgwick's command pulled out, Sumner promised to reverse Scott's order. Indeed, a day or two east of Fort Kearny, the First Cavalry was ordered back to Fort Leavenworth.[22]

Despite his pugnacity, Sumner was a conservative combat officer. His fear of casualties from friendly fire in close combat probably dictated his choice of the traditional saber over modern small arms in his battle with the Cheyennes. A critical tactical lapse was resting his troops after recall instead of vigorously pursuing the defeated enemy. Bull Sumner's Cheyenne campaign was a remarkable feat of frontier soldiering, but he concluded, "I do not think these Indians [Cheyennes] have been sufficiently punished for the barbarous outrages they have recently committed." Afterward, Colonel Harney criticized the Cheyenne Expedition so unmercifully that Sumner challenged him to a duel. Declining the summons, Harney filed charges, but Bull escaped with a mere reprimand.[23]

Most western operations were not so picturesque as the Cheyenne Expedition. Frontier campaigns broke the health of many officers and men and left in their wake bloated carcasses of dead horses, mules, oxen, and slaughtered wildlife. The tactical unorthodoxy of the Sioux Expedition of 1855, commanded by Col. William S. Harney, contrasted sharply with the textbook valor of the Cheyenne Expedition. In this case, the Brule Sioux were the target. The previous year, bands of Sioux had attacked traffic along the Platte River Road, and worst of all was that the Brules had killed every last man in a detachment under 2d Lt. John L. Grattan in August 1854 (see map 1).

The bloody incident began with the slaying of a lame beast by a Sioux warrior. On 18 August the owner reported the depredation to Lt. Hugh B. Fleming at Fort Laramie. Later that day The Bear, a treaty chief of the nearby Brule Sioux, confirmed the story but noted that the cow killer was a Miniconjou Sioux, one of a small band visiting the Brules. The Miniconjous, he declared, were "bad in their hearts" toward the whites. The following day, Lieutenant Fleming, a "shavetail" himself, instructed Grattan to march twenty-nine men of the Sixth Infantry to the Brule camp and arrest the accused warrior. Should the Indians resist, Lieutenant Grattan could "act upon his own discretion," but Fleming prudently advised him to fight only if his detachment could win.

However, Grattan's own belligerence was compounded by a foul-mouthed interpreter named August. En route to the village, August swilled whisky and insulted the Sioux nation to the face of Man Afraid of His Horses, a Brule returning to the village with Grattan's detachment. His patience exhausted, the lieutenant finally snatched the bottle and broke it across his saddle, but August chattered on. When the Grattan detachment reached James Bordeaux's trading post nearby the Brule village, August darted back and forth on his mount, spat lead balls into his hand, and swore he would kill a Miniconjou before sunset. Their honor impugned, a few Sioux warriors began gathering and grumbling. At Bordeaux's insistence Grattan tried to hush his interpreter, but August drove Sioux anger higher and higher.

The bellicose Grattan summoned The Bear to demand the cow killer's surrender and swore that he would take the man or die trying. At The Bear's request, Man Afraid of His Horses tried reasoning with the Miniconjou warrior and his five companions. As Grattan impatiently marched his command to within thirty or forty yards of the Miniconjou lodge, The Bear warned that he would "meet with something very hard," but ignoring the Brule's prediction, the lieutenant arrayed his men in a file to the left and right of two howitzers.

Camp tensions rapidly escalated out of control. Grattan's regulars held their weapons at the ready, The Bear beseeched Grattan to stand down, and Brule warriors surrounded the insolent August the instant he halted his pony. About this time the six Miniconjous emerged from their lodge and loaded their weapons. Prodded by a Brule warrior, Bordeaux leapt on a horse and raced toward the village to intervene.

He was too late. A jittery soldier on the right suddenly stepped forward, fired his musket, and killed a Sioux warrior. The Miniconjous stood their ground. Another Sioux warrior cried out for everyone to hold his fire, but volleys from Grattan's left wing killed four or five Sioux and seriously wounded The Bear. The Brules furiously counterattacked. Bordeaux broke for the rear, while August pleaded with the Sioux to stop shooting. A cannon salvo blew through the Miniconjous' lodge, and when Grattan dismounted to fire the second, a projectile killed him.

Their commanding officer struck dead, the regulars loaded and fired as they retreated to the wagon. One soldier fled on Grattan's horse with August galloping close behind. The Sioux first chased and killed them, and then lit out after the wagon. The regulars resisted furiously, but none survived. Through the night friendly Brules protected Bordeaux, and Little Thunder rode back and forth to hold his warriors in check.[24]

The army had to retrieve its honor from the Grattan debacle. During late spring and early summer 1855, Colonel Harney's expeditionary force of nine companies drawn from the Sixth Infantry, Tenth Infantry, Second Dragoons, and Fourth Artillery slogged over muddy roads to rendezvous at Fort Kearny. On 24 August the Sioux Expedition marched westward to the sand hills of northwest Nebraska, where the Brules were reportedly encamped. At the same time, troops at Fort Pierre on the Missouri River were supposed to march southwest toward Fort Laramie.[25]

On 2 September Harney's regulars made camp at Ash Hollow on the south bank of the North Platte River (see map 1). Across the water several miles to the north, the Brule camp, forty-one lodges strong, lay on the west bank of Blue Water Creek; a dozen lodges of Oglala Sioux stood several miles farther north. Through trader Pierre Louis Vasquez, the Brules informed Harney that "if he wanted peace he could have it, or if he wanted war he could have that." Grimly embracing their challenge, Harney planned to crush the Brules in a hammer-and-anvil maneuver. In his opinion, the only way to impress Indians was to kill a lot of them.[26]

Harney's object was to strike terror into the Brules and, by association, the entire Sioux people. On 3 September at 2:00 A.M., Lt. Col. Philip St. George Cooke forded two companies of Second Dragoons, the light artillery battery, and a company of mounted infantry across the river to the right and deployed them in a line behind the Brule camp. Two and a half hours later, Harney's Sixth Infantry battalion crossed the river, threw out skirmishers, and marched straight toward the village. Brule warriors appeared on the hills to Harney's right. Breaking down their teepees, the Sioux women, children, and elderly began fleeing north but halted.

Brule leader Little Thunder walked forward, and Harney dismounted to talk. The regulars drew up on the east side and the Indian warriors on the west side of the Blue Water. The two leaders parleyed for a half-hour, during which Harney demanded the murderers of the Grattan detail, "the mail party," and several "emigrants." The "day of retribution had come," Harney declared, but Little Thunder could only refuse. The colonel told him to prepare for battle.

After striding back, Harney ordered the advance and then a volley. The long range of the new Sharp's rifles shocked the Sioux, who bolted to bluffs and ravines in their rear. At this moment, clutching the neck of his pony, a Brule warrior rode furiously forward and turned down the regulars' firing line for three hundred yards. "His scalp lock and streamers trailing in the wind," he rose up to bark "his cry of defiance" and quickly disappeared over the crest. His breathtaking ride astonished the regulars and bought his comrades a little time to flee north.

The Brules retreated straight into the fire of Cooke's dismounted dragoons and infantry. Clumping together, the warriors veered down a ravine into which the regulars "poured a plunging fire . . . knocking them out of their saddles, right and left." As braves jumped from their war ponies and "replaced" the wounded on their mounts, dragoons swooped down on them. Todd wrote, "For five miles the fight continued, a perfect melee." That morning, Capt. John Buford learned a valuable lesson about the effective fire of well-armed dismounted dragoons, a tactic that his volunteer cavalry would use at Gettysburg against Confederate infantry commanded by Henry Heth, later a Southern major general but now an infantry captain who fought alongside him in Cooke's "anvil."

Harney pressed the attack. His infantry fired volleys into limestone caves above the creek, but the "piercing cry of a child" stopped the shooting. Lt. Richard C. Drum recalled, "This was the first indication that the women and children were concealed in the caves and under our fire." Dozens of women and children were killed and wounded, but Harney had made his desired violent impression.[27] The regulars killed eighty Sioux, wounded five, and captured seventy. The dead and captives were primarily women, children, and the elderly. Army casualties were "4 killed, 4 severely wounded, 3 slightly wounded and one missing." After establishing Fort Grattan near Ash Hollow, Harney's troops marched to Fort Laramie.[28]

Despite cold and snow, the Sioux Expedition, 450 men, plunged north and east into the northern plains, the western Sioux heartland. The desolate grandeur of the Dakota Badlands leavened an otherwise monotonous march. On 20 October Harney's troops pulled into Fort Pierre, where they spent a miserable winter. The following spring Harney treated with the Sioux, who promised to leave Anglos unmolested on the Platte River Road. The Sioux Expedition set a precedent for winter campaigning, a tactic applied by Philip Sheridan and Nelson A. Miles against Plains Indians after the Civil War.[29]

Harney's attack earned him the epithet "Squaw Killer." Having retired partly to avoid serving under Harney, Ethan A. Hitchcock condemned the colonel's slaughter of Brule women and children. Then an infantry captain at Fort Laramie, William Carlin later wrote, "There were many officers of the expedition who did not approve of the attack." In army circles rumor held that Captain Heth and Maj. Oscar F. Winship goaded Harney into the assault, but Harney's combat record, especially in Florida, was illuminated by brutality.[30] The quest for military glory and personal distinction, combined with the tactical realities of frontier warfare, drove frontier commanders to rash attacks and reckless killing.

To the south in Texas, the Second Cavalry routinely scoured the southern plains for Indians found beyond their treaty reservations. In late 1857 and early 1858, the Comanches and Kiowas escalated their depredations, and Texas authorities demanded their chastisement. That summer Brig. Gen. David E. Twiggs, commanding the Department of Texas, launched the Second Cavalry northward to hunt Comanches between the Red River and north fork of the Canadian.[31]

Twiggs chose Earl Van Dorn, senior captain in the Second Cavalry, to lead this force in the field. Van Dorn was a short, thin, tireless Mississippian with a passion for painting miniatures of friends and family. During August and early September 1858, four companies of the Second Cavalry, two partial companies of the First Infantry, and 135 Indian scouts—Delawares, Tonkawas, Wacos, and other Comanche enemies—rendezvoused at Fort Belknap in north-central Texas. Setting out in September 1858, the Wichita Expedition marched north toward Indian Territory through fire-blackened plains (see map 2). Eight days and 130 miles later, Van Dorn's men reached the south bank of Otter Creek and soon erected a crude stockade called Camp Radziminski in memory of a recently deceased Second Cavalry officer.[32]

On 30 September two Indian scouts reported the location of a Comanche village east of Camp Radziminski. Van Dorn immediately ordered his men into the saddle with two-days' rations. His aim was to attack the camp the following dawn, but thirty-six hours later his cavalry was still coursing eastward over the plains. Near dawn of the second morning, Indian scouts found the Comanche village a short distance away. Van Dorn divided his strike force into four columns a hundred yards apart. The regulars trotted up the hills and walked down the slopes. As they crested the fourth rise, they spotted in the distance the Comanche encampment, a hundred lodges strung along the opposite side of Rush Creek. Fronting into line, the cheering troopers charged the slumbering village while the whooping scouts raced toward the horse herd.

Van Dorn's surprise was complete. The Comanches knew of the expedition's proximity but assumed that they were under the protection of nearby Fort Arbuckle, where they were negotiating peace with the Wichitas. As the early-morning fog lifted, the troopers poured into the encampment, but gullies, ravines, and dense brush broke the charge and gave the Comanches, armed mostly with bows and arrows, time to regroup and counterattack. Regulars and Comanches fought desperately, in close and sometimes hand-to-hand. After running off the Comanche pony herd, the Indian scouts joined the combat. In the din and smoke, the Comanches shot Van Dorn off his horse and wounded him. After an hour and a half, the cavalry concentrated its modern firepower to drive the Comanches completely from the camp.[33]

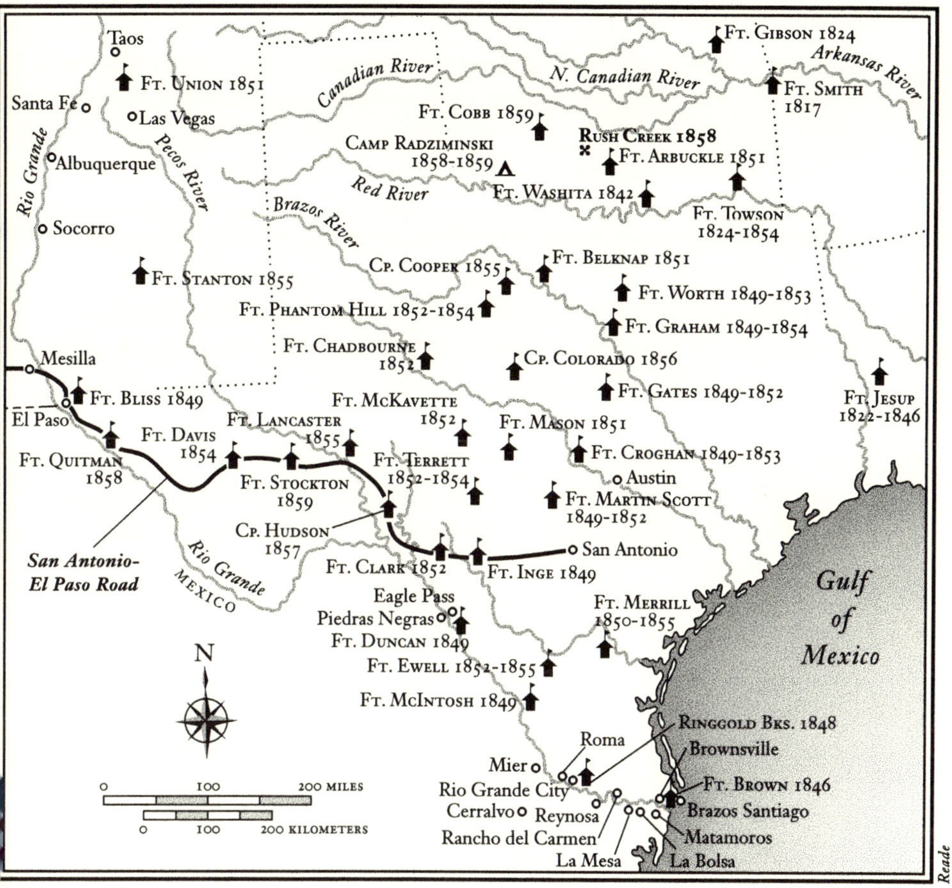

2. Texas and the Southern Plains

Inheriting the battle, Capt. Charles Whiting launched no pursuit but instead ordered all Comanche property heaped and burned. Van Dorn wrote, "Nothing was left to mark the site of their camp but the ashes and the dead." He counted fifty-six slain Comanche warriors. Two Comanche women and two Wichitas were "accidently killed." Army casualties were five dead and nine wounded. The Wichita Expedition returned to Camp Radziminski, from which the Second scouted throughout the winter.[34]

The state of Texas demanded Comanche annihilation, and once winter melted away and cavalry horses fattened, Captain Van Dorn led the Second Cavalry after the Comanches on 30 April 1859. The reinforced Wichita

Expedition comprised six companies totaling 429 men and officers, 58 Indian scouts, a small wagon train, and a remuda of horses and mules. The regulars packed only their blanket and weapons. The column rode directly north over the South and North Forks of the Canadian River and the Cimarron River toward the Arkansas. Scouts and soldiers rode far out in front and on the flanks. After halting in late afternoon, the column relocated a few miles farther on after dark.

Four days out a detachment captured a boy belonging to a Comanche scouting party. Under duress he agreed to lead Van Dorn's troops to an Indian camp north of the Cimarron River. Near the Canadian River, broken ground and heavy rains forced the captain to corral his wagons and resort to pack mules. The soldiers and their mule train crossed the Canadian on 6 May, the North Fork two days later, and the Cimarron near Kansas Territory after another forty-eight hours. Here the scouts surprised a Comanche party, killing one warrior.

A fight seemed imminent. Van Dorn's column rode northwest to Big Sandy Creek and, on the twelfth, made camp at Crooked Creek, "whose sweet waters and green sloping banks, shaded by groves of the thickest foliage" had recently been the site of a huge Comanche encampment. The Second Cavalry, drenched by rain and chilled by a "north wind," tracked northward a "fresh trail" the next morning, but "heavy" and "slippery" terrain and leg-weary horses and mules forced the column to halt at 2:00 P.M.

Thirty minutes later pickets spotted two Indians nearby. Detached to investigate, Lt. William B. Royall and thirty troopers trailed the enemy scouts to a "deep ravine" three miles to the east. These Comanches, a Kotsoteka hunting party, were astonished to see regulars so far north. After dispatching a messenger, Royall drove off the Comanche horse herd and posted troops to blockade both ends of the ravine. Upon receiving Royall's summons, Van Dorn raced the Second to battle.

The regulars had to root out the Comanches. The village lay in a "deep ravine, densely covered with a stunted growth of timber and brambles, through which a small stream, with abrupt banks, meandered from bluff to bluff, on either side." Low sky and rain compounded poor visibility. Armed with bows and arrows, the Comanches concealed themselves in the tangled brush. When the crossfire of skirmishers became dangerous, Van Dorn sealed off the rim and the outlets, and teams of regulars groped forward. At times regulars and Comanches fired simultaneously only yards apart. Outnumbering its foe, the Second shortly located and pinned down most of the Indians. Van Dorn reported, "The Comanches fought without giving or asking quarter until there was not one left to bend a bow." Scouts and regulars plundered and burned the camp.

Showing little mercy, the regulars killed forty-nine Comanches—eight were women—and captured another thirty-six. One trooper was killed outright; one died of wounds later. The wounded included ten enlisted men and two officers, Capt. E. Kirby Smith and 2d Lt. Fitzhugh Lee. The latter, a son of Lt. Col. Robert E. Lee, had shot two warriors in rapid succession, but a third drove an arrow through the young officer's chest. He miraculously recovered from the seemingly mortal wound.

Dividing his command, Van Dorn scouted with several companies to the southwest through the Antelope Hills. Left at Crooked Creek, two other companies under Captain Smith carried the wounded south in easy stages and gathered up the wagon train. The entire Wichita Expedition had rendezvoused at Camp Radziminski by 31 May 1859. In an ironic twist, units of Van Dorn's cavalry protected Comanches and other tribes at the Brazos Reservation from vengeful Texans during the following summer, but the Department of Texas reassigned Captain Van Dorn, and the last cavalry troop departed Camp Radziminski on 23 September.[35]

Far to the northwest in Washington Territory, Col. George Wright commanded the decade's most spectacular campaign. The expansion of settlers and miners east of the Cascade Range triggered war with the Indians of the upper Columbia River. During 1855–56 Wright's regulars waged a grinding war against the Yakamas, but the settlement of the conflict appeased no one.[36] Washington territorial governor Isaac I. Stevens, who once carried Wright from the battlefield in Mexico, accused the army of incompetence, and Wright complained of civilian trespass into military affairs. To keep the peace, Brig. Gen. John E. Wool, commanding the Department of the Pacific, temporarily closed the Cascade country except for the Coleville gold diggings. Two legacies were Forts Walla Walla and Simcoe, from which Wright would launch the climactic campaign to the upper Columbia country.[37]

Tempers simmered throughout 1857. The constant trek of gold seekers to the Coleville mines irritated the Palouses, Spokanes, and other eastern tribes. On 6 May 1858 Maj. Edward J. Steptoe led 158 officers and men—most from the First Dragoons—northward out of Fort Walla Walla. His mission was to march through Palouse country, show the Stars-and-Stripes at the Coleville mines, treat with the Spokanes, and farther east investigate rumors of Mormons—a year into their "rebellion"—inciting the eastern Washington tribes to war.

After crossing the Snake River, Steptoe's command proceeded toward the Palouse River through rolling, grassy prairies but ran headlong into a war party, one thousand strong, on Ingomossen Creek (see map 3). The brightly adorned warriors—Palouses, Spokanes, Coeur d'Alenes, Yakamas, and others—darted on horses back and forth in front of the dragoons and over the hills around them. Steptoe tried to demonstrate his peaceful intentions, but battle was the Indians' objective. The major closed up his supply train, deployed his dragoons on the rear and flanks, and ordered a withdrawal toward the Snake River.

The warriors surged toward the column. Carrying only forty cartridges each, the dragoons beat off charges and counterattacked to drive back the Indians. At day's end the bloodied column entrenched on a small rise besieged by exultant, boasting warriors. Six regulars—two of them officers—were dead, twelve were wounded. Even worse was that each regular had only a few rounds left. Steptoe and his officers agreed to run. After burying the dead and caching the howitzers, the mounted column slipped through a gap in the Indian lines during the night, covered seventy-five miles by 10:00 A.M., and crossed the Snake later that day. The regulars, exhausted and chewed up, reached Fort Walla Walla without additional mishap. Commanding General Winfield Scott roundly criticized Steptoe for packing so little ammunition, and his peers condemned him for walking into a trap.[38]

Brig. Gen. Newman S. Clarke, now commanding the Department of the Pacific from San Francisco, steamed to Fort Vancouver in June. Colonel Wright took over troops north and east of Fort Walla Walla. Clarke wrote him, "You will attack all the hostile Indians you may meet, with vigor; make their punishment severe, and persevere until the submission of all is complete." Simultaneously, Maj. Robert S. Garnett—designer of the California state seal—would lead a punitive expedition into Yakama country. Delivered by Jesuit missionaries, the peace terms—leaving the army and settlers alone, returning federal property, surrendering warriors who initiated the attack on Steptoe, and expelling hostile warriors—were rejected by the upper Columbia Indians.[39]

Throughout July, Wright forwarded troops, supplies, transportation, and livestock from Fort Walla Walla to Camp Taylor at the junction of the Tucanon and Snake Rivers (see map 3). By the third week of August, Wright had congregated 680 troops—190 from the First Dragoons, 400 men of the Third Artillery serving as infantry, and 90 soldiers from the Ninth Infantry. Officers put the men through skirmish drills and target practice. The Third Artillery was armed with the new .58 caliber Springfield rifle; the Ninth

Infantry with the improved Mississippi rifle; and the dragoons with the breech-loading Sharp's carbine and Colt revolver. The Springfield and Mississippi rifles fired the Minié bullet, which would kill hundreds of thousands of soldiers in the Civil War. During 25–26 August, with two hundred packers and drovers tending animals, wagons, and supplies, the Spokane Expedition crossed to the north bank of the Snake River.[40]

Wright drove his men northward over burned plains across the Palouse River and Cow Creek. The route was hot and dusty, the water poor. The confederated tribes gathered for battle when the regulars penetrated the scattered-timber country at the edge of the Spokane Plain. At the crest of a hill just cleared by his foot artillery, Capt. Erasmus Keyes saw an astonishing sight: five hundred mounted warriors—Spokanes, Palouses, Coeur d'Alenes, and others—all dressed in colorful war regalia prancing on the plain below. The regulars' well-aimed rifle fire raked the Indians, who dashed forward individually to fire muskets or arrows. On the right, the Ninth Infantry dislodged Indians concealed in a pine thicket. Wright then cut loose Capt. William Grier's dragoons to clear the field. Calling the engagement the Battle of Four Lakes, Wright estimated Indian losses at eighteen or twenty, but they still retained their pony herds and could field a formidable fighting force.[41]

After several days' rest, the Spokane Expedition struck out again on 5 September. For eight miles, the column skirted a lake and hiked through broken country. Emerging on a plain beyond, the regulars spied a large body of Indians riding along the edge of pine trees some three miles away. Wright deployed his skirmishers across a mile-wide front screened by Grier's dragoons. The Indians set the grass on fire, but foot and horse soldiers leapt through and over the flames, marching forward across the scorched plain.

For seven hours the infantry repulsed frontal and flank attacks, the artillery dislodged warriors from rocks and trees, and the dragoons cut down stragglers. The Indians took a terrible pounding but repeatedly regrouped to make another stand. The regulars drove back the Indians, knocking holes in their ranks with massed rifle fire. When the warriors were forced against the banks of the Spokane River, they scattered and the regulars went into camp. From the initial point of contact, Wright's men had advanced fourteen miles.[42]

The Spokane Expedition refitted for several days and then coursed eastward along the Spokane River to Coeur d'Alene Mission. Wright described his method: "For the last eighty miles our route has been marked by slaughter and devastation; 900 horses and a large number of cattle have been killed or appropriated to our own use; many horses, with large quantities of wheat and oats, also many caches of vegetables, kamas, and dried berries have been destroyed."

Grier's dragoons captured the Palouse pony herd. From afar the warriors had watched in total disbelief the destruction of their corralled horses—approximately six hundred—from volley fire.

At the mission located east of Coeur d'Alene Lake, Wright treated with the Coeur d'Alenes; Father Joseph Joset, S.J., interpreted. The demoralized Indians viewed the flash of Donati's Comet across the sky as a sign of the Anglos' exceptional power and agreed to return United States property and leave the emigrants alone. Taking custody of Coeur d'Alene warriors and their families, Wright pushed southwestward to deal with the Spokanes.

On 23 September at Latah Creek, Father Joset assembled Spokanes, Pend d'Oreilles, Colvilles, and others. The next morning Wright hanged Qualchin, a Yakama war leader implicated in depredations against whites east of the Cascades. Simultaneously, Captain Grier took a detail to investigate the site of Steptoe's battle. The troops recovered the howitzers and the scattered bones of fallen soldiers at the site. That evening, when Palouses began showing up at the Hanging Camp, Wright ordered the seizure of fifteen warriors. He executed six and clapped the other nine in irons.

The Spokane Expedition transported its terror to the Palouse River. The Palouses surrendered the killer of a miner who was slain the previous April, and Wright immediately hanged him. Next he summoned all prisoners and executed several Yakamas and Walla Wallas who had warred on the United States. His warning to the Palouses was to keep the peace. If their depredations ever brought him back, Wright would destroy the tribe.[43]

With Palouse hostages in tow, the Spokane Expedition pulled into Camp Taylor in early October. As the command crossed the Tucanon River, an Indian prisoner sprinted for freedom. An officer gave chase and wounded the warrior, then a dragoon private shot him through the head. Two days later the Spokane Expedition paraded into Fort Walla Walla. Wright's brutal campaign brought the Pacific Northwest Indian wars to a close. The shell-shocked Indians of the Upper Columbia Plateau never again seriously challenged United States sovereignty.[44]

The martial extermination of Indians was never official federal policy, but frontier warfare, unconventional in Euroamerican terms, compelled the army to surprise, attack, and destroy Indian villages and camps. Military units under aggressive commanders such as Sumner, Harney, Van Dorn, and Wright attacked quickly and furiously. Repeating-fire technologies increased the volume of projectiles the regulars could pour into Indian villages and defensive formations. The tactical surprise often guaranteed a heavy toll of women and children and uncomfortably approached a war of slaughter or extermination.

Unclear in later accounts was whether regular troops, both officers and men, regretted the killing of noncombatants.

The frontier campaign was a scout in force—an organized hunt—and professional soldiers often compared the expedition after natives to the chase of wild game. The metaphor's racial logic was foreboding for indigenous peoples, who were less than human in the eyes of the American people and their federal agents, including the regular army. Indeed, the guerrilla tactics and distant homelands of the Indians forced regular troops to reconnoiter large territories, trail their course, and storm the Indians before they fled. However, dehumanizing Indians in the hunting framework sanctioned unorthodox partisan tactics officially frowned upon by Euroamerican soldiers and helped facilitate the grisly destruction of Indian societies by both regular and volunteer armies.

Such racism dovetailed with the imperatives of the army career. Regular officers composed a male cohort of well-educated white professionals, and armed violence was their specialty. Most sought to distinguish themselves among their peers and to earn preferment or promotion in the service. In battle the average line officer found a rare opportunity for demonstrating the skill and courage admired by superior officers. Whatever their moral misgivings, officers still went to war against western Indians, sometimes with enthusiasm. If regulars slew unarmed women, children, and elderly, they blamed unmanly Indian tactics that forced federal troops to ransack desert and mountain sanctuaries and smash into camps and villages. There were almost no professional or political repercussions for the killing of Indian noncombatants in battle, and a standout performance might earn a junior officer notice in his commander's report and in army headquarters' general orders. If the officer was lucky, he might receive a brevet to the next grade or promotion to a higher rank in a newly created regiment. For the ambitious soldier, waging war on Indians was a good professional risk.

4

INTERNAL FISSURES

Soldiers, Politics, and Sectionalism

THE U.S. Army offered men of any class a career path—federal service—that diverged from the hurly-burly of Jacksonian commercial life. The army's seniority system rewarded the patient officer steady employment, regular pay, and eventual promotion, while the sober, literate, and efficient enlisted man rose quickly to the ranks of the noncommissioned officers. An army career was not an ideal professional life, but barring death by disease or combat, it guaranteed economic security unknown to most Americans.

Implied in the army hierarchy, rigidly structured by rank, was a class system coded by ethnicity and education. Dominating the officer corps were middle-class and well-educated Anglo Americans who carried their prejudices from civilian life into military service. The byproducts of their chauvinism—scorn and violence—often targeted enlisted men, who were generally poor whites, both native and European born. The brutality enlisted personnel endured in both civilian and military life gave them exceptional insight into the democratic principles of the Union cause at the outbreak of the Civil War.

Although the army institution was European in design, its personnel were American in content. Rarely did federal military service completely erase the influences of family, society, and section on the soldier. Regulars—enlisted men and officers—absorbed and debated the day's controversial issues, particularly slavery and sectionalism, and witnessed the shock of United States culture on the indigenous peoples of the American West. By decade's end professional soldiers, officers and enlisted men together, held strong opinions and were willing to act on their principles.

To nineteenth-century America, enlisted men were society's flotsam and jetsam. The United States offered boundless economic opportunity, and only the lazy and shiftless, conventional wisdom went, joined the professional army, a haven for loafers. Indeed, as Sgt. Eugene Bandel noted, army ranks sheltered large numbers of men who avoided gainful employment, who were "addicted to drink," or who were otherwise unemployable. Some were hellions and rowdies, "troublesome men," Capt. Edward D. Townsend recalled. These dregs of human society, represented in armies around the world, had given professional soldiering a bad reputation for centuries.[1]

However convulsive and alcoholic some soldiers were, the enlisted ranks were more complex and diverse than the public either knew or admitted. An enlisted man during the 1850s, Augustus Meyers recalled that the average age of his peers was twenty to twenty-five years, and these men came from all over the United States and the world. Often enlisting immediately after immigration, Europeans represented half or more of the men in the ranks. The surgeon general reported that 3,516 foreigners constituted the bulk of the 5,000 soldiers recruited in 1850 and 1851. The Irish and Germans were the two largest nationalities at 2,113 and 678 respectively. The English and Scots were a distant third and fourth at 306 and 126 respectively.[2]

Laborers were the largest category of recruit, but educated and skilled men, generally down on their luck, joined the army as well. Meyers wrote: "Previous occupations ranged all the way from a school teacher to a farm laborer. Some were fairly well educated and others ignorant to the point of illiteracy." Some were "merchants," others were journeymen, and still others were runaway apprentices. A daguerreotypist by training, Sgt. Percival G. Lowe soldiered with a lawyer, printer, draughtsman, and pork packer. While acknowledging the men wedded to whiskey, Lowe remembered his fellow soldiers to be "a remarkably good set of men" and opined, "If these men lacked anything to insure a bright future, it was the strong will and judgment to act independently—to blaze the way and decide their own destiny."[3] These better-educated and trained soldiers formed the core of rugged fighting units in the frontier army.

Comfort, security, employment, and adventure attracted men to the army. One of Lowe's troopers joined up "because he was absolutely hungry—'too proud to beg and too honest to steal.'" Another had met with business reverses and "wanted to hide himself from all his friends" and have "time to think."

Discovering that American streets were not paved with gold, English immigrant George Ballentine enlisted. He recalled, "I was scarcely prepared to find the scramble for the means of living so fierce and incessant, as I found in New York." Adrift in Rochester, New York, James A. Bennett was attracted by the promise of "good board, clothing, medical attention," and free transport "to the 'land of gold,'" California. Enlisting for romance and adventure, Lowe wrote, "Family trouble, disappointment in love, riots and personal difficulties, making one amenable to the law, often caused men to enlist who proved to be the best of soldiers."[4]

Death, disease, desertion, and drunkenness undermined the army's combat readiness and military efficiency. Military service guaranteed an enlistee food, clothing, and steady pay, but it could not promise long life. Diseases, not combat wounds, were the most common killers. Epidemics of malaria, cholera, diarrhea, and dysentery particularly ravaged frontier regulars. In 1849 the army lost 307 men to cholera alone. The cholera epidemic of 1855 swept back and forth through Fort Riley, Kansas, and terrified the survivors. In the summer of 1854 malaria prostrated "every officer, . . . every lady, every soldier, and every laundress" at Fort Merrill in southern Texas. The assistant surgeon wrote, "There are not men well enough for the ordinary garrison duty; a single tour of guard is almost certain to send a man to the hospital." Without the aid of germ theory, army doctors enforced sanitation and hygiene as best they could but were essentially helpless in combating disease epidemics.[5]

Drunkenness and desertion constantly plagued the enlisted ranks. When the American people thought of enlisted men, they imagined illiterate soldiers who spent their pay on "rotgut." Indeed, imbibing alcohol was chronic in the army, and many soldiers eased the monotony, loneliness, and despair of frontier service with liquid spirits. Intemperate in civilian society, alcoholic enlistees brought their disease to the army. Heavy drinking ran counter to midcentury American habits. Influenced largely by the temperance movement, the American people had radically reduced their per capita adult consumption of heavy grain alcohols between 1820 and 1850.

Military doctors complained that excessive drinking was a chief cause of diseases and accidents in the service. In winter quarters especially, First Sergeant Lowe locked up any man on the verge of drunkenness to let him sober up. Lt. William W. Averell overcame habitual unit drunkards by making one a company schoolteacher, designating another company librarian and clerk, drilling the men, holding regular shooting practice, and sponsoring weekly horse races. He also told the most habitual offenders to visit him when they had the urge to imbibe, for he would give them quality alcohol in measured quantities.[6]

The U.S. Army depended on the impoverished classes for most of its recruits, but many commissioned officers brutalized enlisted men with the meanness of unenlightened medieval lords. Enlisted men interpreted their bullying as an index of the private soldier's place in the socio-economic bottom lands of the United States. At Fort Tejon, California, John Xantus bitterly complained, "I did not know [at] that time [of enlistment] the exact position of the army in this country, and I had not the farthest idea that in the American Army only the officers were considered *men;* and the others something like as *last class negroes.*" Likewise, Pvt. Frank Hamilton criticized southern officers, who "looked upon the men and treated them much as they did their slaves upon the plantations."[7]

The harsh discipline and physical abuse of enlisted men were inhumane practices to the public and to many professional soldiers as well. Isolation in frontier posts sorely tested the civility of officers and men, and frontier campaigning hardened everyone's sensibilities. Officers met their men's violence with violence, and the army still resorted to cruel forms of punishment: cropping an ear, standing a prisoner on a barrel, and bucking and gagging being only a few examples. Recalling the penalty of three regulars "for some slight offense," Sgt. James A. Bennett wrote: "A rope was placed around their ankles. The men were stripped first, however, then, thrown head long into the water."[8]

The army had discarded corporal punishment in 1812 only to secure its congressional reinstatement in 1833. The law stipulated that commanders could inflict up to fifty lashes for desertion alone. Although officers resorted to whippings infrequently, no witness, male or female, ever forgot the grisly spectacle. The command formed a square around the whipping post to which the convicted soldier, stripped to the waist, was tied. Usually applied by a musician, the lash hummed through the air and cracked against the prisoner's back, leaving a "purple streak" and drawing a drop of blood. The officer of the day counted off each application while the adjutant tallied it. Some victims endured the whipping with unbelievable stoicism; others howled and writhed in excruciating pain. Squeamish observers, both officers and men, fell out. Sometimes the sentence also ordered shaving the victim's head and branding the letter "D" on his hip. Afterward, the humiliated man was drummed out of the service "to the tune of the 'Rogue's March.'" Upon dismissal, officers and men cursed the "savage spectacle" as they walked away.[9]

If drinking and violence brought the soldier no relief, desertion, if successful, would free him from military torment. Throughout the nineteenth century desertion was a constant irritant to the army. In 1853 Secretary of War Jefferson Davis reported that since the war with Mexico the desertion rate had yearly averaged 16 percent of a ten-thousand-man army. Each deserter cost the army over a thousand dollars, for he usually took his weapons and field kit; the dragoon or cavalry deserter often escaped on his horse. In addition, the army lost the cost of the soldier's recruitment, training, and transport. Desertions, discharges by expiration of enlistment, discharges for disability and other causes, and losses by death forced the regular army to recruit one-third of its ranks each year.[10]

Throughout the nineteenth century the army establishment wrestled with desertion. Cramped and uncomfortable quarters, bad food, backbreaking labor, hard frontier campaigns, public contempt, brutal discipline, and low pay drove men to flight. Congressional penny-pinching and punishing frontier service were the primary sources of misery, and the U.S. Army lacked the moral resources and political backbone to try shaping a public climate favorable to professional soldiering. A centuries-old blemish on armies, savage discipline was ingrained in military culture. Neither the army, Congress, nor the public seemed able to agree on how to resolve the problem.

A West Point graduate and former professional soldier, Secretary of War Jefferson Davis, however, brought some relief. In 1854 he secured a pay increase for enlisted men, raising the monthly stipend of a private to eleven dollars, corporal to thirteen dollars, sergeant to seventeen dollars, and senior sergeant to twenty-one dollars. Enlisted men always complained of low wages, but historian Edward Coffman found that, with emoluments calculated into their base salary, the soldier's pay compared favorably with that of a full-time laborer. However, according to Sgt. Eugene Bandel, "everything" on the frontier was "very expensive" and quickly consumed the soldier's pay. Davis's analysis highlighted a peculiar correlation: the more prosperous the national economy, the higher the desertion rate.

To retain worthy soldiers, Davis also lobbied Congress to ameliorate the conditions of military service. Beyond raising base pay, he urged an additional pay increase for every successive five-year term of enlistment and the promotion of worthy noncommissioned officers to the commissioned ranks. He secured the first two, but Congress rejected the third.[11] Pay increases brought enlisted men some relief, but only a sea change in public attitudes would significantly improve service conditions. Despite Davis's noble efforts, the regular enlisted soldier was underpaid, abused, and unappreciated well into the twentieth century.

Reporting directly to the president, the secretary of war was the army's civilian chief, and with the secretary of the navy, he executed national military policy. He lobbied a stingy Congress for military appropriations and recommended the promotion of officers. He granted the lucrative military contracts that profoundly influenced local economies, and his opinion was critical to the creation and location of frontier army posts.[12]

During the interwar years, William L. Marcy, George W. Crawford, Charles M. Conrad, Jefferson Davis, and John B. Floyd administered the Department of War. Davis and Floyd were its most notable secretaries. Serving the Democratic administration of Pres. Franklin Pierce, Davis was a Mississippian and a Mexican-American War veteran. He was a "slender, tall and erect" man with a lean face, sharp eyes, and high forehead. Although he was an elegant, selfless host, Davis fiercely battled his critics and detractors. During four years of exceptional service, he increased the army by four regiments, secured pay increases for enlisted men, and pushed through significant technological changes.

Davis's successor, John B. Floyd, helped elect James Buchanan and was rewarded with the secretary of war's post. A former Virginia governor, Floyd brought no military experience to the job and generated scandal during his tenure. On the eve of the Civil War, Congress investigated his office for contract irregularities and financial frauds. During the secession winter of 1860–61, Floyd deliberately impeded Union military preparations before he resigned on 29 December 1860 to take up the Confederate cause.[13]

Immediately below the secretary was the General Staff, or the bureau chiefs. These regular army officers were the army's technical experts who supplied, housed, fed, clothed, tried, and paid the troops in the field. The heads of the Adjutant General's Department, Inspector General's Department, the Judge Advocate of the Army, the Quartermaster's Department, Commissary General's Department, the Medical Department, and Paymaster's Department composed the General Staff. Occupying a nebulous position between the staff and the line officers were the Corps of Topographical Engineers, Corps of Engineers, the Ordnance Department, and the military storekeepers. Assigned to Washington, D.C., chiefs of the bureaus and the engineers reported directly to the secretary of war.[14]

Appointed for life, the bureau chiefs were powerful military officials. Secretaries of war came and went, but the chiefs tenaciously sat at their post, some for decades. Q.M. Gen. Thomas S. Jesup served from 1818 to 1860; Chief Engineer Joseph G. Totten from 1838 to 1863; Surgeon General Thomas Lawson from 1836 to 1861; Chief Topographical Engineer John J. Abert from 1834 to 1861; and Adj. Gen. Roger Jones from 1825 to 1852. Their military careers predated the War of 1812. All were capable department heads, but without a retirement system death alone removed Jesup, Lawson, and Jones, while old age and ill health retired Abert and Totten. Over the years the staff chiefs accumulated extraordinary institutional and political power. Within the army, the adjutant general's influence probably exceeded that of the secretary of war.[15]

The chiefs' independence galled the general-in-chief, who nominally commanded both the staff and line. In theory his office centralized army command structure. In practice, however, he exercised no control over the General Staff and only minimal command over line officers and troops. Within a few years of its creation in 1821, the office of commanding general became a ceremonial post; its occupant a figurehead. As the president's civilian deputy, the secretary both administered military policy and managed army personnel with the assistance of the staff chiefs, especially the adjutant general. The commanding general was peripheral.[16]

During the interwar period, the army had only one commanding general, Winfield Scott. He was a brilliant tactician and an audacious commander. At the Battles of the Chippewa and Lundy's Lane during the War of 1812, his regulars and militia—drilled, disciplined, and equipped by him—proved themselves the equals of British regulars. What followed for Scott were years of peacetime departmental command in the East and the West with exceptional diplomatic service during the Nullification Crisis, Patriot War, Cherokee Removal, and Aroostook War. In 1841 he was appointed commanding general of the army. His crowning achievement was the breathtaking invasion of central Mexico in 1847. His brilliant victory made him a national hero and a presidential contender. In 1855, to reward Scott's service in Mexico, Congress passed a bill that bestowed on him the brevet rank of lieutenant general retroactive to the capitulation of Vera Cruz in 1847.[17]

Scott's junior officers worshipped him, and he cultivated their reverence. He bore himself with Caesarian aloofness and condescension and loved the pomp and circumstance of military parades. As he passed along troop formations, his six-foot, four-inch frame draped in glittering dress blues towered over the men, whom he absorbed with alert, blue eyes. Ulysses S. Grant wrote, "I thought him the finest specimen of manhood my eyes ever beheld, the most to be envied." Echoing Grant, David S. Stanley remembered the general-in-chief as "the model for a great hero."[18]

Between the War of 1812 and the Civil War, Scott vigorously advocated the U.S. Army and the professionalization of its officers and enlisted men. Using French, Prussian, and British models, Scott repeatedly preached that education, training, discipline, and system were the cornerstones of an effective professional army. Borrowing heavily from French and British codes, Scott authored the army's first regimented handbook, *General Regulations for the Army of the United States*, published in 1821 and periodically revised until his retirement in 1861. His tactical and ordnance manuals were generally translations of European, particularly French, military works.[19]

For all his military and diplomatic genius, Scott was the quintessence of the aristocratic professional soldier reviled by two generations of American democratic levelers. Scott's ego was the equal of his colossal physique, and he expended enormous time and money scaling and mining the fortresses of political power. Erasmus Keyes, an aide to Scott, declared, "The chief ruling passion of the general was ambition and its uniform attendant, jealousy." No one hated a political enemy—Edmund P. Gaines, Andrew Jackson, James K. Polk, Jefferson Davis, and Alexander Macomb among others—more venomously than did Scott. A Virginia aristocrat, he was first a Federalist and then a Whig, and he never understood why the American people rejected him for the presidency. When Zachary Taylor and later Franklin Pierce, both of whom Scott loathed, entered the White House, he decamped from Washington to New York City.[20]

Scott's departmental, or line, commanders were a diverse and colorful group. They were easterners and westerners, northerners and southerners. Their backgrounds were urban and rural, industrial and agricultural. They hailed from the humble middle class and the exclusive aristocracy. They counted among their ranks Democrats, Whigs, and Republicans, slaveholders, free-soilers, and abolitionists. Their diversity aside, all of these officers cultivated powerful men in their states, the national government, and the professional army to aid their careers. With decades of military service behind them, they were willful, opinionated men dedicated to the service of their nation despite the frustrations, disappointments, and heartbreaks of the American military career. In theory, their years of federal service should have severed their ties to their native states or regions. However, most departmental commanders, southerners especially, retained strong sectional loyalties.

Although southern officers dominated departmental commands, several northerners distinguished themselves. In the Pacific Division, Col. Persifor F. Smith was followed by Ethan A. Hitchcock, colonel of the Second Infantry. The grandson of Revolutionary War hero Ethan Allen, Colonel Hitchcock was the son of a Federalist judge in Vermont. Graduating from West Point in 1817, he taught Jefferson Davis, Robert E. Lee, Joseph E. Johnston, William T. Sherman, and Edgar Allan Poe at the academy in the late 1820s and early 1830s. As General Scott's inspector general in the Mexican-American War, Hitchcock coaxed some order from the chaotic volunteers. Although he served admirably in that conflict as well as the earlier Seminole War, he thought both were waged to expand southern slavery, an institution he abhorred. In politics Hitchcock was a Whig and got on well with Millard

Fillmore and Winfield Scott, but strained relations with the Democratic Pierce administration finally drove him from the army in 1855.

During his years of federal service, Hitchcock earned a reputation for honesty and integrity. An owlish man, he poured over books on philosophy, theology, and metaphysics and daily filled journal pages with speculations on cosmology, ontology, epistemology, morality, and piety. Although he routinely complained about the soldier's life and mulled over retirement, he believed that honest, conscientious men made a difference in the federal service.[21]

Hitchcock's successor to the command of the Pacific Department in 1854 was Brig. Gen. John E. Wool. Born in 1784 he made his home in Troy, New York. During the War of 1812 he distinguished himself at Queenstown Heights and Plattsburgh. Afterward, he served in the Inspector General's Department for twenty years, and during the Jackson administration commanded the Cherokee Removal until Tennessee and Georgia authorities demanded his own removal. His finest moment was at the Battle of Buena Vista during the Mexican-American War. Although Gen. Zachary Taylor rode the victory into the White House, Wool's judicious design of the battlefield and his cool command of the line helped save United States forces from disastrous defeat. He was the rare officer who excelled in both staff and line commands.

Wool returned from the Mexican conflict a national hero. He was a solid Democrat, albeit a northern one. Impeccably connected in Washington and New York political circles, he included William Marcy, Lewis Cass, and Nathaniel P. Tallmage among his closest friends. In 1850, he declined to run for governor of New York, and two years later he was mentioned as a dark horse for the Democratic presidential nomination. His northern roots made him suspect in the eyes of southern Democrats, but after Pierce was elected in 1852 Wool still vaguely hoped that the Democratic party would summon him four years later.

Neat and dapper, Wool stood a little over five feet tall and possessed a cherubic face. David S. Stanley recalled that Wool loved to fleece young lieutenants at cards. Although in his sixties, the energetic general wore out men half his age each day. In the early months of secession, his decisive actions saved Fort Monroe, Virginia, for the Union.[22]

When Wool requested a transfer back to the Department of the East, he was replaced by another northern officer, Brig. Gen. Newman S. Clarke. A native of Connecticut, Clarke began his army career in the War of 1812. During the succeeding thirty years, he plodded up the ranks to become colonel of the Sixth Infantry in June 1846. In the invasion of central Mexico, his brigade of the Fifth, Sixth, and Eighth Regular Infantry did some of the hardest fighting at Churubusco, Molino del Rey, and Chapultepec.

Clarke was one of the more underrated officers in the antebellum army. As department commander he authorized Col. George Wright's Spokane Expedition, which brought the Pacific Northwest Indian wars to a brutal and decisive conclusion, but the Democratic administration of Pres. James P. Buchanan neither took notice nor awarded brevets to Wright and his officers. Like many northern regulars, Clarke thought Presidents Pierce and Buchanan and Congress favored southern officers with undeserved promotions, unearned distinction, and plum assignments. His enmity especially targeted Col. William S. Harney, a darling of the Democratic party. In 1855 Secretary of War Davis awarded Harney the helm of the Sioux Expedition although Clarke, commanding the Department of the West, was the senior officer.[23]

Indeed, George Wright himself was another accomplished but unappreciated professional soldier. Born in Norwich, Connecticut, Wright attended Dartmouth College Academy. In 1818, at the age of fourteen, he enrolled in West Point and studied infantry tactics under Maj. William J. Worth, with whom he later allied himself. Graduating in 1822, he was commissioned a second lieutenant in the Third Infantry. He married Margaret Wallace Foster, a sister-in-law to Col. Edwin V. Sumner, after which he and Sumner became close friends.

The Seminole War turned Wright into a brutal campaigner. In the winter of 1841–42, he drove himself and his unit through Big Cypress Swamp for Worth's extermination campaign. Worth praised his old student's "zeal, energy and talent, patience, and endurance of hardship and privation." In the Mexican-American War, Major Wright won a brevet to lieutenant colonel for his gallantry at Churubusco and Contreras and was wounded while leading Worth's center charge at Molino del Rey. After the war, he served in California's Northern Military District and later the Columbia River District. In 1855 his years of distinguished service were rewarded with the colonelcy of the Ninth Infantry, one of Secretary of War Davis's new regiments.

Wright inherited Worth's enmity for General-in-Chief Scott. In late 1860 he complained to the commanding general about assigning Col. Albert S. Johnston to command the Department of California. Wright believed that his Yankee origins had prejudiced the prosouthern Pierce and Buchanan administrations against him. Eminently fair and just, Wright gave credit to whomever it was due, but his iron-fisted discipline angered some subordinates. Wright's placid face, darkened by hard frontier service, disclosed a taciturn, confident, and experienced senior officer.[24]

The command of the Department of New Mexico occasionally fell to Col. Benjamin L. E. Bonneville of the Third Infantry. Born in Paris, France, he immigrated to the United States in 1802 and graduated from West Point in 1815. He was aide to French hero Lafayette during his celebrated visit to America in 1825. Bonneville served at Fort Gibson, Indian Territory, in the late 1820s and then launched a mysterious fur-trading expedition to the Rocky Mountains during the Jackson administration. His bravery at Contreras and Churubusco, Mexico, earned him a brevet to lieutenant colonel. Between the wars, he hardly cut the dashing figure that Washington Irving painted in *The Adventures of Captain Bonneville.* Some of his junior officers thought him a blarney old fusspot, but his gouty exterior veiled a skillful, wise frontier officer. He personally lead one of the decade's most successful Apache campaigns, the Gila Expedition of 1857.[25]

The most significant northern departmental commander was Edwin V. "Bull" Sumner. Born near Boston, Massachusetts, in 1798, Sumner was a civilian appointment to the Second Infantry at the rank of second lieutenant in 1819. Fourteen years later the Jackson administration appointed him to a captaincy in the elite First Dragoons. Between 1838 and 1842, he commanded the Cavalry School of Practice at Carlisle Barracks, Pennsylvania. Scott thought Sumner one of his most dependable and loyal line officers, assigned him to train the newly created Regiment of Mounted Riflemen, and put him in charge of Harney's Second Dragoons during the invasion of Mexico. At Molino del Rey Sumner's cavalry brigade held Scott's left flank, taking heavy fire and casualties. Scott praised his obedience to authority and enforcement of regulations, though Capt. Richard S. Ewell labeled Sumner a "martinet."

Each morning Sumner greeted his officers in full uniform and with his coat buttoned. Erasmus Keyes believed that Sumner was "one of the best instructed line officers in the army." Totally devoted to the profession of arms, he labored to shield his troops from meddling politicians on the frontier and in Washington. He commanded the Ninth Military Department and the Department of the West during the 1850s.

Sumner was probably a Whig or, at least, was inclined toward that party. His cousin was Charles Sumner, the abolitionist senator from Massachusetts. A favorite of General Scott, Sumner rode next to the commanding general when United States forces marched into Mexico City. His professional allies were John E. Wool, Stephen W. Kearny, and William J. Worth. His bitter enemies included William S. Harney and Joseph E. Johnston, two officers with southern sympathies. During his antebellum career, Sumner never publicly declared a position on slavery, but an acquaintance believed that he was an antislavery man, and his crackdown on border ruffians during "Bleeding Kansas" outraged ultrasoutherners in the Pierce administration. Tall, stout, and grizzled like many cavalry peers, Sumner was a legend in the antebellum regular army.[26]

Dominating the upper echelons of the regular army, however, were officers of southern affiliation or birth like Philip St. George Cooke. Born in Lynchburg, Virginia, he studied Latin, Greek, literature, and natural philosophy. His graduation from West Point in 1827 was followed by an appointment to the Sixth Infantry and frontier campaigning under Maj. Bennet Riley on the Santa Fe Trail. In 1833 Cooke was appointed a lieutenant in the First Dragoons, became the army's cavalry expert, and published *Cavalry Tactics* in 1861. While patrolling the Santa Fe Trail in 1844, he surrounded the Snively Expedition—a group of Texas filibusters preying on Hispano traders—disarmed the pirates, and ordered them back to Texas; Comanches killed several of the unarmed brigands. A decade later, death threats chased Cooke off the Texas frontier.

Cooke was an eccentric soldier. Standing well over six feet, he had a twelve-league step and a nasally voice. A romantic at heart, he pined for the sublimity of armed combat. For that reason his command of the Mormon Battalion—epic but bloodless—in the Mexican-American War gravely disappointed him. The heroic cadences of his official reports and several books disguised the drudgery and hardship of frontier soldiering. At the same time, suffering neither fools nor knaves, he discharged his buckshot tongue at any man or beast that dishonored the nation and army. Whether exploring frontiers, fighting Indians, or policing riots, the Lynchburg dragoon was the army's best all-around antebellum officer.[27]

Although a Pennsylvanian by birth, Persifor Frazer Smith was a Louisianan by marriage. Born in Philadelphia in 1798, Smith was educated at Princeton College, briefly studying law afterward. In 1819 he relocated to Louisiana, and three years later married Frances Jeanette Bureau of New Orleans. Rising quickly in the city's political circles, Smith held a series of judicial and civil offices, including adjutant general of Louisiana, before the Mexican-American War. When the Second Seminole War broke out in 1835, he raised and led a regiment of Louisiana volunteers. That conflict tarnished the careers of many professional and volunteer officers, but Smith's political and military reputation ascended to new heights. When Democratic president James K. Polk created the Regiment of Mounted Riflemen in 1846, he appointed Smith to be its colonel. During the war with Mexico, Smith commanded volunteers and earned brevets to major general in the regular service. At the Battle of Contreras, he engineered the American breakout against a vastly superior Mexican army. After the war, he commanded the Division of the Pacific, the

Eighth Military Department, the Department of Texas, and the Department of the West.

By all accounts, Colonel Smith was a charismatic, intelligent, and courageous regimental commander. Having served as Smith's adjutant in gold-rush California, William T. Sherman recalled, "He was a gentleman of fine social qualities, genial and gentle, and joked at everything." Dabney H. Maury, a lieutenant in the Mounted Riflemen, thought Smith was the "best commander" antebellum America produced. His appointment to the colonelcy of the Mounted Riflemen by the partisan President Polk demonstrated Smith's high esteem in Democratic circles. Indeed, in December 1856 Pres. Franklin Pierce, a Democrat, awarded Smith one of the coveted brigadier general's slots. However, his last few years were marred by failing health, and Smith died in May 1858.[28]

Bull Sumner's successor in New Mexico in 1853 was John Garland, colonel of the Eighth Infantry. A native of Virginia, he joined the army as a lieutenant during the War of 1812 and escorted the defeated Black Hawk to Washington in the early 1830s. During the Second Seminole War, he lured the last significant band to its capture with "a feast" and "liquor." His conspicuous service in four major battles won him a brevet to brigadier general during the Mexican-American War. Upon Worth's death in 1849, he was promoted to the colonelcy of the Eighth Infantry. One of his daughters married Maj. James Longstreet, the future Confederate general. Unlike Sumner, Garland cultivated pacific relations with New Mexico civil authorities.[29]

Taking over the Department of New Mexico from Colonel Bonneville was Thomas T. Fauntleroy, colonel of the First Dragoons. He was a native Virginian who had served in the War of 1812 and returned to civilian life for twenty years. In 1836 he accepted a majority in the Second Dragoons and served in the Seminole War. Unlike most regimental commanders, Fauntleroy received no brevets for Mexican-American War service. In 1850 he became colonel of the First Dragoons. Stubborn and proud, he was less congenial toward civilian officials than Colonel Garland.[30]

Like Fauntleroy, Col. William W. Loring was appointed from civilian life. Although his ancestral roots were in New England, he was born in North Carolina and reared in St. Augustine, Florida, where his parents owned a plantation and sugar mill. In 1832 at age fourteen, Loring enlisted in the Florida Volunteers, campaigned against the Seminoles until the late 1830s, and was nicknamed "Boy Soldier." After three years at boarding school in Alexandria, Virginia, Loring studied law at Georgetown College, practiced law in Florida, and served in the state legislature.

At the outbreak of the war with Mexico, he was appointed a captain in the new Regiment of Mounted Riflemen. At Belen Gate in Mexico City, a musket ball shattered his arm; afterward, he laid aside his cigar and sat impassively as a surgeon sawed off the limb. He was promoted to lieutenant colonel at the war's end and colonel in 1856. At thirty-eight he was the youngest line colonel in the regular army. During the 1850s Loring commanded the Eleventh Military Department (Oregon Territory) and the Department of New Mexico.

William Gwin, Democratic senator from California, labeled Loring a "true Democrat." He advocated the virtues of the Fugitive Slave Law and the Compromise of 1850. Of medium height, Loring was courteous if imperial. His straight black hair slowly receding, he studied his men with condescending yet racing "black eyes." Although one limb short of four, Loring was known for his remarkable stamina and energy. His most memorable feat was commanding the great march of the Mounted Riflemen—1,800 miles—from Fort Leavenworth to Fort Vancouver in 1849.[31]

In early 1861 David E. Twiggs wrote General Scott: "I am a Southern man. . . . As soon as I know Georgia has separated from the Union I must, of course, follow her." Born in Georgia in 1790, Twiggs was an infantry officer in the War of 1812, but lacking an assignment at the war's conclusion, he returned to civilian life for the next decade. Commissioned a major in the First Infantry in 1825, he rose to the colonelcy of the Second Dragoons in 1836 and to brigadier general during the Mexican-American War. He was conspicuous at Palo Alto and Resaca de la Palma and led Scott's vanguard to Mexico City. During the interwar years, he commanded the Eighth Military Department, the Department of Texas, and the Department of the West.

To his men, Twiggs was known as "Bengal Tiger" or "Old Davy." Like Cooke, Harney, Sumner, and Smith, he was a tall, powerful cavalry officer. His scarlet face was framed by a thick head of hair and a heavy beard, both gleaming white. Neither charming nor charismatic, Twiggs was unpopular with both officers and men and extremely "sensitive about his age," which he did not reveal even to his closest associates. William W. Mackall wrote, "All the arts of the barber and tailor were employed to give him the appearance of youth."[32]

Serving three different flags during his life, Albert S. Johnston compiled a remarkable military record. He was a native of Kentucky first educated at Transylvania University and later graduating from West Point in 1826. He resigned in 1834 and went to Texas two years later. In a single year he rose from private to senior brigadier general in the Army of the Texas Republic. Johnston also served as Texas's secretary of war and operated a plantation.

During the Mexican-American War, he led a regiment of Texas volunteers. Reactivating his regular army commission in 1849, he served in the Paymaster Department in Texas until the Pierce administration made him colonel of the Second Cavalry in 1855. Johnston commanded the Departments of Texas, Utah, and the Pacific thereafter.

A Whig before the war with Mexico, Johnston voted for Zachary Taylor in 1848. But the colonel was a slaveholder, southerner, and Texan first, and as the sectional controversy unfolded, he feared the destruction of both the South and the Union by the antislavery North. When Taylor died in 1850, Johnston saw the Democratic party as the protector of those things he held dear. Quiet, confident, and determined, Johnston fussed over the Second Cavalry, and the men returned his affection. Constantly patrolling the frontier, the Second quickly became a crack combat unit.[33]

William S. Harney's antebellum military career was possibly the most sweeping of all. He was born in 1800 into a middle-class, slave-owning family near Nashville, Tennessee. Several miles to the east lay the plantation of Andrew Jackson, Harney's personal friend and mentor. After two years at Cumberland College, Harney was commissioned a second lieutenant in the First Infantry in 1818. A quarrelsome, insubordinate officer, he made enemies of Winfield Scott and Stephen W. Kearny in the 1820s, but at Fort Winnebago in the early 1830s he made a lifelong friend of Jefferson Davis. When Congress created the Second Dragoons in 1836, Harney personally called on President Jackson at the Hermitage to secure the lieutenant colonelcy of the regiment. During the Seminole War, he lost half his company to a Seminole surprise attack, but Harney hunted down the ambushers and hanged six of them, developing a reputation as an unorthodox and aggressive combat leader.

During the Mexican-American War, Harney led an unauthorized and disastrous incursion into northern Mexico. Handing his brigade to Maj. Edwin V. Sumner, Scott suspended and eventually court-martialed Harney, but the general waived the sentence and reinstated him. Harney went on to earn a brevet promotion to brigadier general at Cerro Gordo but forgave neither Scott nor Sumner. After the war, he commanded the Eighth Military Department (Texas), the Department of the West, the Department of Oregon, and the Department of Florida.

Clearly a southern Democrat, he shamelessly exploited his friendships with political allies to advance his career. During the Mexican-American War, President Polk accused General-in-Chief Scott, a Whig, of persecuting Harney because of his Democratic politics. In the 1852 presidential campaign, Harney aided the election of Franklin Pierce, whose administration awarded him the Sioux Expedition in 1855 and the Department of Florida in 1856. Pres. James Buchanan rewarded Harney's political loyalty with a full commission as brigadier general upon the death of Persifor F. Smith in 1858. In the 1820s Harney had married into the wealthy Mullanphy family of St. Louis. The union was frustrating and unhappy, but Harney and his wife owned extensive plantation and slave property. In the sectional dispute, his sympathies were with the South.

Harney's profanity and violence were legendary on the frontier. Prone to sudden, explosive fits of temper, he beat to death his sister-in-law's slave servant in 1834. During the Seminole War, he seemed to thrive on the conflict's brutality. In 1845 his verbal and physical abuse of enlisted men earned the reprimand of General-in-Chief Scott, who condemned his "'vicious habits.'" One of Harney's duties during the Mexican-American War was hanging thirty United States deserters, members of the famous San Patricio Battalion.

Col. Stephen W. Kearny thought Harney had "'no more brains than a greyhound,'" and Colonel Hitchcock was repelled by Harney's butchery, filthy mouth, coarse habits, and uncultivated mind. Junior officers, however, were awed by Harney's towering build and combat prowess. Straight as an arrow, he stood six-feet, three-inches tall—all muscle—with a small head and deep-set, bullet eyes. By the mid-1850s his auburn hair and beard had turned snow white, and toward the end of the decade he began to wear spectacles. At the height of his political and military powers, Harney represented the best and the worst of the regular army during the interwar years.[34]

To the public's mind during the Age of Jackson, the United States Military Academy bred aristocracy. Professionalism smacked of privilege, and the Jacksonians, who exalted unschooled, unorthodox amateurism, ruthlessly attacked both. Critics inside and outside Congress accused the military academy of molding patrician soldiers who imperiled United States democracy. They believed that citizen-soldiers, both more loyal and efficient, were the answer to the Republic's national defense needs. Andrew Jackson, not Winfield Scott, was their soldierly ideal.

The politics of democracy indeed did disgust many professional soldiers. A champion of aristocracy, Commanding General Scott lamented the mongrelization of American politics by Andrew Jackson's followers. After observing Congress in early February 1851, Lt. John W. Gunnison wrote, "The members were in a terrible commotion; the Ohio abolitionist was glorying in the Boston mob and abusing the Secretary of State and this seems to be the order of the day[—]to talk talk & talk about the theoretical notions of Union slavery & liberty." While chasing Apaches in the "deformed and wretched"

Southwest, 2d Lt. Henry Lazelle wrote, "Shame be on Northern and Southern mad-men, those political fools who stand disputing, and endangering the happiness of millions for the possession of a curse!"[35]

Their political reservations aside, regular officers were a middle-class elite. By 1861, 70 percent were graduates of West Point, the most rigorous higher education in antebellum America. The vast majority came from families of average means; their fathers were farmers, merchants, lawyers, artisans, and army officers. Few professional soldiers, despite notable exceptions like Robert E. Lee, William H. Emory, and George B. McClellan, were the scions of wealthy patricians.

Young men joined the army for middle-class reasons: free education, military glory, frontier adventure, personal honor, and economic security. John Pope wanted the engineering education, which had market value in civilian life. Philip Sheridan was swept away by the accounts of Mexican-American War exploits. Although a brilliant soldier, Robert E. Lee believed that an ambitious young man could rise "faster & farther" in the civilian world. After nearly a quarter century in the army he wrote, "Nothing but an unconquerable passion for military life, would induce me to recommend the Military profession." Clawing one's way into the aristocracy was a foolhardy incentive for the army career.[36]

An army commission brought the soldier no romance and little adventure. If he were an engineer, artilleryman, or departmental staff officer, he would likely serve in a city or major installation. The duty might be monotonous, but he would enjoy familiar comforts. If he were an infantry or cavalry officer, his post would probably be a western station, where routine, isolation, and deprivation would test his devotion. Stationed at Fort Humboldt, California, a melancholic Capt. Ulysses S. Grant confided to his wife: "You do not know how forsaken I feel here! . . . I do nothing here but set in my room and read and occationally take a short ride on one of the public horses." Scouts and campaigns broke the boredom, but promising little glory and much fatigue, they also might shatter the officer's health.[37]

Frontier soldering left officers with a lot of leisure. To pass the time, everyone consumed books, journals, magazines, and newspapers, and wrote and read letters. Each day, Colonel Hitchcock and Maj. Samuel P. Heintzelman both composed extensive entries in personal journals. The western deserts, plains, and mountains were an extraordinary wildlife habitat. Officers hunted game both to escape garrison tedium and to stock their mess tables. Ever eager socialites, officers and their wives hosted dinners and dances to entertain themselves, their families, and their neighbors.[38]

Military careers worked hardships on families. Frequent long separations were heart rending. In six years' duty in California and on the northern plains, Capt. Thomas Sweeny saw his wife and children only "nine or ten months." From Camp Yuma on the Colorado River, he wrote his wife Ellen: "I dream of you almost every night. . . . Sometimes my dreams are none of the pleasantest—when you appear to me as a total stranger, caring nothing for me, yet looking on you as one lost to me forever." While Capt. Howard Stansbury surveyed the Rocky Mountains, his depressed wife thought that passing away "with her children beside her" would be a "great relief."[39] Many officers, however, brought their families to the West by steamboat, sailing ship, mule, wagon, or stagecoach. Like pioneer emigrants, military dependents endured the heat, cold, wind, rain, and snow. Yellow fever, malaria, and cholera—not Indians—were their principal killers.[40]

Recreating a middle-class Victorian lifestyle was a priority for military spouses. Frontier posts were constructed from local natural resources: sod on the plains; adobe in the desert Southwest; and lumber in the Pacific Northwest. The Quartermaster Department sometimes furnished flimsy prefabricated "cottages." If an officer received no quarters, he had to house his family in a tent, with civilian neighbors, or in a nearby settlement. To add domestic touches, families furnished their own glass, doors, carpets, chairs, beds, lamps, curtains, china, and other items. Some officers hired servants, and some from the South brought slaves. Although army families often shared their quarters with fleas, mice, snakes, and other wild creatures, they were remarkably resourceful at making comfortable homes on any frontier.[41]

During their off-duty hours, most regular officers drank, gambled, and politicked. At Benicia Barracks in California during 1852, Bvt. 2d Lt. George Crook was appalled that all but two officers were drunk at least once a day. At the wake of Maj. Albert S. Miller—a victim of alcoholism—Maj. Hannibal Day announced, "Well, fellows, Old Miller is dead and he can't drink, so let us all take a drink." Gambling was another common pastime. Regular officers often congregated to play cards, shoot billiards, and imbibe in spirits.[42]

Feeding the intemperance of the officer corps was low pay. Unchanged since the War of 1812, the base salary of a second lieutenant was $25 per month, or $300 per year, supplemented by small living allowances. If the second lieutenant were either an infantry or artillery officer, his allowances for "subsistence and a servant" raised his yearly income to $834. In the mounted arm, his base pay and allowances would equal $1,126. In 1857, bowing to pressure from officers, the secretary of war, and economic inflation, Congress raised the monthly stipend at each officer grade by $20. A second lieutenant now earned $45 per month, $65.50 with emoluments, or $408 per year. A mounted second lieutenant received $420 per year.[43]

Although an officer and his family might live comfortably on his salary and allowances in the East, they struggled to break even in the West. In 1849 from Astoria, Oregon Territory, Theodore Talbot complained: "Prices of everything in Oregon had raised to an enormous height. Eggs are $2.00 a dozen, lumber 250. per M, common blankets $16.00 and so with every article of trade." He later wrote, "Although I am getting $1000 a year now I can barely keep my nose above water." The inflated economy of gold-rush California especially drained the pockets of frontier officers. Feeling pinched, they mustered civilian support for an increase in living allowances. Commanding the Pacific Division, Col. Persifor F. Smith argued that the officer corps should not shoulder the "burthens" of the gold boom, particularly when federal obligations prevented them "from enjoying any benefit."[44]

A regular officer could follow three routes to enlarge his pocketbook: promotion to a higher rank, resignation for civilian employment, or moonlighting during off-duty hours. In the antebellum army, promotion was strictly by seniority; an officer climbed up the ranks by outlasting his peers. The army filled vacancies to the rank of captain by regiment; to field grades of major, lieutenant colonel, and colonel by combat arm, staff department, or corps; and to brigadier general and major general from throughout the army. The Department of War administered neither physical nor aptitude tests to measure the fitness of an officer for promotion. Disgusted with aged officers on the Gila Expedition in 1857, Second Lieutenant Lazelle admitted, "It is to be regretted . . . of our service, that age up to a certain grade, and age alone, gives rank." A first lieutenant or captain might serve in one grade until he was middle-aged and graying before a superior died or retired. Lt. Richard Johnson later recalled, "Officers rarely ever died, and few ever felt that the service could spare them, and hence none resigned."[45]

The seniority system protected mediocre and unfit officers while it held back and frustrated talented young men. In a short time, Lieutenant Crook characterized most commanding officers as small-minded despots who discouraged professional growth in junior officers. Facing a court-martial at Fort Yuma, California, Captain Sweeny complained, "All those old fogies will stand by each other like pickpockets, as they all expect to be in command of posts sometime or other, and wish to [exercise the] prerogative of tyranny over the junior officers under their command." During the 1850s Joseph E. Johnston groused about the resistance of "Fogyism" to tactical and technological innovation in the army.[46]

Slow promotion, low pay, and "fogyism" drove many promising young officers to resign. Fresh from a tour of European armies, Capt. George B. McClellan foresaw only a narrow professional horizon in the army and left the service for a lucrative railroad job in 1856. Although promoted to captain, William T. Sherman became bored with army life and entered the risky world of frontier banking in 1853.[47]

Within the army, officers of all grades moonlighted to augment their monthly stipends. Taking two months' leave in 1849, Sherman surveyed land along the San Joaquin, Cosumnes, and Sacramento Rivers and earned "six thousand dollars." In San Francisco, Capt. Erasmus Keyes invested his savings in real estate and collected one thousand dollars a month in rents. Although he lost all of his structures to the fire of 1851, he immediately rebuilt them and "nearly restored" his "income" by year's end. When Colonel Hitchcock left California in 1854, he consigned "some $45,000" of investments to former captain Sherman in San Francisco. One of the biggest land barons in San Francisco was quartermaster captain Joseph L. Folsom.[48]

Officers throughout the American West tried to exploit frontier economic opportunities. In Washington Territory, Lt. Ulysses S. Grant and another officer lost their money by shipping pigs and cattle to San Francisco. Desperate to bring his family to the Northwest, Grant tried to raise potatoes, but the Columbia River flooded his crop. Maj. Samuel P. Heintzelman helped form the Sonora Mining and Exploring Company in 1857, became its president, and took a two-year leave of absence to direct operations in Mexico. One of the most successful army entrepreneurs was dragoon captain Henry H. Sibley, who patented a conical canvas tent adapted from the Indian tepee. Warm in the winter and cool in the summer, the Sibley tent became standard issue to troops campaigning on the plains. Moonlighting, however, relieved the financial pinch for only a few officers in a big way.[49]

Despite the professional and personal hardships of military life, not many officers could afford financially to resign, for few could accrue savings enough to buy farms or businesses. Although heartsick at long separations, Lt. John W. Gunnison wrote his wife, "It will not do for me to quit my livelihood at present enjoyed, until I can produce another at the place so much the object of affection." Summing up the soldier's conundrum, Cadet Richard S. Ewell wrote his mother in 1839, "The education that we get here [West Point] does not qualify us for any other than military life, and unless a man has money, he is forced to enter the army to keep from starving."[50] Once in the army, a man would likely suffer if he tried to leave.

With professional and economic advancement limited, officers sought other avenues to distinction and preferment. Early in its history, the regular army enacted the brevet promotion to reward bravery, gallantry, and valor in national service, particularly combat. The lieutenant's courage in battle might win him a brevet captaincy; another act might earn him a brevet majority. This system of honorary promotions, however, worked black magic in the army. Although without effect in his own regiment, the lieutenant's brevet rank was activated on "special assignment of the President in commands composed of different corps" or on "courts-martial or *detachments* composed of different corps." If assigned to the detachment at his brevet majority, the young lieutenant outranked captains who lacked equal or higher brevets.[51]

Brevet ranks aggravated the high-pitched jealousies of the officer corps. The army career offered the average officer little power and prestige, and officers keenly felt their vulnerability to superiors. Although schooled in iron discipline, junior officers complained to wives and peers about despotic commanding officers who ignored their "proper" duties but interfered in all "small matters." A "shavetail," or second lieutenant, during the early 1850s, Crook later wrote: "Most of the commanding officers were petty tyrants, styled by some Martinets. They lost no opportunities to snub those under them, and prided themselves in saying disagreeable things. . . . Generally they were the quintessence of selfishness."[52]

Officers placed the highest premium on honor, and their hair-trigger tempers snapped at the slightest provocation. In late 1854 and early 1855 Cols. Edwin V. Sumner and Newman S. Clarke jousted over the command of Jefferson Barracks. Sumner won, and the War Department ordered Clarke, commanding the Department of the West, to St. Louis. Sumner immediately declared "assignable" the quarters of Clarke and his adjutant, Capt. Winfield Scott Hancock. Accusing Sumner of a lapse in "military courtesy and propriety," Hancock wrote, "I have sufficient manliness to let you know that I resent it." Clarke chimed in, "Heretofore I have deemed you a friend." Embarrassed by the "indelicacy," Sumner replied, "I regret this affair altogether; it was unnecessary between officers who have known each other as long as we have."[53]

To create some professional latitude and mobility, officers cultivated personal relationships with powerful politicians and soldiers. The army's most distinguished topographical engineer, Capt. William H. Emory was an intimate of Whig senator Alfred Pearce of Maryland and Jefferson Davis of Mississippi. While stationed in Kennebec, Maine, Lt. Oliver O. Howard developed a close friendship with James G. Blaine, who would secure him the command of a volunteer regiment in the Civil War. Col. Stephen W. Kearny of the First Dragoons kept abreast of forthcoming military policy through Sen. Thomas H. Benton, who chaired the Senate Committee on Military Affairs.[54]

Regular officers secured, or tried to secure, army preferment through powerful civilians and soldiers. In the early 1850s, Lt. Ambrose E. Burnside asked

New Mexico territorial governor James S. Calhoun to recommend him for a promotion. Burnside wrote, "It is a matter of some importance to me, and by using your influence you will confer a great favor." When Congress contemplated army expansion in 1858, Lt. J. E. B. Stuart wanted a captaincy in one of the mounted regiments under consideration and requested the influence of two Virginians, Gov. Henry A. Wise and Secretary of War John Floyd. During the same congressional debate, Capt. Pierre G. T. Beauregard asked Sen. John Slidell of Louisiana to secure him a colonelcy and his friends George B. McClellan, G. W. Smith, and J. K. Duncan majorities or lieutenant colonelcies in the new regiments.[55]

In 1843 Capt. George McCall demonstrated how far antebellum officers would go for a promotion, even a brevet. At the close of the Second Seminole War in 1842, Asst. Adj. Gen. Samuel Cooper recommended McCall for brevet promotion, praising the captain's "zeal, intelligence[, and] capacity for command." When the president submitted the names of McCall and others for brevet consideration, the Senate "confirmed" only a few officers; McCall was not among them. The aggrieved captain concluded that no soldier could gain the "reward of merit" without the agency of "powerful friends."[56]

Determined to get his "due," McCall tapped the political resources of his father, Archibald, who enlisted the aid of James P. Buchanan, Democratic senator from Pennsylvania, the captain's home state. Archibald orchestrated a letter-writing campaign by his influential associates to muster Senate support for his son's brevet. In addition to Buchanan, Senator Sturgeon of Pennsylvania was targeted, and Gov. William Pennington, Sen. William Dayton, and Sen. Jacob Miller—all of New Jersey—were enlisted to campaign for Captain McCall. One other politician, Gouvernor Kemble of New York, lent a hand as well.[57]

Through an infuriating lapse in the military bureaucracy, McCall's name never appeared on Commanding General Scott's master list, which apparently included the names of officers who had never served in Florida. The general-in-chief submitted his recommendations to Pres. John Tyler, who immediately introduced the list to the Senate. After investigating the matter, Kemble told Archibald that the Senate would approve a mere handful and that his son's case was hopeless during the present session. Cursing his bad luck, George wrote his father, "I am not the only one who has felt the unequal action which has been brought about by indulging feeling, of personal friendship, vilely bought favouritism."[58]

Regular officers denied the prevalence of sectionalism in the U.S. Army during the 1850s. Lt. William W. Averell wrote, "The sentiment of loyalty to the flag and love for the nation was universally and unquestionably dominant in the minds and hearts of the army until the winter of 1860–61." Only when "secession and disunion" became likely did "officers of Southern birth" entertain defection to the Confederacy. While fighting Indians on the southern plains, Capt. E. Kirby Smith was unmoved by the slavery debate, so he claimed. In March 1860 he wrote his mother, "A war of the races is surely not reserved for us—there are too many good and conscientious men in both sections . . . to permit it."[59]

The southward flight of one-third of the officer corps, E. Kirby Smith included, belied the common assertion that sectionalism was weak in the regular army. The institution was only as cohesive as the nation that created and sustained it. The exodus of southern officers, the painful wavering of others, the half-hearted sympathies of some Union officers for the Union cause, and the determination of others to crush the South demonstrated how the North-South schism sliced into the heart of the regular army. As a potent weapon of national policy, the army felt the sharp pain of sectional pressures on the Union.

Sectionalism in the army began at West Point. In 1843 Congress placed appointments to the military academy solely in political hands. Each member of the House of Representatives could appoint one candidate from his district every year; the president could select ten aspirants at large. Each family exploited political connections to secure its son's appointment. J. E. B. Stuart, a Virginian, ironically received his position from Thomas Hamlet Averett, the man who defeated Stuart's father, Archibald, in the congressional race of 1848. In Pennsylvania, Winfield Scott Hancock had Congressman Joseph Fornance, one of his father's Democratic cronies, to thank for his berth. From Georgia, Edward P. Alexander was appointed by southern radical Robert Toombs, a neighbor and friend of his father.[60]

Predating the Mexican-American War, sectionalism was an active and visible part of life at the Academy. Cadet John Tidball remembered that the election of 1844 evoked outspoken comment from his peers, especially from southerners who wanted Tennessee expansionist James K. Polk raised to the presidency. Studying at West Point between 1833 and 1837, Edward D. Townsend recalled, "The feeling of the Southerners against the Northerners was quite strong and every now and then broke out in acts of open hostility." On one occasion, two cadets, one southern and the other northern, faced off with quarterstaves. Even before the two combatants had opened their battle, the southern cadet lunged at his opponent, plunging a "dirk" into his stomach. Both fought manfully until the northerner collapsed. The southern combatant was immediately expelled.[61]

Sectional differences also extended into the classroom. Although West Point education stressed mathematics, sciences, and engineering, its entrance requirements were minimal. A sound body and a rudimentary knowledge of reading, writing, and arithmetic were sufficient to earn the nominee a place at West Point. Ninety-three percent of the appointees passed the physical examination and the aptitude test, but one-quarter failed to finish the four-year course. Mathematics and engineering took a heavy toll of southerners and westerners, whose educational preparation was generally inferior to that of their northeastern peers. Tidball, a midwesterner, wrote: "As a rule the New Englanders were what is called smarter than the rest of us. They had more brightness from education." Academic deficiencies drove out nearly one-half of the westerners and over one-third of the southerners. West Point authorities dismissed only one-fifth of the New Englanders for poor marks.[62]

West Point cadets partook avidly, even vehemently, of the political debate over slavery. During the mid-1840s, southerners were constantly speculating "upon politics and the negro," according to Tidball. Of his West Point experience during the 1850s, Oliver O. Howard wrote, "I very soon found that unpleasant feuds existed in the corps of cadets, and, as a rule, the subject of slavery was at the bottom of the controversy." Indeed, southern cadets were touchy about slavery. Howard was an admirer of Free-Soil politician William Seward of New York, and his Bible class, temperance activities, and occasional utterance against the extension of slavery cultivated the enmity of ultra-southerners and their sympathizers. Sectional animosity also infected the cadets' military organization. Academy regulations stipulated that cadets fall into battalions according to their height, but during the 1850s their formations assumed sectional identities.[63]

West Point in the decade before the Civil War, however, was not predominately southern in either its student body or its faculty. Southern-born officers and civilian faculty rarely composed more than one-third of the staff. Of the 155 officers who served at West Point between 1850 and 1861, only 23 resigned their commission to go south. Nor was the body of graduates between 1830 and 1860 unduly southern. The percentage of southern men to finish the course nearly equaled that of southern white males between the ages of fifteen and twenty years of age in the United States population: 23.7 percent versus 23.2 percent respectively. However, some northern cadets, George B. McClellan and Winfield Scott Hancock among them, were admirers and defenders of southern culture and society.[64]

A disproportionate number of officers from slave states held line colonelcies in the regular army during the interwar years. Of the thirty-six regimental commanders, sixteen (44 percent) were born in free states or territories, while seventeen (47 percent) were born in slave states. One line colonel hailed from Washington, D.C., and two others came from Europe. The numbers still favored the slave states if one counted the origin of their appointments: seventeen (47 percent) from free states; eighteen (50 percent) from slave states; and one (3 percent) from Washington, D.C.[65]

Line promotions were strictly by seniority under normal conditions, but they could be influenced by politics under extraordinary circumstances. American expansion to the Pacific Coast in 1848 overtaxed the constabulary capacities of the tiny regular army. Pressured by Secretary of War Davis, Congress legislated four new regiments in 1854: two of cavalry and two of infantry. Pres. Franklin Pierce's endorsement created 138 officers' vacancies.[66]

A mad scramble ensued. Regular officers and civilians began filing applications and making political contacts. In February 1854, writing from New Mexico, Capt. Richard S. Ewell urged brother Ben Ewell to "lobby" for him in Washington. Richard wrote: "I will come down very handsomely, paying all expenses if you fail, and say one thousand dollars for the grade of Major. Wonders are sometimes done by spending a little money judiciously among the proper agents." Winfield Scott Hancock tried to muster the influence of President Pierce, "an old traveling companion in Mexico." Second Lt. John B. Hood, a Kentuckian, sought the support of John C. Breckenridge, a friend since his boyhood and a distinguished senator from his state. Writing for his son, one correspondent told Jefferson Davis, "With your aid I do not fear of success and beg assure you that I will not forget the favor nor hesitate to reciprocate the obligation."[67]

Secretary of War Davis received over one thousand applications. He appears to have enforced an inequitable sectional distribution of the appointments. The origin of birth for sixty-two officers (45 percent) was a free state, while that of seventy-one (51 percent) was a slave state; three (2 percent) were from the District of Columbia and two (1 percent) were from Europe. The origin of the commission slightly evened the percentages between sections. Sixty-one (44 percent) were commissioned from free-states, while sixty-two (45 percent) were commissioned from slave states; two (1 percent) were commissioned from the District of Columbia, three (2 percent) from the western territories, eight (6 percent) at large, and two (1 percent) from the regular noncommissioned ranks. Two-thirds of the nation's population resided in free-states, one-third in the South.[68]

Davis gave nearly half of the slots to men commissioned directly from civilian life. His decision no doubt vexed regular-army officers, who were eager for advancement and generally unimpressed with the military qualifications of civilians. Seventy-five (55 percent) slots went to regular army officers, while sixty-three (45 percent) were granted to civilians. Of these civilians, thirty (48 percent) had fought in the Mexican-American War, seven (11 percent) had served in the regular army, twenty-four (39 percent) lacked any military experience, and one (2 percent) had some West Point training. The civilians with military service were concentrated in the captaincies; those without military service were made lieutenants. To secure the legislation creating the new regiments, Davis had probably promised to commission a large number of men from civilian life.[69]

Davis's appointments reflected the nation's suspicions about the political reliability of the officer corps and its celebration of the citizen soldier. Indeed, despite their national oath, regular officers were hardly apolitical and maintained strong party and sectional loyalties. The schism of the U.S. Army in early 1861 was foretold by the political tumult of its officer corps.

Regular officers generally carried their civilian political attitudes into the army. George B. McClellan, Winfield Scott Hancock, and Thomas Sweeny were outspoken Democratic partisans. Following in his father's footsteps, Hancock idolized Andrew Jackson and saw the Democratic party as the advocate of the "common people." While visiting the nation's capital during the debates over Bleeding Kansas in August 1856, the Irish-born Sweeny blamed the "Black Republicans" for the failure of the military appropriations bill and was certain that they were determined "to either rule or ruin the country." From the South, William S. Harney, William W. Loring, and J. E. B. Stuart were also rock-solid Democrats. Soon after Franklin Pierce assumed the presidency, Stuart wrote a cousin, "I join with you in your best wishes for the success for the Democracy . . . which will secure the permanency of our government and preserve the constitution and the rights of the states inviolate."[70]

The Whig and Republican parties enjoyed proponents among the officer corps as well. While in the army, Ulysses S. Grant was a Whig sympathizer. Although his family owned slaves in Kentucky, Richard W. Johnson echoed its Whig politics. With his "family and friends" predominantly Whig, William T. Sherman championed the party's cause. Ethan A. Hitchcock was another; both he and Grant interpreted the Mexican-American War as a conflict to expand southern slavery, an institution they opposed. Another Whig, Erasmus Keyes, happily sat out that war, teaching artillery tactics at West Point instead. A few officers were Republican. Lt. John W. Phelps, who had turned down a brevet promotion to captain for his Mexican-American War services (the only officer known to do so), resigned his commission in 1859 to crusade fulltime against slavery and masonry. A vitriolic enemy of the slavocracy, Nathaniel Lyon wrote antislavery and pro-Republican manifestos for the *Western Kansas Express*, a newspaper in Manhattan, Kansas Territory.[71]

The election of 1852, pitting Whig Winfield Scott against Democrat Franklin Pierce, stirred the army's political emotions. Major General Scott had engineered the conquest of Mexico City, while Pierce had been one of President Polk's political generals. During the election campaign, party leaders on both sides orchestrated poisonous attacks on the opposition candidate's war record and enlisted the pens of partisan regular officers. The Whigs dug up an altercation between Pierce and Capt. John B. Magruder at the Aztec Club in Mexico City. During a card game, Magruder smacked Pierce in the face and later challenged the general to a duel, but the future president declined. Whigs insinuated that Pierce had skulked away in cowardice. Both William S. Harney and Edward J. Steptoe came to Pierce's defense, though. Harney wrote Pierce, "You could not have acted differently without injury to yourself as a . . . dignified gentleman." A witness to the confrontation, Steptoe asserted to a correspondent, "The allegation that any indignity was offered to Genl. Pierce's person is utterly without foundation." Steptoe's contribution to Scott's demise were newspaper articles in Pierce's behalf.[72]

A loyal Whig since the party's formation, Winfield Scott had been a presidential prospect for a decade. His political managers flooded the country with an anecdotal, illustrated campaign biography and solicited defenses of the general's military record. One correspondent was Colonel Hitchcock, who promised to write articles "on any given point." Scott's campaign, which endorsed the Fugitive Slave Law but ignored slavery in the western territories, cost him crucial votes among disaffected northern and southern Whigs. To his complete surprise, Scott lost the presidential election of 1852. Although he received only 42 of 296 electoral votes, his margin of loss was only three hundred thousand popular votes.[73]

How the officer corps voted is difficult to discern. During the Second Party System, regular officers appeared to divide evenly between the Democrats and the National Republicans or Whigs. However, the politics of slavery challenged their federal oath. Socially conservative and politically cautious, they drifted to the Democratic party—the more moderate organization to their thinking—in greater numbers after 1852. Seventy-five percent or more probably identified with the Democratic party by 1860. Not even their general-in-chief was a political rallying point. Scott—the insufferable egoist, the inspirational soldier, the brilliant statesman—stirred passionate loyalty and bitter enmity. Hardly an officer in the regular army was without a strong feeling about the general-in-chief.[74]

Although federal loyalty and political neutrality were the safest ground, regular officers' sectionalism hardened during the 1850s. In the election of 1856, most probably voted for the moderate-to-conservative Democrat James

Buchanan rather than the radical Republican John C. Frémont, but the cruel blade of sectional schism hung over the corps. During the campaign, while stationed at Watervliet Arsenal in Troy, New York, 2d Lt. Oliver O. Howard of Maine was asked by the sister of his southern host, Lt. William R. Boggs, whether he would cast his vote for Frémont. His affirmation was met with cold stares, and Howard probably concluded that he was sharing the table with nascent secessionists. (Indeed, Boggs would later serve as a Confederate brigadier general.) A loyal federal servant and a Christian gentleman, Howard abruptly discontinued dining at the Boggs residence each evening.[75]

Most officers were racially conservative; few were outright abolitionists. Even Howard and Lyon, both more free-soil than antislavery, sympathized far more with white farmers than African American slaves. The slayer of the Deep South four years later, William T. Sherman wrote in 1860: "He [the African American] must be subject to the white man, or he must be amalgamated or be destroyed. Two such races cannot live in harmony save as master and slave." Although uncomfortable with slavery, some southern officers apologized for it. Richard W. Johnson of Kentucky complained that most slaveholders, having inherited their slaves, were not responsible for the cursed institution and that few could extract themselves from it without incurring ruinous financial losses. In the eyes of Robert E. Lee, slavery was a "moral and political evil" but a necessary instructional tool that would "prepare and lead" the slaves "to better things." Like most southern apologists, Johnson and Lee agreed that slavery was a greater evil to whites than to African Americans.[76]

Bleeding Kansas, the presidential election of 1856, and the emergence of the Republican party made the politics of slavery and the future of the Union a common topic of conversation among regular officers after mid-decade. An infantry captain in the 1850s, William Carlin recalled: "In those days the slavery question dominated all others in the arena of politics. Officers were discussing the question with each other, and the question of disunion was often referred to." No officer publicly declared for "secession or disunion," but none foresaw the election of a "Republican president."[77]

A future hard-fighting Union general, Carlin also remembered a disturbing but "common rumor" that reached Fort Laramie during winter 1855–56. The grisly politics of Bleeding Kansas was boiling over and the critical presidential election was heating up. During that cold, grim season, a few "southern statesmen" began sounding out the loyalty of southern officers. Within the army a well-placed "officer of southern birth," a "reputed favorite of Jefferson Davis," discretely inquired of "his most intimate associates" the side they would take "in the event of an attempted dissolution of the Union." According to Carlin, this southern officer became a "prominent Confederate general." When an unnamed northern officer was approached, he declared for Old Glory and scoffed that the Union would "*pay*" best and muster its great wealth to defend that wealth.[78]

By 1860 officers had earnestly participated in the national dialogue on slavery and sectionalism, and their loyalties were instinctively clear. Earl Van Dorn, John B. Hood, Fitzhugh Lee, and Braxton Bragg were outspoken proponents of secession while they still wore Union blues. In 1858 the haughty P. G. T. Beauregard wrote John Slidell, "We [southerners] have no concessions to make to them—for to us the question of Slavery is one of life or death, to them it is one of fancy—political capital." Equally strong northerners were Erasmus Keyes, Edwin V. Sumner, John Pope, Nathaniel Lyon, Charles Griffin, and David Hazzard. On the Democratic side of the fence, George B. McClellan, Winfield Scott Hancock, and Fitz-John Porter sympathized with southern fears but stood hard and fast by the Union. Professional officers had drawn their political lines on the parade ground long ago.[79]

When the time came to choose between the Union and the Confederacy, most officers were prepared to take sides and could articulate their reasons for doing so. In spite of personal agony, Henry Heth claimed, "I had made up my mind that, in the event of my state, Virginia, seceding, I would cast my fortune with her." A. P. Hill had never owned slaves and despised slavery, but he was a doctrinaire states' rights man and promised his pal, George B. McClellan, that he would fight to the death to defend Virginia. From Camp Colorado, Texas, Capt. E. Kirby Smith wrote his mother, "I am a Southern man in all my feelings and will not stand by the fireside whilst the roof tumbles about my ears."[80]

Other officers drew their swords to defend the Union. For Lieutenant Howard, his choice was simple: All citizens had a duty to defend their country. Richard W. Johnson's parents were slaveholders and Unionists in Kentucky, but critical of secessionists, he declared: "Their rights had not been questioned. No wrong had been done them." A conservative Virginian, Col. Philip St. George Cooke had made his decision in the 1840s: Genuine liberty and freedom lay with the northern cause. His bitter family, including son John Rogers Cooke and son-in-law J. E. B Stuart, disowned him, but Cooke fought for the Union, which he had served with distinction for thirty years.[81]

The defection of one-third of the officer corps to the Confederate States of America indicated structural flaws and ideological weaknesses in the institutional army. Neither the United States Military Academy course of study nor federal service on the western frontiers had sufficiently nationalized the officer corps. For southern officers, loyalty to the Union did not override personal ties to family and section. Numerous forces inside and outside the army undermined its nationalization, professionalization, and cohesion.

Antebellum Americans had not integrated the professional standing army into their political and social consciousness. They scorned the regular army, and politicians inflamed their prejudice. Champions of do-it-yourself soldiering, Jacksonians attacked the regulars' discipline and professionalism as military tyranny and class privilege out of step with the American democracy. In political and social discourse, Jacksonians ignored the glaring failures of the militia system, glorified its few accomplishments, and omitted the hard-won victories of the regulars in the Revolutionary War, the War of 1812, and the Mexican-American War. Those attitudes were unlikely to steel the loyalty of professional soldiers to the Union.

At the national level, Congress enforced its disdain by keeping a tight rein on army pay, manpower, and budgets. Year after year, the United States deployed its army, underfunded, undermanned, and ill-trained, into frontier war zones and demanded the work of a legion from a mere battalion. In officers' eyes the government neither sufficiently compensated nor praised the regulars for their dangerous work. Years of frontier service embittered the regulars, especially the officers, whose members used all available means to secure leaves of absence or preferment that would remove them from their units posted to the frontier. For southern officers such preferment included a commission at a higher rank in the Confederate States Army.

The army, however, generated much of its own misery. Regular officers were proud, vain men, and their petty jealousies and vindictive backbiting slowed army professionalization. Many despised the seniority system but trusted neither Congress to create nor their peers to administer an impartial system of merit promotion. Instead, professional officers stewed over slow promotions till century's end and skirmished with civil and military threats to what little position they enjoyed.

Commissioned officers cultivated relationships with powerful officers and politicians. Junior officers looked to their superiors for favors and protection. Within regiments, officers banded together in cliques, which battled one another for the few available promotions. They formed alliances around sectional origin, political-party affiliation, age, and other commonalities. These personal and professional associations crisscrossed line regiments and staff departments and helped trace the trajectory of the soldier's military career.

Although dreading the personal and national costs of civil war, regular-army officers eagerly anticipated the professional advancement promised by the conflagration. The Union and Confederate armies needed professional soldiers to train and lead their massive armies of green volunteers, and the United

States regular army was the principal source for such experienced officers. The Civil War opened up the seniority system within the U.S. Army and threw open avenues to high rank on both sides. Company-grade officers suddenly rose to field and general ranks. However, sudden and radical promotion did not erase personal pique and professional jealousies. Officers brought their resentments and feuds into the Union and Confederate forces and triggered searing headaches for Pres. Abraham Lincoln and Pres. Jefferson Davis.

Some drunks and scoundrels cursed the private ranks, but their vicious habits generally came from civilian life to army service. Mechanics, artisans, lawyers, schoolteachers, and other skilled and learned men served in the enlisted ranks and benefited the army for a brief time at least. Private soldiers, drunks and effectives, endured hard frontier campaigns and inflicted bloody defeats on American Indians. A significant number of these soldiers—Eugene Bandel, Percival G. Lowe, James A. Bennett, and others—went on to productive civilian careers after their military service.

Even more remarkable was that only twenty-three enlisted men defected to the Confederacy. The poverty, brutality, and prejudice they endured in the antebellum army did not turn them against the Union. Free white men when they joined up, privates and noncommissioned officers bound themselves to a military system that disciplined the ranks with physical terror. Abusive commanding officers such as William S. Harney, Thomas W. Sherman, and Nathaniel Lyon created and enforced an environment of fear, which enlisted men sabotaged and resisted through drunkenness and desertion. Probably better than Union officers, enlisted men implicitly understood the democratic and human principles on which President Lincoln would try to build the Union military effort during the Civil War. Like southerner Philip St. George Cooke, the noncommissioned officers and enlisted men of the regular army understood that the cause of freedom issued from the free North, not the slave South.

II

Border Constabulary

5

STOP THEM

Regulars, Filibusters, and Vigilantes in San Francisco, 1851–1856

CONTRADICTORY presidential policy, sectional politics, and popular will undermined the U.S. Army's intervention against filibusters and vigilantes in San Francisco from 1851 to 1856. Ordered to enforce the neutrality laws on the Pacific Coast, Col. Ethan Allen Hitchcock and Brig. Gen. John Ellis Wool stumbled over federal authorities, local politicians, and California citizens who advocated territorial expansion and admired the filibusters. Especially crippling to the army's constabulary mission was Pres. Franklin Pierce's tacit acknowledgment of unsanctioned imperialism that might benefit the United States. His inconstancy and greed contravened the army's constabulary mission and undercut its developing professionalism. By 1856 the Second Committee of Vigilance in San Francisco had a free hand to invest the city. Democratic-party politics had eroded Wool's prestige and authority to the point that he declined the plea of the Law and Order party to aid the suppression of the vengeful vigilantes.

Manifest Destiny still stirred strong passions throughout the United States during the 1850s. The annexation of Texas, New Mexico, California, and Oregon only whetted American expansionism. From New Orleans to San Francisco, freebooting filibusters—private citizens who set out to invade foreign territories—launched campaigns against Cuba, northern Mexico, and the Sandwich Islands (Hawaii). However, their land piracy, if successful, promised to irritate the explosive issues of territorial annexation and slavery expansion over which southerners and northerners were dangerously divided. Committed to keeping Cuba out of United States hands, Great Britain and France threatened to stop and search American vessels suspected of bearing these invaders. To Pres. Millard Fillmore in 1851, dispersing the filibusters was paramount to preserving the Compromise of 1850—the final word on expansion and slavery in his mind—thus keeping the peace between the North and South and preventing war with any European power.[1]

On 25 April 1851 Fillmore acted against Narciso Lopéz's campaign to Cuba, from which southern expansionists hoped to carve several new slave states. The president condemned Lopez's enterprise, assembling in New Orleans, as a violation of United States "laws and obligations" and demanded its immediate cessation. In the next breath, he mobilized federal authorities to disperse and arrest any filibuster who ignored his executive order. Following the precedents of presidents from George Washington to John Tyler, he ordered the U.S. Army to assist civilian law-enforcement officers.[2]

In early fall 1851, Fillmore's sources in San Francisco reported a military expedition preparing to set sail for the Sandwich Islands. Invoking section 8 of the Neutrality Act of 1818, the president commissioned Colonel Hitchcock, commanding the Division of the Pacific, to deploy all "land forces," regular or militia, against any "expedition or enterprize" with militant designs on a foreign principality, state, colony, district, or people at peace with the United States. Secretary of War Charles M. Conrad instructed Hitchcock to seize all vessels hired to "transport troops, or arms, or munitions of war" and hand them over to the United States marshal. The Sandwich Island expedition had already shoved off in mid-October, but upon receiving Fillmore's commission on 8 January 1851, Hitchcock notified the federal marshal and collector of customs in San Diego and San Francisco about his powers and requested domestic intelligence and law-enforcement assistance.[3]

Recently promoted to colonel of the Second Infantry, Hitchcock had been ordered to join his regiment in California, landing in San Francisco on 7 July 1851. His reputation for scrupulous honesty recommended him to President Fillmore and General-in-Chief Winfield Scott, both of whom wanted to root out financial improprieties practiced by federal authorities in California. Hitchcock, a reformer and humanitarian of national reputation, expected to be sued, abused, and, "failing that," destroyed by civilians, politicians, and federal agents in California, but he confided in his diary, "I shall hold to the right."[4]

During their tenure on the Pacific frontier, Hitchcock and Wool commanded few troops. Upon Hitchcock's arrival, his sprawling division embraced California and Oregon Territory (see map 3). Seven hundred and

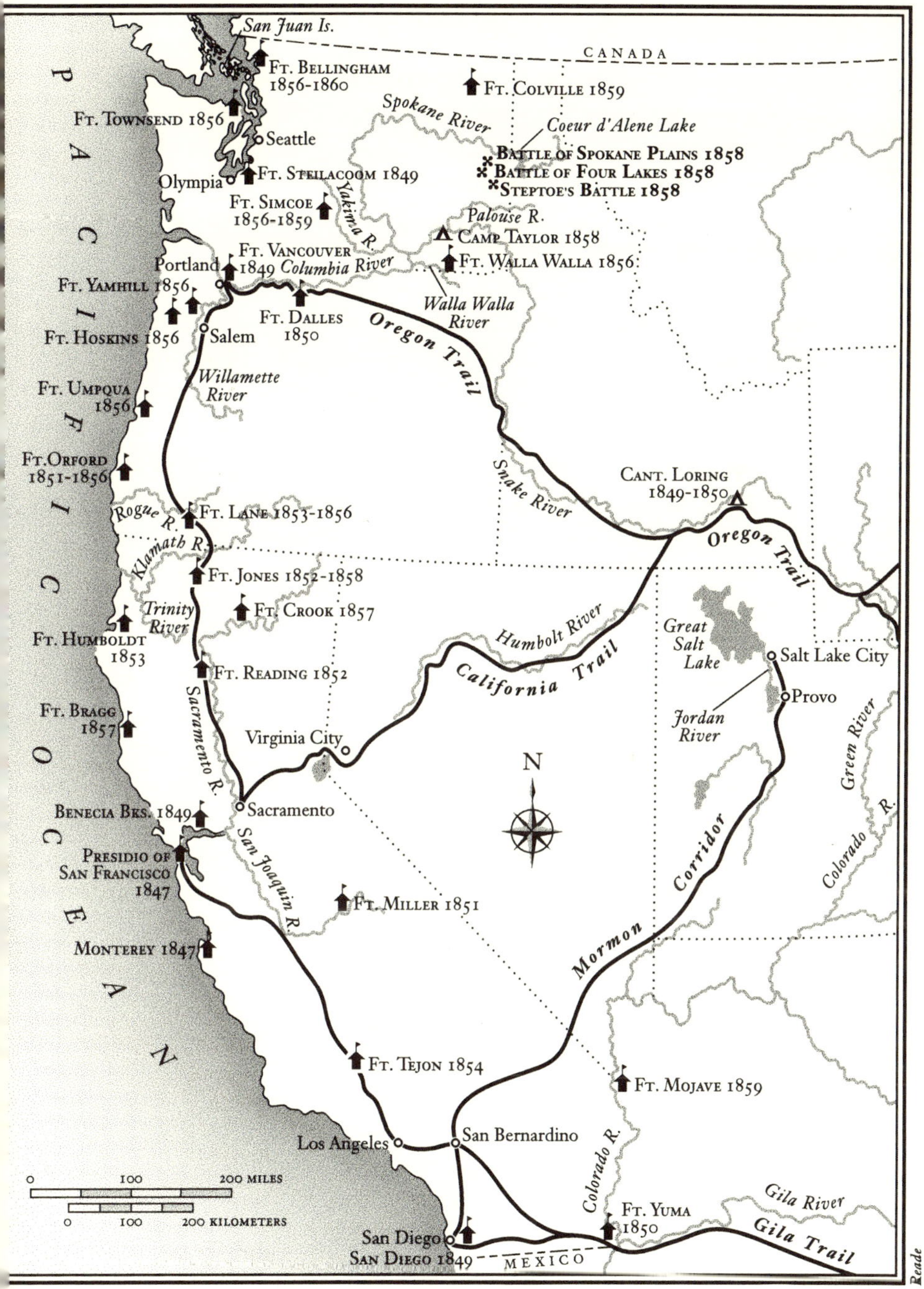

3. The Pacific Coast

thirty-six men and officers composed his entire West Coast constabulary force. The divisional aggregate rose to seventeen hundred in 1852 and remained at that level through 1853. When Wool assumed command on 17 February 1854, the division had recently been renamed the Department of the Pacific, and at year's end, troop levels stood at thirteen hundred.[5]

Tiny garrisons at the Presidio of San Francisco and Benicia Barracks and Arsenal also hampered the army's constabulary mission in San Francisco. Located across the bay to the northeast, Benicia was generally garrisoned by an infantry or artillery company and an ordnance detachment. Between 1851 and 1855, troop levels fluctuated between a low of 56 and a high of 129 men and officers. Perched on the southern shore of the Golden Gate, the Presidio of San Francisco was a one-company post—usually manned by the Third Artillery—in Hitchcock's and Wool's day. From 21 men and officers in 1851, the Presidio's troop aggregate increased to 80 in 1854. The garrisons there and at Benicia were hardly formidable enough to control, overwhelm, or suppress unrest in the city of San Francisco.[6]

Spreading over the sandy hills from the bay's southern shore, San Francisco probably raised Hitchcock's eyebrows. Two years into the gold rush, the city was still the gateway to mines in the river valleys and mountains to the east. Lining the streets in all directions were merchant stores and saloons whose ambitious, calculating owners scrambled to profit off the fluctuating population of restless miners. Struck by San Francisco's ubiquitous gambling establishments in 1853, Ulysses S. Grant recalled, "At all hours of the day and night in walking the streets, the eye was regaled, on every block near the water front, by the sight of players at faro." Standing at approximately forty thousand, the city's population was predominately white European and Anglo American males. Lured by the California promise, Mexicans, Latin Americans, Australians, and Chinese also represented their countries in large numbers.[7]

By 1851 San Francisco already sported a reputation for government graft and corruption, fraudulent Democratic politics, crime, violence, and vice. Hitchcock's landing coincided with the terror of the First Committee of Vigilance. Headquartered across the bay at Sonoma, he generally sympathized with but ignored the extralegal purges of the unwashed and unwanted. The colonel's only involvement was to fill Gov. John McDougal's requisition of two hundred muskets to arm the posse of Sheriff Jack C. Hays, the legendary Texas Ranger, who lost two prisoners to storming vigilantes. His conscience clear, Hitchcock sailed away to Oregon Territory on 20 August 1851. By the time he returned in early fall, the committee had burned itself out.[8]

Proceeding to his new headquarters across the bay at Benicia, Hitchcock began prosecuting his immediate mission, the investigation of federal contracts in California. Over the course of 1852, his headquarters exposed frauds and speculations perpetrated by army officers, Indian agents, and California politicians. Sickened by California's "wholesale butchery" of the Indians, he jealously guarded federal military policy from meddlesome state politicians. At one point, he sharply rebuked the hot-tempered James W. Denver, a Democratic state senator, who dared to influence the placement of army posts. Hitchcock's unpopularity soaring by April 1853, the California legislature memorialized the new secretary of war, Jefferson Davis, for his recall. Through correspondence, the embattled old soldier tested his support in the administration of recently installed Pres. Franklin Pierce, a Democrat. "Military merits alone," Secretary of War Jefferson Davis assured Hitchcock, were the War Department's criteria for evaluating his command of the Pacific Division.[9]

Hitchcock's troubles were soon compounded by "filibusterism," which infected the young men of San Francisco. By 1851 the initial wave of gold-rush miners was exhausting the placer gold in the California river valleys. Impoverished, unemployed, and frustrated, thousands of men drifted back to San Francisco, where dreamy filibusters easily seduced many to enlist or invest in their imperial undertakings. Lying to the south, Sonora, Mexico—sparsely populated, weakly defended, and allegedly endowed with vast untapped mineral wealth—offered would-be conquerors and their followers a new bonanza in gold and land.[10]

From his headquarters at Benicia, Hitchcock conscientiously executed his presidential commission. In mid-April 1852 he ordered Capt. John B. Magruder at San Diego to interdict any American invasion bent on avenging the alleged murder of two Anglos in Baja California. Early the next month, he instructed the commanding officer at the Presidio of San Francisco to break up a party of filibusters organizing in Sacramento if the expedition set off for a foreign country. However, in spring 1852 two sea-borne enterprises, both French, departed San Francisco for Guaymas, Sonora, where the Mexican army routed them. Protesting to the Fillmore administration, angry Mexican officials wondered why federal authorities in California permitted the French filibusters to clear San Francisco harbor. Acknowledging his isolation at Benicia, Hitchcock transferred his headquarters to San Francisco, the regional hub, in mid-June 1852.[11]

Elected in fall 1852, Pres. Franklin Pierce reversed Fillmore's policy on territorial expansion. Although a northern Democrat, Pierce sympathized with land-hungry southerners—his political benefactors—and eagerly sought foreign territory, Cuba especially, to retain their loyalty to his administration and the Union. Inspired by his expansionist rhetoric, some northern Democrats also encouraged Pierce to acquire Cuba, the Pearl of the Antilles, with either gold coin or military might. In summer 1853 the president dispatched James Gadsden to negotiate a land cession on Mexico's far-northern frontier for a southern railroad route to California. A double-edged sword, filibusters complicated official United States negotiations with Mexico for land cessions and the Tehuantepec right of way, but they also placed unofficial, paramilitary pressure on Mexico to sell rights and land desired by the United States. Pierce made a show of reining in the filibusters, but he and Davis sympathized with their cause. Looking ahead to midterm Congressional elections and his own reelection campaign, Pierce was anxious to retain the votes of southerners, many of whom favored territorial expansion and the spread of slavery at any cost.[12]

Although Hitchcock had received his commission from President Fillmore, he intended to exercise his special powers until the Pierce administration revoked them. On 4 April 1853 he alerted Capt. Samuel P. Heintzelman, commanding Fort Yuma on the Colorado River, to a "hostile expedition . . . contemplated from California to Sonora." According to Hitchcock's sources, the lawless column would try to cross the river in the vicinity of Fort Yuma. Should Heintzelman detect the expedition, he should "destroy the supplies, especially the ammunition." Hitchcock leaked the order to the *San Francisco Herald* and compelled William Walker to abandon his overland invasion.[13]

A tiny, birdlike man, Walker would become the United States's most successful and notorious filibuster by decade's end. A Tennessean by birth, the twenty-nine-year-old Walker had practiced law, medicine, and journalism before joining the rush to California in 1850. Fierce editorials against political corruption and a spectacular duel had given Walker local notoriety. His undying ambition was to carve out a southern slave empire in Latin America. Undeterred by Hitchcock's intervention, Walker chartered the brig *Arrow* and promptly started raising money and men for a sea-borne campaign. From Mexico City, Gadsden relayed to Washington, D.C., and San Francisco the Mexican government's displeasure over Walker's hostile preparations, which were jeopardizing United States negotiations.[14]

Indeed, one of Hitchcock's confidential informants confirmed that the *Arrow* was receiving men and arms for a Sonoran invasion, a clear violation of the neutrality laws. Collector Richard P. Hammond kept an eye on the brig, and on the night of 30 September 1853, "with the decided concurrence" of United States District Attorney Samuel Inge, Hitchcock ordered Capt. Erasmus Keyes to seize the *Arrow* and its cargo. His unofficial search uncovering crated "muskets," Keyes handed the ship over to United States Marshal William H. Richardson. In the meantime, Hitchcock urged Inge to libel the ship and impound Walker's supplies, but the district attorney dragged his feet, probably fearing filibuster violence and retaliation.[15]

The army's seizure of the *Arrow* brought down shrill protests from San Franciscans, who generally sympathized with Walker's expedition. Newspapers and politicians scorned the soldier and lionized the filibuster. On 1 October Walker secured a writ of replevin from the California State Court. When the county sheriff served the court order, the federal marshal abandoned the ship, but the sergeant of the regular-army guard defied the lawman and directed him to Hitchcock. Invoking his federal commission, the colonel swore to "hold the vessel against the state's authority," a bold gesture in a nation obsessed with states' rights.[16]

At this point, Democratic politicians began undermining Hitchcock's intervention. After his election President Pierce awarded U.S. senator William M. Gwin the control of federal patronage in California. Gwin's faction was the Chivalry, or Customs House, Democrats, the prosouthern and majority wing of the party in California. A southerner, former slaveholder, and close friend to President Pierce, Gwin advocated the annexation of the Sandwich Islands and portions of northern Mexico. In the midst of the Walker uproar, Gwin personally pleaded with Hitchcock to issue a passport to Henry A. Crabb, a southern lawyer and California state senator who had initiated "an independent move on Sonora." Refusing permission, Hitchcock wrote, "They are either fools or they think I am one." Devoted to the Whigs, Hitchcock had penned defenses of Gen. Winfield Scott, the Whig presidential candidate, against Democratic mudslingers during the election of 1852. He despised the institution of slavery and doubted "Gwin's fidelity to the government."[17]

Senator Gwin, indeed, may have pressured federal civil authorities to ignore Hitchcock's requests for assistance. After the confiscation, swirling rumors foretold an armed seizure of the brig by Walker and his filibuster horde. On 3 October Hitchcock witnessed Gwin buttonholing Collector Hammond on the street. A Mexican-American War veteran, Hammond had resigned his regular-army commission in 1851 to become a surveyor, town builder, lawyer, and politician. Rising to Speaker of the House in California, Hammond was indebted to Gwin for his federal office. That evening, calling at Hitchcock's quarters, the agitated collector begged his wartime comrade to surrender the brig without a fight, but the old soldier flared at Hammond's cowardice, moored the *Arrow* in midstream, and posted a revenue cutter nearby.[18]

District Attorney Inge also backpedaled, "corrupted, probably by Senator Gwin," in Hitchcock's words. Seated behind his desk, Inge admonished the colonel to release the *Arrow* and explained how he had shielded the divisional commander from "the effects of public opinion." Slamming his fist on the table, Hitchcock roared, "Damn public opinion!" and scared Inge into taking out a libel against the brig on 4 October. The son of a southern planter, Inge had represented Alabama in the United States House of Representatives and maintained an interest in northern Mexico; several years later he would lose his personal fortune on a contract to survey Sonora. Hitchcock suspected that Senator Gwin was one of Walker's "secret managers" and that Inge and Hammond became aware of this only after the seizure of the *Arrow*.[19]

Hitchcock's regulars handed the *Arrow* to the U.S. marshal, but several days lapsed before the district attorney inspected the cargo hold, allowing Walker's men to shift some arms, ammunition, and supplies to the nearby *Caroline*. During the night of 16 October, the ship slipped out of the harbor, bearing Walker's little army of American heroes. Although demoralized, Hitchcock took heart that only two hundred men—one of four companies—escaped with Walker to terrorize Mexico.[20]

By mid-October 1853 the uncompromising Colonel Hitchcock might have been the most unpopular man in California. His political isolation, nearly complete, compelled him to write General-in-Chief Scott for a transfer. The public support of "leading politicians" for Walker's filibuster made a mockery of Hitchcock's constabulary mission. Two suits—contempt of court and Walker's thirty-thousand-dollar damage claim—piqued his soldierly honor. His seizure of the *Arrow* fell clearly within the legal parameters of the Neutrality Acts and his presidential instructions. Hitchcock probably placed little faith in his legal counsel, District Attorney Inge, and anticipated losing in frontier courts, which were historically hostile to army officers, but he wrote, "I know I am right and that is enough for me." A bookish, speculative man, he turned to the study of Emerson, Swedenborg, Plato, and Kant for solace.[21]

As Colonel Hitchcock awaited his successor, Inge sprang another surprise. In early November he dropped the libel against the *Arrow* in exchange for the court's waiving all charges against Hitchcock. Local newspapers referred to Inge's deal as "the arrangement," to which a furious Hitchcock, never consulted, publicly denied being a party. In the veteran soldier's mind, quashing the libel was an admission that his authority had never extended to seizing the ship and gave the impression that he "countenanced the unlawful expedition." Inge's legal maneuver was the last straw; Hitchcock washed his hands of enforcing the neutrality laws. Under his direction, Adj. Edward D. Townsend confidentially instructed commanders at San Diego and Fort Yuma not to break up any illegal expeditions until the Pierce administration issued an unequivocal policy on "filibusterism."[22]

Although Secretary of War Davis publicly praised Hitchcock's impoundment of the *Arrow*, the Pierce administration quickly selected his replacement,

Brig. Gen. John E. Wool, commanding the Department of the East. His conferences with Davis left the impression that the Walker filibusters were jeopardizing Gadsden's negotiations; indeed, the secretary of war instructed Wool to employ "all proper means to detect the fitting out of armed expeditions" and to "co-operate with the civil authorities in maintaining the neutrality laws." With a mere seventeen hundred men in the Pacific Department, Wool requested troop reinforcements to maintain "the peace and quiet of the inhabitants," both white and Indian, and desired special authority to prevent violations of the neutrality laws.[23] The Pierce administration granted him a few recruits but no exceptional powers, but on 18 January 1854 the president issued a proclamation denouncing the Walker filibusters then terrorizing Baja California and antagonizing congressional debates over the Gadsden Purchase.[24]

Wool's political identification with Free-Soil Democrats complicated his relationship with the Pierce administration and California Democrats. As the general sailed to New York, he still hoped that the Democratic party would call him back to run for president in 1856.[25] The Department of the Pacific lay far from political epicenters in the East, but the American voters liked to elect military heroes to the presidency, and successfully ending the Pacific Northwest Indian wars and quashing the lawless filibusters might raise his political stock in the public eye and among Democratic-party brokers.

Soon after landing in San Francisco, Wool indeed spoke like a man positioning himself for the Democratic nomination. On 15 February David Broderick, leader of the Free-Soil, or "Tammany," Democrats in California, hosted a dinner honoring two recent arrivals, Wool and Henry S. Foote. Arrayed around the room were Colonel Hitchcock, Mayor Cornelius Garrison, and many Broderick and Chivalry Democrats. During the festivities, when Wool was asked to give a toast, he rose from his seat to predict a sunny future for California, lament the growing sectional schism, and declare: "Indeed I can truly say I have no feelings, principles, or prejudices, that would not make me as much the friend of the one state as the other. I could live with as much pleasure in the South as in the North."

Next in line to speak was Foote. A bald and diminutive southern Democrat, he had been Secretary of War Davis's archrival in Mississippi. Raising his glass, Foote offered, "The Presidential Election of 1856—may it be a man with thoroughly national views." Through the wine and smoke, the Chivalry heard a veiled attack on Pierce, but Wool neither detected a slight nor rose to the president's defense. The following day Chivalry newspapers inveighed against Wool, Foote, Broderick, and the Tammany Democrats.[26]

Wool and Foote had stepped blindly into the middle of the Gwin-Broderick tug of war. In some political circles, Wool and Foote were thought to be disgruntled Democrats whom President Pierce had passed over for higher office. Shut out of federal patronage in California, Broderick Democrats accused Pierce of gross political cronyism. The Chivalry interpreted the dinner, Foote's remark, and Wool's silence as a slap in the president's face. Informed by Gwin's agents in San Francisco, the Pierce administration undoubtedly took note of the divisional commander's political company. In the nation's capital, however, Senator Gwin tried to pat down the administration's ruffled feathers and kept his eye on the biggest prize, military contracts, which Wool awarded, Davis approved, and Congress funded.[27]

His credibility with the Chivalry listing, Wool found the "civil officers"—Attorney Inge, Collector Hammond, and Marshal Richardson—reluctant "to check" the filibusters' expeditions. With or without their help, however, he intended to disperse the brigands. Wool's headquarters kept in touch with naval captain Thomas A. Dornin, commanding the U.S.S. *Portsmouth*. Ordered to intercept the Walker expedition off Baja California, Dornin arrested "Frederick Emory, Walker's secretary of state, and several others" on the coast at Encenada and transported them to San Diego. In late February at San Francisco, Wool initiated the arrest of Col. Henry P. Watkins, Walker's "so called Vice President," and broke up his recruiting station. The judge set Watkins's bail at ten thousand dollars pending a grand-jury hearing. Shorn of reinforcements and resupply, the Walker filibusters were crippled.[28]

Although Wool was vested with no special powers, he promptly began gathering evidence against Count Gaston Raoun de Raousset-Boulbon, Walker's chief rival. The dashing Frenchman had squandered two fortunes during a career that included colonizing, soldiering, politicking, and writing. Now he sought his third fortune in the Americas. For the past year Raousset-Boulbon had been trying to recruit filibusters from the city's hundreds of stranded Frenchmen and Germans, many of whom had been driven from their mining claims by Anglo violence and the Foreign Miners Tax Law. Wool's investigation led him to Luis M. del Valle and Guillaume Patrice Dillon, the Mexican and French consuls respectively. When the government of Mexican president Antonio López de Santa Anna learned about Walker's Baja incursion, it instructed Consul del Valle to raise a force of one thousand Frenchmen—minus the count—for military service on the Sonoran frontier. Their compensation would be regular-army pay and a land bounty. Del Valle secured the aid of Consul Dillon to enlist the volunteers and chartered the ship *Challenge* to convey them to Guaymas, Sonora.[29]

In Wool's mind the scheme was "exceedingly suspicious" and would "lead to difficulties." He was certain that Dillon and Raousset-Boulbon were conspiring to dupe Consul del Valle. Indeed, the French consul was a supporter of French emperor Napoleon III, his imperial ambitions, and French colonies in Sonora. Upon landing in Mexico the French column would transform, Wool anticipated, into a filibuster army commanded by the count. The Mexican consul momentarily became "convinced of the undoubted intrigues," but he pressed ahead with recruitment, much to Wool's dismay. The general's persistence, however, drove the count underground.[30]

Wool infiltrated the French organization by planting a spy. He learned that the *Challenge* was contracted to bear the French expedition to Guaymas. At Wool's request Collector Hammond held the ship until departmental headquarters confirmed the ultimate purpose of the men and supplies. According to a dismissed pilot, Raousset-Boulbon's organization had cached "600 arms and powder" in the "neighborhood of Telegraph hill." On 18 March Wool met with expedition leaders and other interested parties to settle the impasse. Upon exiting, the Mexicans and French thought they had convinced the general to permit the *Challenge*'s harbor clearance. Four days later the ship sailed for Guaymas.[31]

The cagey Wool never doubted that the Frenchmen were filibusters. Confident that the *Challenge* would break "the laws of revenue," Wool instructed the navy to return the ship to port. Indeed, customs officers found dozens of violations and recorded fines in excess of $16,500. On 29 March the United States marshal processed a libel on the *Challenge*, seizing the ship and its cargo to liquidate the fines. French newspapers charged Wool with boosting his presidential chances at the expense of law-abiding Frenchmen. Two days later Wool consented to releasing the vessel after he and Collector Hammond received "positive assurances" that the French column was "exclusively an emigrating party, and would proceed without arms or ammunition to Guaymas."[32]

Raising the legal stakes, Wool initiated the arrest of Consul del Valle. District Attorney Inge complied. Taken into custody by the United States marshal on 31 March, del Valle was charged with "enlisting [men], within the territory of the United States, into the service of a foreign government." The court convicted del Valle for violations of the neutrality laws but let him off lightly. Wool's hope was that court convictions would "put a stop to filibustering" by del Valle, Dillon, Watkins, Emory, and others. Still at large, Count Raousset-Boulbon was the general's high-priority target. Secretly assembling a new expedition, the elusive Frenchman, however, "accomplished ends through the medium of others."[33]

During the trial del Valle's counsel subpoenaed Consul Dillon. Invoking international immunity, the Frenchman refused to appear and was charged with contempt of court. Arrested in public, the insulted consul hauled down the French tricolor, and his countrymen in the city talked openly of a rescue. Wool ordered the emplacement of "ten heavy guns . . . on Alcatrazas Island, and ten 32-pounders at Fort Point" to receive any "French men of war" that might try to repay the insult.[34]

Del Valle's conviction did not deter the indefatigable Count Raousset-Boulbon. Despite Consul Dillon's protestations to the contrary, Wool was convinced that he and the count were linked in "nefarious schemes." With Wool's body of incriminating "facts" in hand, District Attorney Inge rearrested Consul Dillon on 13 May 1854. To Secretary of War Davis, Wool wrote, "His interference and aid in his endeavors to fit out expeditions against Sonora left me no other course." Dillon's trial commenced eleven days later, the very day that Count Raousset-Boulbon stole away from San Francisco toward Sonora.[35]

The Dillon trial was inconclusive. His immunity waived by the court, the angry consul stuck to his story: the Mexican government requested the recruitment of a French colony to defend Sonora against United States filibusters, Walker's men in particular. Despite his vigorous investigations, Brigadier General Wool's vague testimony failed to link Dillon and the count and was of no help to District Attorney Inge. After deliberations, the jury voted 10 to 2 for Dillon's conviction, but on 29 May, probably to save face for himself and his president, Inge filed a nolle prosequi, a decision to waive prosecution, and the judge discharged Dillon.[36]

Wool also had to mop up the backwash from Walker's violent and disastrous campaign in Baja, California. Surrendering to the regular army in San Diego during the first week of May 1854, the wispy imperialist and thirty-three destitute, whipped followers were transported to San Francisco. Upon receiving the prisoners, federal authorities paroled the rank and file and a grand jury indicted Walker on violations of the neutrality laws. Walker posted a ten-thousand-dollar bail, and the U.S. District Court granted a trial postponement until the fall judicial term.[37]

Wool's bold charge against the filibusters had displeased the Pierce administration. Reports from the general and other federal authorities gave Davis the impression that the army was dictating the intervention to civil officers. The legal protocol was that Wool should respond to their summons for a military posse. Indeed, Wool seemed to be the primary force behind the del Valle and Dillon arrests and the *Challenge* libel. On 14 April Secretary of War Davis scolded the general for exceeding his military powers. Wool's role, Davis lectured, was not to "originate arrests and prosecutions for civil misdemeanors" but simply to "aid the civil authorities" upon their request.[38]

Davis's reprimand was both personal and political. Probably privy to the Broderick dinner by early April, he may have feared Wool's lending—whether inadvertently or consciously—his prestige to Free-Soil Democrat Broderick, who aspired to the United States Senate. At the same time, the Pierce administration was furiously battling for congressional passage of the Kansas-Nebraska Act and the Gadsden Purchase Treaty. To Pierce, Davis, and other friends of the South, the passage of both was critical to placating southern secessionists and preserving the Union. Wool's zealous prosecution of Walker had the potential to alienate archsoutherners. Davis let everyone know that the president was a champion of expansion and the South.[39]

Far away in California, a seething Wool fired back a written defense. Neither demands on civil authorities nor arrests of filibusters, he informed Davis, originated from headquarters. Only when the evidence seemed to warrant some legal action did Wool make a "written application" to District Attorney Inge, who then made the decision to secure an arrest warrant. To prove his point, the general solicited endorsements from District Attorney Inge and Marshal Richardson. In the presence of Wool, Inge wrote that the general was never "officious, coercive, or dictatorial" and that he never "interfered" in the duties of civil authorities. Likewise, Richardson praised Wool's "mild and conciliatory" conduct during the filibuster unrest.[40]

His blood boiling, Davis tried to embarrass and isolate Wool. The general's unauthorized construction contracts and his staff's high living expenses came under the secretary's scrutiny. Arguing economy and efficiency, Davis ordered Wool to remove departmental headquarters to Benicia and close down the Presidio. Bristling with indignation, the general argued that his "presence alone" kept hundreds of idle men "from organizing" and launching "against Sonora." Davis's order smacked of malicious punishment for the Broderick dinner and would be impractical and costly to carry out. With the backing of his staff and the community, Wool suspended the removal order on 21 June. His friend and professional colleague in Washington, General-in-Chief Scott, who hated Secretary Davis, endorsed Brigadier General Wool's justifications, but Davis, moved by neither Wool's reasoning nor Scott's opinion, stood by the transfer order. Satisfied that the public had heard and accepted his appeal, Wool shifted his headquarters to Benicia Barracks on 2 September 1854. Still unresolved, the Davis-Wool skirmish sizzled and popped in official correspondence, neither man budging, through the fall and winter.[41]

Davis's rebuke, however, had one intended effect. In August 1854 the general received alarms from Minister Gadsden and Collector Hammond about filibusters to Mexico and the Sandwich Islands fitting out in San Francisco. His powers "restricted" by the Pierce administration, a chastened Wool had to "await the call of civil officers," the United States district attorney or marshal specifically. Hammond pledged his office to help Wool "check the evil in question," but no other civil officer exerted himself to disperse filibusters. Neither operation materialized, and Wool's restraint earned Davis's praise.[42]

Into spring 1855 partisans on both sides waded into the Wool-Davis brawl. The general called on James Stewart, William L. Marcy, Lewis Cass, and others. From the nation's capital, Senator Gwin and Sen. Milton Latham confirmed that Davis had censured Wool for consorting with Foote and Broderick. In July 1854, although a Pierce man, Senator Gwin promised to help steer through Congress Wool's military contracts—Californians badly wanted the federal dollars—which lawmakers ultimately funded. On the East Coast, a correspondent for the *New York Daily Times* accused Brigadier General Wool of jealousy and spite: during the late war with Mexico, Wool had commanded Davis, who now commanded him. Defending the general in the same paper, "Amicus" noted that Davis's specious critique of the general's conduct was to be expected from a "country lawyer." Wool had executed the secretary's instructions to the letter, but his service, Amicus accurately noted, seemed to have been "precisely what the Department [of War] did not want."[43]

During his political skirmishes, Wool received unlikely editorial assistance from William Walker. Feeling exploited and abandoned, Walker attacked Pierce, Davis, Gwin, and the Chivalry in the San Francisco *Commercial Examiner* and the *Democratic State Journal*, both Broderick newspapers. One of Walker's articles condemned Davis's abuse of Wool and accused the president and secretary of "flagrant folly and imbecility." The editorial attacks and defenses by Wool and his partisans drove District Attorney Inge, a loyal Pierce man, to distraction. In a bitter letter to Davis, he wrote of Wool, "To speak frankly on this subject the old man is in his dotage and the monomaniacal idea that he is [a] prominent candidate for the Presidency has taken complete possession of him."[44]

Showing his gratitude, Wool did not press the government's case against Walker. In October 1854 a federal jury acquitted America's would-be imperialist of breaking the neutrality laws. His defense probably benefited from a gush of public sympathy for Count Raousset-Boulbon, who was captured and executed by the Mexican army in Sonora. Undeterred by federal law or the count's demise, Walker organized a new expedition, this one bound for Nicaragua. Approached by Walker, both Inge and Wool examined and approved his "colonization" contract; the general even offered his hearty congratulations.

On 4 May 1855 Walker and fifty-three followers—all armed to the teeth—set to sea.[45] Wool had one less headache in his unruly division.

Still, the Pierce administration ordered Wool through one final humiliating exercise. The government of Napoleon III of France sharply protested the arrest and trial of Consul Dillon to Minister John Y. Mason, the head of the United States legation in Paris. Probably still smarting from the Ostend Manifesto debacle, Mason urged U.S. armed forces to salute the French flag in San Francisco harbor. The French foreign minister agreed. In mid-September 1855 Adj. Gen. Samuel Cooper wrote Wool, "I am further instructed by the Secretary of War to say that you will carry out the arrangements made for an exchange of national courtesy." Swallowing his pride, Wool dutifully ordered his artillerists to salute the French flag with volleys of cannon when the French Pacific fleet entered the bay on 26 October.[46]

Walker's departure gave Wool a year-long respite in San Francisco, but in spring 1856 the Second Vigilante Movement invested the city. Two spectacular public shootings—the murder of U.S. Marshal Richardson by Charles Cora on 17 November 1855 and the critical wounding of James King of William by James P. Casey on 14 May 1856—sparked civil insurrection. When the municipal police handed the two assailants to Sheriff David Scannell, angry mobs threatened to lynch Cora and Casey. Mayor Van Ness summoned three hundred city militia and requisitioned musket cartridges and several cannon shot from the Presidio. Without Wool's permission, 1st Lt. Horatio G. Gibson filled the order. As Ness tried to calm his constituency, he asked federal authorities to guard Casey, but they declined further involvement.[47]

Two days later on 16 May, the Second Committee of Vigilance came to life. Dominated by importers and merchants, it boasted military organization, discipline, and secrecy. The vigilantes' mission was to clean up municipal government and to smash the hold of the Broderick Democrats—Irish-dominated—on the city. Sheriff David Scannell tried to raise a posse from the Law-and-Order party, while Gov. J. Neely Johnson appointed banker William T. Sherman major general of the California militia. Most local militia, however, deserted to the committee, leaving Sherman only a few men and fewer arms. From the roof of the International, he, Johnson, and Ness watched helplessly as armed vigilantes coerced the surrender of Casey and Cora, who were lynched four days later on 22 May. Sherman returned to his bank and Johnson steamed back to Sacramento "in disgust."[48]

The execution of Cora and Casey was only the opening salvo. From a fortified building on Clay Street, the vigilantes ordered the seizure, trial, and banishment of others, especially Broderick operatives. One committee prisoner, Yankee Sullivan, committed suicide. Sherman recalled "a feeling of general insecurity" in the city. Over a short time, some four thousand armed men enrolled in the vigilante organization. Fearing death and ruin, Law-and-Order representatives recalled Governor Johnson to San Francisco.[49]

With municipal and county power usurped, Johnson turned to the regular army. On the evening of 30 May at Benicia, Wool, Sherman, Johnson, and Secretary of State David F. Douglass played cards and discussed the vigilantes in Wool's quarters. The general and governor hypothetically talked about arming state militia with federal weapons. The president retained that power, Wool said, but given California's isolation, the departmental commander had some latitude to exercise the responsibility himself. If guaranteed federal arms, Sherman promised to raise a militia and "command a dispersion" of the vigilantes. The slippery Wool evaded a firm commitment.

The following day, Wool showed Johnson, Sherman, and Douglass the small arms, cannon, ordnance, and ammunition housed in Benicia Armory. At some point Wool vaguely promised Johnson—in the presence of Douglass—all the arms he wanted. That evening, as the general escorted his three guests to the wharves, Wool described the legal protocol that would lead to his arming Sherman's troops. If the Committee of Vigilance defied a writ of habeas corpus and refused to obey the governor's dispersal order, and if the governor called out the state militia, the general would fill his arms requisition and deduct the weapons from the state quota. Now confident, Sherman said: "That is all I want.—Now, Governor, you may go ahead." Johnson and Douglass returned up river to Sacramento; Sherman sailed back to San Francisco.[50]

The following day, Sheriff Scannell tried to serve a writ of habeas corpus on one of the vigilantes' prisoners, but the committee refused to release him. When notified, Governor Johnson declared San Francisco in a state of insurrection, commanded the Vigilance Committee to disperse, and summoned the San Francisco County militia. On 4 June Johnson informed Wool that the state, destitute of arms and ammunition, needed federal guns. Sherman published his muster order and smugly received panicked vigilante representatives beseeching him to call off the state guard.[51]

Some pundits doubted the honor of Wool's word. Indeed, when Johnson's aide-de-camp, F. A. Rowe, delivered the state requisition, the general reneged. On 5 June Wool explained that the president alone had the legal authority to fill a state requisition. Civil authorities, Johnson replied, had fulfilled their legal obligations: A state of insurrection now invested San Francisco. The exasperated governor resubmitted the requisition and boarded the steamer *Antelope* to Benicia.[52]

On the morning of 6 June, while conducting business at his bank, Sherman learned of Wool's about-face and demanded an explanation, but the general made no reply. Two days later Sherman crossed the bay and confronted Wool. When representatives of the San Francisco Conciliatory Committee filed into his quarters, Wool reluctantly handed the banker a letter denying "any promise of arms," and Sherman stalked away under the belief that Wool had "deliberately" lied. Walking to a nearby hotel, he listened to Governor Johnson, Chief Justice Terry, and others curse Wool's treachery. Seeing the Law-and-Order cause as "powerless for good," Sherman resigned his state commission and never again engaged in California politics.[53]

Governor Johnson wrote off the general and returned to Sacramento on 9 June. Later, Wool pleaded an "imperfect recollection" of the federal statutes; a fresh reading indicated that he had "no discretionary power whatever." The president alone had the authority to lend federal troops and weapons to state and territorial governments. That very week the Democratic party convened to nominate a presidential candidate, and Wool wanted neither to risk another reprimand from Secretary of War Davis nor to embarrass the Democrats, mired in Bleeding Kansas, with another frontier civil war.[54]

Wool turned his back on the vigilante unrest. Federal troops guarded the mint, customs house, post office, Presidio, and harbor fortifications but observed strict neutrality otherwise. On 19 June Governor Johnson complained directly to President Pierce that his government was powerless to protect citizens and punish the vigilantes' "lawless acts of aggression and disobedience." Handed the issue by Pierce, Attorney General Caleb Cushing ruled that the president was legally bound to enforce only the U.S. Constitution, that the Vigilance Committee had broken only California state law, and that Governor Johnson had failed to exhaust all legal powers to suppress the insurrection. On 19 July Secretary of State William Marcy informed Governor Johnson that the president would not intervene to suppress the Second Committee of Vigilance.[55]

As Johnson awaited the president's response, committee outrages mounted. In mid-June vigilantes seized state arms and ordnance stored in the harbor and in two city arsenals, and they arrested and convicted Chief Justice David S. Terry for murdering a vigilante policeman. When the victim recovered, however, the justice was quietly released.[56] In early July, Sherman sensed exhaustion creeping into the committee and wrote his brother, John, "I do not think there is any necessity for the interference of the federal authorities, but that before we can hear from Washington the matter will be over and forgotten." Indeed, on 18 August 1856 the committee officially adjourned. Its three-month terror had killed four men, expelled twenty-eight others, and crushed Broderick's Democratic organization.[57]

In late summer, when the federal court charged two vigilantes with piracy for the seizure of state arms in the bay, their comrades vowed "to protect them at all hazards." The federal marshal appealed to Wool for troops "to protect the court" and enforce "its authority," but Wool forwarded the request to Secretary of War Davis. In November Davis replied that President Pierce, a lame duck, had no instructions on the matter.[58] In the meantime Wool and Johnson skirmished over the state arms requisition. The general held his ground, and Johnson mailed the statements of Sherman, Douglass, and Rowe—eyewitnesses to Wool's Benicia promise—to President Pierce. Focused on Kansas and the presidential election, Pierce let the Wool-Johnson exchange sputter to a close.[59]

At civil-military intersections, the U.S. Army officer generally perceived himself as a neutral and apolitical federal agent.[60] In unstable frontier locales, however, his command decisions were anything but neutral. The location of a post or intervention against lawlessness often carried far-reaching political, economic, and social consequences for frontier peoples. In antebellum America, states and other smaller jurisdictions often had their way in disputes with the federal government. Despite their presidential instructions, Hitchcock and Wool surrendered their enforcement of the neutrality laws in the face of local opinion and opposition, and Wool realized that the Pierce administration would probably favor the vigilantes' destruction of the Broderick machine and withdrew his promise to arm the California militia. Sensitive to states' rights, the Pierce administration lent neither Hitchcock nor Wool any assistance, moral or military. Their interventions crumbled in the backrooms of San Francisco and Washington, D.C.

Like their professional peers, Hitchcock and Wool were still very political.[61] The former, a Whig, barely veiled his contempt for California Democrats, and Pierce's capitulation to the southern slavocracy prompted the colonel to resign from the army in 1854. His gloomy premonition of failure coming true, Wool carried too much Democratic-party baggage to be apolitical. Although any northern officer would have made the Chivalry faction nervous, Wool's affiliation with northern Democrats elevated their jealousy and suspicion to a shrill pitch. He returned to the Department of the East in 1857 after three tumultuous years in California.[62] After Wool, no Pacific commander tried to intervene against California filibusters. Civil constabulary duty in San Francisco was a futile exercise.

Winfield Scott, the Soldier's Soldier. Scott boasted a profound understanding of strategy, tactics, logistics, and diplomacy. *Courtesy of the Library of Congress, LC-USZ62-110151*

John M. Washington, the Tragic Soldier. Washington was New Mexico Territory's first military commander after the Mexican-American War. In 1853 he and other soldiers drowned near Cape Horn when stormy seas swamped their ship on the way to California. *Courtesy of the Library of Congress, LC-USZ62-10104*

Samuel Cooper, the Bureaucrat. As adjutant general of the army, Cooper wielded enormous institutional influence. Defecting to the South in 1861, he became adjutant and senior general in the Confederate army. *Courtesy Kansas State Historical Society, Topeka*

Edwin V. Sumner, the Obedient Servant. Shown here as a Civil War major general, Sumner loved the regular army and idolized General-in-Chief Winfield Scott, his mentor. Engraving after a painting by Alonzo Chapell. *Courtesy Museum of New Mexico, Santa Fe, neg. no. 11010*

Philip St. George Cooke, the Western Horse Soldier. Endowed with a fiery tongue, Cooke was at his best when calling the bluff of frontier mobs. *Courtesy Massachusetts Commandery Military Order of the Loyal Legion and the United States Army Military History Institute, Carlisle Barracks, Pennsylvania*

Fort Leavenworth, Kansas Territory, the Gateway to the American West, circa 1852. Military roads leading west and southwest originated at Fort Leavenworth. *Courtesy Kansas State Historical Society, Topeka*

Fort Craig, New Mexico Territory, Southwestern Combat Station, circa 1866. Regular-army patrols launched from here routinely skirmished with Apaches and Navajos. *Courtesy Museum of New Mexico, Santa Fe, neg. no. 14514*

William S. Harney, the Squaw Killer. Buffeted by violent swings of emotion, Harney could slaughter his enemies one moment and dote on the survivors the next. *Courtesy Massachusetts Commandery Military Order of the Loyal Legion and the United States Army Military History Institute, Carlisle Barracks, Pennsylvania*

George Wright, the Quiet Destroyer. Wright brutally applied fire, steel, lead, and rope to terrorize and subdue the Pacific Northwest Indians in the late 1850s. *Courtesy Massachusetts Commandery Military Order of the Loyal Legion and the United States Army Military History Institute, Carlisle Barracks, Pennsylvania*

Fort Laramie, High Plains Watchdog, 1858. Harney brought his Sioux Expedition here after crushing the Brule Sioux in 1855. Its walls propped up, old Fort John stands to the left of the parade ground.
Courtesy Wyoming Division of Cultural Resources, Laramie

Fort Vancouver, Washington Territory, Pacific Northwest Outpost, 1853. The army post stands on the hill to the left. Both Harney and Wright commanded troops from Fort Vancouver during the 1850s. Lithograph by Gustave Sohon. *From* Reports of Explorations and Survey . . . for a Railroad from the Mississippi River to the Pacific Ocean, *vol. 12, pt. 1, p. 155*

David E. Twiggs, the Traitor. No officer or enlisted man liked the rancorous, spiteful Twiggs. His surrender of U.S. Army supplies, ordnance, installations, and personnel to Texas state forces and his subsequent commission in the Confederacy blackened Twiggs's name in the North. *Courtesy Massachusetts Commandery Military Order of the Loyal Legion and the United States Army Military History Institute, Carlisle Barracks, Pennsylvania*

Earl Van Dorn, the Cavalry Gallant. Van Dorn's Second Cavalry struck like a knife into the heart of Comanche country, but his alleged affair with another man's wife triggered Van Dorn's murder during the Civil War in 1863. *Courtesy Massachusetts Commandery Military Order of the Loyal Legion and the United States Army Military History Institute, Carlisle Barracks, Pennsylvania*

Albert S. Johnston, the Monument. Johnston's proud, stony demeanor cultivated the reverence of officers and men in the antebellum army, long before a Union bullet martyred him at Shiloh in the Civil War. *Courtesy Massachusetts Commandery Military Order of the Loyal Legion and the United States Army Military History Institute, Carlisle Barracks, Pennsylvania*

Randolph B. Marcy, the Wilderness Regular. Marcy stood second only to Philip St. George Cooke as an expert on frontier military campaigning and survival skills. *Courtesy Massachusetts Commandery Military Order of the Loyal Legion and the United States Army Military History Institute, Carlisle Barracks, Pennsylvania*

The Army of Utah, Tormentor of Saints, 1858. Pictured here at Yellow Creek, the regular army spied on and needled the Mormons through the Civil War. The artist, Joseph Heger, was a German American private in the Regiment of Mounted Riflemen. *Courtesy William Robertson Coe Collection of Western Armericana, Yale University, New Haven, Connecticut*

Benicia Barracks, California, Pacific Coast Depot. Benicia's facilities warehoused quartermaster, commissary, subsistence, and ordnance stores. An armory also stood on the military reservation. Lithograph by Charles Koppel. *From* Reports of Explorations and Survey . . . for a Railroad from the Mississippi River to the Pacific Ocean, *vol. 5, frontispiece*

John E. Wool, the Card Shark. Wool bluffed California filibusters and Pacific Coast politicians with mixed results. *Courtesy Massachusetts Commandery Military Order of the Loyal Legion and the United States Army Military History Institute, Carlisle Barracks, Pennsylvania*

Ethan A. Hitchcock, the Cosmologist. Hitchcock groused about the burden of federal service but devoted nearly his entire adult life to the army and the Union. *Courtesy Massachusetts Commandery Military Order of the Loyal Legion and the United States Army Military History Institute, Carlisle Barracks, Pennsylvania*

Samuel P. Heintzelman, Soldier-Entrepreneur. A Union major general in this image, Heintzelman policed the American frontier with one hand and exploited its economic opportunities with the other. *Courtesy Massachusetts Commandery Military Order of the Loyal Legion and the United States Army Military History Institute, Carlisle Barracks, Pennsylvania*

6

RIDING THE LINE

Regulars on the Texas-Mexico Border

THE Treaty of Guadalupe Hidalgo brought no peace to the Mexican-American border. In the wake of the American invasion and withdrawal, the United States expeditionary force left behind social chaos, political paralysis, and restless Anglos, Mexicans, and Indians along the international frontier. Indian raids and counter-raids, livestock theft, racial prejudice, brigandage and banditry, smuggling, slavery and slave catching, and filibustering generated violence and mayhem on both sides of the border.

Entangled in the politics of slavery, filibusters were especially problematic. Neither the American nor Mexican government was able to control its border citizens. On the American side, the federal government ordered its regular army to quell these private martial enterprises, particularly the Carvajal expedition and the Cortinista rebellion.[1] In the human stew along the Texas-Mexico border, race and ethnicity informed the army's response to civil crisis. However much the army distrusted and disliked Anglo Texans, regular troops never crushed their lawless expeditions with armed force, but armed uprisings of Tejanos and Mexicans suffered the entire length of the federal sword.

The Mexican government tried to enforce sovereignty over its northernmost frontier. Along the Rio Grande after the war, Anglos, Tejanos, and Mexicans conducted a lucrative and unrestricted trade in sugar, coffee, tobacco, cotton, flour, and other commodities. Vexing border merchants, the Mexican central government legislated prohibitive tariffs on tobacco, cloth, and other items. On occasion zealous Mexican customs officials blockaded the entry of some merchants and seized the goods of others. The pleas of entrepreneurs to legislate fair tariffs fell on deaf ears in the Mexican government, which created special border guards to tighten enforcement. Smuggling boomed.[2]

Into this unrest stepped José M. J. Carvajal in 1851. He was a dreamy schemer, a good friend of Stephen F. Austin, and a political fixture in southern Texas and northeastern Mexico. Teresa Griffin Vielé, the wife of an army officer, described Carvajal as "a small man" with "an eagle eye" and "an astute intellect." Educated in the United States, Carvajal joined the Texas Revolution against Mexico but commanded Mexican troops during the Mexican-American War. His driving ambition was to carve from Mexico's far northern frontier an independent republic that would conduct liberal trade with the United States.[3]

Carvajal's opportunity came in late September 1851. Convening at La Loba, Mexican insurgents—*Pronunciados*—demanded the deflation of customs duties and the elimination of import prohibitions by Mexico City. Chosen to lead the revolt, Carvajal fled authorities and established headquarters in Rio Grande City, Texas (see map 2). Raising money and men, he pledged his republic, once established, to revising the outrageous tariff, offering commercial advantages, and outlawing the harboring of fugitive slaves. In a short time his force of Americans and Mexicans captured Camargo, Mexico, where John S. "Rip" Ford and approximately thirty Texas Rangers joined him. Next occupying Reynosa, Carvajal immediately promulgated a new tariff schedule that placated the Rio Grande merchants.[4]

Reports of border unrest soon reached Whig president Millard Fillmore, who was committed to enforcing the Fugitive Slave Act on the one hand and to blunting southern expansionism on the other. The Carvajal movement, like southern filibuster designs on Cuba, threatened to unravel the delicate weave of the Compromise of 1850 and undermine American negotiations for a railroad right of way across Mexico's Isthmus of Tehuantepec. The Mexican government demanded intervention.[5]

President Fillmore acted. On 22 October Fillmore exhorted the public not to join expeditions of military conquest against Mexico and warned that captured Americans— particularly Rip Ford's rangers, whose participation greatly irritated the president—would be left to the mercy of Mexican justice. That same day, invoking the Neutrality Act of 1818, he ordered Brig. Gen. David E. Twiggs, commanding the Division of the West, and Col. Persifor F. Smith, commanding the Eighth Military Department (Texas), to check and disperse illegal military invasions with any part of the "land and naval forces of the United States or of the militia" at hand.[6]

With Twiggs stationed in New Orleans, federal enforcement fell to Colonel Smith headquartered at San Antonio. On 21 October he assigned Col. William S. Harney to cut off the resupply of Carvajal's army from the United States and block its reentry from Mexico. Harney led several companies of the Second Dragoons to Ringgold Barracks a half mile below Rio Grande City and consulted with Mexican officers from Camargo. Harney's units patrolled the lower Rio Grande and guarded ferries and fords. The filibusters, however, had eight hundred miles of shallow, fordable river available.[7]

As Harney established pickets and patrols, Carvajal attacked Matamoros with three hundred men, including Rip Ford's rangers and a few U.S. Army deserters. The bloody house-to-house fighting between Mexican federals and Carvajal's insurgents started fires that consumed some of the city's finest structures. The United States consul, James F. Waddell, caught a buckshot in the cheek as he helped retrieve stores from the burning customs house. In the heat of battle, Carvajal accused Capt. John W. Phelps, commanding Fort Brown across the river, of aiding Mexican troops and made an impassioned plea to the people of Texas and Matamoros. Ten days after launching his attack, Carvajal suddenly pulled his Pronunciados upriver. Along the way, they attacked Cerralvos before they withdrew individually and in bands to Texas.[8]

In Washington, D.C., Secretary of State Daniel Webster assured Mexican minister Luis de la Rosa of the United States's sincere desire to stop the invasion. De la Rosa condemned his host for winking at the filibusters, and Webster had to admit that the desertion of regular troops to Carvajal and Mexico was hampering army intervention. The repulse of the Pronunciados relaxed Letcher's diplomatic embarrassment and strengthened the Mexican government.[9]

Ever buoyant, Carvajal raised and equipped a new army, aided by Rip Ford in the Texas legislature. On 20 February 1852 Carvajal's approximately three hundred troops skirted Ringgold Barracks and forded the Rio Grande a few miles below Rio Grande City. In a sharp battle Mexican infantry and cavalry scattered the Pronunciados. During the first week of March, 1st Lt. John Gibbon arrested Carvajal near Brownsville, but the filibuster walked free on five-thousand-dollars bail and immediately campaigned to outfit a new expedition. His acquittal in June 1852 infuriated the Mexican government, which turned completely against the Tehuantepec treaty.[10]

From southern Texas, Colonel Harney urged President Fillmore to place the Texas-Mexico border under martial law. However, such a draconian policy, departmental commander Colonel Smith feared, would only stir up the home-rule prejudice of Texans. What civil and military authorities needed most were the legal tools to enforce the law and clearly defined constabulary "powers and duties" for regular troops. In the meantime, Smith ordered five companies of Mounted Riflemen "to sweep the whole country between the Nueces" and the Rio Grande.[11]

Secretary Webster agreed with Smith, but the potential political repercussions probably deterred President Fillmore.[12] Creating domestic law enforcement powers for the United States Army would have mortified antislavery radicals resisting the controversial Fugitive Slave Act in the North and slaveowners fearing federal dismemberment of slavery in the South. The army would have to patrol the frontier with its hands tied and powers vague.

For the remainder of 1852, Mexican authorities routinely warned American officials about Carvajal's preparations for a new campaign. In early 1853 Mexican army detachments chased Carvajal and eighty men back into Texas, and on 26 March a gang under Carvajal associate A. H. Norton attacked Reynosa and ransomed the alcalde. Burdened with plunder, Norton's men sparred with Mexican federals but escaped across the river.[13]

After the Reynosa raid, federal authorities took drastic measures. On 31 March at 2:00 A.M., Maj. Gabriel R. Paul marched four companies of mounted infantry and two of Mounted Riflemen from Ringgold Barracks to nearby Rio Grande City. Company F of the Mounted Rifles sealed off the plaza while the other regulars searched from house to house for Carvajal. If denied access to a dwelling, Paul's men broke down the door. The surprise descent worked. Bursting into one home, the soldiers finally captured an undressed Carvajal and handed him over to Major Paul. Detained in the plaza, three hundred men—a "desperate looking" lot one trooper recalled—were disarmed and released.

Major Paul quickly dispatched his star prisoner to Brownsville, but lacking an arrest warrant, the federal marshal set Carvajal free. The filibuster's confidence soared, and the roguish Norton crowed and bragged in Brownsville's streets. Their rosy fortune grayed, however, when the Mexican consul filed a complaint against the two for the sack of Reynosa and the marshal immediately arrested them. Acquitted once again, Carvajal ultimately went south to join the northern Liberal revolt against Pres. Antonio López de Santa Anna. That summer, officially surveying the Texas-Mexico border, topographical engineer Lt. William H. Emory jousted with Mexican authorities, who sometimes mistook him and his men for *filibusteros.* Indeed, Emory employed many ex-Carvajal soldiers, "young men, whose tastes for civil pursuits had been destroyed by the Mexican War."[14]

Always rickety, the border was now destabilizing. Despite Carvajal's inactivity, "exiled Mexicans and sundry foreigners" on Texas soil made Mexican authorities jittery. General border banditry and horse thieving was complicated by the Liberal revolt and United States expansionism. In 1852 the

American people had elected Franklin Pierce president on an expansionist platform. His well-publicized desire to acquire Cuba and a slice of northern Mexico had inspired filibusters everywhere, Carvajal included. The transfer of Colonel Smith's Regiment of Mounted Riflemen from southwest to north Texas in 1855 opened Bexar and Comal Counties to Indian raiders, especially Lipan Apaches, from Mexico. Incensed Texans demanded federal protection and summary retaliation. In response to Colonel Smith's petition, Gov. E. M. Pease enlisted eighty-eight Texas Rangers under James H. Callahan on 20 July 1855. Smith labeled these rangers men "of entirely different character" than the riff-raff flocking to the filibusters.[15]

However, these rangers were no different. In early October 1855, Callahan's company crossed into Mexico below Eagle Pass either to pursue Lipan Apaches or recover fugitive slaves (see map 2). After skirmishing with Mexican troops, the rangers occupied, plundered, and burned Piedras Negras to slow their pursuers. Commanding Fort Duncan at Eagle Pass, Capt. Sidney Burbank unlimbered four cannon to cover the rangers' fording of the Rio Grande. Although Governor Pease dismissed Callahan, furious Mexican officials condemned Burbank and the U.S. Army.[16]

The barrage of Mexican complaints frustrated Colonel Smith. His troops investigated countless rumors but detected few filibusters. Smith's troops could detain only expeditions demonstrating hostile intent. Most adventurers secretly schemed on United States soil but hatched their enterprises in Mexico to avoid arrest. Carvajal recently crossed into Mexico, but his object was to join the Liberal rebellion in Monterey. In April 1856 Smith handed the Texas command to Col. Albert S. Johnston and prepared to return to the East.[17]

Carvajal's exit did not end violence in southwest Texas. In 1856 slaveowners in the region accused Mexican Americans of abetting the flight of fugitive slaves to Mexico, where human bondage was outlawed. After uncovering the plot for a slave revolt in Columbus, Texas, in September 1856, hysterical Texans expelled Mexican American families from Matagorda County, San Antonio, and the San Antonio River area. Racial tensions escalated.

In spring 1857 Anglo Texans turned their hostility on Tejano cartmen operating between San Antonio and the gulf ports. Angry at being underbid, Anglo freighters organized to terrorize, ambush, rob, pillage, and burn the Tejano columns. At one point, "men with their faces blackened" assaulted an army train, killed a Tejano, and wounded four others. The widespread violence forced Brig. Gen. David E. Twiggs, now commanding Texas, to deploy patrols on the road and Governor Pease to secure special legislation combating the atrocities. When Anglo settlers became targets, vigilantes captured and executed the depredators and ended the Cart War.[18]

The Tejano evictions and the Cart War wringed ethnic tensions ever tighter in southwest Texas. In July 1859 these exploded in Brownsville when Juan N. Cortina, fed up with Anglo violence and prejudice, shot and wounded Marshal Robert Shears as he pistol-whipped a Tejano. Influential and distinguished, Cortina's family had settled the Camargo area under Spain, and Juan was a leader among the vaqueros and ranchers in the Brownsville-Matamoros region. Standing five feet, eight inches tall with "reddish blonde hair and grey eyes," Cortina applied his exceptional "native intelligence" to great advantage. To Anglos he was a lawless desperado; to Mexicans and Tejanos he was a folk hero.[19]

On 28 September 1859 at 4:00 A.M., Cortina and approximately fifty men rode into Brownsville from Matamoros to avenge unpunished Anglo crimes against Tejanos and Mexicans (see map 2). Riding up and down the streets, they hunted Anglos—especially Adolphus Glavecke and Deputy Sheriff Robert Shears—on Cortina's death list. They killed two Anglos who had murdered Tejanos, a jailer and the Hispano who tried to protect him, and a Mexican cart driver. One raider died. Contrary to popular belief, Cortina's men neither sacked nor plundered the town. At daylight General Carvajal, the former filibuster but now a Mexican soldier, crossed the river from Matamoros to intervene. He and a Mexican delegation gave Cortina two options: evacuate his men or suffer the attack of the Matamoros militia.[20]

Obliging the powerful Carvajal, Cortina and his followers withdrew to his mother's Rancho del Carmen eight miles above Brownsville. On 30 September he issued a proclamation justifying the raid and the killings as an act of "self-preservation" by Mexican Americans. Brownsville harbored, he declared, a "league" of unscrupulous men conspiring to harass and dispossess citizens of "Mexican origin." His quarrel, indeed blood feud, was with the frontier lawyers, who in collusion with Cameron County politician Adolphus Glavecke, Cortina's relation by marriage, had been stealing Tejano land. (Cortina's mother had waged a bitter court battle against Brownsville developers to retain her portion of a Spanish land grant.) Cortina would not ride into Brownsville to kill these creatures, but he thought they should be punished for their crimes.[21]

The city anticipated the worst. Women and children fled to Matamoros while 150 men stayed behind to form a militia. Town fathers petitioned Pres. James P. Buchanan to order the army's reoccupation of Fort Brown, Ringgold Barracks, and Fort McIntosh on the lower Rio Grande. They also solicited the aid of New Orleans merchants and politicians and southern Texas newspapers. One thousand vengeful Mexicans, they feverishly warned, were gathering to sack and burn Brownsville.[22]

To the contrary, Brownsville residents went on the offensive. In early October a night patrol captured Cortina confident Tomas Cabrera. Then on 24 October 135 Anglos, allied Mexican-Americans, and Matamoros militia sallied forth from Brownsville to disperse the vaquero "army." Routed by Cortinistas at Rancho del Carmen, the "Brownsville Tigers" abandoned two pieces of artillery and fled hysterically back to town. Spreading north and east were shrill stories that Cortina's "banditti" had stormed Brownsville, killed one hundred defenders, and left behind stinking corpses and smoldering ashes. Briefly convinced, Brigadier General Twiggs reported the unverified rumors to the War Department.[23]

Although cautious at first, Secretary of War John Floyd ordered two artillery companies from Fort Clark to Fort Brown on 25 October. The alleged sacking of Brownsville prodded Twiggs to create a constabulary battalion from the First Artillery, First Infantry, and Second Cavalry—some 150 men. The regulars were to rendezvous at "old Fort Merrill" with Maj. Samuel P. Heintzelman, the expedition commander.

A veteran of thirty-three years, Heintzelman was an able frontier soldier with salt-and-pepper hair and a "fatherly appearance." In 1850 he had successfully established remote and forlorn Fort Yuma at the confluence of the Gila and Colorado Rivers in California despite quarrelsome junior officers. Heintzelman's instructions were to hunt and "collide with the Mexican, Cortina," who was apparently on "the Arroyo Colorado." If in "hot pursuit" of Cortina's men, Heintzelman's force could pursue them over the Rio Grande into Mexico.[24]

In Washington, D.C., the Buchanan administration cut orders to transfer troops from Fort Monroe, Virginia; Fort Leavenworth, Kansas; and north Texas to the lower Rio Grande. Still pouring into the capital were stories of bloodthirsty Cortinista hordes besieging desperate Anglos, but on 20 November, steaming into New Orleans from the lower Rio Grande, the captain of the *Arizona* reported that Brownsville was secure and standing. In San Antonio, Twiggs confirmed the news, and Secretary of War Floyd canceled the transfer orders.[25]

Earlier, on 12 November, a hundred Texas Rangers under Capt. William G. Tobin had occupied Fort Brown. The following night they lynched Cabrera; Cortina may have executed three captives in retaliation. At Palo Alto four rangers died in a firefight with Cortinistas, and Tobin's men burned Santa Rita, a Tejano community, the next day. On 22–23 November a mile above Rancho del Carmen, Cortina's force of 250 men repulsed a body of nervous Texas Rangers, many of whom afterward went home. An exultant and self-confident Cortina declared, "*Mexicans!* . . . the voice of revelation whispers to me that to me is entrusted the work of breaking the chains of your slavery." His army grew to approximately five hundred Tejanos and Mexicans.[26]

In the meantime, the regulars converged on Brownsville. Dispatched by steamer from New Orleans, Capt. James B. Ricketts's First Artillery company marched into Brownsville on 17 November. Hysterical politicians, he concluded, overdrew the Cortinista threat, and he criticized the rangers' lynching of Cabrera, bungled attacks, and vicious atrocities. Commanded by Major Heintzelman, the Brownsville Expedition pulled into town on 5 December. Whipped twice, the mutinous rangers refused to scout northward, but Heintzelman's information indicated that "three hundred and fifty" Cortinistas, with two artillery pieces, were dug in "across the river road, nine miles above town."[27]

On 14 December at 2:00 A.M., the major led 165 regulars and 120 rangers northward. Short of Rancho del Carmen, the rangers cowered in the cold darkness until Heintzelman personally led them into the deserted "breastwork of ebony logs and earth mixed with brush." He next ordered the rangers into the chaparral to cover his flanks and launched the regulars straight up the road. As they advanced, the rangers fell in behind, unable to make any headway through the thick chaparral.

Three miles farther at El Ebonal, "a burst of smoke and a round shot" startled the combined force. The major deployed rangers and regulars to flank the gun, but the chaparral was too dense. Working their artillery "most gallantly," the Cortinistas, approximately sixty men, launched four-pound balls "straight down the road" into men, animals, and wagons. A lead shot struck a mule, lodged in an ammunition wagon, and set a box of "friction tubes" on fire. Heintzelman's left and right wings easily repulsed Mexican and Tejano flankers, and regular artillery soon drove the Cortinista cannoneers from the field.

Heintzelman wanted that Tejano gun. After a two-hour rest he launched the rangers forward. A couple of miles north, they and regulars chased the Cortinistas out of the houses at Vincente Guerra's ranch and dogged them beyond Jesus Leon's place. At one point, to Heintzelman's dismay, the rangers charged the 4-pounder, dismounted forty yards short, and popped away with small arms—"the gun with two horses & two mules soon ran away." The skirmish ended.

Augmented by Maj. Rip Ford's ranger company, Heintzelman's troops chased the Cortinistas a few miles toward San Jose. However, heavy rains and rumors that Cortina was menacing Brownsville—probably started and fanned by the rangers—made Heintzelman return to the town. Expedition casualties were one dead ranger and two wounded regulars; Cortina was absent the whole time. Dissatisfied with the campaign, Heintzelman complained: "I am mystified at the little we have done with near 300 men. . . . We would undoubtedly have done better without the Rangers." Their burning out of "friends and foes" especially peeved and embarrassed the major.[28]

After refitting his troops, Heintzelman struck out northward again in chilly, wet weather on 21 December. His information was that Cortina had "concentrated his whole force" and "was retiring up the river to lay waste to the country." One hundred and fifty regulars and 198 rangers marched through the Baston on the twenty-third and Edinburg on the twenty-fifth, the Cortinistas continually retiring beyond. Ranchos and towns were abandoned, some burned. The following day, while bivouacked at Las Cuevas Ranch eighteen miles below Rio Grande City, Heintzelman learned that approximately four hundred Cortinistas were "occupying Ringgold barracks and Rio Grande City."

That night at 12:00 A.M., Heintzelman's troops stole a night march to surprise the Cortinistas. Halting the column three miles below Rio Grande City, he instructed Ford and 85 rangers to swing far to the right and get behind the town on the road to Roma. The regulars, their artillery unlimbered, advanced toward Cortina's front along the main road. Captain Tobin and 113 rangers guarded Heintzelman's right flank.[29]

Unable to penetrate the chaparral east of Rio Grande City in the thick fog, Ford hastily attacked Cortina's left wing a little beyond town. Captain Tobin's command soon joined the fray. During the fierce skirmish, Ford sat astride his horse and rallied his men, balls zipping in all directions. At one point, Cortinistas nearly encircled the rangers, but the sight of regular troops cresting the hill behind the town compelled Cortina to withdraw his men toward Roma. Many dashed straight for the river.

Heintzelman exploited the Cortinista collapse. The rangers pursued and captured two pieces of artillery. Armed with Sharp's rifles, Capt. George Stoneman's Second Cavalry shot up several companies of Cortina's infantry huddling under a river bank, slaughtered men swimming the river, and dropped others rising on the opposite bank.[30]

Heintzelman's surprise was complete. In all, Cortina's army lost sixty men to wounds and drowning. The rangers suffered sixteen slightly wounded. Heintzelman crowed, "We captured his guns, ammunition and baggage carts, provisions, everything . . . and entirely dispersed his force." Escaping over the river, Cortina gathered a few men and menaced Roma, but a detachment of regulars held them at bay. Heintzelman remained at Roma until 15 January 1860, when his troops began the six-day march back to Brownsville. Along the way he saw only a few occupied ranchos. All others were either burned or deserted.[31]

Although routed, Cortina was hardly finished. He gathered, rearmed, and resupplied some followers at La Bolsa, a bend in the river thirty-five miles north of Brownsville. Regular cavalry under Stoneman and two ranger companies under Ford patrolled the 120-mile stretch between Brownsville and Roma. Small parties of Mexicans and Tejanos drove cattle and horses, some their own, from Texas to Mexico. At least one band intercepted and rifled the mail.

On 4 February the steamer *Ranchero* sailed into a skirmish between Cortinistas and rangers firing from opposite sides of the river. A regular-army detachment banged away from the deck. One ranger died. Federal authorities accused Cortina of attempted robbery, but such intent was unlikely. Later, Major Ford led forty-nine rangers over the river to drive the Mexicans off La Bolsa. Once across, the rangers scattered the Cortinistas but bumped into a Mexican police force and returned to Texas. Located several miles farther downstream, Captain Stoneman's regulars "hastened" to reinforce the rangers and protect the steamer.[32]

Alarmed by the La Bolsa fight, Texas declared that war with Mexico was imminent. From Austin, Gov. Sam Houston blamed the turbulence on impotent Mexican authorities and threatened to invoke "the indefeasible right of self-preservation," raise an army of "ten thousand" Texans, "repel" Mexican aggressions, and occupy portions of northern Mexico. Houston later offered "5,000" Texas volunteers to the federal government and requisitioned percussion rifles, Sharp's rifles, Colt revolvers, and cavalry accouterments. Protecting the federal purse, the Department of War declined the men and refused the requisition.[33]

However, Houston's threats spurred the Buchanan administration to action. First, the War Department ordered the Third Infantry, ten companies in all, to reoccupy Fort Brown, Ringgold Barracks, and Fort Clark along the lower Rio Grande. Second, it put Lt. Col. Robert E. Lee, fresh from his capture of John Brown at Harper's Ferry, Virginia, in command of the Department of Texas. Adjutant General Cooper ordered Lee "to put a period to the predatory operations" of Cortina's "outlaws." His discretion extended to throwing his force over the river to chastise "any band of banditti on the Mexican side."[34]

Lee left San Antonio for Fort Duncan on 15 March but steered toward Eagle Pass. Cortinistas, he learned, were preparing to assault the settlement. Once there, he reported, "Everything in this section of [the] country is quiet." Escorted by two Second Cavalry companies, he reconnoitered the Rio Grande southward. The border country was at peace, but all ranchos, Anglo and Hispano, were in ashes. As he passed down the river, Lee warned Mexican authorities that his force would ford the river to punish brigands if Mexican troops neither dispersed nor arrested them. Mexican officials assured Lee that Cortinistas had vacated the river settlements.[35]

While these U.S. regulars rode toward Eagle Pass, Captain Stoneman led a strike into Mexico. Working on a tip from a Mexican officer, Heintzelman sent Stoneman and four companies—two cavalry and two ranger—across the river forty miles toward La Mesa Rancho the night of 17 March. Arriving a half-hour before sunup, the Americans spooked a sentinel and attacked the ranch right away, but the adversary there turned out to be Mexican national guardsmen. One Mexican soldier was wounded; one Mexican woman, mortally. The Americans lost "four horses."[36]

After daylight 150 Mexicans, infantry and cavalry, marched to the edge of the Stoneman's encampment. The Mexican commander, Vargas, had been dispatched by Matamoros authorities to cooperate with Stoneman, but the American distrusted him. Against Vargas's wishes, Stoneman's troops scoured the area for Cortina as far as "Cayentano Rancho, 42 miles from the river." The combined force of regulars and rangers recrossed the Rio Grande on 21 March. Shortly thereafter, four ranger companies made a dash to Maguey, twenty miles south of Matamoros, but failed to trap Cortina.[37]

Lieutenant Colonel Lee pulled into Fort Brown on 11 April. The frontier was clear of "bands of armed men on either side" of the border, he reported. Nine companies of regulars guarded the Mexico-Texas line from Fort Brown to Ringgold Barracks. The rangers' term of service would soon expire, and the Texas government, strapped for funds, wanted them federalized. Lee doubted that the Mexican government could control bandits and Indians on its side, but lacking authority, he refused to enroll the rangers, who were mustered out at Goliad.[38]

For all intents and purposes, Lee's duty on the Rio Grande was finished. Cortina was now dodging authorities in northern Mexico. In early May, Lee learned of Cortina's return to Matamoros and threw two companies of regulars across the river to snare him, but Cortina slipped away. (During the French intervention in Mexico, Cortina became a staunch Juarez supporter, a general in the Mexican army, and the governor of Tamaulipas.) A few days later, Lee traveled to San Antonio and returned to the normal duties of a departmental commander.[39]

The military interventions against the Carvajal filibusters and Cortinista uprising demonstrated the army's disparate responses to frontier upheaval. Well-connected to the economic and political elite of southern Texas, Carvajal enjoyed the support of many Anglo Texans, particularly merchants, whose commercial fortunes would benefit from an independent Liberal republic in north Mexico, and Texas Rangers joined Carvajal's little army of invasion. Given the Anglo Texan involvement among the Carvajal filibusters, the regular army could ill-afford to assault his expeditions. Killing Texans would have created a fierce political backlash in both Texas and the United States against the army. At the same, U.S. Army officers generally supported Manifest Destiny in principle and probably sympathized with Carvajal's imperial ambitions. Their interest in corralling Carvajal extended little beyond fulfilling the mission ordered by President Fillmore.

Racism motivated the aggressive operation against Cortinistas. Manifest Destiny championed Anglo civilization at the expense of Hispanos, Indians, and "others," and the officer corps generally shunned middle- and lower-class Tejanos and Mexicans. Major Heintzelman blamed Anglo Texan outrages for the Cortinista uprising, but visions of a race war between Anglos, Tejanos, and Mexicans spurred the Buchanan administration and the regular army to suppress Cortina's insurgency. Always trying to placate the slave South, President Buchanan shared southern Texas plantation owners' fears of losing slaves to northern Mexico in a general Hispano uprising along the international border. With North-South acrimony spiraling out of control, the president prudently avoided full-scale war with Mexico.

Likewise, far to the northwest off the coast of Washington Territory, the United States faced a serious challenge from a traditional imperial rival, England. A small fleet of Her Majesty's warships were confronting U.S. troops entrenched on San Juan Island.

7

IT IS OURS

The Army and the San Juan Island Dispute

THE United States Army cultivated cautious, conservative commanding officers. In no way could the secretary of war micromanage his departmental commanders posted two to three thousand miles west of Washington, D.C. The telegraph stopped at Fort Leavenworth and New Orleans, and roundtrip postal communication with New Mexico, California, and the Pacific Northwest took six to eight weeks. Autonomy and latitude were critical to a commander's departmental administration, but the secretary and president depended on his sobriety and prudence to keep the peace, particularly along the international frontiers with Mexico and Canada.

The army had failed, however, to tame Brig. Gen. William S. Harney, a maverick in the regular service and a man of volcanic temper. The administration of Pres. James P. Buchanan dispatched Harney to finish the Pacific Northwest Indian wars, but his national chauvinism nearly precipitated a war with Great Britain when he unexpectedly ordered the occupation of San Juan Island by regular troops. Cool heads, both British and American, defused the tense standoff, and although the president recalled his errant general, Harney ultimately prevailed. Neither the president nor the army could discipline Harney, a line brigadier, a forty-two-year veteran, and a hero among southern Democrats.

The San Juan Archipelago lay to the east of the Strait of Juan de Fuca and south of the forty-ninth parallel (see map 3). When Great Britain and the United States signed the Oregon Treaty of 1846, the agreement set the boundary between British Columbia and Oregon Territory at forty-nine degrees north latitude and granted the English control of Vancouver Island. However, it left unclear the sovereignty over the many islands—principally San Juan, Lopez, and Orcas—of the archipelago. Did the international boundary run southward through the Strait of Rosario between the continent and the islands as the British contended, or did it run farther westward and then southward through the Haro Strait between Vancouver Island and the archipelago as the United States claimed? The status of the three islands did not matter in 1846, British and American diplomats tacitly agreed. They had leapt the major international hurdle between the two countries at the time.[1]

The fruit of their procrastination ripened in the early 1850s. Granted the right to colonize Vancouver Island in 1849, the Hudson's Bay Company (HBC) soon began governing the archipelago as part of its jurisdiction, but the firm collided with American farmers, loggers, and fishermen eager to exploit San Juan's resources. In 1853 the Oregon territorial legislature claimed the islands, and two months later lawmakers in newly created Washington Territory sketched the boundaries of Whatcom County to embrace the archipelago. Fortifying the HBC's sovereignty, Sir James Douglas, chief factor and governor of Vancouver Island, chased away American loggers on Lopez Island in 1853 and established a sheep farm on San Juan Island later the same year.[2]

Other confrontations quickly followed. In September 1853 U.S. Collector of Customs Isaac N. Ebey landed on San Juan to assess a tax on HBC sheep. Ebey quarreled with Charles J. Griffin, the HBC rancher, left behind a deputy, and departed for the continent. Responding several months later in 1854, Governor Douglas commissioned Griffin justice of the peace and magistrate for the islands.

The nonpayment of United States taxes was intolerable to Washington territorial authorities. Backed by a posse, Sheriff Ellis Barnes went to the island, confiscated thirty company sheep, and auctioned them for taxes. The loss infuriated Governor Douglas, who demanded restitution from Washington Territory's hotspur, Gov. Isaac I. Stevens. Scoffing at Douglas's charge, Stevens proclaimed United States sovereignty over the archipelago and referred the impasse to Secretary of State William L. Marcy.[3]

Neither the British nor Americans were prepared to wage war over several inconsequential islands. After consultations, their governments assigned commissioners to explore the shipping channels and negotiate a boundary. Both Stevens and Douglas were instructed to sustain their country's sovereignty over the San Juans in principal but not to the point of war. Although American prospectors taxed Douglas's patience during the Fraser River gold rush of 1858, British and American officials kept an uneasy peace on the disputed islands. The boundary commissioners surveyed the shipping lanes but reached no formal agreement. This status held through 1858.[4]

Into this quiet yet unstable mixture stepped bellicose, undiplomatic Brig. Gen. William S. "Squaw Killer" Harney at the end of the year. The Department of War had assigned Harney to command the newly created Department of Oregon with headquarters at Fort Vancouver on the Columbia River. His command portfolio boasted missions in some of the American frontier's hotspots—Texas, Kansas, Florida, and the northern plains. His instructions were to bring the region's messy Indian wars—his specialty—to a close through diplomacy or war.[5]

Taking over the department on 25 October 1858, Harney was six weeks too late. In early September Col. George Wright had broken the back of Indian resistance through the Spokane Expedition, one of the decade's most brutal and skillful campaigns. Harney was left with mopping up small pockets of resistance, policing Indian reservations, and regulating Indian-white contact—unheroic, tedious constabulary duties to the glory-hungry general.[6]

American settlers expected the new commander to champion their regional interests. His predecessors on the Pacific Coast, Brig. Gen. John E. Wool and Col. Newman S. Clarke, had enforced a moratorium on settlement east of the Cascade Mountains to pacify the frontier, a policy that had infuriated the region's politicians and settlers. In 1858 Congress lifted the ban. On 10–11 December 1858 the Oregon territorial legislature praised United States lawmakers for reopening the Cascade country and celebrated the creation of the Department of Oregon and the assignment of Harney. Quickly advertising their expectations, Oregon lawmakers declared, "We have entire confidence in the ability and willingness of General Harney to protect, by every means in his power, such of our Atlantic friends as may wish to immigrate to our country, and therefore entreat him to establish Garrisons on the Emigrant route, and particularly at or near Fort Boise."[7]

Once the winter lifted and the ground firmed, Harney toured his new department. His inspections eventually took him to posts guarding Puget Sound and to Vancouver Island, where he interviewed Governor Douglas. On 9 July he sailed to San Juan Island. Alarmed American settlers, numbering about twenty-five families and led by United States Customs Inspector Paul K. Hubbs, probably fired Harney's indignation with stories of Indian atrocities and HBC intrigue. Indeed, a few men had died violently, but the authorities did not know whether sea-borne Indians or frontier riff-raff had killed the victims. Instead, American inhabitants solely blamed "marauding northern Indians" incited by the HBC. A "detachment of twenty men," they pleaded, would "give them a feeling of security."[8]

The Anglophobic Harney fulfilled their wish. Upon his return to Fort Vancouver, former governor Stevens, now territorial delegate to Congress, encouraged Harney to garrison the island. On 18 July the general ordered Company D, Ninth Infantry, to occupy Griffin Bay on the southeastern end of the island. The mission of its captain, future Gettysburg legend George E. Pickett, was twofold: to deflect the northern Indians from San Juan Island and Puget Sound and "to resist all attempts at interference by the British authorities" in American affairs on the island. Harney advised Pickett's company to pack "doors, window-sash, flooring," and other domestic comforts, indicating that United States occupation might be longterm.[9]

Harney's precipitous act was puzzling. He seemed to snort at the British navy's overwhelming superiority in the north Pacific. From Illinois George B. McClellan surmised that Harney and Stevens wanted to start a war that would unite the country and overshadow the sectional crisis. Capt. Granville O. Haller believed that Harney, Stevens, and other southern sympathizers tried to handcuff the North in a bloody war and hand the South trouble-free secession. However, Harney, a steadfast Union man, was hardly that Machiavellian, and Stevens, although a proslavery Democrat, would rush to the Union flag at the outbreak of civil war. Instead, Harney's reaction was born of an explosive temper, self-conscious personal and national honor, and violent frontier prejudice against the British in general and the HBC in particular.[10]

His temper, honor, and prejudice mixed potently in a more immediate way. In mid-June on San Juan, American settler Lyman Cutler shot an HBC boar that had repeatedly grubbed in his potato patch. A. G. Dallas, a company official and Governor Douglas's son-in-law, allegedly threatened Cutler with British arrest if he did not pay restitution. Uncritically accepting the Cutler story, Harney labeled British behavior "an outrage upon the rights" of American citizens. He saw himself as the defender of United States interests in Puget Sound against British tyranny.[11]

Captain Pickett's infantry landed at San Juan Island aboard the steamer *Massachusetts* on 27 July 1859. Once his troops came ashore, the captain declared San Juan a United States possession, warned away the Indians, and declared American codes the law of the island. These were bold declarations for a soldier who graduated dead last in the West Point class of 1846, McClellan's year no less. A swashbuckling Virginia dandy, Pickett generally wore long hair in ringlets and sported a mustache and goatee. Brevetted twice for gallantry at Contreras, Churubusco, and Chapultepec, he was a brave, if reckless, combat officer. Since the war, his service had taken him to frontiers in Texas and the Far West.[12]

Pickett's occupation shocked Governor Douglas, but Harney's unilateral act mystified him. On 2 August 1859 Douglas proclaimed "against the occupation" and declared "the sovereignty of the island of San Juan . . . to be in the crown of Great Britain." Harney scoffed. His presidential instructions, he replied, enjoined him to protect American citizens from domestic and foreign enemies and authorized him to station troops on the island. British threats to seize and try Cutler, an American citizen, were an outrageous affront to United States honor. Harney reported the insult to President Buchanan.[13]

Both bristling with indignation, the governor and the general sparred through the mails. Douglas denied ever dispatching an HBC employee to detain "an American citizen" for trial in the British courts. Why had the general been silent on the Cutler affair during his recent visit to Victoria? Harney replied that the insult to Cutler did not come to his attention until he toured San Juan. Although Pickett's regulars fortified their position under the eyes of three British warships, they would remain on the island until President Buchanan communicated his wishes.[14]

Harney put Pickett in a tight spot. Determined to sustain British sovereignty over San Juan, Governor Douglas dispatched Maj. John de Courcy aboard the HMS *Tribune*, a thirty-gun frigate, to Griffin Bay. A justice of the peace and magistrate, de Courcy's charge was to enforce British law and evict American settlers. Douglas instructed Capt. Geoffrey P. Hornby, commanding the *Tribune*, to prevent the reinforcement of Pickett's detachment. Hopelessly outgunned and undoubtedly scared, Pickett seemed to laugh at his predicament. On 30 July he humorously wrote Lt. Col. Silas Casey, "It is not comfortable to be lying within range of a couple of war steamers." He put in a requisition for "tools," probably spades and pick axes for trenching.[15]

Douglas underestimated the captain's tenacity and his general's resolve. Pickett brushed off an HBC official sent to shoo away his command, driving the governor to dispatch the HMS *Satellite* and HMS *Plumper*. Likewise, Harney defied the British flotilla by sending Pickett 120 men aboard the *Massachusetts*, which landed under the guns of the *Tribune*. Douglas had instructed the ship's commander to fire on any United States run, but before British gunners sent a shot across the *Massachusetts* bow, the captain of the *Plumper* delivered a countermand from the Vancouver Island Legislative Council. United States regulars came ashore safely.[16]

Captain Hornby, commanding the British flotilla, extended the courtesies of a gentleman, but Pickett refused to vacate his station and confer with him aboard the *Tribune*. Instead, practicing good British etiquette, Hornby and two junior officers called on Pickett at two o'clock in the afternoon of 3

August. In the spirit of fair play, Hornby recommended "joint military occupation" to mitigate "a collision between the forces or authorities of the two countries."

His hands tied, Pickett politely but firmly called the British bluff. Neither would he agree to joint occupation nor would he allow any British troops to come ashore. His hope was that the "pill" he dispensed would buy him a little time. In typical good cheer, Pickett wrote Harney: "I had to deal with three captains, and I thought it better to take the brunt of it. They have a force so much superior to mine that it will be merely a mouthful for them."[17]

Harney subsequently threw more fuel on the fire. In addition to requisitioning all "available" United States warships on 7 August, he ordered Silas Casey, lieutenant colonel of the Ninth Infantry, to reinforce Pickett's command with four companies of the Third Artillery the following day. On 9 August, transporting Casey's command, the steamer *Julia* was menaced by the British steamer *Active* but landed the lieutenant colonel's troops, artillery, and supplies on San Juan in a dense fog. The British again held their fire.[18]

Lieutenant Colonel Casey was no friend to Harney. Born and raised in Rhode Island, he believed that Harney and other southern officers had received undue brevets and promotions under Democratic presidents while he and other northern officers had soldiered in obscurity and without reward. Even so, brevetted three times in Mexico, Casey was a seasoned combat officer capable of commanding a spirited defense of San Juan. However, fighting the Royal Navy probably looked suicidal, and Harney seemed to be provoking a fight. Unaware of Hornby's orders to hold his fire, Casey "resolved to make an attempt to prevent so great a calamity" and to confer with Adm. Robert L. Baynes, who had recently arrived aboard the HMS *Ganges.*[19]

On 11 August Casey and Pickett steamed twenty-five miles aboard the *Shubrick* to Esquimalt, the British naval station on Vancouver Island. The Rhode Islander's proposal was to urge on Harney a withdrawal of United States reinforcements in return for a British promise not to harass Pickett's constabulary. With Governor Douglas at his side, Baynes refused to leave the *Ganges*, anchored "100 yards" away, and call on the American field officer. The snubbed Casey and Pickett, both "dressed in full uniform," returned to San Juan under a cloud.[20]

Expecting battle, Casey ordered his regulars to dig in. Overmatched in manpower and artillery, he requisitioned "five full companies of regular troops, with an officer of engineers and a detachment of sappers." Probably miffed, the general ordered Casey to offer the British no olive branches and secured the Washington territorial governor's pledge of volunteers to fight the British should war erupt.[21]

Under no circumstances would Baynes attack U.S. regulars fortified on San Juan. Like the British Admiralty, he valued the free navigation of the neighboring straits over the ownership of the San Juan Archipelago. When he had learned of Douglas's warlike preparations, Baynes responded, "Tut, tut, no, no, the damned fools." He ordered Hornby not to harass American troops. Occupying San Juan was not a precondition to claiming sovereignty.[22]

By the time of Baynes's arrival in Puget Sound, any British assault would have been costly. Four hundred and fifty well-entrenched U.S. regulars, eight 32-pounders, one 6-pounder, and five mountain howitzers faced five British ships of war having a combined 167 guns and approximately two thousand sailors, marines, and royal engineers. A landing party would have boasted a three-to-one advantage at most; five to one was the recommended assault ratio. Casey's defenders, armed with rifles, would have inflicted heavy British casualties.[23]

Scratching his head on the other side of the continent, President Buchanan was completely stumped by Harney's "decided" maneuver. Had the general consulted Commissioner Campbell before he ordered the occupation? Like the United States and England, the general was expected to "suffer" the "status" until a joint commission settled the boundary question. In the administration's eyes, defending American "rights" and curbing Indian "incursions" were the only reasonable explanations Harney could give the British for occupying San Juan Island. The president for his part wanted to reassure the British that he was not "prejudging" the boundary question.[24]

Harney's occupation of San Juan dumbfounded Commissioner Campbell. In idle conversation the commissioner unofficially opined that the "mid-channel" of the Haro Strait was the international boundary, but the joint commission alone was credentialed to settle the issue. Occupying San Juan—never Campbell's intention—would "somewhat embarrass" the sovereignty question. Now on the defensive, the prickly Harney roundly disabused Campbell of his niggling technicalities. Removing himself from Harney's line of fire, Campbell decided to tour the less dangerous forty-ninth parallel as far as Fort Coleville to the east.[25]

Having lost faith in Harney, the Buchanan administration turned to General-in-Chief Winfield Scott, a gifted diplomat. Although he harbored an ego the size of a man-o-war, Scott was remarkably skilled at defusing international tension, especially with the British. While giving Scott wide "discretion," the acting secretary of war instructed him to seek "a joint occupation of the island," even if hostilities had commenced. His one charge was to guarantee the rights of American settlers on San Juan Island until Great Britain and the United States could draw a boundary.[26]

Scott took great pleasure in retrieving the incompetence of his political and military peers. He suspected that Harney, an old professional enemy, was grandstanding for high political office. Taking along Lt. Col. Lorenzo Thomas and Lt. Col. George Lay, Scott struck out from New York on 20 September 1859, crossed from the Gulf of Mexico to the Pacific Ocean by way of Panama, and reached Fort Vancouver on the steamer *Northerner* on 20 October. The following morning the general-in-chief interviewed Harney. Puget Sound was tranquil, and the British had withdrawn all ships but the *Satellite* from Griffin Harbor.[27]

Going on the offensive, Scott immediately extended an olive branch to Governor Douglas. From Fort Townsend on 25 October, Scott proposed joint occupation of "separate" parts of the island with "a detachment of infantry, riflemen, or marines, not exceeding one hundred men, with their appropriate arms only." Although noncommittal, Douglas signaled his receptivity to negotiations. Several days later from Victoria, he laid before Scott "a joint civil occupation, composed of the present resident stipendiary magistrates." Douglas wanted all "military and naval forces" recalled from the island and Marcy's status restored.[28]

The status was not all Douglas desired: He wanted Harney's head as well. The governor had never intended to enforce English law on American residents. No British act or policy warranted Harney's "aspersion"; the general occupied San Juan without just cause. Scott probably read attentively. Douglas's accusations handed him the ammunition to terminate Harney's command or, at least, to humiliate him.[29]

Rejecting joint civil occupation as clumsy, Scott reiterated his original proposal. The general believed that the Indian threat was very real, although Douglas downplayed it. Two detachments, one British and one American, would enforce law and order among their own citizens on San Juan. Douglas lacked the authority to negotiate a treaty, but he made a suggestion that surely gratified Scott. If the general-in-chief removed the "menacing" force now on San Juan, Douglas would "withdraw the British naval force" and would try neither to take "possession of the island" nor to assert "any jurisdiction." The United States withdrawal would gall Harney.[30]

Two days later on 5 November, Scott ordered all U.S. troops back to the continent. He had originally intended Pickett's company to stay, but the gallant Virginian was probably too much identified with Harney and the San Juan fiasco for the British to stomach. Under Scott's instructions, Company D vacated the island and Capt. Lewis C. Hunt's Fourth Infantry company remained behind. (Four years later at Gettysburg, Hunt's brother, Henry J. Hunt, would "blunt" Pickett's Charge with shells and grapeshot.)[31]

Douglas accepted Scott's troop reduction on San Juan, but he insisted that no United States civil or military authority harass British citizens. Likewise, British authorities would "abstain" from any "acts of interference or of exclusive jurisdiction." Indeed, Scott expected Hunt to interdict any "functionary of Washington Territory" who tried to "interfere with any British subject" on the island. The one exception proscribed illegal liquor sales to U.S. regulars by British citizens. Hunt was permitted to detain any culprits and turn them over to British authorities; he could "expel" them "without further ceremony" should they reappear "without permission." Satisfied with this arrangement, Scott steamed for San Francisco in the second week of November 1859.[32]

The disposition of Brigadier General Harney, however, was unfinished business. During the negotiations, Scott kept Harney completely in the dark. Before departing, he instructed his brigadier not to trifle with "the sovereignty of the island," but Harney's removal, the general-in-chief anticipated, would be a British precondition to any boundary settlement. On 15 November, as he steamed southward, Scott penned a "conditional order" returning Harney to the Department of the West in St. Louis, his preferred command and residence. Scott planned to merge the Departments of Oregon and California anyway; a Pacific Northwest military district had no need for a brigadier general.[33]

Scott's order was a favor to Harney, who nevertheless believed that he still enjoyed Buchanan's unconditional support. Upon Scott's departure, Harney began shoring up his image and testing his strength. First, the Council of Washington Territory endorsed his San Juan venture as "prudent and proper." Second, Harney set out to enlist the adjutant general, president, and Washington territorial council against Scott's proposed military reorganization of the Pacific military frontier. Reducing his department to a district, Harney argued, would open the region to violent Indian wars. In the meantime, he requested the "indulgence" of a leave to visit his family in the East.[34]

His pride stinging, Harney looked for an opening to undo Scott's diplomacy. The general-in-chief had placed Captain Hunt on the island because of his reputation "for firmness, discretion, and courtesy," but in early April 1860 Harney removed Hunt's company. The general's pretext was a complaint lodged by San Juan "citizens" against "the gross and ungentlemanly conduct of Captain Hunt." The protestors accused Hunt of "stopping trade" and "endeavoring to drive the inhabitants from the island."[35]

Harney seized the opening. He ordered Hunt to report all actions "taken against the citizens of San Juan Island." Backed by former justice of the peace D. F. Newsom, Hunt labeled his accusers "illicit liquor dealers" whom he had driven from camp. The three worst offenders were defendants in a civil suit filed by him. A petition raised by "bona fide" settlers registered "full confidence in the judgment and discretion of Captain Hunt." According to Newsom, civil power was impotent against the lawless liquor vendors and "itenerant boatmen" who plagued San Juan. He recommended the appointment of some United States officer to exercise "summary power" on the island.[36]

Harney sneered. Without consulting Scott, Cooper, or Buchanan, he ordered Hunt's company to Fort Steilacoom and Pickett's company back to San Juan. Scott had not notified Harney about the San Juan settlement; the latter denied its official existence. Contrary to Scott's understanding with Douglas, the Oregon commander asserted United States sovereignty over San Juan Island and ordered Pickett to "acknowledge and respect the civil jurisdiction of Washington Territory." The general dared the commander of British marines on San Juan to "ignore this right of the Territory."[37]

Captain Hunt was staggered; Lieutenant General Scott was flabbergasted. From San Juan Island Hunt wrote Scott, "No cause is assigned for this disturbance of the arrangements made by the general-in-chief." Headquartered in New York City, Scott ordered Hunt's letter and five enclosures publicly disclosed and complained to Secretary Floyd, "I found both Brigadier General Harney and Captain Pickett proud of their *conquest* and quite jealous of any interference therewith on the part of higher authority." As Scott had feared, he could not trust Harney to execute the "pacific arrangement" with Great Britain. British "forbearance" alone would prevent a clash of arms.[38]

Harney exhausted Buchanan's good will. The general's recall of Hunt and reassertion of sovereignty irked Douglas and the British. On 8 June 1860, Secretary of War Floyd ordered Harney "to repair to Washington city without delay." In his own defense, Harney argued that the general-in-chief never briefed him about the joint occupation and the British marine landing on San Juan was completely unexpected. The publication of his departmental correspondence particularly infuriated him. Returning to the Department of the West, Harney would cause grave anxiety in U.S. Army Headquarters and the Lincoln administration in Washington during the early days of the Civil War.[39]

On 5 July 1860 Harney turned over the Department of Oregon to Col. George Wright. Instead of rotating Pickett's company to the mainland, Wright allowed it to remain on the island. Pickett and British officers observed "amicable" relations; regulars and marines were "on very pleasant" terms. Pickett's greatest headaches were unruly, lawless frontiersmen. At his wit's end, he pleaded unsuccessfully for a permanent civil magistrate. The dashing

Virginian would remain on San Juan Island until he resigned to serve in the Confederate States Army.[40]

President Buchanan probably sighed in relief at Scott's diplomatic solution. Since his inauguration in March 1857, one crisis after another had wracked his administration: the Dred Scott Decision; the Lecompton Constitution and guerilla violence in Kansas; the Mormon Rebellion in Utah; John Brown's raid on Harper's Ferry, Virginia; and the Cortina uprising in Texas. Ongoing during the second half of the decade were Indian wars from Washington Territory to Texas. A war with Great Britain over San Juan Island would have been a crowning embarrassment.

Harney's behavior indicated problems in the army high command. Known for insubordination, the general never acknowledged his failed judgment and seemed honor-bound to unravel the diplomacy of Major General Scott. Harney's personal enmity overwhelmed his military professionalism. Scott's mission originated with the president, but the frontier general's insubordination was a conscious acknowledgment of the general-in-chief's institutional isolation. By the late 1850s, Scott boasted little bureaucratic clout in the army or political influence with Congress. Despite the San Juan fiasco, Harney still commanded political prestige in the Democratic party as a military hero and institutional power in the army as a line brigadier. Forty years of federal service protected him with seniority. Harney's court-martial, suspension, or dismissal, all probably desired by Scott, would have ignited a nationwide row, a public conflagration from which the Buchanan administration, already battered and bruised, stood to gain nothing. His return to the command of the Department of the West was a simple and trouble-free political solution to Harney's diplomatic blunder and military outrage.

III

Civil Intervention

8

TREAT THEM AS ENEMIES

Regulars and Saints in Utah

FROM Cantonment Loring a few miles above old Fort Hall on the south bank of the Snake River, an angry Capt. Andrew Porter reported "a hostile feeling" toward the federal government in the Mormon settlements to the south. His unfriendly neighbors would sell his Mounted Riflemen neither fodder nor vegetables. At river crossings Mormon ferrymen gouged military trains. The Saints even "hissed" Porter's troops and encouraged desertion. The United States Army, the beleaguered captain predicted, would have to occupy the Great Salt Lake Valley to tame such Mormon "mischief."[1]

The Mormons belonged to the controversial Church of Jesus Christ of Latter-day Saints. Violently purged from Illinois in 1845–46, the Saints followed their prophet-president, Brigham Young, over the Oregon Trail beyond the Rocky Mountains to the Great Salt Lake Valley (see map 4). These zealous Protestants saw themselves as a chosen people distinct from the "Gentiles," the nonbelievers who persecuted them. At the end of the Mexican-American War, Mormon leaders created a constitution and petitioned Congress for statehood, which would grant them local control of their political affairs.[2]

Penned in October 1849, Captain Porter's accusations worried the federal government. The Oregon Trail, the principal overland road to the Pacific Coast, coursed through the Great Salt Lake Valley.[3] Keeping the road open to emigrants and merchants and clear of resistance Indian or otherwise was a federal priority in the American West, and the United States distrusted the

Mormons, whose primary loyalty was to the Church of Latter-day Saints and Brigham Young. Chilly after the Mexican-American War, federal-Mormon relations first slowly and then quickly froze during the next eight years. The frontier army was the primary federal weapon to breach the united Mormon front and coerce their obedience to United States sovereignty.

During the interwar years, the regular army operated with extraordinary restraint in Utah Territory. Mormon resistance to federal sovereignty was more centralized and organized than that of any other opposition movement in the American West, and the Gentile critique of Mormon culture, particularly polygamy, was vitriolic and cross-sectional. However, the regulars committed no heinous atrocities against these peculiar Americans. In part, race shielded the Saints. Unlike Cortinistas in Texas or American Indians in general, the Mormons were white, and in the 1850s neither the U.S. government nor its army was willing to wage a full-scale war on white Americans.

In spring 1849 topographical engineer Capt. Howard Stansbury rode to the Great Salt Lake Valley with forty-niners and Mounted Riflemen on their way respectively to California and to Oregon. Pres. Zachary Taylor wanted to know the condition of the Salt Lake Mormons and Indians and the disposition of each toward American emigrants and the U.S. government. A native of New York City, the forty-three-year-old Stansbury had been a topographical engineer for twenty-one years both as a civilian and regular. Like his topographical peers, he approached the American West as an empirical scientist, Romantic poet, and United States nationalist.[4]

During the late summer, the legendary Jim Bridger guided Stansbury from Fort Bridger across the Wasatch Range into the northern Great Salt Lake Valley (see map 4). Fearing dispossession, the suspicious Saints grumbled, and when Stansbury heard about plots to assassinate him, he "undeceived" President Young in Great Salt Lake City on 28 August. To maximize information gathering, the captain needed Mormon provisions, labor, and guides. Young laid the matter before the Mormon council, which promised its cooperation but monitored the captain's every triangulation.[5]

Stansbury's assistant, Lt. John W. Gunnison, surveyed the country from Salt to Utah Lakes until cold weather drove the expedition back to the city. At one point Stansbury loaned weapons, ammunition, and a few regulars to a Mormon punitive expedition against Indians in Provo Valley. When spring thawed the snow and ice, he traversed the northern and western shores of Great Salt Lake while Gunnison triangulated the valley. In late July the Stansbury Expedition returned east along a route south of the Oregon Trail. Bridger led the party through Green River Valley and the south-central Wyoming desert across the mountains to Fort Laramie. From there Stansbury followed the Platte River Road to Fort Leavenworth.[6]

During the winter of 1850–51, he and Gunnison wrote their official report. In private, the ambitious lieutenant also began composing a short book on the Mormons. Their combined work, remarkably restrained, offered Americans the first glimpses of Mormon Utah. Both officers praised Mormon friendship, loyalty, and hydraulic and civil engineering, but the officers were troubled by Mormon theocracy, which concentrated civil and ecclesiastical power in the same hands. Under President-Governor Young, the Saints were totally devoted to their religious mission, the creation of the Kingdom of God on earth. The two explorers worried that the Mormons would exclude other Christians from political power if Deseret, the name Saints gave to their territory in 1849, achieved statehood.[7]

Stansbury and Gunnison diverged on Mormon polygamy. The scientist in Stansbury withheld moral judgment. Plural marriage was hardly the "gross licentiousness" declaimed in the East, and he witnessed no "petty jealousies, envy, bickerings, and strife" among the wives. However, polygamy was loathsome to Gunnison, who sensed alienation and loneliness in Mormon women. Privately to his wife Martha, he condemned polygamy as the immoral, arbitrary traffic in women. The Church seemed able to dispense females at will to chosen men.[8]

Science and politics tempered Stansbury and Gunnison. Each officer tried to speak as a scientist, especially given that antagonizing the Mormons might place overland emigrants at risk. At the same time, congressional passage of the Compromise of 1850 temporarily closed the door to political debates over the western territories, southern slavery, and Mormon polygamy. However, Stansbury confirmed plural marriage to easterners, and as the sectional crisis heated up, it joined southern slavery as one of the "twin relics of barbarism." As the decade unfolded, Democratic politicians would flog polygamy to divert public attention from slavery.[9]

Denying Deseret statehood, the Compromise of 1850 created Utah Territory in its place. President Fillmore appointed Young territorial governor and four other Mormons to federal offices. Arriving in summer 1851, three Gentile appointees watched in disbelief the public practice of polygamy, but what most enraged them was Mormon theocracy. The territorial legislature quickly passed the Utah Judiciary Act, which extended the jurisdiction of probate courts from civil to criminal cases. Young promptly filled the probate benches with Mormon bishops and alienated federal courts from judicial power.[10]

The Mormons had legitimate gripes as well. Gentile authorities publicly flaunted their prejudice. Territorial Secretary Broughton D. Harris withheld the twenty-five thousand dollars given him for government operations, and Associate Justice Perry E. Brocchus publicly impugned the morality of Mormon women. The Saints' hostility finally drove out these Gentiles. The "runaways" filed reports critical of Mormon hegemony, but a doubtful Fillmore defended Young and appointed better-qualified, less-vitriolic men, who generally cooperated with the governor and Church.[11]

Into this climate came John W. Gunnison, now a captain, author, and commander. He was in charge of the thirty-eighth parallel survey, one of four lines in the Great Railroad Survey Congress entrusted to the regular army in March 1853. His course would take his expedition into the Mormon kingdom. Service with Stansbury and publication of *The Mormons, or, Latter-day Saints, in the Valley of Great Salt Lake* had made Gunnison a national expert on the Great Basin and Mormonism, all of which earned him the thirty-eighth-parallel command.[12]

Gunnison's fragile health as a youth had compelled his parents, New Hampshire farmers, to steer him toward an army career. In their opinion soldiering was less taxing than agriculture or commerce. Driving himself to several physical and emotional collapses, Gunnison finished second in the West Point class of 1837. Now forty-one years old, he was ordered to reconnoiter a rail line through the southern Rockies into the Great Basin. Missouri representative Thomas H. Benton and St. Louis merchants were keenly interested in this central road, which would originate in Missouri.[13]

As Gunnison assembled his scientists, artists, guides, and supplies in St. Louis during spring 1853, he worried over Mormon grousing about his book and apprised Brigham Young of the survey. On 23 June the Gunnison Expedition departed Fort Leavenworth (see map 4). During the next few months the expedition passed Bent's Fort to the Arkansas River headwaters; crossed Sangre de Cristo Pass, the San Luis Valley, Cochetopa Pass, and present-day western Colorado and eastern Utah; explored passes through the Wasatch and Pavant Mountains; and eased into Pavant Valley. Riding ahead, Gunnison pulled into Manti, Utah, a Mormon settlement, on 18 October. Here he learned of a war between the southern Mormon settlements and the Ute Indians.[14]

Several days later, Gunnison's men bivouacked near Fillmore, Utah. The local bishop warned Gunnison of a Pavant war party on the loose to the northwest, but the captain assumed that his friendship with the Pavants, cultivated three years earlier, would guarantee his expedition's safety. After a few days of rest and recovery, the survey rode northwest toward the Sevier River, where it camped at Gunnison Bend. On 25 October one wing explored the area

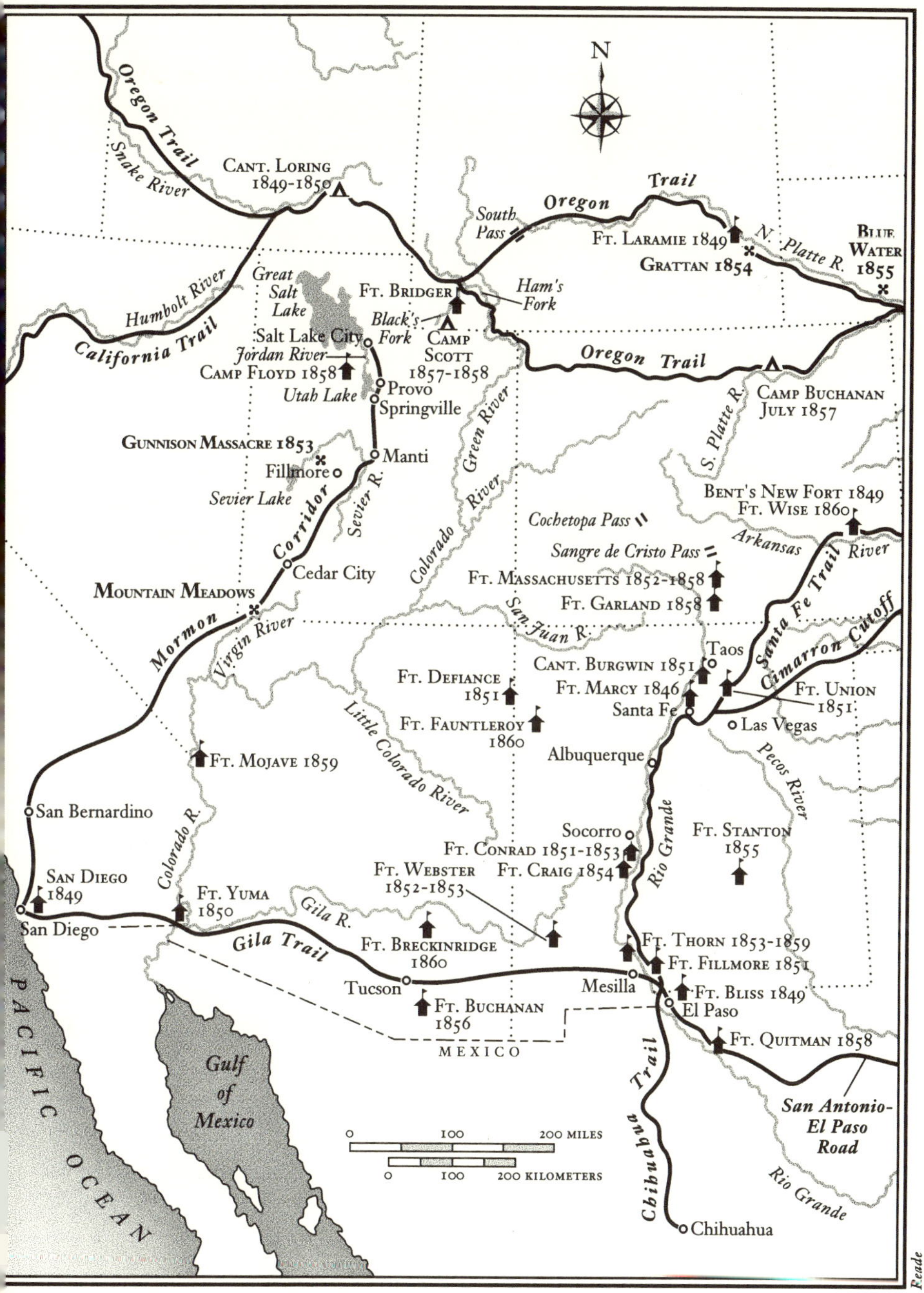
N
Oregon Trail
Snake River
Cant. Loring
1849-1850
Oregon
Trail
South
Pass
Ft. Laramie 1849
Grattan 1854
N. Platte R.
Blue
Water
1855
Humbolt River
California Trail
Great
Salt
Lake
Ft. Bridger
Ham's
Fork
Black's
Fork
Camp
Scott
1857-1858
Salt Lake City
Jordan River
Camp Floyd 1858
Utah Lake
Provo
Springville
Oregon Trail
Camp Buchanan
July 1857
S. Platte R.
Gunnison Massacre 1853
Fillmore
Manti
Sevier Lake
Sevier R.
Green River
Colorado River
Corridor
Mormon
Cedar City
Mountain Meadows
Virgin River
Cochetopa Pass
Sangre de Cristo Pass
Bent's New Fort 1849
Ft. Wise 1860
Arkansas
River
Ft. Massachusetts 1852-1858
Ft. Garland 1858
San Juan R.
Santa Fe Trail
Cimarron Cutoff
Taos
Cant. Burgwin 1851
Ft. Marcy 1846
Santa Fe
Ft. Union
1851
Las Vegas
Ft. Defiance
1851
Ft. Fauntleroy
1860
Little Colorado River
Ft. Mojave 1859
Albuquerque
Pecos River
San Bernardino
Colorado R.
Socorro
Ft. Conrad 1851-1853
Ft. Craig 1854
Rio Grande
Ft. Stanton
1855
San Diego
1849
San Diego
Ft. Yuma
1850
Gila R.
Ft. Webster
1852-1853
Gila Trail
Ft. Breckinridge
1860
Ft. Thorn 1853-1859
Ft. Fillmore 1851
Tucson
Mesilla
Ft. Bliss 1849
El Paso
Ft. Buchanan
1856
Ft. Quitman 1858
Mexico
Pacific Ocean
Gulf
of
Mexico
Chihuahua Trail
San Antonio-
El Paso
Road
Rio Grande
Chihuahua
0
100
200 miles
0
100
200 kilometers
Reade

upstream while Gunnison led the other down toward Sevier Lake. Each party traveled about fourteen miles in opposite directions that cold, snowy day. Gunnison's party camped in a grassy glade in the narrow river bottom.[15]

No one sensed danger as dawn trickled through the trees. Topographer Robert H. Kern and botanist Frederick Creutzfeldt warmed themselves at the fire as the camp cook set up the tripod and kettles. Four regulars strolled over to check on the horses hobbled nearby. As Captain Gunnison awakened and stirred in his tent, a hail of arrows and bullets instantly killed Kern, Creutzfeldt, and the cook. A camp hand, a Mormon guide, and three privates were soon slain. Totally surprised, Gunnison bravely sprang from his tent and called out to cease firing, but a fusillade of arrows riddled and dropped him. The regulars tending the horses fled with Pavants in hot pursuit. The assailants remaining behind stripped the bodies. Some ten days later, Pavant leader Moshoquop realized his party had killed Gunnison, his friend.[16]

Racing northward, the survivors stumbled into Lieutenant Beckwith's camp the morning of 27 October. Capt. Robert M. Morris, commanding the escort, assembled a rescue party and rode into Gunnison's camp that evening. All were dead and scavengers had mutilated the bodies. Morris withdrew his detail the next day, and the reunited survey made for Fillmore. Soon investigating the site, Mormon militia found the corpses unburied and the bones "promiscuously" scattered.[17]

Gentiles accused the Saints of complicity in the killings. From San Francisco in early 1854, Andrew J. Gunnison, the captain's brother, wrote Martha, "The story has been rife that the Mormons were connected with that horrid affair." The stories of four men who claimed to have been in Fillmore, Utah during the massacre seemed to implicate the Mormons, but the grieving Andrew gave no details.[18]

Young and the Saints skillfully turned the odium on the army. In a consoling letter to Martha, the Mormon leader enclosed a lock of hair clipped from her husband's "unburied" corpse. In San Francisco, Utah territorial delegate Almon W. Babbit assured Andrew that no Mormons had conspired against his brother. Indeed, the Saints viewed Morris's unmanly flight as naked "cowardice." Babbit asked Andrew if he was aware that Lieutenant Beckwith had sold some of the captain's property to clear expedition debts. Once in Washington, D.C., Babbit submitted the same account to the Pierce administration.[19]

Mormon accusations incensed the army. On 1 May 1854, in a letter to Martha, Beckwith defended Morris's response but, obviously troubled, added that he would have interred the remains "beneath the blue waters of the Sevier." The aftermath of the Gunnison killings cut any remaining strands of harmony between the army and Mormons. In the army's opinion, the

Pavant atrocity was a Mormon-Indian enterprise plotted and unleashed by the Saints' hierarchy. The army was now a full participant in the federal-Mormon struggle.[20]

The national spotlight now fell on Governor Young's administration of Utah, particularly Indian affairs. Since Mormon settlement, he had unilaterally conducted Great Basin Indian policy and had advocated "patience and forbearance" toward the Indians. President-Governor Young hoped to civilize indigenous peoples and helped establish instructional farms for the Great Basin Indians. Mormon missions among the Indians, however, worried the Gentiles, including Agent Garland Hurt, who suspected the Saints of turning the natives against the United States.[21]

Democratic president Franklin Pierce decided to investigate Mormon polygamy, theocracy, and arrogance in Utah Territory. Southern Democrats, his benefactors, wanted to replace Young, whose term would expire at the end of 1854. Pierce assigned an old friend and loyal Democrat, Maj. Edward J. Steptoe, to observe the Young administration's prosecution of Gunnison's assailants. Steptoe carried a governor's commission, which he could invoke at his discretion to remove Young.[22]

At the head of federal troops, Major Steptoe entered Great Salt Lake City on 31 August 1854. Throughout the fall he criticized the Gunnison investigation and trial. Federal authorities prosecuted eight Pavants, but the jury acquitted five and convicted three of manslaughter only. The court sentenced them to thirty-six months imprisonment, the maximum penalty. All three Indians eventually escaped.[23]

Camped at the city's edge, the regulars caused the Mormons much anxiety. Soldiers and Saints brawled in the streets, and elders feared the rape and seduction of their women; Mormon authorities threatened Lt. Sylvester Mowry, who was trying to woo one of Young's daughters-in-law. On New Year's Day 1855, a gunfight between soldiers and Saints wounded several men. The Mormon militia, the Nauvoo Legion, turned out, and the regulars dug in. Several tense days later, army and Mormon authorities arranged an amicable settlement.[24]

Young's prospects looked bleak, but Steptoe recommended his reappointment and even signed a pro-Young memorial endorsed by other federal authorities, regular army officers, and "prominent citizens." The major had come to admire Young's administrative genius and probably realized that governing the Saints was beyond his grasp. Young's reappointment signaled Mormons and southerners that, under the Pierce administration, the federal government would not interfere with peculiar domestic institutions—that is, polygamy in Utah and slavery in the South. Closer to home, Pierce needed the southern Democracy, his political heart, to battle free-soil militancy in Kansas Territory.[25]

President Pierce appointed three new non-Mormon officers. In a short time, Chief Justice John F. Kinney complained about Mormon tyranny. In addition, Associate Justice William W. Drummond declared the Utah Judiciary Act unconstitutional; he also consorted with a prostitute, even on his court bench, to the shock of the Saints. Drummond's legal and moral challenge coincided with severe drought, grasshopper plagues, and bitter cold. Hungry, penniless, despairing Mormons began sitting on federal juries to earn hard currency. Drummond must have smiled.[26]

To the wrathful Young, God was punishing Mormon backsliding. From his pulpit the prophet exhorted all Saints to reform, repent, and rebaptize. By spring 1856 a religious revival, orchestrated by Jedediah Grant, was electrifying Mormon country. His invocation of Old Testament blood atonement terrified both new converts and Gentiles. Whipped up by Grant, a Mormon mob ransacked the office of Associate Justice George P. Stiles, stole court documents, and burned the papers and library of a recently excommunicated lawyer. Mormon hostility discomfited Surveyor David Burr and Agent Hurt in outlying settlements. During late 1856 Drummond, Burr, Kinney, and Stiles bolted for the East, where they reported a Mormon rebellion. After rebaptizing thousands of Saints in cold mountain streams, Grant died from pneumonia, but he had purged Zion of Mammon.[27]

Democratic president James P. Buchanan took notice of this second wave of federal runaways from Utah. Unlike his predecessor, he had to deal with the Mormon challenge. The election of 1856 had riveted the nation's attention on the "twin relics of barbarism"—slavery and polygamy. For different reasons both Democrats and Republicans furiously assailed plural marriage. The Buchananite assault signaled to southern extremists that the new administration would act decisively against all secessionism.[28]

The infamous Dred Scott decision, handed down two days after Buchanan's inauguration on 4 March 1857, raised antislavery hysteria to an operatic pitch. Kansas Territory was in upheaval, and the Democratic party, the only cross-sectional political institution, threatened to split. Throughout the land the American people saw their country collapsing. On 20 May, acting decisively, Buchanan fired Governor Young, suspended Utah's federal mail service, and ordered the regular army to the Great Salt Lake Valley.[29]

Buchanan's reasoning was a mystery. Pundits pondered military contracts, political kickbacks, and secessionist plots. A plausible explanation was that unrest in Utah handed Buchanan a way to unite the country—especially Democrats—behind anti-Mormonism and divert attention from the divisive politics of slavery. Buchanan and Secretary of War John B. Floyd envisioned the Mormon masses streaming toward the "freedom" of federal lines and their gratitude translating into provisions and shelter for the regulars. Even more likely was that no president—Whig, Democrat, or Republican—could allow Indians, outlaws, or Mormons to threaten or even to close the California-Oregon Trail, the principal road to the Far West.[30]

Maj. Gen. Winfield Scott advised against mounting the expedition in 1857. The year was too advanced, and twenty-five hundred regulars, the requisite number, could not safely reach Utah before winter. Either Buchanan ignored or Secretary of War Floyd pocketed Scott's letter, and soldiers, supplies, and transportation arrived at Fort Leavenworth throughout June. Capt. John W. Phelps, an abolitionist, observed ruefully that Buchanan lacked "the firmness" to be president in such a troubled epoch.[31]

Secretary of War Floyd initially selected Col. William S. Harney to command the Utah Expedition. A seasoned plains campaigner with a violent reputation sure to terrify the Saints, Harney foresaw a winter disaster and resisted the command, lecturing Scott that the Utah operation violated "well settled" logistical and tactical dictums. In the meantime, the Second Dragoons, Fifth Infantry, Tenth Infantry, Fourth Infantry, and Phelps's battery rendezvoused at Fort Leavenworth. Scott wanted the rear guard on the road no later than 21 July 1857. Sorely needed in Kansas, Harney remained there and Buchanan looked for a replacement.[32]

On 18 July the vanguard—five hundred men, ninety-seven wagons, and six hundred animals—marched out of Fort Leavenworth and covered the 625 miles to Fort Laramie in six weeks. The officers quarreled, however, and morale plummeted. Col. Edmund B. Alexander, an elderly veteran who remained cloistered in his ambulance, seemed oblivious to imminent hardships.[33]

On 21 September at the Sweetwater River, Alexander's command encountered Capt. Stewart Van Vliet of the Quartermaster Corps. He had arrived in Utah in July to secure quarters and stockpile provisions for the troops and had received a polite but firm rebuff. The Saints promised to burn homes and crops if the regulars crossed the mountains. Van Vliet reported snow at Fort Bridger and recommended wintering there, but Alexander and his officers scoffed at the Mormon sympathizer. Indeed, having witnessed no "Mormon rebellion," Van Vliet would lobby Buchanan and Congress for peace.[34]

Governor-President Young unofficially learned of the Utah Expedition on the tenth anniversary of Mormon entry to the Great Salt Lake Valley. The dumbfounded Young cursed President Buchanan, who had neither notified him of removal nor investigated the charges of rebellion. Officially still governor, the prophet mobilized the Saints for war. Mormon communities stockpiled arms, ammunition, food, and clothing. Outlying settlements stripped territorial approaches bare and withdrew to the interior valley. With devastating results, Mormon authorities mobilized the Indians against the federals and activated the Nauvoo Legion, some twelve hundred men, who fortified Echo and Emigrant Canyons. Mormon rangers burned Forts Bridger and Supply and harassed the federal column, but the prophet admonished his rangers not to draw blood.[35]

Despite his vitriol, Young sought peace. Through a Mormon delegation, he ordered the army either to retire beyond the territory or to disarm before wintering on Black's Fork and departing in spring. Capt. Jessie A. Gove fussed to his wife Maria: "The old fool! . . . We will show him on which side of his bread the butter should be spread." In October the guerrillas struck several lightly guarded supply trains, burned fifteen hundred tons of food, and bought the Saints precious time. Now the army faced a mountain winter on half rations.[36]

The federal vanguard was in disarray. Anticipating Harney's arrival, Alexander had no instructions for active operations. On 7 October, pressed by his officers, he ordered the command up Ham's Fork toward Mormon outliers. In bitter cold, soldiers hacked out a road while Mormon guerrillas set grass fires around them. The six-mile-long column had advanced a mere three dozen miles when a blizzard struck ten days later. The men and animals suffered terribly. Alexander finally ordered a retreat to Henry's Fork on 19 October. Dozens of animals died, teamsters burned wagons and cargos, and officers smoldered.[37]

At this point, Colonel Alexander was contacted by the new expedition commander, Col. Albert S. Johnston of the Second Cavalry. Pulled from duty in Texas, Johnston was ordered to escort civil officers to Utah and help them restore law and order. Racing out of Leavenworth on 17 September, Johnston rendezvoused with the frostbitten army at the confluence of Ham's and Black's Forks on 4 November. His immediate order was to treat "as enemies" all Saints met in arms. The 1857 campaign finished, the regulars followed Johnston through a violent winter storm into quarters near Fort Bridger, leaving behind hundreds of dead draught animals.[38]

Following in Johnston's wake over the Platte River Road were the new governor and other civilian authorities. For governor, Buchanan tapped Alfred E. Cumming, former mayor of Atlanta and superintendent of Indian affairs. Obese and imperious, Cumming declined Johnston's offer to escort him to Utah. Instead, the governor and his officers traveled with six companies of Second Dragoons under Lt. Col. Philip St. George Cooke. Through heavy rain and ferocious blizzards, Cooke cheerfully led his dragoons and civil officers across the plains, through South Pass, over Green River, and to Fort

Bridger in nine weeks. The Second Dragoons lost 130 of 274 horses to "starvation" and 77 men to "desertion." Cooke's leadership was remarkable, but the march was a waste of men and horses. The dragoons' arrival brought Johnston's force to two thousand men.[39]

Colonel Johnston immediately began planning the spring campaign. To remount his cavalry, he sent Capt. Randolph B. Marcy of the Fifth Infantry to Fort Union, New Mexico, the nearest source of horses and mules. An experienced frontier explorer, Marcy led forty soldiers, twenty-five mountain men, and five Mexican packers south and east into the western slope of the southern Rockies on 27 November. The men crawled through snowdrifts, ate "mule-steaks," and followed a Mexican packer over Cochetopa Pass to the eastern slope. Two men, Mariano and Miguel, went forward to Fort Massachusetts and returned on "fresh horses" eleven days later. They passed out jerky, tobacco, and other luxuries to the starving, delirious men. Despite the hardships, only one man died—from gluttony too soon after starvation. Marcy himself lost forty pounds, but his winter crossing of the Rocky Mountains was the Utah Expedition's only triumph.[40]

In winter quarters at Camp Scott, Colonel Johnston and Governor Cumming agreed that a rebellion gripped Utah Territory and military force alone would exact Mormon submission. Anticipating war in the coming spring, Cumming requested that Secretary of State Lewis Cass clearly spell out his "military rights and duties" in the case of conflict with the Mormons. At Camp Scott, Johnston marginalized the governor, treated Utah Territory like a theater of war, and expected civilian deference. Returning Cumming's earlier snub, the colonel copied him none of his correspondence with Mormon or federal authorities. Likewise, the governor hinted to Cass that army paralysis alone held him in check. In the meantime, he awaited a political opening.[41]

His opportunity came from Pennsylvanian Thomas Kane, a Gentile philanthropist to the Mormons. The snow-bound expedition, cost overruns, national financial panic, and the Lecompton controversy had embarrassed Buchanan. The public now clamored for peace, and Kane offered to help. Buchanan wrote him an unofficial introduction, and shortly after Christmas 1857 Kane traveled by way of Panama and California to Utah, passing through Mormon and federal lines on 14 March 1858. That first evening he observed strict silence. The officers and men suspected Kane for a Mormon spy. The petulant Captain Gove wrote, "My men want to hang him."[42]

The Kane-Johnston relationship was clumsy from the outset. The day after his arrival, the stranger went straight to Cumming and took up residence with him. The regulars resented the cold shoulder, and Kane likewise distrusted the army. A few days later he mistook a dinner invitation, garbled by a German orderly, as an arrest and challenged Johnston to a duel. The colonel clarified his message, and Kane withdrew his summons.[43]

Another comedy almost cost Kane his life. In the evening of 17 April, while returning to camp from a meeting with a Mormon messenger, he squeezed off several pistol rounds to signal that he was lost. The balls passed over camp, the long roll was sounded, and skirmishers sallied forth to beat the woods. During their search, a Private McCarty stumbled upon Kane and fired a round. Hauled in by the guard, the shaken diplomat accused McCarty of attempted murder. The rattled private probably had to explain his damnably poor marksmanship, not his decision to fire, to his commanding officer, Captain Gove.[44]

As winter progressed, Brigham Young and Kane wooed Governor Cumming. The Saints still prepared to implement the Sebastopol Plan, a scorched-earth policy, but Young invited Cumming forward without the army, and Kane reassured him of Mormon sincerity and his own safety. Seizing the opening, Cumming left Camp Scott under a veil of secrecy on 5 April 1858. The regulars—officers and men—felt betrayed. Left behind, Mrs. Cumming felt a chill from the army.[45]

After a week-long journey, the governor was received graciously in Great Salt Lake City. The Mormons "recognized" him as "Governor" and restored all federal property and records, but northern Saints were still evacuating to the south while young men stood ready to fire structures and fields. In early May the governor proclaimed peace restored and the Oregon-California Trail reopened, but Johnston complained to General-in-Chief Scott, "He gives me no information with regard to . . . the adjustment of the Mormon difficulties." With the Nauvoo Legion still entrenched at Echo Canyon, the army would continue to treat the Saints as enemies.[46]

Putting little stock in Cumming and Kane, Buchanan still prepared for a war against the Great Basin Mormons. Throughout winter and spring the army concentrated regulars and stockpiled supplies at Fort Leavenworth for the approaching campaign. In late May and early June 1858, seven columns of freight wagons and troop guards left for Utah. Harney and his staff followed on 12 June.[47]

Johnston communicated only by letter with Cumming and Kane upon their return to Camp Scott on 16 May, and the governor still shared no information. Under the pseudonym "Argus," Gove disparaged Cumming to the *New York Herald*, but opting for peace, President Buchanan stole the governor's thunder by dispatching a pair of federal negotiators, Ben McCulloch and Lazarus Powell. Their instructions were to demand Mormon submission in return for a presidential pardon of all rebellion-related crimes. Despite Cumming's protests, the commissioners arrived at Camp Scott in late May.[48]

On 10 June in Great Salt Lake City, the commissioners and governor met with the Mormon First Presidency, which included Young. The Saints' only choice was to submit to federal law or suffer the bayonet. In exchange the president would pardon them for all rebellion-related crimes and guarantee their constitutional rights and safe return home. Young denounced the previous federal appointees but accepted the pardon for burning the supply trains. The Mormon people would reluctantly welcome the new authorities and federal troops. All parties appeased, Commissioners McCulloch and Powell invited the army into the valley.[49]

Johnston's regulars were already on the march. He had no news from McCulloch, Powell, or Cumming, but the early arrival of supply trains, troop reinforcements, and Captain Marcy's New Mexico horses and mules compelled Johnston to launch the Utah Expedition toward the valley on 13 June. At Bear River the regulars intercepted the declaration of peace, and Johnston proclaimed the army's pacific intent. After a two-day rest, the Utah Expedition took to the road again.[50]

Johnston's movement outraged Cumming. Federal negotiators had reassured Young that the army would stay put until they summoned it. Mustering a tortured justification, Johnston ordered no about-face. On 26 June the Utah Expedition, nearly three thousand men, debouched from Emigrant Canyon and descended into the valley. Another four miles brought the regulars to deserted Great Salt Lake City. Pvt. Charles A. Scott wrote, "It was like entering a Graveyard, silence reigned supreme." The men strained to see women but spotted only a small Mormon police force left behind to irrigate gardens, pastures, and fields, and to fire all structures should the army attempt an occupation. No soldier, however, broke ranks to loot or scavenge.[51]

The regulars nonetheless indulged in their passage through Great Salt Lake City. At the column's head, the regimental bands played martial strains. The men filed proudly behind their lively regimental banners—Third, Fifth, Sixth, and Tenth Infantry, Fourth Artillery, Second Dragoons, First Cavalry, and the Mounted Riflemen. At one point an irreverent adjutant ordered a bandmaster to strike up "One-Eyed Riley," an old bawdy tune. Riding at the head of his Second Dragoons, Lieutenant Colonel Cooke removed his hat to honor the Mormon Battalion.[52]

The expedition crossed the Jordan River and bivouacked three miles south. Several weeks later a board of reconnaissance recommended Cedar Valley, forty miles to the south, as the best location for a permanent post. As the column marched south along the Jordan River, it encountered trains of

Mormons returning northward. Officers physically disciplined any man who disparaged, robbed, or assaulted the Saints. A boon to the local economy, the army hired hundreds of Mormon laborers and purchased adobe bricks, lumber, fodder, and food from Mormon contractors to build and supply Camp Floyd. Local Saints sold and bartered produce, meat, hay, barley, wheat, corn, "cotton yarn boots shoes hats hardware and other items." Nearby Fairfield became "Frogtown," a den of saloons, grog shops, theaters, and brothels, but Camp Floyd steadily infused hard currency into the impoverished Mormon economy.[53]

With the rebellion settled, Johnston hoped Harney would relieve him, but Secretary Floyd recalled Harney and left Johnston to administer the Department of Utah. While the War Department redeployed troops, Johnston granted leaves of absence to Cooke, Alexander, Gove, Marcy, and others.[54] However, smoldering behind the fatigue details and blue uniforms was army bitterness over the winter retreat and the federal pardon.

In the wake of peace, Young, Cumming, Johnston, and other authorities skirmished over federal courts and land rights. The U.S. government had granted no settler legal title to any Utah land, and Johnston reserved the right to graze army livestock in the "Rush, Cedar, Tintie, and Goshen valleys" but promised that "actual settlers" would suffer no military eviction. In Rush Valley, however, Johnston ordered Daniel Spencer's herd removed by 15 April 1859, and Lt. Louis H. Marshall, commanding the grazing detail, sent a squad to expel a Spencer employee from his shanty. When menaced with a pitchfork, Sgt. Ralph Pike fractured Howard Spencer's skull with a rifle. From Great Salt Lake City, Governor Cumming complained that Daniel Spencer had a "right to occupy" the land.[55]

Sergeant Pike was thereafter a marked man. Indicted for "riotous assault," he was arraigned before a federal judge in Great Salt Lake City on 11 August. Afterward, as the sergeant's party walked up East Temple Street toward the Salt Lake House, Howard Spencer barked Pike's name, walked briskly toward him, and drew a revolver. His holster flap fastened, Pike wheeled to run, but Spencer's pistol exploded and the ball crashed into his side. The regulars chased the assailant, but a Mormon crowd closed ranks to let him flee. Assisted to his room, Pike died several days later.[56]

Federal and Mormon authorities let the commotion run its course. No regulars marched on the city. Johnston worried that Mormons would take hostage the soldiers already there under Maj. Fitz-John Porter. After Sergeant Pike died and tensions relaxed, Porter's detail returned to Camp Floyd. Enraged by the murder of their company sergeant, however, some of Gove's men vandalized property and stock at nearby Cedar Fort. Army authorities quickly condemned their vengeance and briefly restricted all soldiers to Camp Floyd.[57]

The Cumming-Johnston feud came to a head over military posses during the spring and summer of 1859. In early March, Associate Justice John Cradlebaugh requisitioned a regular detachment to guard federal prisoners at Provo, Utah, which had no jail according to Cradlebaugh. Johnston detached Capt. Henry Heth's company of the Tenth Infantry, which encamped in a "corral near the court-house." Insulted Provo citizens declared, "We regard a military despotism the most dangerous of all conceivable forms of government." A vitriolic Mormon hater, Cradlebaugh defended the "quiet, orderly" regulars.[58]

Cradlebaugh's court was investigating the Mountain Meadows Massacre. In September 1857, as the army bore down on Utah, a combined force of Paiute warriors and Mormon militia besieged the Fancher party, 130 Arkansas emigrants on their way to California, in Mountain Meadows on the California Road. After several days' siege, Mormon Indian agent John D. Lee lured the emigrants into an ambush laid by the Paiutes and the militia, who spared only eighteen children under the age of ten. The victims were stripped and their bodies heaped in shallow graves. Mormon killers swore themselves to secrecy, but travelers, horrified Saints, Indians, and others gradually leaked news of the atrocity.[59]

Worried about peace unraveling, Governor Cumming arrived in Provo on 14 March. The townsmen declared that they had offered Justice Cradlebaugh every assistance. Cumming demanded the "immediate" withdrawal of Heth's force, but Johnston and Heth ignored him. The captain even instructed his men to shoot Mormon rock throwers. The Provo mayor's arrest, however, nearly brought forth a Mormon posse of "two hundred" men. Ratcheting up the pressure, Colonel Johnston deployed seven infantry companies with artillery and dragoons to aid Cradlebaugh and Heth. The captain afterward reported "a very great change" in "the public pulse."[60]

However, the Mormons "thwarted" U.S. Marshal P. K. Dotson's efforts to serve Cradlebaugh's warrants. Turning to Johnston, Dotson secured 50 dragoons and 150 infantry as a federal posse. On 29 March the detachment "surrounded" and entered Bishop Aaron Johnson's residence at Springville. His "harem of nine wives" sharply scolded the officers, who laughed and jigged. However, Dotson returned to Provo emptyhanded.[61]

Never consulted by Cradlebaugh or Johnston, Governor Cumming beseeched Secretary Cass to clear up the "discrepancy" between federal departments in Utah. Indeed, Buchanan made Cumming the supreme territorial authority. Secretary Floyd ordered Johnston to detach military posses only on

Cumming's order, "not otherwise," and Attorney General Jeremiah S. Black revoked the authority of Justices Cradlebaugh and Sinclair to requisition federal troops. At Camp Floyd, Johnston released all federal prisoners. Governor Cumming won a major victory.[62]

Throughout 1858 and 1859, the Bureau of Indian Affairs, the Attorney General's Office, and the War Department investigated the Mountain Meadows Massacre. Under congressional pressure, the War Department ordered Johnston to assist in the recovery of surviving children living with the Indians or Mormons. Preoccupied with overland trails, Johnston handed the task to Dr. Jacob Forney, superintendent of Indian affairs in Utah Territory. By fall 1858 he had secured ten children. During April and May 1859, Dr. Forney, Justice Cradlebaugh, and the army simultaneously descended on southern Utah.[63]

Two separate army detachments participated. From Camp Floyd, Capt. Reuben P. Campbell led dragoons and infantry to Santa Clara. At Meadow Creek, Campbell met Forney, who now had custody of sixteen Arkansas children between the ages of three and ten. Riding with Campbell, Justice Cradlebaugh interviewed the survivors at Corn Creek, Forney's nearby agency. The testimony of the oldest children incriminated Mormons, especially John D. Lee and Isaac C. Haight, in the siege and slaughter. Marching on, Campbell's expedition pulled into grassy Mountain Meadows during the first week of May 1859.[64]

The scene appalled even the most combat-seasoned soldier. Captain Campbell reported, "Here I found human skulls, bones, and hair scattered about, and scraps of clothing of men, women, and children." Assistant Surgeon Charles Brewer, who had visited the Fancher train near O'Fallon's Bluff in June 1857, studied skeletal remains at four sites. A ravine northwest of the wagon corral held "many bodies, skulls, bones, and matted hair" of the men. Another site farther on contained "another assembly of human remains," mostly women and a few children. Hair, bonnets, lace, muslin, calicoes, and other material littered the ground here. Brewer wrote, "Many of the skulls bore marks of violence, being pierced with bullet holes, or shattered by heavy blows, or cleft with some sharp-edged instrument." Male skulls "showed that fire-arms had been discharged close to the head." No recovered article betrayed a single victim's identity. On 6 May a burial detail interred the remains of a mere twenty-six victims. Campbell's command then encamped on the Santa Clara River.[65]

The second command of regulars was led by Capt. James H. Carleton of the First Dragoons. Escorting a paymaster across the southern Great Basin from Fort Tejon, California, the dragoons rendezvoused with Campbell's command at Mountain Meadows on 16 May. Upon arrival Carleton interrogated the Hamblins, whose ranch house stood four miles south of the meadows. They downplayed Mormon complicity and emphasized Paiute culpability, but they also noted the comings and goings of Lee and other Mormons. Other nearby residents claimed to have been harvesting during the massacre or to be only recently arrived in the area from the north. However, a Santa Clara Paiute participant, Jackson, stated that Lee, Haight, and sixty Mormons—all "painted and disguised as Indians"—helped besiege and slaughter the Fancher emigrants. According to Carleton, Young gave the order, and Lee and Haight "led and directed" the assault.[66]

Carleton considered the massacre Mormon "vengeance on the people of Arkansas." In May 1857 popular Mormon apostle Parley P. Pratt had been arrested for wife abduction and then murdered by the enraged husband near Fort Smith, Arkansas. When President Young opened emigrant trains to attack in late summer 1857, the Arkansans became "the authorized, if not legal, prey of the inhabitants." Innocently rolling into a war, the Fancher train, "a rich one," invited plunder and slaughter by Saints dizzy with "hatred."[67]

Carleton ordered another search for remains. His detail combed the "sage bushes" a mile back from either side of the road to Hamblin's house. Their additional finds filled a wagon bed. Carleton reported: "I gathered many of the disjointed bones of 34 persons. The number could easily be told by the number of pairs of shoulder blades and by lower jaws, skulls, and parts of skulls, etc." The regulars then interred them.[68]

Sending a message to the Saints, Carleton raised a "rude" cross over the grave. The inscription read, "Vengeance is mine; I will repay, saith the Lord." The Saints were white people, but Captain Carleton had broken through his racial barrier against killing renegade Anglos. His recommendation was that the federal government exterminate the Mormons: "Give them one year, no more; and if after that they pollute our soil by their presence make literally Children of the Mist of them." Carleton returned to Fort Tejon and wrote a detailed report later published by Congress.[69]

Johnston soon recalled Campbell's detachment to Camp Floyd. Governor Cumming became alarmed that armed Mormons were collecting in the mountains around the Great Salt Lake Valley. Wrapping up his inquiry, Justice Cradlebaugh concluded that he could squeeze no further incriminating evidence from the Mormons on his own. The army then provided light spring wagons, a baggage wagon, and a small guard to return the surviving children to Arkansas.[70]

Johnston's command of the Department of Utah drew to a close in early spring 1860. Captain Tracy thought his leaving was good riddance, but most officers and men who had endured the hard winter of 1857–58 were saddened by his departure. On 1 March 1860 the Camp Floyd garrison drew up along the road for one final review. Sitting proudly astride his horse, Johnston praised their fortitude and devotion. Captain Heth wrote, "I do not believe there was a dry eye in that line." After traveling overland to California, Johnston sailed to New York and joined his family in Louisville, Kentucky, after a separation of nearly three years.[71]

Despite their official standoff, the army and Saints engaged in brisk commerce. The Department of Utah was far away from army depots in California, the Pacific Northwest, and Missouri, and hard currency or cash was in short supply in the Mormon economy. The Quartermaster and Commissary Departments contracted with local suppliers for building materials and food supplies. The Mormons may have wished away federal troops, but desperately poor, they cheerfully exploited the economic opportunities generated by the federal occupation. In short, the Mormons and the army needed one another in the Great Salt Lake Valley.

Marching through Utah to California, Pvt. Eugene Bandel recalled his detachment being met by "numerous Mormons with provisions to sell, of which they made quick sales at stiff prices." Captain Tracy found that, even during the Springville occupation, the Saints were always "on the alert to profit at every point as they say, from our presence." Individual troops and companies bartered with the Mormons for "fried fish, buttermilk, pies, vegetables, butter, eggs and 'Valley Tan' whiskey" and paid for the items with "money, clothing, tea and coffee, pieces of iron, and stoves."[72]

The army poured hundreds of thousands of dollars into the Mormon economy. The Quartermaster Department hired hundreds of men to erect quarters, manufacture adobe bricks, blacksmith, and perform other skilled and unskilled tasks. The church profited handsomely from lumber and grain contracts. Although it never charged the army a toll on the Provo Canyon Road, agents of the church collected fees on the scores of Russell, Majors, and Waddell freight wagons. The periodic army surplus sales of "iron, tools and equipment, livestock, stock feed, . . . beans, flour, and other food" boosted the Mormon economy as well.

When Philip St. George Cooke, now a full colonel, withdrew the garrison from Fort Crittenden (formerly Floyd) at the start of the Civil War, he disposed of "$4,000,000 worth of property for approximately $100,000." Large supply wagons, completely outfitted, sold for $6.50. The Utah Expedition came to subjugate the Mormons but instead subsidized their economy and eased their plight in the difficult early years of settlement.[73]

The federal government's guiding principle in Mormon relations was enforcing United States sovereignty in the Great Salt Lake Valley and Great Basin. Outside Fillmore, no president completely trusted the Mormons to foster federal interests—to pacify the Indians and protect the California-Oregon Trail—in Utah Territory. Taylor, Pierce, and Buchanan deployed the regular army to reconnoiter, or spy on, Mormon Utah, and intelligence gathering was a critical charge in the missions of Stansbury, Gunnison, Steptoe, and Johnston. Supplemented by the observations of other Gentile authorities, their reports described the culture of the Mormons—a deviant people—to the United States government and its constituency. The official reports, personal letters, and private publications of army officers helped shape federal policy and public opinion toward the Church of Latter-day Saints, particularly the institution of polygamy.

As a coercive federal arm, the regular army occupied the Great Salt Lake Valley but broke only Mormon military resistance. Gentile authorities gained control of the federally commissioned territorial government, but the hierarchy of the Mormon Church—a parallel theocratic government—still commanded the allegiance and obedience of its congregation, a bond that no federal bayonet could sever. The church and the federal government would skirmish politically for another quarter century.

Throughout the 1850s, the U.S. Army was more a velvet glove than mailed fist in Mormon Utah. Regular troops had waged war on the British, American Indians, and Mexicans, but shooting down Anglo or white citizens was forbidden territory. Mormon haters painted the Saints as ignorant, superstitious, promiscuous barbarians not unlike the Indians or African Americans. Although regular troops anticipated active campaigning against a subhuman people in the Great Salt Lake Valley, they witnessed instead a white Protestant society, albeit peculiar, and came to admire Mormon thrift, order, and industry, qualities antebellum Americans associated with Anglo-Saxon civilization.

In addition to racial and cultural barriers, the politics of slavery partly inhibited the federal response to Mormon unrest in Utah Territory. Presidents respected the American suspicion of standing armies and political tyranny, disguised their militant civil actions as federal moral intervention, and cautioned field commanders against shooting anyone. Democratic presidents Pierce and Buchanan especially worried about any federal military intervention possibly alienating their southern supporters. Abolitionists, free-soilers, and slavocrats saw that a bloody civil action against the Mormons would set a far-reaching precedent for violent federal operations against all domestic opposition parties. During the interwar years, the United States was unwilling and unable to prosecute a vigorous war on other white Americans.

9

SUPPRESS THEM

Regulars and Partisans in Bleeding Kansas

ON 5 December 1855 at 1:00 A.M., Col. Edwin V. "Bull" Sumner, commanding Fort Leavenworth, received an emergency dispatch from Wilson Shannon, governor of Kansas Territory headquartered at Shawnee Mission. Proslavery militia had rendezvoused on the Wakarusa River to storm Lawrence, Kansas, and free-state minutemen were entrenching to repulse them (see map 1). The governor urgently requested the deployment of the regular troops between the belligerents. Colonel Sumner promised to mobilize his First Cavalry and meet the governor at Delaware Crossing later that evening.[1]

Governor Shannon had foolishly activated the "Kansas Territorial Militia" on 27 November 1855 after Sheriff Samuel Jones lost a prisoner to outraged free-soil settlers and reported a massive rebellion underway. Fifteen hundred Missourians—"border ruffians" or "pukes" to free-staters in Kansas—responded to the summons and plundered neighboring free-soil homesteads. When Shannon interviewed free-state leaders in Lawrence, he quickly saw the monkey Jones had made of him.[2]

Leading the cavalry to the rescue seemed politically risky upon reflection, and Sumner rescinded the marching orders to await presidential instructions. Pleading morality, the governor wrote, "It is peace, not war, that we want, and you have the power to secure peace," but Sumner stood pat and Pres. Franklin Pierce left Shannon to negotiate an end to the so-called Wakarusa War. The governor's feverish diplomacy secured a truce and raised the siege, but he and Sumner knew that, come spring, warfare would return.[3]

For the next five years, the U.S. Army routinely intervened against violence between proslavery and free-soil partisans in Kansas Territory. The national stakes of the political contest made this constabulary action the army's most charged intervention during the interwar years. The United States Military Academy indoctrinated future officers to conduct themselves and their units in the national interest, but presidents and governors deployed the regulars to achieve partisan goals, specifically to defeat free-soil opposition and establish Democratic supremacy and southern slavery in Kansas. Federal military intervention, however, backfired on the slavocracy. Instead of aiding the presidents' prosouthern agents, the regular-army constabulary, particularly its northern-born officers, guaranteed the survival and ascendancy of the free-state party in territorial politics.

Hotly contested in Congress, the Kansas-Nebraska Act opened those two territories to settlement in May 1854. Upon statehood bona fide residents would vote for a state constitution that either allowed or prohibited slavery. Popular sovereignty was the democratic panacea to sectional division over slavery in the new western territories, but the bill's repeal of the Missouri Compromise shocked the North and triggered a desperate sectional battle centered in Kansas. While the New England Emigrant Aid Society of Massachusetts mobilized antislavery families for settlement in Kansas, southern slavocrats vowed to plant and cultivate slavery there.

Citizens of neighboring Missouri, a slave state, simply assumed Kansas was theirs. Organized by former senator David Atchison, they invaded eastern Kansas and elected a proslavery legislature. The Democratic territorial administration shut out free-soil settlers, on whom Pres. Franklin Pierce, a Democrat, blamed Kansas anarchy. With nowhere to turn, antislavery Kansans created a shadow government in Topeka. Most settlers, whether proslavery or free-state, took up arms more to protect their land claims than to champion slavery or freedom.[4]

With Atchison controlling the militia, Shannon personally lobbied Pierce to secure access to regular troops the following spring. The failure of popular sovereignty would split the Democratic party, and Pierce gambled that southern Democrats would perceive federal deployment as a crackdown on the free-soil rebellion. His legal foundation was the "Cushing doctrine"—that the U.S. Constitution empowered federal courts to employ national military forces and state militia as a posse comitatus when popular mobs obstructed the federal legal process.[5] In the end Pierce's policy satisfied no one.

On 11 February 1856 President Pierce proclaimed Kansas Territory in a state of insurrection and authorized Governor Shannon to deploy regulars against illegal, armed associations should the federal marshal need their assistance. From Fort Leavenworth, Colonel Sumner advised the Pierce administration to disperse all armed mobs, especially the Kansas militia, but Adj. Gen. Samuel Cooper, a southern sympathizer, curtly informed the colonel to obey the governor.[6]

With the spring thaw, thousands of new emigrants staked homesteads in Kansas. Mercenaries Henry Titus of Florida and Jefferson Buford of Alabama led several hundred armed southerners to liberate Kansas for slavery. The Republican-controlled House of Representatives dispatched the Howard Commission to investigate voter fraud the previous year. The warm weather inspired Sheriff Samuel Jones to arrest free-soilers, but Lawrence residents expelled him on 19–20 April. Once back in Lecompton, Jones reported their defiance to Governor Shannon, who requested a military posse. Colonel Sumner reluctantly detached eleven regulars but cautioned their commanding officer, twenty-eight-year-old 1st Lt. James McIntosh, "Use great circumspection . . . and do not resort to violence if it can possibly be avoided."[7]

Late afternoon on 23 April, Jones and the cavalry rode into Lawrence. By sundown he had arrested six individuals and jailed them in a local residence. McIntosh's troopers encamped in a lot behind the house, but that evening a "secret assassin" shot Sheriff Jones. Stunned Lawrencians posted a five-hundred-dollar reward for the shooter and nursed the sheriff. Sumner immediately dispatched another eleven men to McIntosh.[8] Hard on their heels came the colonel, the governor, and two cavalry squadrons. After soothing frazzled nerves, Sumner assigned McIntosh's squadron to Governor Shannon.

The proslavery response was swift and shrill: "HIS DEATH MUST BE AVENGED." In Lecompton, Shannon accused free-soilers of spreading murder and mayhem, kept the First Cavalry at Leavenworth, and handed vengeance to United States Marshal Israel Donelson, who summoned a citizen posse to serve warrants in Lawrence. A mob—mostly Missourians—gathered at Lecompton.[9]

On 12 May Sumner witnessed the "great excitement" and offered to arrest anyone under federal indictment, but Shannon saw a chance to crush the free-soil menace and refused to intercede. He explained that citizens, not soldiers, ought to make the arrests. Disparaging the marshal's "partisans," Sumner anticipated a "serious collision." Lawrence residents begged Sumner to intervene, but a stickler for law and regulations, he would act only on a legal summons from the governor or marshal.[10]

The posse was free to act. On the morning of 21 May, Donelson's deputies, five hundred strong, fell in behind red banners on Mount Oread overlooking Lawrence; the home of Charles Robinson, the Free-State governor, burned in the background. At 11:00 A.M., with a clutch of men in tow, Deputy

United States Marshal William Fain successfully arrested a handful of free-soilers. Afterward, Donelson dismissed the deputized army, which was immediately sworn in by Sheriff Jones—miraculously risen from the dead. At midafternoon he led the posse—including Atchison, Titus, Buford, and other proslavery luminaries—downhill into Lawrence. Under Jones's direction they destroyed the Free-State Hotel and the offices of the *Herald of Freedom* and *Kansas Free State*. Once dismissed, his whooping deputies plundered the town. Expressing no remorse, Shannon posted regulars near Lawrence, Lecompton, and Topeka to "check" free-state retaliation.[11]

The Sack of Lawrence dovetailed with the bloody assault on abolitionist senator Charles Sumner, the colonel's cousin, on the Senate floor by Rep. Preston Brooks of South Carolina. Freed on bail, Brooks was lionized and feted as a defender of southern honor. To horrified northerners the sack and assault illustrated southern desperation to extend slavery into the "virgin" West.[12]

Headquartered at Osawatomie, Kansas, abolitionist John Brown decided to avenge the two attacks. On the night of 24 May, Brown, four sons, and two others hacked to death five proslavery settlers along Pottawatomie Creek. In his wake hundreds of Missourians crossed the border to protect friends and family and to hunt Brown. Opportunists on both sides gutted farms and murdered enemies. As the Democratic party assembled in Cincinnati, President Pierce chastised Shannon for indulging Donelson's posse and helplessly watched Kansas implode.[13]

Governor Shannon handed peacekeeping to the First Cavalry, which patrolled the roads between Lawrence and Missouri. Accused of inactivity in St. Louis newspapers, Sumner complained to Adjutant General Cooper, "If the armed civil posses had not been allowed to act, as I earnestly advised the Governor, these disturbances would not have happened." Two days later, Shannon issued a law-and-order proclamation, but Pierce lost the Democratic presidential nomination to Pennsylvanian James P. Buchanan. As United States minister to England, Buchanan was untainted by the politics of Bleeding Kansas.[14]

Chaos reigned in the territory. At Black Jack, Brown's reinforced gang captured two dozen members of the Westport Rangers, a partisan company from western Missouri, and marched them to Ottawa Creek, where 150 free-soilers joined him. Sumner soon galloped up with three cavalry troops, including Lt. J. E. B. Stuart. When Old Bull threatened to wade into the free-soilers with sabers, Brown released the rangers. Turning to Deputy Marshal Fain, Sumner asked for the warrants on Brown and others, but the lawman produced none, and the chagrined colonel let Brown go. Taking exception, Henry

C. Pate, captain of the rangers, stepped onto a log to editorialize, but Sumner roared, "I don't want to hear a word from you, sir," and ordered everyone to clear out.[15]

Sumner next steered his regulars toward proslavery militia two miles away. Kansas territorial delegate J. W. Whitfield stood at the head of 250 men. Invoking presidential and gubernatorial proclamations, Sumner pointed the way to Missouri and ordered the men home. Out of sight, however, half regrouped and sacked Osawatomie, Brown's settlement. Visited by regulars earlier, one resident complained, "The soldiers came without our request and went away just in the only time they were at all wanted."[16]

During June, the First Cavalry lifted the proslavery blockade of free-soil towns. On the Westport Road, Lieutenant McIntosh intercepted numerous Missouri mobs, one sweep turning up several "abolitionist corpses." That officer wrote Shannon, "If this Missouri movement could be stopped, I would have some hopes of more quiet times." By the end of the month, the frustrated Missourians relented, and only a few "freebooters"—Sumner's term—still plundered and robbed.[17]

After Pierce lost the nomination, his cabinet divided over Kansas pacification. Ultrasoutherners, led by Secretary of War Davis, wanted to withdraw the First Cavalry and to make popular sovereignty benefit the South and Democrats. A second camp, Buchananites, urged military protection of all bona fide settlers, free-soil and proslavery. Naked southern aggression, the Buchanan camp feared, would scare remaining northern Democrats into Republican arms.[18]

Pierce decided to replace Sumner, who was rumored to be sympathetic to free-staters. The old regular was hard on both sides, but his intervention was retarding Democratic interests. In the Senate, John J. Crittenden and others proposed that General-in-Chief Winfield Scott pacify Kansas, but Pierce and Davis hated the general. In late June the president posted an old friend, Col. Persifor F. Smith, to Kansas Territory. His Pennsylvania roots, Louisiana wife, Democratic politics, and southern sympathies placated both northern and southern Democrats. Pierce assumed that Smith would pursue the Democratic agenda.[19]

Still in command, Sumner faced one final unpalatable task. Defying the governor, the free-state legislature planned to convene in Topeka on Independence Day. Governor Shannon instructed Sumner to scatter the body should it "reassemble and enact laws." Shannon then skulked away to St. Louis. On 3 July Sumner and four companies of First Cavalry rendezvoused with Acting Gov. Daniel Woodson and Marshal Donelson outside Topeka.

Woodson issued a proclamation forbidding the free-state body to assemble and create law.[20]

On Independence Day, Marshal Donelson mounted the stairs to Constitution Hall, where the presiding officer read the president's and governor's proclamations. Nobody moved and Donelson stalked out. Returning to camp, he handed the dispersal order to Sumner. At noon the colonel led four cavalry troops and an artillery section into Topeka's town square. As the cannoneers unlimbered their howitzers, Sumner dismounted his horse and strode into the hall. Standing erect, Sumner announced, "Gentlemen, I am called upon this day to perform the most painful duty of my life." The assembly had to disband immediately. Recalling his dispersals of border ruffians, Sumner declared, "God knows I have no party feeling." His eyes straight ahead, Colonel Sumner marched out the door, mounted his horse, and ordered his troops to move out.[21]

Ten days later Bull Sumner went on leave, but free-state accusations of military tyranny dogged him to his home in Syracuse, New York. The *National Anti-Slavery Standard* compared him to English dictator Oliver Cromwell, and Secretary of War Davis reprimanded him. Defending himself, Sumner explained that he acted upon the marshal's summons and that his order was directed at the illegal legislature, not the unarmed assembly. Sensing Atchison behind his censure, the colonel wrote, "When they [Missouri Democrats] found that I would be strictly impartial, that lawless mobs could no longer come from Missouri, and that their interference with the affairs of Kansas was brought to an end, then they immediately raised a hue-and-cry that they were oppressed by the United States troops."[22] Pressed with Kansas unrest and Pacific Northwest Indian wars, Davis and Cooper dropped their quarrel with Sumner.

In Sumner's absence Kansas disintegrated. Proslavery guerrillas intensified their war from stockades inside Kansas while free-soil chieftain James H. Lane reinvigorated free-state resistance. Everyone carried a weapon, and farmers worked their fields in armed teams. Throughout the summer, the struggle rushed toward climax.[23]

Colonel Smith assigned Maj. John Sedgwick of the First Cavalry to command the field constabulary. A Connecticut native, Sedgwick had been critical of free-state forces, but a Sumner protégé, he practically invited their reduction of the proslavery blockhouses. On 16 August free-soilers attacked Fort Titus, killed one partisan, wounded Titus and another, burned down the stockade, and took their prisoners to Lawrence. The entire time Sedgwick and his First Cavalry watched with amusement from a distance. Shannon reached the scene in time to see the smoldering ruins.[24]

The following day he and Sedgwick visited Lawrence to recover Titus and his marauders and saw eight hundred armed men gathering to destroy Lecompton. Governing Kansas seemed hopeless, and soon thereafter Shannon resigned. His "removal" was imminent anyway. In late July Pierce had begun seeking a new man to pacify Kansas before the presidential election. To that end he appointed John W. Geary.[25]

As Geary politicked in Washington, D.C., Congress adjourned without passing a military appropriations bill. The Howard Commission had exposed the fraudulent Kansas election held the previous fall and the abuse of power by Pierce's appointees. The Republican-controlled House responded by amending the appropriations bill to forbid the army's enforcement of the Kansas legal code. The Democratic-dominated Senate struck the amendment, but Congress adjourned before compromising. Left with no army budget, the president called a special session on 21 August and browbeat enough Know-Nothing members to pass the bill shorn of the amendment.[26]

With Shannon gone, Acting Gov. Daniel Woodson, a nail-spitting proslaver, declared war on free-soilers and summoned the territorial militia. Free-state forces checked two Missouri columns at Fort Scott and Bull Creek; a third proslavery army sacked Osawatomie and killed Frederick Brown. Both sides murdered, burned, and looted, but Colonel Smith pulled back his regulars, ordering them to intervene against the Kansas militia only upon a summons by civil authorities. From Fort Leavenworth Capt. John P. Hatch wrote his father, "He [Smith] is old and so broken down by disease that he had not the nerve to interfere unless he has orders to do so."[27]

However, on 18 August Smith augmented Sedgwick's cavalry at Lecompton with the Second Dragoons under Lt. Col. Philip St. George Cooke and several First Cavalry squadrons under Lt. Col. Joseph E. Johnston. Smith expected this enlarged force, now under Cooke's command, to protect Lecompton and sidestep the Kansas militia. To the romantic Cooke, chasing guerrillas was unsoldierly, and when he was ordered by Acting Governor Woodson to invest Topeka, he bluntly refused to wage war on American citizens.[28]

Lane's mob at Lawrence was a genuine threat. As proslavery armies recoiled toward Missouri, Lane led six hundred free-soil militiamen toward Lecompton on 5 September. In the late afternoon Cooke intercepted the vanguard a mile south of the capital. Lane faded into the ranks while Samuel Walker proclaimed their mission: to liberate free-soilers wrongly held in federal custody. But unlike Atchison's partisans, Cooke's regulars would fight, and Walker led the lieutenant colonel to Lane. When the deputy marshal rode up to demand Lane's arrest, Cooke retorted, "Go to _____, or rather back to camp." President Pierce had ordered the release of all free-state prisoners, and Cooke personally guaranteed their safe return. He then ordered everyone back to Lawrence.[29]

Gov. John W. Geary arrived at Fort Leavenworth on 9 September. The desolation and chaos in eastern Kansas stunned him: "In isolated or country places, no man's life is safe. The roads are filled with armed robbers, and murders for mere plunder are of daily occurrence. Almost every farm house is deserted, and no traveler has the temerity to venture upon highways without an escort." Geary had fought in Mexico and later served as mayor of San Francisco, where he suppressed the "Hounds," rampaging Australian miners. He stood "six feet five" and weighed "approximately two hundred and sixty pounds." A Pennsylvania Democrat like Smith, he too was acceptable to both wings of the Democratic party. His mission was to pacify Kansas and salvage popular sovereignty before the presidential election.[30]

Geary stepped resolutely into Kansas. He released all free-soil prisoners, reorganized and federalized the Kansas militia, and dispatched agents to deactivate any territorial troops still operating in the field. On the evening of 12 September, a Geary messenger located the Kansas militia, twenty-five-hundred strong, massing to destroy Lawrence—the evening before, three hundred horsemen had approached Lawrence but suddenly retreated toward Franklin. Rousing Cooke at 1:35 A.M., Geary rushed to Lawrence with four hundred dragoons and cavalry. After soliciting free-soil cooperation, Geary rode back to Lecompton in the company of Cooke's regulars.[31]

At sundown the following day, the governor received another urgent message: proslavery militia were closing on Lawrence, again from Franklin. Lieutenant Colonel Johnston ringed Lawrence with regulars while Geary and Cooke rode to Franklin, where twenty-five-hundred well-armed Missourians, Atchison at their head, had rendezvoused to destroy the "Black Republicans." Would-be generals denounced the president, governor, and army, but Cooke swore to uphold Geary "at the cannon's mouth," and Atchison's army disbanded. As Geary returned to Lecompton, he encountered freshly sacked homesteads, at one of which he interviewed a gut-shot farmer who reported that the Kickapoo Rangers, a proslavery company, had just assaulted him and stolen his horses.[32]

On 14 September in Geary's absence, Capt. Thomas J. Wood rode after free-soil partisans operating around Osawkee and Hickory Point. Setting out at 9:00 P.M. from Leavenworth Crossing of the Grasshopper River, Wood located the free-state camp near Hickory Point and divided his command. Wood reported, "By a rapid movement the three parties concentrated on the camp before there was time to make any preparation for resistance or escape." The marshal arrested 101 free-soil partisans and marched them to Lecompton.[33]

Throughout the summer Kansans anticipated the arrival of Lane's "Army of the North," a massive force he purportedly recruited during a tour of free states the previous spring. Even Geary envisioned "1,000 men" invading from Nebraska and Iowa to fight for free soil. Patrolling the border in October, Cooke's regulars stopped a wagon train of 240 emigrants—only five were women—who claimed to be "*bona fide* settlers." The federals confiscated dozens of new saddles, a tool chest, 242 percussion muskets, numerous Hall muskets and Sharps carbines, sixty-one sabers, fifty Colt's revolvers, and four boxes of ball cartridges. Arrested by the federal marshal, the emigrants were escorted to Topeka, where Geary harangued them. Afterward, Lane's Army of the North scattered to their homesteads.[34]

Geary's peace policy worked. By late September his administration had enrolled two companies of militia at Lecompton and one at Lawrence and negotiated peace between Walker and Titus. With tranquility blanketing the prairies, Geary invited back all displaced citizens. In early November Colonel Smith mustered out the militia, and Geary retained only a cavalry squadron and an infantry company at Lecompton.[35]

The governor now waged political war on the Atchison Democrats, who had conspired to force slavery on Kansas "*at all hazards.*" The citizen majority, Geary believed, wanted a free Kansas. Only the "honest application" of the Organic Act would permanently restore peace and faith. The Atchison machine ostracized the governor, President Pierce withdrew his support, and Colonel Smith abandoned him. When menaced by a disgruntled office seeker, the governor requested additional troops to patrol Lecompton, but Smith, recently promoted to brigadier general by Pierce, refused.[36]

In a desperate bid for support, Geary reiterated his charges against Pierce appointees to the incoming president, but his plea failed to win Buchanan's hand. Ahead of death threats, the governor fled Kansas in early March 1857, leaving his office to Secretary Daniel Woodson, who once again became acting governor. Lionized in the North by Free-Soilers, Geary went on to distinguish himself in the Union army during the Civil War and served two terms as Republican governor of Pennsylvania.[37]

President Buchanan aimed to hold the Union and the Democratic party together in face of shrill abolitionists and fire-eating secessionists. Despite his reservations, he committed his administration to championing popular sovereignty in Kansas. He also committed his presidency to upholding the Dred Scott decision, futilely hoping that it would settle the issue of slavery in the western territories for all time. However, stripping all African Americans, free and slave, of political and civil rights; declaring the Missouri Compromise line unconstitutional; and throwing open the territories to slavery was anything but settling and drove thousands of northern Democrats into the Republican party.[38]

Buchanan saw light in Kansas nonetheless. That territory's demographics, heavily Midwestern, destined the future state for freedom, but the president still needed to win free-soil Kansans to the Democracy. To that end he courted fifty-six-year-old Robert J. Walker, a Pennsylvania native, Mississippi plantation owner, former United States senator, and treasury secretary, to be the next governor of Kansas. Hard pressed by Buchanan, Walker set aside financial speculations to accept the office, but he extracted three conditions from the president: the appointment of Frederick Stanton as territorial secretary; the submission of Kansas slavery or freedom to a territorial plebiscite; and the assignment of Col. William S. Harney to Kansas.[39]

Colonel Harney was contentedly hunting Seminole Indians in the Florida swamps when the Department of War reassigned him to Kansas. He labeled his new assignment the "grave-yard" of commands, but Walker and Buchanan trusted his politics. The colonel's brutality, the cynical Walker believed, would terrorize radical free-staters. When Harney reached Kansas in spring 1857, he informed Walker that his command would serve no "partisan interests." Adjutant General Cooper instructed him to help federal authorities keep the peace, enforce the law, and detach Lieutenant Colonel Cooke's Second Dragoons specifically to serve Walker.[40]

Upon reaching Kansas in early May 1857, Walker began wooing moderate free-soilers. In public he acknowledged that the Kansas majority was free-state and committed his administration to its demand: a plebiscite on the entire state constitution, not the slavery clause alone. Walker's position enraged slavocrats everywhere. At his inaugural dinner, L. A. McLean, a tall, red-headed bully, reminded Walker, who stood only five feet, two inches tall, that Atchison Democrats had broken three governors—even the gigantic Geary. Walker's commitment exceeded Buchanan's policy, but the president wanted Kansas a free-soil Democracy and pledged his support.[41]

Walker flitted between Kansas settlements to solicit free-soil voting in the June election for delegates to the constitutional convention. Free-soil leaders trusted neither Walker nor the legislature and called an election boycott that handed the convention to proslavery Democrats. Despite this setback, Walker focused on coaxing moderate free-state voters into the fall territorial elections, but James Lane spooked the governor with a radical town-charter movement, and Walker ordered the occupation of Lawrence by Cooke's dragoons on 15 July. Seven companies deployed around the town but encountered no "revolutionary proceedings."[42]

Appearing compulsive and foolish, Walker nonetheless felt besieged by radicals on both sides. The constitutional convention and its radical proslavery leadership lay beyond his legal control, while Lane reportedly was raising an insurrectionary army. Walker demanded Buchanan's unconditional support and two thousand regulars. Honest elections alone, he believed, would politically offset the controversial constitutional convention.[43]

In Walker's mind he could trust only the army. He threatened to resign in mid-July when Harney was assigned to the Utah Expedition; Buchanan, desiring a pacific Kansas, canceled the transfer. Throughout the summer Walker pestered Secretary of State Lewis Cass for troop reinforcements. Reiterating the president's fidelity, Cass promised Walker "a fully adequate" regular force. The War Department, however, lifted the Lawrence occupation and ordered the Second Dragoons to Utah in early September. An outraged Walker again threatened to quit.[44]

He stayed, however, and Secretary of War John B. Floyd delivered the promised troops, most of whom were concentrating at Fort Leavenworth for the spring campaign against the Mormons. On 10 September the governor announced his intention to guard "the polls against any attempt at insurrection or violence." Harney committed twenty-two companies, approximately nineteen hundred officers and men, or one-eighth of the army's strength, to constabulary duty. Heavy patrols watched the Missouri border while squadrons and companies policed polling stations.[45]

Walker's strategy worked. Free-soilers voted in droves and the Missourians stayed home, but proslavers still eked out a legislative majority. Free-state leaders accused Democrats of voter fraud. Indeed, Walker threw out illegal ballots in Johnson, Douglas, and McGee Counties, giving the legislature to free-staters. At Kickapoo and Marysville, desperate proslavery officials had induced a handful of regulars to cast ballots. Previous to the election, Walker concluded that regulars stationed at Fort Leavenworth "had a legal right to vote," but the law was unclear. The Kansas Organic Act forbade regulars from voting if military service alone brought them to Kansas, while Kansas territorial statutes set the legal qualification at six month's residence. Of two thousand regulars on patrol, only sixty to eighty voted, and Harney never mentioned the controversy.[46]

Proslavery Democrats still controlled the legal constitutional convention. When the delegates met at Lecompton in early November, six companies of First Cavalry under Major Sedgwick policed swirling, menacing free-state mobs. Supported by Walker, Superintendent John C. Calhoun, the convention manager, sought a plebiscite on two documents: a constitution with slavery and one without slavery. Taking control, radical slavocrats allowed a referendum only on the slavery clause. Otherwise the constitution left unmolested slave property already in Kansas and stipulated that Kansans could not amend the document until 1864. Twisting the knife, the convention also took the referendum from Walker's control.[47]

Angry, ill, and exhausted, the governor left Kansas in November 1857. On the twenty-sixth he explained to Buchanan the convention's mockery of popular sovereignty, but the president was adamant about submitting the Lecompton Constitution to Congress. Stalking out, Walker next conferred with Sen. Stephen H. Douglas to plot congressional resistance. On 21 December Republican and Democratic free-soilers boycotted the polls, again policed by regulars, and "Kansans" voted overwhelmingly to be a slave state.[48]

After Walker resigned, Acting Governor Stanton called a special session of the new free-state controlled territorial legislature, which enacted a plebiscite on the Lecompton instrument. An enraged Buchanan fired Stanton and replaced him with John W. Denver, an Indian commissioner and a Democratic-party regular. On 4 January 1858, with troops guarding the polls, nine thousand citizens voted against the Lecompton Constitution. After a fierce political struggle in both houses, Congress returned the document in the guise of a land-grant bill, which Kansans overwhelmingly rejected on 2 August 1858.[49]

Militant tensions relaxed in the Lawrence-Lecompton area after the new year, but bloody guerrilla violence erupted around Fort Scott in southeastern Kansas (see map 1). During 1856–57, proslavery partisans had driven out the free-soil minority and squatted on vacant homesteads. In subsequent claim-dispute cases, Democratic justice Joseph Williams always ruled against free-soilers. In summer 1857 James Montgomery organized antislavery partisans, the so-called Jayhawkers, to skirmish with proslavery guerrillas, evict proslavery settlers, and preside over squatter courts. By winter Jayhawker terror had brought southeast Kansas to a standstill.[50]

In late December 1857, the pleas of Justice Williams and Deputy Marshal John Little brought Major Sedgwick and three companies of the First Cavalry to Fort Scott. After soothing jangled nerves the regulars pulled out, and the Jayhawkers resurfaced to lynch, plunder, and burn out their enemies, even raiding Fort Scott itself in February 1858. Dispatched by Lt. Col. John Munroe, Capt. George T. Anderson led two companies of First Cavalry troopers to Fort Scott in mid-February. Little, Anderson, and the regulars responded vigorously to frequent Jayhawker alarms, but the brigands always vanished into the prairie.[51]

Governor Denver blamed unchecked Jayhawking on the "culpable neglect" of judges and peace officers. His requests for military reinforcements, however, fell on deaf ears in the Buchanan administration, which was consumed by the Lecompton Constitution and the Utah Expedition. At Fort Riley Bull Sumner wanted Anderson's two companies withdrawn. He seemed to think the captain, a Georgian, was seeking vengeance on free-soilers.[52]

Anderson got his chance on 21 April. That day, as Montgomery and seventeen guerrillas evicted proslavery settlers along the Marmaton River, a runner reported the depredations to Deputy Marshal Little at Fort Scott. Riding southward to investigate, Anderson's regulars surprised the brigands near the river. The Jayhawkers took cover in the timber along Yellow Paint Creek, and the captain ordered his twenty troopers to charge with pistols drawn. Free-soilers and regulars simultaneously fired a volley. Hit by balls, several cavalry mounts threw their riders; one trooper was killed outright and several others, Anderson included, were wounded. A cavalryman soon waved a white flag and the Jayhawkers slipped away.[53]

The humiliated Anderson now wanted to place southeast Kansas under martial law, but Munroe rejected the idea. Unlike Sumner, Sedgwick, Cooke, Wood, and other officers, Anderson had tried to shoot up the partisans and thus compromised the army's moral authority at Fort Scott. Harney replaced him with Captain Wood and added two sections of artillery and a company of the Second Dragoons to the Fort Scott detachment.[54]

Anderson returned to Fort Leavenworth under a cloud. Although withholding the source, Sumner informed him that someone was circulating "reports prejudicial to his reputation." Indeed, free-soilers in the Fort Scott area complained of threats, intimidation, and abuse from Anderson. His pride aching more than his wound, the captain applied for a court of inquiry but resigned his commission on 11 June 1858. Three years later he joined the Confederate army and became a reliable brigade commander under James Longstreet.[55]

The violence in southeast Kansas crescendoed during May and June. Charles Hamilton, a tall, handsome, violent Georgia aristocrat, led forty proslavery partisans into Blooming Grove, Kansas, and herded eleven free-soilers into a dry gulch off the Marais des Cygnes River. On Hamilton's order his guerrillas fired a volley that killed four men and wounded six. In quick retaliation Lane futilely marched his militia into Westport, Missouri, Hamilton's staging ground, while Montgomery's Jayhawkers sacked stores and homes from Lawrence to western Missouri. Near Blooming Grove Captain Wood's regulars dispersed a few Jayhawkers but made no arrests.[56]

The alarmed Governor Denver dispatched his aide-de-camp, 2nd Lt. Joseph P. Jones, to investigate southeast Kansas. The young regular, a North Carolinian, was awestruck by the devastation around Fort Scott. Between the Marais des Cygnes and Osage Rivers, guerrillas had robbed, plundered, or burned every single homestead, and dozens of proslavery families had fled to Missouri. Completely intimidated, marshals and sheriffs were impotent, and Justice Williams—"fiddling" Williams as he became known—disarmed and dispersed all settlers banded together for mutual protection. Too few in number, the regulars left many settlements exposed to partisan atrocity. Jones recommended withdrawing federal troops and arming a coalition of free-soil and proslavery moderates.[57]

By late spring the emboldened Montgomery captured a mail carrier bearing arrest warrants for him and several others to Governor Denver. Penning a letter, the abolitionist chieftain threatened to burn down Fort Scott if the governor did not withdraw the regulars and place the town under free-soil protection. On the night of 6 June, the Jayhawkers rolled a burning wagon against the Fort Scott Hotel, hid in a nearby ravine, and peppered away at regulars extinguishing the flames. Taking cover, the soldiers fired back. The hotel escaped the flames, and the Jayhawkers withdrew to the Marmaton River, the regulars following at a safe distance.[58]

Montgomery's attack brought Governor Denver south. As his carriage rolled toward Fort Scott, a lone horseman trotted up alongside and confessed to being James Montgomery. After some chitchat, Denver again refused his demands and Montgomery jogged away. The chaos and desolation shocked the governor. Jayhawkers had depopulated entire communities, and impoverished refugees jammed the streets of Fort Scott. Denver wrote, "The people seemed to have forgotten that they had a civil government." Denver promised energetic government to combat the gangs; Fort Scott residents promised to serve in posses and on juries. When peace was restored, Denver would withdraw federal troops.[59]

The governor left his pacification program in the hands of Capt. Nathaniel Lyon, a radical free-soiler who publicly despised Buchanan, Harney, and the slavocracy. During his watch, the proslavery–free-soil fusion reestablished government and peace around Fort Scott. Appearing only once, the Jayhawkers fired a few shots toward the regulars, but Lyon scattered them with an artillery round. In late June the Department of the West tried to transfer Lyon's companies to Minnesota, but Governor Denver's vigorous opposition forced the Buchanan administration to countermand the order. On 9 August, confident that peace would hold, Denver replaced the regulars at Fort Scott with mounted volunteers. After Kansans voted down the Lecompton Constitution, he resigned on 1 September 1858.[60]

Government at Fort Scott worked too well. When the county sheriff incarcerated Jayhawker Benjamin Rice for murder in early November 1858, his comrades rose again to plunder Linn and Bourbon Counties with impunity. Six weeks later a hundred Jayhawkers, led by Montgomery and augmented by John Brown's gang, rode into Fort Scott, released Rice, and fired into a few homes; a stray round killed Marshal Little. Despite citizen pleas, Acting Gov. Hugh Walsh refused to send regular troops and admonished the people to defend themselves.[61]

Walsh relinquished his office to a new territorial governor, Samuel Medary, on 18 December 1858. The citizens of Lykins County pleaded "in the name of High Heaven" for federal intervention, and a shaken Justice Williams urged a declaration of "martial law." Instead, Medary dispatched four companies of the First Cavalry to Fort Scott and Lieutenant Jones to Washington, D.C. Medary urged the release of six hundred muskets to volunteer companies and the appointment of Philip Colby to the federal marshalcy. Buchanan filled Medary's arms requisition, and heavily armed civilian posses drove the Jayhawker "horde" into hiding, Montgomery surrendering himself to a territorial commission. When John Brown liberated slaves from several west Missouri plantations in late January 1859, Deputy Marshal Colby and twenty-six regulars unsuccessfully dogged his trail toward Nebraksa.[62]

Frontier regulars in Kansas enjoyed an unusually long respite from constabulary duties until 1860. That fall the election of Abraham Lincoln emboldened Montgomery to threaten all federal officials who tried his Underground Railroad associates under the Fugitive Slave Act. Acting Gov. G. M. Beebe wrote, "Nothing short of the death of the ring-leader of the band will give quiet to the Country." He requested martial law and "three hundred" dragoons to eradicate the Jayhawkers. On 23 November 1860 Brigadier General Harney ordered Maj. Henry Wessells, commanding Fort Riley, to march dragoons and infantry to Fort Scott. A week later Harney joined him. Montgomery's band had broken up neither the land office nor the federal court, but the Jayhawkers had murdered seven men, and Justice Williams had fled into Missouri. Civil officers were issuing warrants for the killers.[63]

Regular troops, Lyon's company included, encamped near Mound City, Montgomery's headquarters, to help the federal marshal arrest the Jayhawkers. A Republican and Lincoln supporter by this time, Lyon was writing political columns for the *Western Kansas Express* in Manhattan and had joined the "Wide Awakes," a nationwide Republican political arm. He had cultivated a vitriolic hatred for Harney and was determined to redress federal injustices against free-soil Kansans. Risking court-martial and dismissal, Lyon tipped off Montgomery, Charles Jennison, and other Jayhawkers. The United States marshal and his military posse found neither the guerrillas nor their arms caches. The empty-handed Wessells left Lyon's company in Mound City. In his absence Lyon aided the free-soilers, even loaning federal horses to the Underground Railroad.[64]

Harney left Capt. William Steele in command of troops at Fort Scott, but in mid-December 1860 Steele wrote, "The opinion is prevalent that nothing can be done here but protect this town with the Land Office." No one had seen Montgomery, and by the end of the month, Justice Williams had decided to serve no warrants on any Jayhawker. Lyon relieved Steele and commanded an uneventful occupation of Fort Scott until he was called to defend the St. Louis Arsenal in early 1861.[65]

The military intervention in Kansas was the most blatant political manipulation of a field army during the interwar period. The deployment of United States troops to civil constabulary duty in Kansas was a serious investment of military manpower and political capital. Presidents Pierce and Buchanan tried to shape the political landscape of Kansas through the appointment of commanding officers and territorial governors. Both chief executives ultimately failed. No regular-army unit, no matter how many thousands of troops filled it and how many Smiths or Harneys officered it, was going to intimidate the free-soil majority and make Kansas a proslavery-dominated state.

The David Atchison machine operated to create a Democratic Kansas with slavery; individual officers of the U.S. Army helped thwart Atchison agents and supporters. The administration of Kansas by Pierce appointees generally disgusted regular-army officers including prosouthern ones such as Colonels Smith and Harney. Southern officers, excepting Captain Anderson, maintained a low profile in Kansas, but the operations of Colonel Sumner, Lieutenant Colonel Cooke, Major Sedgwick, and Captain Lyon undoubtedly—and sometimes consciously—aided the survival of free-soil settlers, their political party, and their cause. There was no organized regular-army conspiracy to create a free or slave Kansas, but the even-handed operations of regulars partially shielded the Free-Soil party and its followers from the heavy-handed policies of Democratic presidents Pierce and Buchanan and their most vicious appointees until the free-staters got the political upper hand in the territory during the winter of 1857–58.

The Kansas intervention probably damaged the army's reputation in the antislavery North. Serving two prosouthern presidents and several Democratic territorial administrations, the regular army became identified with the

South among free-soil activists and sympathizers. Chasing Jim Lane, Sam Walker, John Brown, James Montgomery, and the Jayhawkers, who were folk heroes to many northerners, cast suspicion on the loyalties of the regular army. When the Civil War broke out, loyal federal officers, especially those with a constabulary background in Kansas, had to battle the stigma of their service to the Pierce and Buchanan administrations.

10

SCHISM

The Frontier Army and the Civil War

THE election of Abraham Lincoln to the presidency on 6 November 1860 threw the nation into a panic. Associating his Republican party with abolition, southern states threatened secession. Although many pundits scoffed at the idea, many others—Commanding General Winfield Scott included—seriously listened and fretted. Better than any federal statesman, he knew the United States was unprepared militarily, politically, and ideologically for a war on the South, and he foresaw the likely schism of the regular army should the South leave the Union. The lurching, chaotic federal response to the early months of secession confirmed Scott's worries and left portions of the West vulnerable to Confederate seizure.

A Virginian by birth and a southerner by education, he knew that the South was earnest. As early as 29 October, Scott urged Pres. James P. Buchanan to reinforce federal installations "below New Orleans, at Mobile, at Pensacola, at Savannah, and at Charleston," but Buchanan feared that any federal reinforcement would precipitate war. As the secession winter grayed and then darkened, three cabinet members treaded water until their states seceded. One was Secretary of War John B. Floyd of Virginia, who probably pocketed Scott's recommendations and ran military affairs without him.[1]

When Scott dispatched Maj. Robert Anderson, a Kentucky Unionist, to command the Union harbor defenses at Charleston, South Carolina, in November, he had no instructions from the administration to transmit. On 20 December South Carolina seceded from the Union, and Anderson withdrew the Fort Moultrie garrison to Fort Sumter. Scott and other Unionists praised his resolve, but Secretary Floyd and administration southerners flew into a rage. Disgraced by financial scandal, however, Floyd resigned on 29 December, and by the second week of January 1861, the departure of most remaining southerners left the Buchanan cabinet in Unionist hands.

Scott's recommendations impressed the pro-Union cabinet. Buchanan sent a relief ship to Fort Sumter, ordered the defense of Forts McRae and Pickens at Pensacola, Florida, removed archsoutherner Maj. Pierre G. T. Beauregard from the West Point superintendency, and rescinded Floyd's orders to transfer cannon from Pittsburgh to forts in Mississippi and Texas.[2] At the same time, Scott contacted the incoming Lincoln administration and consulted with William Seward, Edwin Stanton, and Charles Sumner. The general-in-chief prepared the security for Lincoln's trip from Springfield to Washington and hired Pinkerton detectives to ferret out potential assassins.[3]

From Springfield, Illinois, to Harrisburg, Pennsylvania, the president-elect was guarded by four Republican army officers including Col. Edwin V. "Bull" Sumner. During the trip, Pinkerton agents uncovered an assassination plot in Baltimore and urged Lincoln to pass unnoticed through the city to Washington. Skulking was cowardice to Bull Sumner, who proposed carving safe passage with cavalry sabers, but slipping Sumner's tyrannical grasp, Lincoln reached the nation's capital during the night under Pinkerton care.

Scott and Sumner also coordinated the inauguration-day security. On 4 March 1861 President Buchanan picked up President-elect Lincoln at the Willard Hotel. Army engineers led and loyal Washington volunteers escorted their carriage down Pennsylvania Avenue to the Capitol. On a parallel street, Scott commanded regular cavalry and artillery units. Sumner's cavalry guarded the cross streets. Perched on rooftops, sharpshooters watched the crowds. Secessionists had threatened disruptions, but Lincoln was peacefully sworn in by Chief Justice Roger B. Taney, the author of the Dred Scott Decision.[4]

In the meantime, southern officers defected to the Confederacy. Adj. Gen. Samuel Cooper, a New Yorker by birth but southerner by marriage, resigned three days after Lincoln took office. Only ten months after his promotion to brigadier general and quartermaster general, Joseph E. Johnston left the U.S. Army when Virginia seceded in April 1861. Both officers bore invaluable knowledge of Union army organization and logistics to the Confederacy. No other bureau commanders defected to the southern service.

No resignation pained Scott more than that of Robert E. Lee. Returning from Texas on 1 March 1861, Lee probably told Scott that he would follow his home state. While Virginia delegates sat in secret session in mid-April, the Lincoln administration offered Lee the command of seventy-five thousand troops at the rank of major general, but he would not make war on the South. During a personal interview, Scott declared, "Lee, you have made the greatest mistake of your life; but I feared it would be so." Virginia seceded on 19 April. The next day Lee wrote Scott, "Save in defense of my native State, I never desire again to draw my sword."[5]

Virginians now expected General Scott, a native son, to fly across the Potomac to their defense. However, he had never owned slaves, now claimed New York as his home, and remained "stubbornly loyal to the Union." During fifty-three years of federal service, he had fought southern Democrats tooth-and-nail and would desert neither the Union nor its army. After Scott rebuffed a Virginia delegation sent to lure him south on 20 April, he was burned in effigy at the University of Virginia. Scott's nephew, Col. Joseph W. Harper, ordered slaves to destroy his portrait at the family home.[6]

The Union paid a heavy price for Buchanan's procrastination. The federal government lost forts and arsenals throughout the South. While Scott recalled regiments from western stations, he tried to prevent the loss of western territories to the Confederacy. The vacillation of some officers, the treachery of others, and the incompetence of still more jeopardized the hold of the Union over Missouri, Texas, and New Mexico. However, the vigorous measures of loyal officers salvaged most of the West for the federal government.

On 15 December 1860 Brig. Gen. David E. Twiggs arrived in San Antonio to relieve Lt. Col. Robert E. Lee in the Department of Texas. The seventy-year-old Twiggs, a Georgian, hated General-in-Chief Scott and had no stomach for serving a Republican president. In his mind Union collapse and Texas secession were imminent, and he may have come to San Antonio with a mind to surrender the department to Texas secessionists.[7]

For a month the paralyzed Buchanan administration left Twiggs uninstructed despite his entreaties from the Texas frontier. Finally, he resigned his commission, requested a berth in the Georgia state militia in mid-January, and awaited his relief by the Department of War.[8] A week later, while a Texas convention pondered secession, Twiggs threatened to surrender "arms and other property" to state agents upon Texas's departure. Now in Unionist hands, the Buchanan administration officially relieved Twiggs in late January and scrambled to extract "five companies of artillery" stationed on the lower Rio Grande. On 1 February the convention overwhelmingly passed a secession ordnance.[9] Twiggs's headquarters ordered an inventory of all "munitions of war" and "quartermaster's stores" in the department and appointed three officers to confer with Texas commissioners, but talks broke down. Two weeks later Twiggs received the order relieving him.[10]

During the night Texas state troops under Col. Ben McCulloch occupied San Antonio and surrounded Twiggs's headquarters and the federal arsenal. Lacking the inclination to resist them, the general capitulated. Former major Earl Van Dorn and 1st Lt. John B. Hood, both archsoutherners, rejoiced, but Twiggs's surrender shocked pro-Union and most pro-Confederate army officers. On his way to Washington, Lee pulled into San Antonio the same day. Tears filling his eyes, he asked a female acquaintance, "Has it come so soon as this?" and escaped the occupied city.[11]

Twiggs's replacement, Col. Carlos A. Waite, a New Yorker, arrived in San Antonio from the Texas frontier on 18 February. His 2,684 regulars were strung out from the Gulf of Mexico to El Paso to Indian Territory. Waite planned to embark most of them for the East at Brazos Santiagos and at Indianola. However, slowing the withdrawal were Texas seizures of arms, livestock, wagons, and other property including a $30,000 army payroll.[12] By early May, around 2,100 troops had sailed for the East. When Confederates fired on Fort Sumter, Texans captured approximately 400 soldiers in and around San Antonio. Officers were soon paroled but enlisted men were held, some until 1863; none deserted to the Confederacy.[13]

Twiggs's capitulation lost the Union "15,000 stands of arms, 80,000 pieces of ordnance, 1,200 horses, $55,000 in specie, plus mules, wagons, tents, provender and munitions of war." The general also handed over 2,600 men and nineteen posts. On 1 March President Buchanan cashiered Twiggs "for his treachery to the flag of his country." Returning to New Orleans, the general promised to settle the score with Buchanan in Pennsylvania by personal combat. However, he was the oldest officer to defect to the Confederate army, and his infirmities kept him from the field. After briefly commanding the district of Louisiana, he retired to a farm near Augusta, Georgia, where he died on 15 July 1862. His family interred him on his childhood farm.[14]

The Union surrender emboldened Texans to go on the offensive to the north. Anticipating their maneuver, General-in-Chief Scott dispatched Lt. Col. William H. Emory of the First Cavalry to concentrate all federal troops in Indian Territory at Fort Washita. If Arkansas seceded, the Fort Smith garrison should relocate beyond that state's borders. Emory, a Marylander, was the nation's preeminent military geographer-explorer. His parents were wealthy plantation- and slaveowners, and he counted Jefferson Davis among his closest friends. Like many southern officers, he had decided to follow his native state's fortunes.[15]

Lieutenant Colonel Emory left Washington by stage on 22 March and traveled by steamer from Memphis, Tennessee, south down the Mississippi River and northwest up the Arkansas. Earlier in March Arkansans had rejected secession, but pro-Confederate sentiment was strong in the flatland south. While en route, Emory ordered troops at Fort Arbuckle to fall back to Washita and the commanding officer at Fort Cobb to march a company to Fort Washita. On 13 April 1861 reports of the Confederate bombardment of Fort Sumter reached Fort Smith, Arkansas. Secession hysteria swept the state, and as Scott and Emory had feared, pro-Confederate Arkansans confiscated a year's worth of federal supplies destined for Fort Smith.[16]

The outbreak of war prompted Emory, by then at Fort Smith, to request his own recall to Washington, D.C. Northern officers such as Capt. Samuel D. Sturgis, commanding Fort Smith, justifiably questioned his loyalties. In the meantime, Emory rode alone at night 150 miles southwestward to Fort Washita, Indian Territory. On 23 April at 9:00 P.M., just ahead of Arkansas volunteers, Sturgis brought out the Fort Smith garrison, two companies of First Cavalry, and left behind "the ordnance sergeant, hospital steward, chief bugler, sick and laundresses." His command reached Fort Washita a week later.[17]

In the wake of the Confederate bombardment of Fort Sumter, Texas secession and Arkansas waffling jeopardized the military frontier in the Indian Territory. On 17 April General Scott ordered the withdrawal of the garrisons there to Fort Leavenworth and cast about for an officer to bear his instructions through Missouri and Arkansas. His aides—Maj. Irvin McDowell and Maj. Fitz-John Porter—plucked Lt. William W. Averell of the Mounted Riflemen from a game of billiards at the Willard Hotel to undertake the mission.[18]

On the afternoon of 17 April, dressed in civilian clothes, Averell secretly left Washington for St. Louis. At Rolla, Missouri, he changed into "a good suit of butternut clothing" and boarded the stage to Fort Smith, which he reached four days after Sturgis's evacuation. Chaotic Confederate militia jammed the streets, but Averell got away on a frisky horse, followed the road to Fort Washita, dragged his exhausted mount through the San Bois Mountains, and skirted Perryville. On the road south from deserted Fort Arbuckle, he encountered the vanguard of Emory's retreating column. Capt. Eugene A. Carr, who did not recognize Averell, conducted him to Emory. Averell recalled, "The Colonel was in the saddle, looking as grim as a grizzly bear." When the astonished Emory recognized the weary rider, Sturgis, Carr, David Stanley, and other officers rode over to greet Averell. After delivering his dispatches, the lieutenant dismounted and fainted.[19]

Anticipating Scott's orders, Emory had initiated the withdrawal of the Washita garrison toward Fort Arbuckle on 16 April. In the wake of Twiggs's treason, the captains of the First Cavalry agreed to arrest their colonel should he betray any sign of surrendering to Texas militia, four thousand strong, who were following only a day behind. After gathering troops from Forts Cobb and Arbuckle, Emory's force—six companies of the Fourth Cavalry, five of the First Infantry, and "150 women, children, teamsters, and other non-combatants"—fell back toward Fort Leavenworth, guided by Delaware scouts Possum and Black Beaver.[20]

During the retreat, Emory's scouts reported four "escaped slaves" from the "Chickasaw Nation" trailing the column at some distance. Thrown into "a great stew," Emory envisioned his court-martial for violating the Fugitive Slave Act. He loosed "the camp followers"—gamblers and other riffraff—to capture them and collect the reward money. However, the African Americans heroically beat off their assailants, one man dying in the melee. The news stunned and disgusted Emory's officers, and Captain Stanley threatened to charge Emory with accessory to the murder. The assault had taken place in free-soil Kansas, and one African American was a legally free man. In concert with Capt. Delos B. Sackett, Emory approached Stanley, and all agreed to say "nothing about the matter."[21]

The following day Emory received another shock: The president had accepted his resignation. Before leaving for Indian Territory, the lieutenant colonel had placed his resignation letter with his wife, father-in-law, and brother. When the Sixth Massachusetts Regiment fired on pro-Confederate rioters in Baltimore on 19 April, brother John assumed Maryland would secede and forwarded the letter to the War Department without consulting Emory. On the Kansas prairies, Emory's officers let him lead the column to Fort Leavenworth. To honor his appeal regimental officers signed a petition requesting Emory's reinstatement. Indeed, President Lincoln reappointed Emory partly as a gesture of good will to his powerful family and the people of Maryland, a critical border state. Emory went on to become an accomplished Union combat officer.[22]

In January 1861 Col. Albert Sidney Johnston took command of the Department of the Pacific from the deceased Col. Newman S. Clarke. Outside some minor Indian unrest, Johnston's department was quiet. He had 2,245 men present for duty in California, Oregon, and Washington. Rumors of secessionist conspiracies flitted about Johnston during January and February, but nothing came of them.[23]

That Johnston, a southerner by birth, intended to seize arms and Alcatraz for the Confederacy was just one fantastic story among many. To the contrary, he mounted all available artillery at Fort Point overlooking the harbor entrance, moved "10,000 rifled muskets, accouterments [*sic*] and ammunition" to Alcatraz, and garrisoned that island with 120 regulars. However, the Texas surrender put Johnston, a former Texas planter, under suspicion in panic-stricken Washington, D.C.[24]

To investigate conditions in California, General-in-Chief Scott dispatched Edwin V. Sumner, one of his trusted protégés. During the secession winter, Sumner's own loyalties had come under the scrutiny of Republican witch hunters, who probably recalled his dispersal of the Kansas free-state government in 1856, but Lincoln acknowledged his fealty with promotion to brigadier general—Twiggs's slot.[25] Leaving on 1 April, Sumner traveled anonymously through Panama to California, probably passing Johnston's resignation letter in transit. Landing in San Francisco three-and-a-half weeks later, Sumner relieved Johnston, reported California tranquil, praised the Texan's administration, and recommended Col. George Wright, Sumner's brother-in-law, for the Pacific command.[26]

This secret mission dishonored Johnston, who afterward took his family to Los Angeles. When the Lincoln administration learned of his fortification of the San Francisco harbor, it hoped to win him back, but his resignation was approved in early May, and Scott ordered his arrest should he try to cross the Far Southwest to Texas. Indeed, at the end of June, Johnston left Warner's Ranch with thirty-three men including Lewis A. Armistead, Aaron B. Hardcastle, and six other former officers. Through scorching summer heat, they marched over the Mojave Desert to Pima Village, thence to Tucson, and finally entered Mesilla, where they linked up with Lt. Col. John Baylor's Texans, who had just captured federal troops northeast of Fort Fillmore. Johnston traveled on to Richmond, Virginia, and became a full general in the regular Confederate army.[27]

Although little worried about the Confederate threat in California, Sumner nevertheless isolated pockets of southern sympathizers. He drilled the California militia, concentrated troops near Los Angeles, spied on suspicious ships and persons, rooted out known traitors, participated in Union rallies, and made all officers sign the oath of allegiance, a Lincoln policy. By June his vigorous measures had pushed Confederate sympathizers into Nevada and Southern California.[28]

At Los Angeles Capt. Winfield Scott Hancock faced the strongest den of California secessionists. A good friend to the South, Hancock blamed secession on the North and raised no hand to stop the Johnston party. He had parted sorrowfully from his best friend, Maj. Lewis A. Armistead, whom Hancock's own Union troops would mortally wound at Gettysburg two years later. A staunch Unionist nonetheless, Hancock organized and armed loyalists to hold local Confederates at bay until the arrival of the First Dragoons from Forts Mojave and Tejon.[29]

Sumner was irked by the "arrival" of southern officers on leave from "remote" posts in Oregon, Washington, and California. He ordered Colonel Wright to grant no leave until the president approved an officer's resignation. At Fort Crook, California, Capt. John Adams filed his resignation on 31 May 1861 but did not leave California until late July.[30] Posted to San Juan Island, Capt. George Pickett of Virginia tendered his resignation on 20 June 1861 but did not reach Richmond, Virginia, until mid-September.[31] Sumner's policy, although inconvenient, did not stop the hemorrhage. His son-in-law and aide-de-camp, Armistead L. Long, resigned on 10 June and went on to become Lee's military secretary in the Army of Northern Virginia. Sumner's own adjutant, Capt. William W. Mackall of Maryland, resigned on 3 July and rose to chief of staff for both Braxton Bragg and Joseph E. Johnston in the Army of Tennessee.[32]

Too old and weak to command, General-in-Chief Scott reached to the Pacific Coast for his replacement, Henry W. "Old Brains" Halleck, a California lawyer and land baron. An ex-regular-army officer, Halleck had published *Elements of Military Art and Science* in 1846, impressing Scott with his grasp of the theory and practice of war. A Democrat, Halleck hoped that the war would not become an antislavery crusade. He reached the East in fall 1861 and eventually became a problematic general-in-chief of the Union armies.[33]

Northern officers stationed on the Pacific Coast also chomped at the bit to reach the eastern theater of war. At Fort Yamhill in northwest Oregon, 1st Lt. Phil Sheridan anxiously awaited his summons. Frontier rumors wildly embellished the conflict: "Forty thousand men killed and wounded, and none were reported missing nor as having run away." In September 1861 he received a captain's commission in the regular army and a desk job in Missouri, although he later rose to military immortality assailing Missionary Ridge in Tennessee and the Shenandoah Valley in Virginia.[34]

No officer pined for an eastern field command more than George Wright, colonel of the Ninth Infantry and commander of the Department of Oregon. While the Department of War ignored his request for higher rank and reassignment, it promoted and transferred younger officers below him in rank. Smoldering with resentment, Wright blamed Scott for his banishment. In fact, Brig. Gen. John Denver, former Democratic governor of Kansas Territory, was slated to take over the Department of the Pacific, but Sumner distrusted him and recommended Wright for the Pacific command. Promoted to brigadier general of volunteers, Wright never went east again and died in a shipwreck off the coast of northern California in summer 1865.[35]

Upon landing in California, Sumner immediately requested an eastern command. A forty-two-year veteran, the sixty-four-year-old soldier passionately loved the Union and the regular army, and he burned to erase the dishonor of his two sons-in-law, 1st Lt. Armistead L. Long and Capt. Eugene E. McLean, both of whom had defected to the Confederacy. Brought east in October 1861, Sumner was one of the Republican generals Lincoln posted around Maj. Gen. George B. McClellan and fought gallantly in the Peninsular Campaign, the Seven Days' Battles, Antietam, and Fredericksburg. At sixty-six years the oldest corps commander in the Union army, he asked to be relieved after the Union carnage at Fredericksburg and died in Syracuse, New York, on 21 March 1863. A steady hand and a hard fighter, Bull Sumner represented the best the antebellum regulars gave to their government and nation.[36]

Col. Thomas T. Fauntleroy of the First Dragoons resigned his commission in March 1861 and handed the Department of New Mexico to a Floridian, Col. William W. Loring of the Mounted Riflemen. Despite bad departmental credit, unpaid troops, Indian wars, and many resignations, he thought affairs "tranquil enough," but Unionists doubted Loring's loyalty and feared a repetition of the Texas surrender. At one conference Loring told his officers that he would join the Confederacy but honor his federal commission until then.[37]

If there was any secessionist conspiracy in New Mexico, Maj. Henry H. Sibley was one of the orchestrators. He penned his resignation at Taos in late April and first embraced "the glorious banner of the Confederate States of America" a month later. From El Paso he encouraged Loring to permit Confederate seizures of federal military stores in southern New Mexico. However, on 11 June Loring relinquished the department to Col. Edward R. S. Canby and traveled south to Fort Fillmore. Sibley's letter fell into the hands of Canby, who futilely ordered the arrest of all suspected conspirators including Colonel Loring.[38]

The real threat to New Mexico was military invasion from Confederate Texas. Canby concentrated all federal troops in southern New Mexico at Fort Fillmore near Mesilla. By the end of June, Maj. Isaac Lynde commanded seven companies of the Seventh Infantry and 99 Mounted Riflemen, but paralyzed with fear he made no military preparations to receive the Texans gathering at El Paso during the month of July. Forty-five miles away, Confederate lieutenant colonel John R. Baylor decided to launch 258 men toward Fort Fillmore on the night of 23 July, but a deserter gave away their approach. After scouting Baylor's position at Mesilla, Lynde half-heartedly attacked with six companies of infantry and two of Mounted Rifles on 25 July. Under cover in "jacals and cornfields," the Texans easily repulsed the regulars, and Lynde led his troops back to Fort Fillmore.[39]

Baylor intended to bombard Fillmore, which was surrounded by hills, but the terrified Lynde ordered the fort burned, and his troops marched toward Fort Stanton on 27 June. Heat and thirst knocked infantrymen out of line near San Agustín Pass, and Baylor's Texans cut off the retreat. A beaten man, Lynde considered his situation "hopeless" and capitulated to Baylor. His officers protested, but Lynde's adjutant, a Confederate sympathizer, kept on copying down the terms. The major surrendered 476 officers and men.

After Lt. Alfred Gibbs of the Mounted Riflemen was paroled, he made his way to Missouri and charged Lynde with dereliction of duty and cowardice in the face of the enemy. By order of the president, Major Lynde was dropped from the army rolls for abandoning his post and surrendering his men to an inferior insurgent force. His inept command had opened the Southwest to the Confederacy.[40]

Nowhere in the trans-Mississippi West were the military stakes of secession higher than in St. Louis, where Brig. Gen. William S. Harney and Capt. Nathaniel Lyon sparred for the reins of the Department of the West. During his years of regular-army service, Harney had made his home in St. Louis and had married into the Mullanphy family, aristocratic, prosouthern, and slaveholding. He was an iron-willed Unionist, but his southern Democratic politics made him suspect in Republican circles. His hawkish diplomacy and boorish insubordination in the Department of Oregon had triggered his recall and humiliation in 1859. Now he wanted peace and appreciation, but the Department of War unwittingly cast him into a boiling cauldron of the early Civil War.[41]

The state of Missouri occupied a precarious place during the secession crisis. Slave owners were a small minority in the state, but secessionism dominated rural Missouri. Tied to the Northeast by the railroad, St. Louis was the state's commercial and urban center. Its large population of Germans and other European immigrants were staunch Unionists and free-labor partisans. Heating up in early 1861, the struggle for St. Louis dramatized that rural-urban and ethnic division.[42]

Commanding the Department of the West from St. Louis, Harney acted with uncharacteristic restraint. In his eyes Missouri would remain loyal so long as no arbitrary federal coercion drove its citizens into the Confederacy. Secessionists inside and outside Missouri, however, hoped to arm Confederate troops with rifles, cartridges, powder, field batteries, and heavy guns housed in the St. Louis Arsenal. In late January 1861 Scott instructed Harney to "give particular attention" to the arsenal's defense and to post Capt. Nathaniel Lyon's company of the Second Infantry there. Some five hundred radical secessionists had organized themselves into "Minute Men" and boasted of capturing the installation. Commanding the arsenal guard, Capt. Thomas "Fightin' Tom" Sweeny declared, "I'll blow it [the arsenal] up and you with it before I surrender; there are only forty of us to die."[43]

During January, prosouthern governor Claiborne F. Jackson pushed Missouri toward disunion. The state legislature called for the election of delegates to a secession convention and promised to resist any federal coercion of the South. Gen. Daniel M. Frost of the state militia convinced Maj. William H. Bell, the arsenal commander and a North Carolinian, to surrender the post and its weapons upon Missouri's demand.[44]

The arsenal's vulnerability alarmed Frank P. Blair Jr., a scion of the influential Republican Blairs. Frank helped create "Union Clubs"—all predominantly German in membership—and secretly drilled and armed the men, while his brother, Postmaster General Montgomery Blair, secured Bell's removal. However, Bell's replacement, Capt. Peter V. Hagner, was another southern sympathizer and forbade the augmentation of arsenal defenses. Arriving on 7 February, Lyon immediately clashed with Hagner, but Harney supported the arsenal commander. While appealing to the War Department, Lyon aided Blair's pro-Union militia.[45]

Harney downplayed the Confederate danger. Secessionists were "a decided minority in St. Louis," and the Union militia outnumbered the Minute Men by almost three to one. By mid-February, under Scott's order, the arsenal garrison had increased to 488 officers and men. Sharing none of Harney's complacency, Blair and Lyon labeled most Missouri Unionism "conditional" and undependable, and the Minute Men daily provoked fights with the Union guard. Under Blair family pressure, however, the new Lincoln administration placed Captain Lyon in command of arsenal defenses. Piqued by the order, Harney put the ordnance department firmly in Hagner's hands.[46]

The Harney-Lyon battle escalated. The general worried that Lyon would provoke a war and tried to banish him to Fort Leavenworth, but he about-faced when the Republicans lost control of city government to the conservative Constitutional Unionists—secessionists to his mind. Harney kept Lyon at the arsenal, instructed him to strengthen defenses, and ordered Hagner to fill Lyon's requisitions. In early April the regulars erected platforms, reinforced them with sandbags, and placed artillery pieces at commanding points. Captain Sweeney wrote, "We *may* get whipped, but we'll see."[47]

Still, Harney soft-pedaled the secessionist threat. Neither the Confederate bombardment of Fort Sumter, Governor Jackson's refusal to fill Lincoln's militia requisition, nor Unionist pleas in St. Louis invigorated Harney's defense of the arsenal and the federal position in the state. He explained to Lt. John Schofield, "Why, the State has not yet passed an ordnance of secession; she has not gone out of the Union." In Schofield's opinion "Harney's Union principles" were unequal to the critical "situation." Indeed, pro-Confederates seized the arsenal at Liberty, Missouri, and under pressure from General Frost, Jackson ordered state troops to assemble at convenient locations.[48]

Lyon and Blair took matters into their own hands. On 16 April and behind Harney's back, Lyon contacted Illinois governor Richard Yates to request that his militia be prepared to receive arsenal arms and deploy to St. Louis. Traveling to Washington, Blair successfully lobbied for Hagner's removal, and the arsenal command fell fully to Lyon. On 21 April the Lincoln administration removed Brigadier General Harney and recalled him to Army Headquarters in Washington, General Scott's office. While en route, Harney's train was stopped and boarded by Virginia Confederates, who tried to woo him with a high command, but he resolutely refused and his train went on. Despite his loyalty, the Confederate interview probably weakened his credibility with the Lincoln administration.[49]

In Harney's absence Captain Lyon took over St. Louis. By seniority departmental command went to Col. Edward B. Alexander several weeks away at Fort Laramie. The adjutant general wrote Lyon, however, "The Secretary of War directs that you execute immediately the order previously given to arm loyal citizens." The captain soon had three thousand troops under arms and the authority to declare "martial law in the city." By 8 May at Camp Jackson in west St. Louis, the state militia numbered seven hundred men and officers. That same day Frost received cannon and ammunition captured at the Baton Rouge Arsenal.[50]

Lyon set out to subdue the secessionists. The next day, disguised as a woman, he scouted their position from a barouche and later learned that Harney, reinstated by Scott, would arrive in St. Louis in two days. On 10 May in midafternoon, seven thousand Union troops converged on Camp Jackson. Lyon gave General Frost, a West Point classmate, thirty minutes to surrender. About the same time, a freak horse kick incapacitated Lyon, and one-armed Captain Sweeny took over. His militia surrounded, outnumbered, and outgunned, Frost soon relented, and the Unionists confiscated three 32-pounder guns, one mortar, three mortar beds, shot and shells, 1,200 rifle muskets, 6 field pieces, 25 kegs of powder, 30 to 40 horses, camp equipments, and baggage.[51]

Lyon's Unionists marched "some 50 officers and 639 men" toward the arsenal. William T. Sherman, an eyewitness, recalled that angry men and women crowded, cursed, and jostled the Union volunteers, especially the Germans. In the midst of the tumult, a drunken spectator fired a shot and the volunteers returned fire. When Lyon and the regulars reestablished order, twenty-five civilians and one volunteer lay dead. Lyon paroled the Missouri militia the following day.[52]

Brigadier General Harney returned to a tense St. Louis on 11 May. Although he detested Lyon, he officially approved his "conduct" at Camp Jackson, but the general issued a conciliatory proclamation and promised federal noninterference in state and city affairs. Testing Harney, the Missouri legislature subjected every "able-bodied" man to state military service and gave the governor absolute control over the militia. To Harney the bill was an "indirect secession ordinance," and he promised to smash any state treason. With Blair's endorsement, Harney requested authority to raise a regiment of Irish volunteers to offset local prejudice against the Germans.[53]

Harney acknowledged that "loyal men" were suffering secessionist violence but still prosecuted a peace policy. On 21 May in St. Louis, he signed a joint proclamation with Sterling Price, major general of the Missouri militia. Price promised to quell disruptive secessionists and unionists, while Harney promised to refrain from any sudden "military movements" so long as state troops were pacific. Governor Jackson and Major General Price, however, were merely buying time to strengthen and arm the Missouri militia for secession.[54]

Harney seemed satisfied with Missouri neutrality, but stories of secessionist atrocities poured into Blair's and Lyon's headquarters. In Washington, D.C., the Lincoln administration, discomfited with the Harney-Price accord, thought Missouri "too far committed to secession." On 16 May General Scott drafted an order to remove Harney, and Lincoln reluctantly commissioned Frank Blair to invoke the order at his discretion. Blair never doubted the general's loyalty but distrusted his political judgment. When Harney declined the services of fully armed Union Zouaves, Blair dispatched an agent to deliver Special Order No. 135 relieving Harney of departmental command.[55]

Although dumbfounded, Harney retired to his farm in Jefferson County. A week later, declaring himself a "true and loyal soldier," he bitterly wrote, "My countrymen will be slow to believe that I have chosen this portion of my career to damn with treason my life." To mend his honor, he requested a Pacific command, but Harney remained unassigned until his retirement in 1863.[56]

Departmental command devolved on Lyon, now a brigadier general of volunteers. His force totaled ten thousand men, while Price's state militia numbered one thousand men poorly armed. Fearing Lyon's wrath, Jackson and

Price met with him and Blair at the Planter's House on 11 June. If Lyon confined his volunteers to areas they already occupied, Jackson pledged to enforce Missouri neutrality and disband his home guard. Recalling state treachery, however, Lyon would tolerate no curbs on Union power and replied that he would visit war on every man, woman, and child to enforce federal supremacy. He grabbed his hat, wheeled around, and stalked from the room. Jackson, Price, and Blair had witnessed the coming fury of the Civil War. Two months later, while leading a federal charge, Brigadier General Lyon was shot off his horse at the Battle of Wilson's Creek in southwestern Missouri. He was the Civil War's first Union martyr.[57]

Nathaniel Lyon represented a new kind of professional soldier. The nation-state was his master; his loyalty was to the federal government alone. In his mind the Union army—regulars and volunteers—was an instrument of the federal will. Ahead of his time, General Lyon was willing to enforce national authority against white citizens—that is, to kill rebels and destroy property—in their home states. The unconditional federal loyalty of soldiers such as Lyon and Sumner, however, was the exception in the U.S. Army. In early 1861 most Union officers, whether of southern or northern origin, were ideologically and legally uncertain about how aggressively and violently they should prosecute a civil war against other white Americans to preserve the Union. During the first two years of the conflict, their indecision weakened the federal defense of the American West and Union cause generally.

By custom and indoctrination, the U.S. Army, like its federal government, had tread lightly on and around states' rights. In antebellum America state sovereignty was generally inviolable or sacred. Unclear to commissioned officers such as Harney, Twiggs, and Emory was whether they could legally lead their troops into battle against states that wanted to expel federal agencies, the army included, and secede from the Union. Nor did subordinates know whether they could arrest superior officers who negotiated with secessionists or refused to defend federal sovereignty with vigor. Although northern and southern officers deplored Twiggs's surrender of the Department of Texas, no one—not even hard-core Unionists—organized to arrest him or the Texas commissioners or to stop their proceedings. Nor did Colonel Waite and pro-Union officers seem to consider seriously shooting down Texas secessionists to defend United States installations, property, and honor. Ideological and legal deficiencies undermined federal and army resolve in Texas, Indian Territory, New Mexico, and Missouri.

The experience of armed constabulary duty on the interwar frontier added almost no spine to departmental commanders contending with determined secessionist threats. Regular troops across the West had operated to quell civil disturbances, but in nearly all instances, unit commanders only threatened armed force to disperse the mobs. Race helped identify legitimate human targets. In California, Kansas, Texas, and Utah, the civilian agents of lawless enterprises and uprisings were generally white Euroamericans whom the national government and its standing army—comprised of free white males—resisted shooting down to enforce federal law. White or Anglo ethnicity likewise protected southern secessionists in Missouri, Indian Territory, and Texas, or complicated the act of their suppression by regular officers and enlisted men. Nearly four years of bloody civil war were necessary to galvanize the American people and the army into unleashing the full fury of federal sovereignty—political and military—on the South.

The Lincoln administration turned over the military West largely to volunteer troops during the Civil War. George Wright, James H. Carleton, and other western commanders fought Confederate troops and Indians with citizen soldiers. While holding the Texans at bay in southern New Mexico during the war, the federal government continued developing the social, political, and economic resources of the American West.[58] Handing over their frontier posts to western volunteers, regular troops marched eastward to wage war on the Confederate army. Around these regular units, the Lincoln administration built the Union army, which brought the South to its knees after four years of grisly war.

CONCLUSION

THE interwar army's experience of small wars, counterinsurgencies, and constabulary duty was not an aberration but the norm in the United States Army's history. Conventional wars such as the War of 1812, the Mexican-American War, and the Civil War were temporary diversions from the army's traditional mission of policing the frontier, suppressing internal resistance, and enforcing national sovereignty. The United States was an expanding nation whose people demanded the elimination of all geographical and human obstacles to Euroamerican progress in the West. On the antebellum frontier, the regular army was the most active federal agent of political and cultural incorporation.

The North American frontier, a zone of military and cultural conflict, pitted Euroamericans against American Indians and sometimes Euroamericans against one another. The American people insisted that their standing army make war on American Indians and crush social and political rebels, but Congress and its constituency were loath to back the army's war effort with adequate financial, human, and logistical tools to execute its mission against American Indians and other resistance to frontier expansion, national sovereignty, and federal law. Lawmakers and their constituencies never acknowledged that the American frontier was in a state of war and that the suppression of indigenous populations and their incorporation was a martial campaign of terror. Instead, they considered the Indians a savage roadblock to progress, and the federal government deployed regular troops, however inadequately prepared, to remove the obstruction.

The regular army coped with and overcame cultural prejudice, institutional deficiencies, western geography, and indigenous military resistance by improvising tactics that escalated levels of state-sanctioned violence. Army strategy was one of total warfare against American Indian people and their resources. Regular troops stole up on Indian camps and villages and killed as many people and destroyed as much food stores and personal belongings as possible before retiring from the field. Infantry units such as those at Blue Water and Spokane Plain conducted some combat operations, but dragoons, cavalry, and mounted rifles, each operating as frontier rangers, were the staple army combat unit in western warfare. When they targeted a specific American Indian population, the regulars' maneuvers resembled a partisan raid—a swift, bloody assault designed to inflict maximum damage, casualties, and terror in the shortest possible time. The Euroamerican hope was that the Indians would stop raiding white settlements or relocate to a federal reservation.

To some degree the bloodletting of frontier warfare revolted the United States Army officer corps. Since the Enlightenment, the western European military ethic advocated conflict between professional armies that applied the principles of war in clearly demarcated combat zones. Armed conflict between gentlemen-scientists would create a controlled combat environment that contained the violence and destruction to the battlefield. On the North American frontier, Indian warriors and Euroamerican soldiers—militia and professional—fought in ill-defined fields of war, targeted settlements and villages, and killed women and children. Total warfare between Euroamericans and American Indians seemed less a military science practiced by educated gentlemen than a blood sport indulged by benighted savages.

Frontier raiding and sacking also seemed unbecoming of the modern nation-state, particularly one such as the United States predicated on the rule of law. However, western terrain, distances, and culture drove the U.S. Army to transform its troops and tactics from the geometric evolutions and volley fire of heavy infantry preferred by European armies to the punishing hunt and bloody raid of partisan cavalry demanded by the North American frontier. During a decade's campaigning, military policymakers did not totally abandon European martial codes and systems, but the wisest frontier commanders grafted regular-army discipline and modern small arms to unorthodox operations that gave their troops tactical flexibility against the Indians under taxing conditions.

The tactical reservations of the officer corps, however, could be reasoned away with race. In the officers' minds, federal troops were the foot soldiers of Manifest Destiny and civilization, a culture superior to the American Indian way of life. Indigenous peoples were ultimately a little less human than

Euroamericans, and the advancement of democracy and Christianity in North America justified the tragic toll of Indian autonomy and lives. In the eyes of most army officers, the demise of the American Indians was regrettable but necessary.

The resistance of indigenous peoples to United States sovereignty presented only half of the frontier threat to the nation's internal security. Euroamerican social unrest and political riot also challenged the rule of law on the western frontier and triggered the intervention of regulars to aid federal and county law enforcement officers. The scale of such operations ranged from expelling a single family trespassing on an Indian reservation to quelling organized mass resistance such as that practiced by free-soilers in Kansas, Mormons in Utah, and Hispanos in Texas.

In some ways these federal military interventions confirmed republican fears of a standing army acting against its own people to squash dissent. Between the Mexican-American and Civil Wars, however, the regular army never stepped in on its own volition but deployed against civil riot only at the order of its civilian masters, the secretary of war or the president. The sectional, political, and socio-economic heterogeneity of the officer corps prevented the United States Army from brewing and advocating a distinct position on divisive antebellum issues, and no frontier army commander crushed political opposition to advance an army agenda. The frontier regular army was a law enforcement tool, applied by federal appointees, that generally enforced the law and often enacted the political policy of the president.

As a coercive instrument of the state, the regular army bore the political will of the president when he sent federal troops into the field. His agenda might be national, partisan, personal, or any combination of the three. The suppression of the *Cortinistas* and Mormons received the support of most Americans; the electorate, North and South, generally despised the Mexicans and Saints as alien and mongrel peoples. Quelling the Texas and California filibusters and Kansas partisans was a trickier mission; each movement enjoyed mass support among political partisans and regional sections. Sometimes that support issued unofficially from the president who ordered the army to suppress the unrest. Although a federal military unit detached to civil constabulary duty carried the presidential stamp, individual commanding officers often mediated the president's political agenda—their political convictions influenced the vigor of the unit's response to the crisis.

Civil constabulary duty did not end with the outbreak of Civil War. Instead, the army occupied the conquered South during and after the conflict and aided the reintegration of the South into the United States. Between 1868 and 1876, the regular army was the principal agency administering congressionally mandated Reconstruction. At the same time, frontier regulars helped civil law-enforcement authorities chase and arrest outlaws in the turbulent American West until Congress passed the Posse Comitatus Act in 1876 and the federal government withdrew the army from the South in 1877. Both acts extracted the regulars from law enforcement for short time, but when federal courts began applying to the president for the enforcement of labor injunctions during the Gilded Age, they sucked the regular army into policing labor unrest across the country.[1]

As the army marched into the twentieth century, it remembered the myths and romance, not the hard service, of its hundred years on the American frontier. With Indians no longer a threat in the West, popular culture celebrated army triumphs in art, fiction, film, and history, and many forgot the bitter memories of political mayhem, broken health, lost life, and shattered societies. As the United States Army and Navy both took up imperial missions overseas, the American military probably seemed less a domestic political menace to the public. The regular army was finally incorporated into national mythology, particularly those stories inspired by the frontier experience.

The United States and its army took few concrete military lessons from the frontier into the twentieth century. A professional army, however well supplied and trained, could not make up for the failures and imprudence of poorly conceived diplomatic, political, and social policy. Did professional officers and noncommissioned officers who served in the last years of the Indian wars bring any wisdom to the Filipino Insurrection or the Pershing Punitive Expedition? If anything, one hundred years of frontier service had taught the regular army adaptability, tenacity, and survival. Those skills ensured its longevity to the end of the twentieth century, the bloodiest years on human record.

Abbreviations

4Cav.	Fourth Cavalry
9MD	Ninth Military Department
ACAB	*Appleton's Cyclopaedia of American Biography*
ACP	Appointments, Commission, and Personal
ACPB	Appointments, Commission, and Personal Branch
AGO	Adjutant General's Office
CAB	*Cyclopaedia of American Biography*
Cav.	Cavalry
DAB	*Dictionary of American Biography*
DMO	Department of Missouri
DNM	Department of New Mexico
DOR	Department of Oregon
DPac	Department of the Pacific
DTex	Department of Texas
DUtah	Department of Utah
DWest	Department of the West
EFB	*Encyclopedia of Frontier Biography*
HED	House Executive Document
HEH	Henry E. Huntington Library, San Marino, California
HSP	Historical Society of Pennsylvania
KSHC	*Kansas State Historical Collections*
LC	Library of Congress
LR	Letters Received
LS	Letters Sent
NA	National Archives
NPS	National Park Service
OR	*War of the Rebellion: A Compilation of the Official Records of the Union and Confederate Armies*
PR	Post Return
RG	Record Group
RLS	Regimental Letters Sent

RSW	*Annual Report of the Secretary of War*
SED	Senate Executive Document
WWWCW	*Who Was Who in the Civil War*

Notes

PREFACE

1. The system of military rank in the nineteenth-century army was a bewildering maze of actual rank and brevet rank (an honorary promotion providing no increase in pay but sometimes greater authority). To simplify the identification of regular soldiers in the text, I employ their actual rank to the exclusion of brevet rank, even when their duty entitles them to command troops under the latter.

2. Judd to 1st Lt. John H. Dickerson, 16 August 1849, LR, 1849, 9MD, Records of U.S. Army Continental Commands, RG 393, NA, M1102, roll 1.

3. Major historical works dealing with warfare on the frontier and in the West are Utley, *Frontiersmen;* Utley, *Regulars;* Bender, *Empire;* Prucha, *Sword.* Works covering the army's civil interventions are: Coakley, *Role;* Ball Sr., "Military Posses"; Ball Jr., "'Embroilments'"; and Laurie, "Filling." Prucha's *Broadax* and Tate's *Frontier* each include a chapter on the army as a frontier law-enforcement agency but consider constabulary duty nonmartial. An exception is Hutton, *Sheridan,* which explores the regular army's mission as both war maker and peacekeeper.

4. Some of the major works in military history informing this book are: Millis, *Arms;* Cunliffe, *Soldiers;* Weigley, *Army;* Weigley, *American Way;* Ganoe, *History;* Dupuy, *Compact;* Leach, *Arms;* Higgenbotham, *Independence;* Royster, *Revolutionary;* Martin and Lender, *Respectable;* Kohn, *Eagle;* Prucha, *Sword;* Prucha, *Broadax;* Crackel, *Jefferson's;* Utley, *Frontiersmen;* Utley, *Regulars;* Goetzmann, *Exploration;* Coffman, *Army;* and Skelton, *Profession.*

5. Military historians have downplayed sectionalism in the officer corps. See Skelton, *Profession,* chap. 18; and Coffman, *Army,* 92–96.

INTRODUCTION

1. Secretary of War John B. Floyd to Pres. James P. Buchanan, 5 December 1857, *RSW,* SED 11, serial 920, 3–4.

2. Merk, *Manifest,* 24.

3. Adj. Gen. Roger Jones to Secretary of War George W. Crawford, 28 November 1849, *RSW,* SED 1, serial 549, 1–2; Secretary of War Charles M. Conrad to Pres. Millard

Fillmore, 30 November 1850, *RSW*, HED 1, serial 595, 3; Secretary of War Jefferson Davis to Pres. Franklin Pierce, 1 December 1853, *RSW*, SED 1, serial 691, 3; Secretary of War Jefferson Davis to Pres. Franklin Pierce, 3 December 1855, *RSW*, SED 1, serial 811, pt. 2, 3; Secretary of War John B. Floyd to Pres. James P. Buchanan, 1 December 1859, *RSW*, SED 2, serial 1024, 3; and Secretary of War John B. Floyd to Pres. James P. Buchanan, 3 December 1860, *RSW*, SED 1, serial 1079, 3; and Utley, *Frontiersmen*, 12–13.

4. Utley, *Frontiersmen*, 22.

5. Scott to Secretary of War Charles M. Conrad, 30 November 1850, *RSW*, HED 1, serial 595, 114–15.

6. For a description of the uniforms, arms, and equipment of the mounted regiments in the 1850s, see Steffen, *Horse*, vol. 2, chaps. 6 and 7.

7. For these figures and others, see Jones to Crawford, 28 November 1849, 179–80; General Return, 1850, *RSW*, HED 1, serial 595, 116; General Return, 1853, *RSW*, SED 1, serial 691, 111; Secretary of War Jefferson Davis to Pres. Franklin Pierce, 4 December 1854, *RSW*, SED 1, pt. 2, serial 747, 3; General Return, 1854, *RSW*, SED 1, serial 811, 131; Secretary of War Jefferson Davis to Pres. Franklin Pierce, 1 December 1856, *RSW*, HED 1, serial 894, 3; Floyd to Buchanan, 5 December 1857, 3; General Return, 1857, *RSW*, SED 11, serial 920, 67; General Return, 1859, *RSW*, SED 2, serial 1024, 597; and General Return, 1860, *RSW*, SED 1, serial 1079, 213.

8. For a description of the military frontier in 1846, see the maps in Prucha, *Sword*, xii–xiii, 194–99; Prucha, *Broadax*, chaps. 4 and 5; and Frazer, "Jesup," "Leavenworth," and "Snelling," *West*, 56, 60–62, 67–68.

9. Scott to Crawford, 3 November 1849, *RSW*, SED 1, serial 549, 98–99; Floyd to Buchanan, 5 December 1857, 3–6; and Utley, *Indian*, chap. 1.

10. Maj. Gen. Winfield Scott to Secretary of War George W. Crawford, 3 November 1849, 98–103; Frazer, "The Department of New Mexico, 1853," *Mansfield*, 26.

11. Frazer, "Smith," "Presidio of San Diego," "Leavenworth," "Brown," "Vancouver," *West*, 16–18, 30, 56, 144–45, 176–77.

12. A description of Fort Leavenworth in 1850 is Orlando B. Willcox, "Plains Journal," 18 June 1850, Garth, *Forgotten*, 137. Another description is Peck, "Recollections," 485. See NPS, "Fort Leavenworth, Kansas," *Soldier*, 145–48.

13. For Fort Kearny see Osborn Cross, "Journal," 31 May [1849], Settle, *March*, 55–56. See also NPS, "Fort Kearny, Nebraska," *Soldier*, 206–7. Cross also described Fort Laramie: "Journal," 2 June [1849], Settle, *March*, 98; a historical sketch of this post is NPS, "Fort Laramie National Historic Site, Wyoming," *Soldier*, 373–79. For Fort Bridger see NPS, "Fort Bridger, Wyoming," *Soldier*, 365–67. Frazer, "Dalles," *West*, 127; and NPS, "Fort Churchill, Nevada," *Soldier*, 213–14. Camp Floyd, Utah Territory, was later renamed Camp Crittenden. Frazer, "Crittenden," *West*, 166. The distances are from Israel Moses, "Journal of Distances," Settle, *March*, 346–50.

14. A classic history of the Santa Fe Trail is Duffus, *Trail*. Military activity on the trail is explored in Oliva, *Soldiers*, and Chalfant, *Dangerous*. Henry Heth describes Fort Atkinson in *Memoirs*, 86–87. See Frazer, "Wise," "Atkinson," "Larned," *West*, 41–42, 50–51, 55.

15. Bender describes the New Mexico defense network in "Frontier," 249–72, 345–74. Marc Simmons sketches the Chihuahua Trail in "Santa Fe and Chihuahua Trail," Lamar,

Reader's, 1084–85. Averell knew Fort Craig intimately. See Averell, *Saddle*, 123–44. A recent article on Fort Craig is Ball Jr., "Craig." Two inspector generals toured New Mexico in the early 1850s. See McCall, *New Mexico*, ed. Frazer, and Frazer, *Mansfield*, chap. 1; NPS, "Fort Buchanan, Arizona," "Fort Fillmore, New Mexico," "Fort Bliss, Texas," 66–67, 226, 318–19. Frazer, "Marcy," *Forts*, 100–101.

16. For the travels of the Army of the West and the Mormon Battalion, see U.S. House, *Notes*, HED 41, serial 517, and Cooke, "Journal," Bieber, *Exploring*. See Dobyns, ed., *Hepah* for a little-known expedition through the Far Southwest by Maj. Lawrence P. Graham's brigade of regulars from Monterey, Nuevo Léon, Mexico, to Los Angeles, California, in 1848–49. Forts Buchanan and Yuma were the edge of the world for frontier regulars. NPS, "Fort Buchanan, Arizona," "Yuma Crossing, Arizona-California," *Soldiers*, 66, 81–85. Thomas Sweeny spent several years at Fort Yuma. Sweeny, *Journal*. An excellent historical account of life at Fort Buchanan is Pfanz, *Ewell*, chap. 8; a first-person account is Tevis, *Arizona*.

17. Troops and their families generally sailed from New York to the Texas coast to reach the Department of Texas. See Vielé, *Following*, chaps. 4–10; Lane, *Married*, chaps. 1–2; and Helen Chapman to Mother, 2, 9, 11, 19 January 1848, Coker, *News*, 3–8. For Lane quotation, see Lane, *Married*, 22.

18. Lane, *Married*, 25. She and her husband, 1st Lt. William B. Lane, traveled the San Antonio–El Paso Road and passed up the Chihuahua Trail to Cantonment Burgwin near Taos, New Mexico. See chaps. 7–8. In 1850 Turnley was in charge of one of the first military trains—"300 teams" and wagons, "500 beef cattle," "1800 mules"—to roll between San Antonio and El Paso. See Turnley, *Reminiscences*, 117–20. The distances between Indianola and other posts are from Secretary of War Charles M. Conrad to Pres. Millard Fillmore, 29 November 1851, *RSW*, HED 2, serial 634, 105–15.

19. Crook, *Autobiography*, 7; Frazer, "The Department of the Pacific, 1854," *Mansfield*, 120, 153–59; NPS, "Benicia Barracks and Arsenal, California," *Soldiers*, 89–91.

20. See Mansfield's description of California frontier in Frazer, "Department of the Pacific," *Mansfield*, 105–14, 120–22, 132–70. Strobridge, *Regulars*, recounts the history of the antebellum army in northern California.

21. Talbot to Sister, 10 May 1849, and Talbot to Mother, 25 May 1849, Hine and Lottinville, *Soldier*, 120–29; Frazer, "Department of the Pacific," *Mansfield*, 114–15, 170–75; NPS, "Vancouver Barracks," *Soldiers*, 355–58.

22. Talbot's letters during four years in Oregon are a blistering indictment of white settlement. Hine and Lottinville, *Soldier*, 118–82. Inspector General Mansfield's report on the Oregon military frontier is in Frazer, *Mansfield*, 115–20, 167–82. In 1858 Mansfield returned to inspect the Pacific frontier. Frazer, "Dalles," "Bellingham," "Coleville," "Simcoe," "Steilacoom," and "Townsend," *West*, 127–28, 167–68, 172, 174–77. As an infantry lieutenant, Phil Sheridan spent seven years in the Pacific Northwest. Sheridan, *Personal*, chaps. 4–7.

23. NPS, "Fort Hoskins, Oregon," "Fort Lane, Oregon," *Soldier*, 287–88; Frazer, "Umpqua" and "Yamhill" in *West*, 132–34.

24. [Tables of Organization for Eastern, Western, and Pacific Divisions], *RSW*, HED 1, serial 549, 188c-e; Thian, *Notes*, 25, 30 31.

25. Thian, *Notes*, 79, 86, 88, 98, 100, 105.

26. [Table of Organization for Western Division and Military Departments Nos. 6 and 7 in 1849], *RSW*, HED 1, serial 549, 188d; [Table of Organization for Western Department, 1860], *RSW*, SED 1, serial 1079, 216–17; Thian, *Notes*, 44–45, 46, 105–6.

27. [Tables of Organization for Western Division and Military Department No. 8 in 1849], *RSW*, HED 1, serial 549, 188d; Thian, *Notes*, 48, 98–99; [Table of Organization for Department of Texas, 1860], *RSW*, SED 1, serial 1079, 218–21.

28. [Tables of Organization for Western Division and Military Department No.9 in 1849], *RSW*, HED 1, serial 549, 188d; Thian, *Notes*, 49–50; [Table of Organization for Department of New Mexico, 1860], *RSW*, SED 1, serial 1079, 222–23.

29. [Tables of Organization for Pacific Division and Military Department No. 10 in 1849], *RSW*, HED 1, serial 549, 188e; Thian, *Notes*, 50–51.

30. Thian, *Notes*, 53–54; [Table of Organization for Department of California, 1860], *RSW*, SED 1, serial 1079, 228–29.

31. [Tables of Organization for the Pacific Division and Military Department No. 11 in 1849], *RSW*, HED 1, serial 549, 188e; Thian, *Notes*, 51.

32. [Table of Organization for Department of Oregon, 1860], *RSW*, SED 1, serial 1079, 226–27; Thian, *Notes*, 85–86.

PROLOGUE

1. Johannsen, *Frontier*, 17–19; Bauer, *Mexican*, 387; Potter, *Impending*, 54, 68–69, 76, 85. Richard Griswold del Castillo discusses the background to the treaty in *Treaty*, chaps. 2–4.

2. Heitman, "Zachary Taylor," *Register*, 1:949. For Taylor's northern Mexico campaign, see Bauer, *Taylor*, chaps. 7–10; and Bauer, *Mexican*, chaps. 3–4, 9. For Taylor as a slave owner, see Elbert Smith, *Presidencies*, 20, 27–28. Taylor's views on the Far West, slavery expansion, and the Wilmot Proviso are found in Bauer, *Taylor*, 224, chap. 15; and Elbert Smith, *Presidencies*, 28, 40, 101–4.

3. Bauer, *Taylor*, 291–92; Elbert Smith, *Presidencies*, 101–2.

4. Ball, "Interwar," chap. 1; Grivas, *Military;* Twitchell, *Military;* Secretary of War William L. Marcy to Col. Richard B. Mason, 9 October 1848, *California*, HED 17, serial 573, 258–59.

5. Washington to Secretary of War William L. Marcy, 8 November 1848, *RSW*, SED 1, serial 549, 104; Chamberlain, *Confession*, 239, 255; Lamar, *Southwest*, 71, 72.

6. Lamar, *Southwest*, 65–66, 72; Ruxton, *Rockies*, 180; Ball, "Interwar," 80–81; Ganaway, *Controversy*, 40–41.

7. Ganaway, *Controversy*, 40–41; Lamar, *Southwest*, 72.

8. Larson, *Quest*, 18–21; Chamberlain, *Confession*, 44; Lamar, *Southwest*, 73; Washington to Adj. Gen. Roger Jones, 25 September 1849, *RSW*, SED 1, serial 549, 111–12. For the Washington campaign see McNitt, *Navajo*.

9. Espinosa, "Memoir," 7; Howard, *Autobiography*, 1:78–79; Heitman, "John Munroe," *Register*, 1:736; Bauer, *Mexican*, 37, 39, 47–48, 58, 215.

10. Secretary of War William L. Marcy to Commanding Officer, 12 October 1848; and Secretary of War George W. Crawford to Commanding Officer, 26 March 1849, *California*, HED 17, serial 573, 261–62, 272–73; Elbert Smith, *Presidencies*, 33–34, 98, 152–53. Historical background to the boundary dispute and the Texas claim is found in Stegmaier, *Texas*, chaps. 1–2.

11. Neighbors to Munroe, 23 February 1850; and Munroe to "the several officers commanding posts in and near the territory claimed by the State of Texas," *Letter*, HED 66, serial 577, 2; Edrington, "Military," 385. Stegmaier discusses the Neighbors mission in *Texas*, chap. 3.

12. Edrington, "Military," 385; Elbert Smith, *Presidencies*, 98.

13. Headquarters, U.S. Army, Special Orders No. 69, 8 November 1849, McCall, *Letters*, 485; Secretary of War George W. Crawford to McCall, 18 November 1849, McCall, *Letters*, 486; McCall to M______, 12 March, 29 August 1850, McCall, *Letters*, 492, 523. McCall's report on the Ninth Military Department is reproduced in McCall, *New Mexico*.

14. Larson, *Quest*, 39–40; Twitchell, *Military*, 162; Lamar, *Southwest*, 73–74; McCall to M______, 13 May 1850, McCall, *Letters*, 493.

15. Larson, *Quest*, 30–31; Munroe, "Proclamation," 23 April 1850, *Message*, SED 60, serial 561, pt. 2, 2–3; Lamar, *Southwest*, 77; Robert S. Neighbors to Munroe, 15 April 1850, *Message*, SED 56, serial 561, 15. A recent discussion of the statehood movement is Stegmaier, *Texas*, 5.

16. Larson, *Quest*, 50; Twitchell, *Military*, 161; Lamar, *Southwest*, 78.

17. Larson, *Quest*, 50; Lamar, *Southwest*, 78; Elbert Smith, *Presidencies*, 152–53.

18. Pleasonton to Thurlow Weed, 22 September 1876, Barnes, *Weed*, 180; Elbert Smith, *Presidencies*, 153; Hamilton, *Taylor*, 2:380.

19. George McCall to M______, 29 August 1850, Santa Fe, McCall, *Letters*, 524; Bauer, *Taylor*, 316; Elbert Smith, *Presidencies*, 156–57, 182; Twitchell, *Military*, 161.

20. Secretary of State John M. Clayton to King, 3 April 1849, *California*, HED 17, serial 573, 10–11; Crawford to Smith, 2 April 1849, K-1, Box 1, 1849, LR DPac (no. 3584), pt. 1, U.S. Army Continental Commands, 1821–1920, RG 393, NA.

21. Heitman, "Bennet Riley," *Register*, 1:831; Heidner, "Bennet Riley," *DAB*, 15:608–9; Maury, *Recollections*, 43; Bauer, *Mexican*, 265, 293, 295–96, 312.

22. Lieutenant Colonel Riley to 1st Lt. William Sherman, 13 April 1849, D-11; Lieutenant Colonel Riley to Adj. Gen. Roger Jones, 11 June 1849, D-24; Lieutenant Colonel Riley to 1st Lt. William Sherman, 16 April 1849, D-14; and Lieutenant Colonel Riley to Adj. Gen. Roger Jones, 25 April 1849, D-17, Box 1, 1849, LR DPac (no. 3584), pt. 1, RG 393, NA.

23. 2d Lt. Alfred Gibbs to Lieutenant Colonel Riley, 24 May 1849; Smith to Riley, 8 June 1849; and Gibbs to Riley, 9 June 1849, vol. 1/4*, LS DPac (no. 3578) (no. 3578), RG 393, NA, 62–65; Riley to Jones, 30 June 1849; and Riley, "Proclamation," 3 June 1849, *California*, HED 17, serial 573, 748–51, 777–80.

24. Secretary of War George W. Crawford to Lieutenant Colonel Riley, 26 June 1849; Secretary of War Crawford to Lieutenant Colonel Riley, 24 August 1849; Lieutenant Colonel Riley, "To the People of California," 22 June 1849; and Halleck to Dimmick, 3 September 1849, *California*, HED 17, serial 573, 276, 280, 785, 822–23; [Item], CT 2485, Box 63, Couts Papers, HEH.

25. Harlow, *California*, 339–46; Grivas, *Military*, 212–16; Sherman, *Memoirs*, 1:79; Garnett to Lyon, 30 September 1849, HM 46545, HEH.

26. Riley, "Proclamation," 12 October 1849; and Crawford to Riley, 28 November 1849, *California*, HED 17, serial 573, 858–59, 281–82; Grivas, *Military*, 218–20.

27. Potter, *Impending*, 112.

1. Crampton, *Interior*, i, 4–5, 10–11, 13.

2. Prucha, *Father*, 1:319–23.

3. Utley, *Indian*, 37.

4. A summary of the Indian-white relationship during the 1850s is Utley, *Indian*, chap. 2. A classic survey of the overland emigration is Unruh, *Plains*.

5. Merk, *Manifest*, 24–34.

6. Utley discusses the creation and implementation of the new reservations in *Indian*, chap. 2. Two book-length studies also explore this policy. See Trennert Jr., *Alternative;* Hoopes, *Affairs*.

7. Prucha, *Father*, 1:342–45; Utley, *Indian*, 60–61.

8. Prucha, *Father*, 1:372–73. For the Treaty of Laguna Negra with the Navajos, see McNitt, *Navajo*, chap. 14, app. c.

9. Utley, *Indian*, 51–52; Prucha, *Father*, 1:385–90. The most influential federal official on California Indian policy was Edward F. Beale. See Thompson, *Beale*, chaps. 4–5.

10. Utley, *Indian*, 52–55; Prucha, *Father*, 1:397–409.

11. Crook, *Autobiography*, 15–16.

12. Averell, *Saddle*, 156.

13. Utley, *Frontiersmen*, 10–11; Bender, *Empire*, 29. Ethan A. Hitchcock and Edward D. Townsend blamed settlers and miners for most of the violence in California. See Hitchcock, *Diary*, 396; Townsend, *California*, 56.

14. Millett and Maslowski, *Common*, 236–39.

15. Johnson, *Reminiscences*, 63–64; Meyer to James [Walden], 14 February 1855, Clary, "Texan," 43; J. E. B. Stuart to Jack Hairston, 31 March 1855, Hairston, "Stuart's," 328.

16. Hardcastle Journal, 20 May [1859], CT 2511, Box 65, Couts Papers, HEH; Hitchcock, *Diary*, 395; Townsend, *California*, 68.

17. Marcy, *Life*, 62, 66; Johnson, *Reminiscences*, 137–39.

18. Sweeny to William Bodge, 14 February 1858, SW 850 (115), Box 8, Letterbook, Sweeny Papers, HEH; William Sherman to John Sherman, 20 March 1856, Thorndike, *Letters*, 56.

19. Townsend, Journals, 29 May, 8 June [1838], HM 41695 (5–6), Townsend Papers, HEH; Grant to Julia [Dent Grant], 19 March 1853, Simon, *Grant*, 1:296.

20. Hardcastle, Journal, 17 May [1859], CT 2511, Box 65, Couts Papers; Crook, *Autobiography*, 16.

21. Heitman, "Edwin Vose Sumner," *Register*, 1:936; Warner, "Edwin Vose Sumner," *Blue*, 489–90; Stanley, *Sumner*, chap. 2; Secretary of War Charles Conrad to Lt. Col. Edwin Sumner, 1 April 1851; and Sumner to Adj. Gen. Roger Jones, 24 October 1851, Abel, *Official*, 383–84, 416–17.

22. Sumner to Secretary of War Charles Conrad, 24 October 1851, Abel, *Official*, 416–19.

23. Munroe to Calhoun 9 Ap[ri]l 1851; Calhoun to Munroe, 10 April 1851; Calhoun to Lt. Col. Edwin Sumner, 4 August 1851; Lt. Col. Edwin Sumner to Calhoun, 8 Aug[us]t [18]51; Calhoun to Secretary of State Daniel Webster, 15 September 1851; Calhoun to Commissioner of Indian Affairs Luke Lea, 1 Oct[obe]r; and Calhoun to Lt. Col. Edwin Sumner, 10 November 1851, Abel, *Official*, 324–25, 396–98, 425–26, 432–33, 447–49.

24. Sumner to Jones, 20 November 1851, Abel, *Official*, 445.

25. Lt. Col. Edwin Sumner to Secretary of War Charles Conrad, 24 October 1851; Lt. Col. Edwin Sumner to Gov. James S. Calhoun, 10 November 1851; Lieutenant Colonel Sumner to Morris, 1 April 1852; and Lt. Col. Edwin Sumner to Adj. Gen. Roger Jones, 3 February 1852, Abel, *Official*, 416–19, 452, 516–17, 479.

26. Gov. James S. Calhoun to Commissioner Luke Lea, 31 March 1852; Gov. James S. Calhoun to Lt. Col. Edwin Sumner, 7 April 1852; Lt. Col. Edwin Sumner to Gov. James S. Calhoun, 8 April 1852; Lt. Col. Edwin Sumner to Adj. Gen. Roger Jones, 9 April 1852; Lt. Col. Edwin Sumner, "Proclamation," 7 April 1852; Gov. James S. Calhoun to Lt. Col. Edwin Sumner, 12 April 1852; Lt. Col. Edwin Sumner to Adj. Gen. Roger Jones, 22 April 1852; Gov. James S. Calhoun to Lt. Col. Edwin Sumner, 18 April 1852; and Lt. Col. Edwin Sumner to Gov. James S. Calhoun, 19 April 1852, Abel, *Official*, 513, 517–528.

27. Lt. Col. Edwin Sumner and Gov. James S. Calhoun to the Public, 21 April 1852; Lt. Col. Edwin Sumner to Secretary of State Daniel Webster, 8 May 1852; Lt. Col. Edwin Sumner to Adj. Gen. Roger Jones, 8 May 1852; Lt. Col. Edwin Sumner to Capt. James H. Carleton, 20 May 1852; and Agent J. Greiner to Commissioner Luke Lea, 31 May 1852, Abel, *Official*, 528, 535, 537–538.

28. Lt. Col. Edwin Sumner to Conrad, 27 May 1852, *RSW*, HED 1, serial 674, 23–26; Lt. Col. Edwin Sumner to Adj. Gen. Roger Jones, 24 September 1852, quoted in Stanley, *Sumner*, 168–69.

29. "The Big Bug of Albuquerque," *Santa Fe Weekly Gazette*, 19 February 1853; Stanley, *Sumner*, 180.

30. Hitchcock, *Diary*, 396; Crook, *Autobiography*, 16.

CHAPTER 2

1. Keyes, *Observation*, 253.

2. Floyd, Journal, 18 April 1859, HM 19334, HEH.

3. Frazer, "Department of New Mexico," *Mansfield*, 48–49, 67.

4. Ibid., 163–65, 184–85.

5. A discussion of the army as a cheap labor force is in Prucha, *Broadax*, chap. 8, and Wooster, *Soldiers*, 29–30. The employment of enlisted men on post construction continued into the late nineteenth century. Rickey, *Forty*, 93–96. Nowhere was the post-farm program more vigorously applied than in the Ninth Military Department under Lt. Col. Edwin V. Sumner. The farms were generally a failure. Frazer, *Mansfield*, 62–64; Frazer, *Supplies*, chap. 4; Prucha, *Broadax*, chap. 7.

6. Coffman, *Army*, 156–57; Utley, *Frontiersmen*, 41–42; Charles [Whilden] to William [Whilden], 28 August 1855, Moore, "Clerk," 143.

7. Lowe, *Dragoon*, 76; Bennet, 1 November [1850], *Forays*, 17.

8. Averell, *Saddle*, 59, 131–32.

9. Glisan, *Journal*, 54–55.

10. Marcy, *Life*, 283–84; Bandel to Parents, 19 October 1856, Bandel, *Frontier*, 80.

11. The best discussion of frontier defense is Utley, *Frontiersmen*, 53–58. See *RSW*, SED 1, serial 691, 5–6; and Wooster, "Strategy," 5–15.

12. Secretary of War Charles M. Conrad to President Zachary Taylor, 30 November 1850, *RSW*, HED 1, serial 595, 8–9.

13. Jesup to Secretary of War William H. Crawford, 10 November 1849, *RSW*, SED 1, serial 549, 193–95; Jesup to Secretary of War Charles M. Conrad, 20 November 1852, *RSW*, HED 1, pt. 1, serial 674, 70; Frazer, *Supplies*, 4–5, 189–90.

14. Jesup to Crawford, 10 November 1849, 194; Conrad to Pres. Millard Fillmore, 30 November 1850, 5.

15. Kearny to Adj. Gen. Roger Jones, 15 September 1845, *RSW*, SED 1, serial 470, 212.

16. Ibid.

17. Scott to Secretary of War Charles M. Conrad, 21 November 1851, *RSW*, HED 1, pt. 2, serial 611, 161–62; Scott to Secretary of War Jefferson Davis, 18 November 1854, *RSW*, SED 1, pt. 1, serial 747, 51.

18. Sumner to Jones, 24 October 1851, Abel, *Official*, 416–19; Clarke to Father, 29 September 1852, Miller, *Above*, 42–43.

19. Lt. Col. Edwin Sumner to Adj. Gen. Roger Jones, 24 October 1851, Abel, *Official*, 416–19.

20. Ibid. For Davis's proposal see *RSW*, SED 1, serial 691, 5–6. Other officers made the same proposal. Q.M. Thomas Jesup to Secretary of War Charles Conrad, 20 November 1852; and Col. Thomas T. Fauntleroy to Q.M. Thomas Jesup, 31 July 1852, *RSW*, HED 1, pt. 1, serial 674, 70, 127–28; Capt. Rufus Ingalls to Q.M. Thomas Jesup, 22 November 1855, *RSW*, SED 1, pt. 2, serial 811, 162.

21. Kip, *Army*, 51; Marcy, *Life*, 68; Glisan, *Journal*, 327–28.

22. Lowe, *Dragoon*, 81.

23. Meyer to James [Walden], 14 February 1855, Clary, "'Texan,'" 42; Price, *Across*, 64; Roland, *Johnston*, 178–79.

24. Price, *Across*, 44–45, 50–51, 54–56, 61–63; Lee to Johnston, 25 October 1857, Sibley, "Lee," 104–5; Frazer, "Mason," *Forts*, 155.

25. Hood, *Advance*, 8–14.

26. McQuaide to Porter, 25 July 1857, P7/1, 1857; and Porter to 1st Lt. John D. Wilkins, 13 February 1860, P6, 1860, LR DNM (M1120), RG 393, roll 6; Heitman, "Hugh McQuade," *Register*, 1:681; Hugh McQuade [McQuaide], Returns from Regular Army Cavalry Regiments (M744), Records of the Adjutant General's Office, RG 94, NA, roll 27.

27. McQuaide to Capt. Andrew Porter, 25 July 1857, P7/1, 1857, LR DNM (M1120), RG 393, roll 6.

28. Capt. Andrew Porter to Maj. George Crittenden, 17 February 1857, C6/1; and 2d Lt. Matthew L. Davis to Maj. George Crittenden, 20 February 1857, C6/2, ibid.

29. Robert H. Stapleton to Porter [enclosure], 10 January 1860, P2, 1860, LR DNM (M1120), RG 393, roll 12; Utley, *Frontiersmen*, 168–70; McNitt, *Navajo*, 328–29, 334–62.

30. McQuaide to Porter [enclosure], 13 February 1860, P2; and Porter to 1st Lt. John D. Wilkins, 13 February 1860, P6, 1860, LR DNM (M1120), RG 393, roll 12; Fort Craig PR, February 1860, Returns from Military Posts (M617), RG 94, roll 261.

31. McLane to 1st Lt. John Hatch, 11 February 1860, P6/1, 1860, LR DNM (M1120), RG 393, roll 12.

32. Porter to Wilkins, 11 February 1860, P5; and Porter to Wilkins, 13 February 1860, P6, LR DNM (M1120), RG 393, roll 12.

CHAPTER 3

1. Peck, "Recollections," 484–85.

2. Capt. Henry Wharton to Deas, 1 September 1856, W61; Capt. Henry Wharton to Ass[istan]t Adj[utan]t Gen[era]l, Sioux Expedition, 10 June 1856, W61/2; Capt. Henry Wharton to Ass[istan]t Adj[u]t[ant] Gen[era]l, Sioux Expedition [enclosure], 7 June 1856; and Capt. George H. Steuart to Capt. Henry Wharton, 27 August 1856, W61/3, 1856, Box 4, LR DWest (no. 5486), United States Army Continental Commands, RG 393, NA.

3. Head-Quarters of the Army, New York, Army General Order No. 5, 4 April 1857, Chalfant, *Cheyennes*, 333–34; Peck, "Recollections," 485, 503.

4. Col. Edwin Sumner to Sedgwick, 17 May 1857, vol. 1, RLS NM-93, 4Cav. (no. 719), United States Army Mobile Units, RG 391, NA.

5. Peck, "Recollections," 488–89; Heitman, "John Sedgwick," *Register*, 1:872.

6. Peck, "Recollections," 488–93; Chalfant, *Cheyennes*, chap. 5.

7. Sumner to Ass[istan]t Adj[utan]t Gen[era]l, 20 September 1857, vol. 1, RLS 4Cav. (no. 719), RG 391; Peck, "Recollections," 494; Chalfant, *Cheyennes*, 359. For the Utah Expedition, see chapter 8 of this book.

8. Peck, "Recollections," 494; Col. Edwin Sumner to Ass[istan]t Adj[utan]t Gen[era]l, 20 September 1857; Lowe, *Dragoon*, 201–2.

9. Peck, "Recollections," 494; Col. Edwin Sumner to Assistant Adjutant General, Headquarters of the Army, 20 September 1857, *RSW*, SED 11, serial 920, 98–99. A map of Sumner's pursuit and strike is in Chalfant, *Cheyennes*, 134.

10. Peck, "Recollections," 495; Col. Edwin Sumner to Assistant Adjutant General, 20 September 1857, 98–99.

11. Peck, "Recollections," 495; Girardi and Hughes, *Carlin*, 18–19; Sumner to Assistant Adjutant General, Headquarters of the Army, 9 August 1857, *RSW*, SED 11, serial 920, 96–97.

12. Peck, "Recollections," 496; Col. Edwin Sumner to Assistant Adjutant General, 9 August 1857, 96–97.

13. Sumner to Assistant Adjutant General, 9 August 1857, 96–97; Peck, "Recollections," 495–96.

14. Peck, "Recollections," 496–97; Sumner is quoted on 496. Sumner to Assistant Adjutant General, 9 August 1857, 96–97.

15. Adjutant General's Office, Washington, D.C., General Orders No. 13, 15 August 1855, quoted in Steffen, *Horse*, 2:34–35. For the First Cavalry in Bleeding Kansas, see chapter 9 of this book.

16. Sumner to Assistant Adjutant General, 9 August 1857, 96–97; Peck, "Recollections," 497; Stanley, *Memoirs*, 43–44; Girardi and Hughes, *Carlin*, 19–20; Chalfant, *Cheyennes*, 192.

17. Sumner to Assistant Adjutant General, 9 August 1857, 96–97; Stanley, *Memoirs*, 43–44; Peck, "Recollections," 497. Attacking with edged weapons is explored in Crossman, *On Killing*, chap. 5. He also notes that killing humans is an unnatural act for the majority of men. See his *On Killing*, chap. 3.

18. Rodenbough, "Fourth," 202; Stanley, *Memoirs*, 44–45.

19. Chalfant, *Cheyennes*, 197–98.

20. Peck, "Recollections," 500–501; Girardi and Hughes, *Carlin*, 21; Sumner to Assistant Adjutant General, 9 August 1857, 96–97; Stanley, *Memoirs*, 45–46.

21. Sumner to Assistant Adjutant General, 9 August 1857, 96–97; Col. Edwin Sumner to Assistant Adjutant General, Headquarters of the Army, 11 August 1857, *RSW*, SED 11, serial 920, 97–98; Col. Edwin Sumner to Assistant Adjutant General, Headquarters of the Army, 20 September 1857, 98–99; Peck, "Recollections," 501–3.

22. Sumner to Assistant Adjutant General, 20 September 1857, 98–99; Peck, "Recollections," 503–4.

23. Sumner to Assistant Adjutant General, 20 September 1857, 98–99. Harney kept copies of Sumner's series of written challenges and introduced them as evidence of his conduct unbecoming an officer and gentleman. The original challenge is Sumner to Harney, 14 Dec[ember] 1857, Box 1, Sumner Family Papers, LC. Copies of Sumner's letters to Harney and Harney's "Charges and Specifications" against Sumner are in the same location.

24. This account of the Grattan debacle is pieced together from the following reports by officers at Fort Laramie and statements by eyewitnesses: Maj. William Hoffman to Page, 19 November 1854; Bordeau[x], Statement, n.d. [enclosure]; Fleming to Hoffman, 19 August 1854, [enclosure]; and Obridge Allen, statement [enclosure], n.d., H-69, Box 1, 1854, LR DWest (no. 5486), pt. 1, Records of the United States Army Continental Commands, RG 393, NA. See also Man Who Is Afraid of His Horses, statement, n.d., enclosure to Maj. William Hoffman to Page, 7 January 1855, H-11, Box 2, 1855, LR DWest (no. 5486), pt. 1, RG 393.

25. Todd, "Harney," 92–100, 108–10; Clow, "Mad," 133–38.

26. Todd, "Harney," 110; Clow, "Mad," 138.

27. Primary accounts of the engagement on Blue Water Creek include: Harney to Lt. Col. Lorenzo Thomas, 5 September 1855, *RSW*, SED 1, pt. 2, serial 811, 49–51; Todd, "Harney," 111–14; Drum, "Reminiscences," 143–51; Philip St. George Cooke, "Personal Recollections—Campaign of 1855–60," Rodenbough, *Everglade*, 181–84; Bandel to Parents, 19 October 1856, Bandel, *Frontier*, 82–88; and Heth, *Memoirs*, 123–28.

28. Harney to Thomas, 5 September 1855, 49–51; Todd, "Harney," 114 n, 115–16; Bandel to Parents, 19 October 1856, 82–88; Clow, "Mad," 141.

29. Todd, "Harney," 117–25; Clow, "Mad," 141–46.

30. Hitchcock, *Diary*, 414–15, 418–19; Girardi and Hughes, *Carlin*, 14. According to Heth, Harney originally intended to leave the Brule camp unmolested and march on to Fort Laramie, but Heth's appeal to Harney's manliness sparked him to order the attack. See Heth, *Memoirs*, 127–28.

31. Chalfant, *Without*, 30–37.

32. Eliza Johnston, the wife of Col. Albert Sidney Johnston, reported that Captain Van Dorn painted miniatures. See Roland and Robbins, "Diary," 493 (30 March 1856 entry). For a description of the expedition's march to Otter Creek, see Van Dorn to Capt. John Withers, 26 September 1858, quoted in Chalfant, *Without*, 119–20. Frazer, "Belknap," *Forts*, 142; Kajencki, "Radziminski," 389.

33. For a description of the march and battle, see Van Dorn to Capt. John Withers, 5 October 1858, Chalfant, *Without*, 122–23; Chalfant, *Without*, 41–44.

34. Van Dorn to Withers, 5 October 1858, 122–24; Chalfant, *Without*, 43–44.

35. The foregoing narrative leans heavily on Chalfant, *Without*, chaps. 5–8. See also Van Dorn's reports: Van Dorn to Capt. John Withers, 13 May 1859; and Van Dorn to Capt. John Withers, 31 May 1859, Chalfant, *Without*, 135–36, 137–40. A brief summary is in Utley, *Frontiersmen*, 133–35.

36. Schlicke, *Wright*, 180.

37. For an instructive account of the Yakama War, see Utley, *Frontiersmen*, 187–200; Frazer, "Simcoe" and "Walla Walla," *Forts*, 174, 177.

38. For secondary accounts of the Steptoe fight, see Utley, *Frontiersmen*, 201–3; and Schlicke, *Wright*, 144–53. A summary of the engagement is in Kip, *Army*, 9–12. Lt. John Mullen examined the Steptoe battle site, and his cartographer sketched a map of Steptoe's advance and retreat. See Mullen to Capt. William W. Mackall, 9 October 1858, M100, 1858, Box 14, LR DPac (no. 3584), pt. 1, RG 393, NA.

39. Utley, *Frontiersmen*, 203–4; Schlicke, *Wright*, 154–55. Brigadier General Clarke's charge to Wright is quoted in Schlicke, *Wright*, 155.

40. Keyes and Kip discuss the target practice with the new rifles. See Keyes, *Observation*, 265; and Kip, *Army*, 23–24. For the modern weapons issued to the troops of the Spokane Expedition, see Schlicke, *Wright*, 164. For the expedition's order of battle, see Kip, *Army*, 44–45.

41. For accounts of the Battle of Four Lakes, see Keyes, *Observation*, 267–68; and Kip, *Army*, 51–60. For Wright's official report, see Wright to Capt. William W. Mackall, 2 September 1858, *RSW*, HED 2, serial 998, pt. 2, 386–90.

42. Wright to Capt. William W. Mackall, 6 September 1858, *RSW*, HED 2, serial 998, pt. 2, 390–93; Keyes, *Observation*, 269–70; Kip, *Army*, 64–72; Schlicke, *Wright*, 170–72.

43. Wright to Capt. William W. Mackall, 10 September 1858; and Wright to Capt. William W. Mackall, 15 September 1858, *RSW*, HED 2, serial 998, pt. 2, 393, 396–97. For Wright's negotiations with the Coeur d'Alenes, Spokanes, and Palouses, see Kip, *Army*, 75–106; and Schlicke, *Wright*, 176–84.

44. Kip, *Army*, 105–6; Schlicke, *Wright*, 183–85.

CHAPTER 4

1. Bandel to Parents, 17 March 1857, Bandel, *Frontier*, 114; Townsend, ["Memoir of Early Life to the Mexican War"] (HM 41697), Townsend Papers, HEH; Prucha, *Broadax*, 36–37; Prucha, *Sword*, 320–24; Utley, *Frontiersmen*, 35–36; Utley, *Regulars*, 22; Rickey, *Forty*, 18; Millett and Maslowski, *Common*, 133.

2. Meyers, *Ranks*, 37; Utley, *Frontiersmen*, 39–40; Prucha, *Broadax*, 41–42. Army recruiting statistics support Meyers's observation: The average age was twenty-four to twenty-five years. Senate, *Statistical*, SED 96, serial 825, 632.

3. Meyers, *Ranks*, 37; Lowe, *Dragoon*, 14–15, 23, 38–39. Army data support the observations of Meyers and Lowe. See Senate, *Statistical*, SED 96, serial 825, 631–32. Dragoon Samuel Chamberlain described "three classes" of soldiers: "DEAD BEATS," "OLD SOLDIERS," and "DARE DEVILS." The first were untrustworthy, the second were "quiet" and "mechanical," and the third were the "pride of the officers and the admiration of their companions." Chamberlain, *Confession*, 186–87. Another curious figure in the enlisted ranks of the army was John Xántus, a Hungarian immigrant who enlisted at Fort Leavenworth

in 1855. Xántus became one of the Smithsonian Institution's most accomplished field collectors and, while an enlisted man, was sponsored for membership in the Academy of Natural Sciences in Philadelphia. See Zwinger, *Xántus*.

4. Lowe, *Dragoon*, 3, 5, 8, 21; Ballentine, *Autobiography*, 1; Bennet, *Forays*, 3.

5. Coffman, *Army*, 183–84, 187–88. For cholera at Fort Riley, see Lowe, *Dragoon*, pt. 5. Capt. William Carlin's unit suffered cholera deaths on the march to Fort Laramie in spring 1855. Girardi and Hughes, *Carlin*, 11. A detailed army medical history in the mid-nineteenth century is Senate, *Statistical*, SED 96, serial 825; the Fort Merrill example is found on 353.

6. Coffman, *Army*, 191–92; McPherson, *Battle*, 29; Lowe, *Dragoon*, 97–98; Averell, *Saddle*, 130–32.

7. Louis de Vésey [John Xántus] to [Spencer Baird], 1 August 1858, Zwinger, *Xántus*, 158; Hamilton, *Reminiscences*, 41.

8. Several officers recalled applying force to subdue an unruly soldier: Alexander, *Fighting*, 19; Averell, *Saddle*, 90–91; and Maury, *Recollections*, 79–81. For a description of dunking, see Bennett, *Forays*, 12. Another discussion of such harsh punishments is found in Coffman, *Army*, 196–97.

9. See War Department, "Extracts from Acts of Congress," *Regulations*, paragraphs 3–4. For descriptions of whippings, see Averell, *Saddle*, 61; Roland and Robbins, "Diary," 467 (29 October 1857 entry); Hamilton, *Reminiscences*, 45–46; and Ballentine, *Autobiography*, 28. Meyers (*Ranks*, 131–32) and Chamberlain (*Confession*, 193–96) describe their punishments for refusing to execute a corporal sentence. The branding of a deserter is described in Meyers, *Ranks*, 42–43; and Bennett, *Forays*, 5, 38.

10. *RSW*, SED 1, pt. 2, serial 691, 7–8; Coffman, *Army*, 193. Of twelve hundred troops serving in California in 1849, the first year of the gold rush, two-fifths deserted to the mines. See *RSW*, SED 1, serial 549, 90.

11. For Davis's analysis of the desertion problem, see, *RSW*, SED 1, pt. 2, serial 691, 7–8. Coffman compares enlisted pay and emoluments with civilian wages and the cost of living in *Army*, 153–55. Bandel to Aunt, 11 March 1859, Bandel, *Frontier*, 266–67.

12. Weigley, *Army*, 88–89, 134–35; Millett and Maslowski, *Common*, 89, 120–22.

13. Weigley, *Army*, 189–95, 558; Strode, *Davis*, 1:252, 258; Warner, "John Buchanan Floyd," *Gray*, 89–90.

14. Weigley, *Army*, 134–35; Millett and Maslowski, *Common*, 121. A legal history of the general staff is Thian, *Legislative*.

15. Heitman, *Register*, 1:39–44. See also Heitman, "John James Abert," "Thomas Sidney Jesup," "Roger Jones," "Thomas Lawson," and "Joseph Gilbert Totten," *Register*, 1:150, 573, 582, 619, 966. Warner, "Joseph Gilbert Totten," *Blue*, 509–10; Goetzmann, *Exploration*, 432. Weigley, *Army*, 135; Utley, *Frontiersmen*, 48–49.

16. Millett and Maslowski, *Common*, 120–21; Weigley, *Army*, 138–39.

17. Elliott, *Scott*, 164–65, 180; Arthur Smith, *Fuss*, 119, 184, 205–12, 213–16, 218–24, 229; Johnson, *Quest*, 218. Scott's *Memoirs* are unsatisfactory. Two recent biographies of Scott are Eisenhower, *Agent*, and Johnson, *Quest*. Townsend, Journal, 8 June 1838, HM 41695(6), Townsend Papers.

18. The foregoing sketch is compiled from the memoirs of several professional soldiers. Keyes, *Observation*, 2, 7; Grant, *Memoirs*, 1:41; Averell, *Saddle*, 35; Stanley, *Memoirs*, 19–20.

19. Johnson, *Quest*, 43–46, 68–71, 76–79. This work is a solid, insightful biography of Scott.

20. Keyes, *Observation*, 11, 173; Winfield Scott to Edward Townsend, 14 May 1849, Box 2, HM 41658, Townsend Papers; Arthur Smith, *Fuss*, 4, 160, 225–28; Elliott, *Scott*, 210–11, 212–14, 287–88, 373–76, 382, 595–96, 645, 648–49; Johnson, *Quest*, 91–103, 108–10, 145–46, 217–19.

21. *CAB*, s.v. "Hitchcock, Ethan Allen"; *DAB*, s.v. "Hitchcock, Ethan Allen"; Hitchcock, *Diary*, 382, 390, 404, 411–12, 414–15, 418; Hitchcock to Thomas, 6 October 1855, "Ethan Allen Hitchcock" ACP 1893, LR ACPB (M1395), Records of AGO, RG 94, NA, fiche ACP 70; Weems, *Conquer*, 33–34; Satz, *Indian*, 160–61, 192–94.

22. Hinton, "Wool," 5, 10, 11, 18–23, 34–35, 37–38, 45, 65, 114, 233, 251, 278–79, 280, 281, and chap. 3; "Honors to Gen. Wool," *New York Daily Times*, 2 January 1854, p. 1; "The Visit of Kossuth—Gen. John E. Wool," *New York Daily Times*, 18 February 1852, p. 4; "Democratic Candidates for the Presidency," *American Whig Review* 15 (April 1852): 311–16; Stanley, *Memoirs*, 34–35; Weems, *Conquer*, 293–94; *DAB*, s.v. "Wool, John Ellis"; Bauer, *Mexican*, 209, 214.

23. Heitman, "Newman S. Clarke," *Register*, 1:307; *ACAB*, s.v. "Clarke, Newman S."; Thian, *Notes*, 86; Justin Smith, *War*, 2:112, 113, 144, 572; Hancock, *Reminiscences*, 21.

24. Schlicke, *Wright*, 8–11, 23, 39, 57–59, 63, 76, 79–80, 214, 221, 230; Wright to James W. Nesmith, 11 June 1860; and Wright to Col. James A. Hardie, 29 November 1861, Schlicke, *Wright*, 220–21, 230; Keyes, *Observation*, 275. Wright complained about the brevet as late as 1864. See Wright to Edwin Stanton, 14 November 1864, W1099 CB 1864, LR ACPB AGO (M1064), RG 94, roll 134.

25. *DAB*, s.v. "Bonneville, Benjamin Louis Eulalie"; Thrapp, "Bonneville," *EFB*, 1:136; Reeve, "Puritan," 23:288, 24:25, 29. Averell, however, thought Bonneville impressive. Averell, *Saddle*, 146.

26. Stanley, *Sumner*, 5–6, 48, 53, 91, 102–3, 106, 122; Long, "Sumner," vi, vii, 5, 24, 48–50, 59–60; Rodenbough, *Everglade*, 158; Bennett, *Forays*, 38; Howard, *Autobiography*, 1:182–83; Keyes, *Observation*, 470; Ewell to Ben [Ewell], 12 February 1847, Hamlin, *Making*, 60–61; Tucker, *Superb*, 24, 26, 47; Jordan, *Hancock*, 10; Stanley, *Memoirs*, 43; Govan and Livingood, *Valor*, 17, 21–22, 25; Ball Jr., "'Embroilments,'" 37–38; Carr, "Reminiscences," 381. Sumner was one of the Republican generals during the Civil War. Williams, *Lincoln*, 65.

27. Young, *Cooke*, 14, 18–19, 21–24, 26, 36–66, 68, 117–23; Clarke, *Kearny*, 87; Maury, *Recollections*, 109; Tom [Swords] to John [Abraham Johnston], 26 March [18]44, Meyers, "Crack," 200; Roberts, *Mormon*, 85.

28. *DAB*, s.v. "Persifor Frazer Smith"; Maury, *Recollections*, 85; Sherman, *Memoirs*, 1:66; Smith to Pierce, 23 January 1857, series 3, Pierce Papers, LC, roll 5.

29. Sanger and Hay, *Longstreet*, 12–13; Thrapp, "John Garland," *EFB*, 2:537; McNitt, *Navajo*, 237–38.

30. Heitman, "Thomas Turner Fauntleroy," *Register*, 1:415; Sifikas, "Thomas Turner Fauntleroy," *WWWCW*, 214; *ACAB*, s.v. "Fauntleroy, Thomas T."; Thian, *Notes*, 79.

31. Wessels, *Born*, 2–4, 6–8, 13–19; Warner, "William Wing Loring," *Gray*, 193–94; Senator Gwin to Pres. Franklin Pierce, 7 July 1852, series 3," Pierce Papers, LC, roll 4; Averell, *Saddle*, 110; Maury, *Recollections*, 37.

32. *DAB*, s.v. "Twiggs, David Emanuel"; Warner, "David Emanuel Twiggs," *Gray*, 312; French, *Autobiography*, 102; Mackall, *Recollections*, 133–34; Twiggs to Scott, 15 January 1861, *OR*, ser. 1, vol. 1, 581.

33. Johnston, *Life*, 177, 257, 258; Johnston to Son [William Preston], 12 September 1856; and Johnston to Will[iam], 23 November [1856], Johnston, *Life*, 189–190; Johnson, *Reminiscences*, 107–8; Warner, "Albert Sidney Johnston," *Gray*, 159–60.

34. Adams, "Harney," passim; Richmond L. Clow, "William S. Harney," Hutton, *Soldiers*, 46–48; Reavis, *Life*, 90; Thian, *Notes*, 48, 63, 86, 106; Polk, *Diary*, 2:384–87; Harney to Pierce, 22 September 1852, "confidential," series 4, Pierce Papers, roll 5; Elliott, *Scott*, 449–50; Weems, *Conquer*, 426–27; Hitchcock, *Diary*, 174 n, 415, 418–19; Myers, "Crack," 209 n. 130; Browne, "Utah," 365. For the comments of junior officers and men on Harney, see Keyes, *Observation*, 287; Maury, *Recollections*, 43–44; Meyers, *Ranks*, 75; Averell, *Saddle*, 88–89; Howard, *Autobiography*, 1:75–76; and Heth, *Memoirs*, 127.

35. Timothy Johnson, *Quest*, 109–10, 145–46; Ambrose, *Duty*, 111–13, 115; James Morrison, "*Best*," 61–62; Weigley, *Army*, 153–56, 157–58; Millett and Maslowski, *Common*, 129; Gunnison to [Martha Delony Gunnison], 7 February 1851, HM 17069, Box 1, Gunnison Papers, HEH; Reeve, "Puritan," 295 (6 May 1857 entry).

36. James Morrison, "*Best*," 15, 22, 61–62; Ambrose, *Duty*, 119; Coffman, *Army*, 46–48; Hutton, *Sheridan*, 3–4; Morris, *Sheridan*, 14–15; Schutz and Trenerry, *Abandoned*, 6–7; Lee to Markie [Martha Custis Williams], 16 September 1853, Craven, "*Markie*," 37.

37. Coffman, *Army*, 81; Weigley, *Army*, 168–69; Utley, *Frontiersmen*, 42, 45. Smith's letter to his mother is in Parks, *Smith*, 66–67. Grant to Wife [Julia Dent Grant], 2 February 1853 [1854], Simon, *Grant*, 1:316.

38. Johnson, *Reminiscences*, 44, 65; Meyer to James [Walden], 4 April 1855; and Meyer to James [Walden], 26 September 1855, Clary, "'Texan,'" 51, 72; Meyers, *Ranks*, 101–2; Averell, *Saddle*, 131; Sweeny to Ell[en Swain Sweeny], 25 February 1851, Letterbook (SW 850[9]), Box 8, Sweeny Papers; Hancock, *Reminiscences*, 11; Sedgwick to sister, 25 September 1860, *Correspondence*, 2:24; Schofield *Forty-six*, 22; Alexander, *Fighting*, 20; Grant to Wife, 2 February 1853 [1854]; Crook, *Autobiography*, 11. The journals of Ethan A. Hitchcock are in Hitchcock Family Papers, 1755–1902, Missouri Historical Society Collections, St. Louis, Missouri. The journals and diaries of Samuel Peter Heintzelman are located in his Papers, 1822–1904, LC. See the papers of John Williams Gunnison and Thomas William Sweeny at HEH for letters to their wives, friends, and family.

39. T[homas Sweeny] to Ell[en Swain Sweeny], 28 March 1851, Letterbook (SW 850[11]); and Sweeny to Bodge, 5 June 1856, Letterbook (SW 850[110]), Box 8, Sweeny Papers; Gunnison to Wife [Martha Delony Gunnison], 10 June 1849, HM 17060, Box 1, Gunnison Papers, HEH; Coffman, *Army*, 117–19.

40. For primitive conditions and disease, see Gunnison to Alice [Gunnison], 10 November 1841, HM 17085, Box 1, Gunnison Papers; Roland and Robbins, "Diary," 463–500; Lane, *Married*, passim; Vielé, *Following*, passim; Parks, *Smith*, 80; Lowe, *Dragoon*, pt. 5; King, *War*, 18–19; Coffman, *Army*, 119–22.

41. Hancock, *Reminiscences*, 5; Johnson, *Reminiscences*, 77, 78; Sweeny to Bodge, 10 February 1856, Letterbook (SW 850[102]), Box 8, Sweeny Papers; Averell, *Saddle*, 156; Lane, *Married*, 29, 30; Roland and Robbins, "Diary," 490 (15 January 1857 entry); Ewell to Ben [Ewell], 21 July 1852, Hamlin, *Making*, 75–76; Stanley, *Memoirs*, 54; Meyer to James [Walden], 3 January 185[5], Clary, "'Texan,'" 34; Sheridan, *Memoirs*, 1:25–26. Two

volumes on the Quartermaster and Commissary Departments have appeared in recent years: Frazer, *Supplies*, and Miller, *Soldiers*. Coffman, *Army*, 94, 125, 127–28.

42. Crook, *Autobiography*, 7; Johnson, *Reminiscences*, 65; Meyer to James [Walden], 26 September 1855, 72; Averell, *Saddle*, 130; Utley, *Frontiersmen*, 30–31, 46; Coffman, *Army*, 63–64.

43. Coffman, *Army*, 49–50, 59–60; Utley, *Frontiersmen*, 31.

44. Talbot to Sister, 10 May 1849; and Talbot to Mother, 25 Sept[ember] 1850, Hine and Lottinville, *Soldier*, 122, 147; Smith to Capt. William Freeman, 28 January 1850; and Smith to Jones, 1 April 1850, vol. 1/4* LS DPac (no. 3578), RG 393, pp. 175, 194–95.

45. Utley, *Frontiersmen*, 31–32; Coffman, *Army*, 49; Johnson, *Reminiscences*, 41–42, 87, 91; Reeve, "Puritan," 29 (21 May 1857 entry); War Department, *Regulations*, art. 4, pars. 19–21.

46. Crook, *Autobiography*, 10; Sweeny to Ell[en Swain Sweeny], 27 May 1853, Letterbook (SW 850[57]), Sweeny Papers; Govan and Livingood, *Valor*, 23.

47. Sears, *McClellan*, 50; Sherman *Home*, 133; Sherman, *Memoirs*, vol. 1, chaps. 3–5.

48. Sherman, *Memoirs*, 1:73–77; Keyes, *Observation*, 242; Glisan, 17 January 1855, *Journal*, 212; Sherman to Hitchcock, 16 Aug[ust] 1854; and Sherman to Hitchcock, 31 May 1854, Box 2, General Correspondence, Hitchcock Papers, LC. For the specific amounts of money that Sherman oversaw for Hitchcock, see the colonel's endorsements on Sherman to Hitchcock, 31 May 1854; and Sherman to Hitchcock, 1 Sept[ember] 1854, Box 2, Hitchcock Papers.

49. Sweeny, 26–28 [June 1851], *Journal*, 117; T[homas] Sweeny to Ell[en Swain Sweeny], 12 May 1851, Letterbook (SW 850[14]), Box 8, Sweeny Papers; Lewis, *Grant*, 316–18; Coffman, *Army*, 83; Jerry Thompson, *Fight*, 12–14; Jerry Thompson, *Sibley*, 102–7, 131–33.

50. Col. James A. Hardie to Capt. Joseph Folsom, 27 April 1853, HM 19072; Col. James A. Hardie to Peter Van Winkle, 27 April 1853, HM 19073; and Capt. Joseph F[olsom] to Peter Van Winkle, 27–30 April 1853, HM 19073, Grabhorn Collection, HEH; Gunnison to [Martha Delony Gunnison], 28 February 1846, HM 17055, Box 1, Gunnison Papers, HEH; Ewell to Mother, 3 October 1839, Hamlin, *Making*, 27.

51. Utley, *Frontiersmen*, 32–33; Weigley, *Army*, 110–11; War Department, *Regulations*, art. 2, par. 10.

52. Capt. Thomas Sword to Lt. Abraham Johnston, 10 November 1844, Myers, "'Crack,'" 202; Crook, *Autobiography*, 10.

53. The correspondence between Hancock, Clarke, and Sumner is quoted in Hancock, *Reminiscences*, 22–24.

54. Norris, et al., *Emory*, 2, 94, 97–99; Goetzmann, *Army*, 129–30; Carpenter, *Sword*, 13; McFeely, *Yankee*, 39; Clarke, *Kearny*, 88–89, 284.

55. Burnside to Calhoun, 23 January 1850, RI 369, Ritch Papers, HEH; Emory Thomas, *Bold*, 59–60; Beauregard to Slidell, 9 February 1858, HM 24506, HEH.

56. Cooper to [Adj. Gen. Roger Jones], 25 April 1842, HM 42583; and McCall to father [Archibald McCall], 10 January 1843, HM 42611, McCall Papers, HEH.

57. Buchanan to Archibald McCall, 10 January 1843, HM 42578; Gen. T. Cadwalader to Sen. William Dayton, 24 January 1843, HM 42579; Pennington to Jacob Miller and William Dayton, 24 January 1843, HM 42579; T. Cadwalader to A[rchibald] McCall, 24 January 1843, HM 42579; John Briden to Archibald McCall, 30 January 1843, [no

accession number]; Sen. William Dayton to Gen. T. Cadwalader, 13 February 1843, HM 42587; and Kemble to Gen. T. Cadwalader, 20 February 1843, HM 42600, McCall Papers, HEH.

58. Kemble to Cadwalader, 20 February 1843; Kemble to Archibald McCall, 20 February 1843, HM 42601; and George McCall to Archibald McCall, 5 March 1843, HM 42612, McCall Papers.

59. Averell, *Saddle*, 237; Smith to Mother, [?] March 1860, Parks, *Smith*, 105.

60. Morrison, "*Best*," 62–63; Emory Thomas, *Bold*, 15; Tucker, *Superb*, 19–21; Jordan, *Hancock*, 7; Klein, *Alexander*, 3–4, 9; Alexander, *Fighting*, 4–5.

61. Townsend, "Memoir," HM 41697, Townsend Papers; Morrison, "Cadet," 312.

62. Morrison, "Cadet," 312; Morrison, "*Best*," 63, 181–82; Morrison, "Educating," 108–11.

63. Morrison, "Cadet," 312; Howard, *Autobiography*, 1:48, 49, 52–53; McFeely, *Yankee*, 33; Carpenter, *Sword*, 9–10; Morrison, "Struggle," 141.

64. Morrison, "Struggle," 144–45; Sears, *McClellan*, 6; Jordan, *Hancock*, 10.

65. This data is compiled from Heitman, *Register*, vol. 1, passim.

66. *Pay*, HED 22, serial 851, 22–26, 54–56.

67. Ewell to Ben [Ewell], 25 February 1854, Hamlin, *Making*, 78; Jordan, *Hancock*, 23; McMurray, *Hood*, 14–15; R. Patterson to Davis, 19 April 1854, Davis Papers, LC, roll 1.

68. I have compiled these statistics from two sources: Heitman, *Register*, vol. 1, passim; and *Pay*, HED 22, serial 851, 22–26, 54–56.

69. Heitman, *Register*, vol. 1, passim; *Pay*, HED 22, serial 851, 22–26, 54–56; Utley, *Frontiersmen*, 34 n. 60.

70. Sweeny to Ell[en Swain Sweeny], 20 August 1856, Letterbook (SW 850[113]), Sweeny Papers; Tucker, *Superb*, 26; Jordan, *Hancock*, 5–6; Sears, *McClellan*, xii, 58, 117–18; Polk, *Diary*, 2:385; Gwin to Pierce, 7 July 1852; Stuart to Cousin [Bettie Hairston], 7 May [1853], Hairston, "Stuart's," 294.

71. Grant, *Memoirs*, 1:53–54, 214–15; Johnson, *Reminiscences*, 22, 71; Sherman to [Ellen Boyle Ewing], 17 September 1844, *Home*, 27. See also Sherman to [Ellen Sherman], 31 May 1855, *Home*, 142; Hitchcock, *Diary*, 404; Keyes, *Observation*, 203, 289; Warner, "John Wolcott Phelps," *Blue*, 368–69; Phillips, *Damned*, 104, 106–7, 116, 124.

72. Elliott, *Scott*, 629; Harney to Pierce, 22 September 1852, roll 5; Steptoe to Pierce, 30 June 1852, roll 4; Steptoe to Pierce, 2 July 1852, roll 4; Pierce to Steptoe, 20 September 1852, roll 5; Mason to Steptoe, 23 September 1852, roll 5; Steptoe to Mason, 23 September 1852, roll 5; and Steptoe to Pierce, 27 July 1852, [confidential], series 3, Pierce Papers, roll 5; Casdorph, *Magruder*, 79; Winders, *Polk's*, 70.

73. Townsend, [Notes on Winfield Scott], HM 41702, Box 2, Townsend Papers; Hitchcock, *Diary*, 375–76, 382; Elliott, *Scott*, 622–23, 627, 634, 642, 645; Smith, *Fuss*, 353; Johnson, *Scott*, 216.

74. Coffman, *Army*, 90–91; Skelton, *Profession*, 350, 353; Skelton, "Officers," 38, 48. Edward J. Steptoe reported to Pierce that officers sitting on a court-martial with him were "Democrats, with but one exception," and were "heartily" supporting his campaign. Steptoe to Pierce, 30 June 1852. Steptoe was undoubtedly currying future favor with Pierce.

75. Averell, *Saddle*, 71; Carpenter, *Sword*, 13; Skelton, "Officers," 48 n. 52; Coffman, *Army*, 91.

76. Averell, *Saddle*, 71; Longstreet, "Old Army," *New York Times*, 19 August 1894, Sanger and Hay, *Longstreet*, 16–17; McFeely, *Yankee*, 32; Phillips, *Damned*, 105; Sherman to [Ellen Sherman], 10 July 1860, *Home*, 178–79; Johnson, *Reminiscences*, 74–75; [Lee] to [Mrs. Lee], 27 December 1856, Jones, *Lee*, 82–83.

77. Girardi and Hughes, *Carlin*, 16.

78. Ibid., 16–17.

79. Hartje, *Van Dorn*, 75–76; Keyes, *Observation*, 178–79, 289; Beauregard to Slidell, 9 February 1858; Carr, "Reminiscences," 381; Williams, *Lincoln*, 65; Schutz and Trenerry, *Abandoned*, 59–60; Phillips, *Damned*, 106; Sears, *McClellan*, 66; Warner, "Fitz John Porter," *Blue*, 378–80; Girardi and Hughes, *Carlin*, 15–16.

80. Heth, *Memoirs*, 149; Hassler, *Hill*, 27; Smith to Mother, 15 September 1860, Parks, *Smith*, 109–10.

81. Carpenter, *Sword*, 21; Johnson, *Reminiscences*, 132; Young, *Cooke*, 166.

CHAPTER 5

1. An overview of filibusters is Brown, *Agents*. See also Robert E. May, "Manifest Destiny's Filibusters," *Manifest Destiny and Empire: American Antebellum Expansionism*, ed. Sam W. Haynes and Christopher Morris, The Walter Prescott Webb Memorial Lectures no. 23 (College Station: Texas A&M University Press, 1997), 146–79; and May, "Males," 857–86. For Fillmore's position on expansion and filibusters, see Brown, *Agents*, 40, 94, 106. Potter, *Impending*, 180–81. Acting Secretary of State John J. Crittenden outlines Fillmore's policy on expansion and Cuba in a letter to Count de Stargis, 22 October 1851, Manning, *Diplomatic*, 6:460–63.

2. Pres. Millard Fillmore, Proclamation, 25 April 1851, quoted in *The San Francisco Daily Herald*, 11 June 1851. A study of the Lopéz expedition is Tom Chaffin, *Fatal Glory: Narciso Lopéz and the First Clandestine U.S. War against Cuba* (Charlottesville: University of Virginia, 1996). Fillmore's proclamation against private campaigns to Mexico is in Severance, *Fillmore*, 1:310. A recent overview of the Carvajal expedition is Ball Jr., "Interwar," 280–89. A pathbreaking underground classic on frontier military constabulary duty is Ball Sr., "Military Posses." For military intervention in antebellum civil unrest, see Coakley, *Role*, chaps. 1–10. See also two general works: Marvin S. Reichley, "Federal Military Intervention in Civil Disturbances" (Ph.D. diss., Georgetown University, 1939); and Bennet Rich, *The Presidents and Civil Disorders* (Washington, D.C.: Brookings Institution, 1941).

3. Acting Secretary of State William Derrick to Robert Letcher, 24 September 1851, Manning, *Diplomatic*, 9:96; Rolle, "California," 257, 259; Fillmore to Hitchcock, 18 November 1851; and Conrad to Hitchcock, 19 November 1851, "Hitchcock" ACP 1893, LR ACPB (M1395), RG 94, fiche ACP 70; Hitchcock to United States Marshal and Collector of Customs, 8 January 1852, vol. 2/5*, LS DPac (no. 3578), pt. 1, RG 393, NA.

4. Warner, "Ethan Allen Hitchcock," *Blue*, 230–31; *DAB*, s.v., "Hitchcock, Ethan Allen"; Adj. Gen. Roger Jones to Hitchcock, 15 May 1851, LR DPac, RG 393; Hitchcock, *Diary*, 380–82.

5. Thian, *Notes*, 25, 86. Divisional troop aggregates are taken from *RSW*, HED 2, serial 634, 213; *RSW*, HED 1, serial 674, 62–63; *RSW*, SED 1, pt. 2, serial 691, 122–23; and *RSW*, SED 1, pt. 2, serial 747, 122–23.

6. Frazer, "Presidio of San Francisco," *Forts*, 30–31. Troop aggregates for the Presidio of San Francisco and Benicia Barracks and Arsenal are taken from *RSW*, HED 2, serial 634, 208–9; *RSW*, SED 1, pt. 2, serial 691, 122–23; and *RSW*, SED 1, serial 747, 62–63. In late 1852 Benicia Barracks had 222 officers and men, a larger garrison than usual. The additional men were probably in transit to interior posts. *RSW*, HED 1, serial 674, 62–63.

7. Senkewicz, *Vigilantes*, 12–15, 18, 32–33; Grant, *Memoirs*, 1:208.

8. Townsend, *California*, 73; Bean, *California*, 139–41; Senkewicz, *Vigilantes*, 75–78, 82, 84–88; Hitchcock, *Diary*, 386–87; Bancroft, *Popular*, 1:332–33, 350, 352, 363.

9. Hitchcock to Denver, 28 May 1852; Hitchcock to Adjutant General Cooper, 8 February 1853; and Hitchcock to Adjutant General Cooper, 21 April 1853, "Hitchcock" ACP 1893, LR ACPB (M1395), RG 94, fiche ACP 70; Davis to Hitchcock, 3 June 1853, Crist and Dix, *Davis*, 5:18, 18 n. 2; Hitchcock, *Diary*, 393; Warner, "James W. Denver," *Blue*, 120.

10. Brown, *Agents*, 159, 191; Bancroft, *California*, 6:583.

11. Hitchcock to Magruder, 21 April 1852; and Hitchcock to Maj. Charles Merchant, 8 May 1852, vol. 2/5*, LS DPac (no. 3578), pt. 1, RG 393, pp. 116, 135; Metcalf, "California," 5–7, 11–16; Bancroft, *California*, 6:585, 587–88.

12. Brown, *Agents*, 109, 116–17; Nichols, *Pierce*, 265–66; Potter, *Impending*, 181–82; Bailey, *Diplomatic*, 291–92.

13. Hitchcock to Capt. Samuel P. Heintzelman (confidential), 4 April 1853, vol. 2/5*, LS DPac (no. 3578), pt. 1, RG 393, pp. 243–44; Bolaños-Geyer, *Walker*, 2:198.

14. Manuel Diez de Bonilla to Gadsden, 20 August 1853; Manuel Diez de Bonilla to Alfred Conkling, 8 August 1853; Alfred Conkling to William Marcy, 9 August 1853; Manuel Diez de Bonilla to Gadsden, 20 August 1853; and Gadsden to Manuel Diez de Bonilla, 22 August 1853, Manning, *Diplomatic*, 9:601–2, 598–99, 600, 601–2, 602–3; Hitchcock to District Attorney Inge, 24 October 1853, "Hitchcock" ACP 1893, LR ACPB (M1395), RG 94, fiche ACP 70. A sketch of Walker's background is Stout, *Liberator*, 81–83.

15. Hitchcock to Inge, 24 October 1853; and Hitchcock to Adj. Gen. Samuel Cooper, 1 October 1853, "Hitchcock" ACP 1893, LR ACPB (M1395), RG 94, fiche ACP 70; Hitchcock to Hammond, 22 September 1853, vol. 2/5*, LS DPac (no. 3578), pt. 1, RG 393, p. 505; Townsend, *California*, 93; Hitchcock, *Diary*, 400–401.

16. Townsend, *California*, 93; Hitchcock, *Diary*, 400–401.

17. Thomas, *Between*, 46–48; Hitchcock, *Diary*, 382, 390, 402, 411; Williams, *Broderick*, 74–75, 75 n. 18; Gwin, "Memoirs," ed. Ellison, 178. In 1857 Crabb and fifty-nine followers died in an expedition to Sonora. Wyllys, "Crabb," 183–84, 190–91.

18. Hitchcock, *Diary*, 401; Hitchcock to Hammon[d], 3 October 1853, LS DPac (no. 3578), pt. 1, RG 393, p. 518; *National Cyclopaedia*, s.v. "Hammond, Richard Pindell."

19. Hitchcock, *Diary*, 401; *National Cyclopaedia*, s.v. "Inge, Samuel Williams."

20. Hitchcock to Inge, 10 October 1853; and Hitchcock to Hammond, 8 October 1853, vol. 2/5*, LS DPac (no. 3578), RG 393, pp. 521–22, 519; Townsend, *California*, 93–94; Hitchcock, *Diary*, 401–2; Bolaños-Geyer, *Walker*, 2:212.

21. Hitchcock to Inge, 8 October 1853; and Hitchcock to Inge, 10 October 1853 vol. 2/5*, LS DPac (no. 3598), RG 393, pp. 521–22; Hitchcock to Inge, 24 October 1853 "Hitchcock" "ACP 1893, LR ACPB(M1395), RG 94, fiche ACP 70; Hitchcock, *Diary*, 402–4; Prucha, *Broadax*, chap. 4.

22. Inge to Hitchcock, 5 November 1853; and Hitchcock to Adj. Gen. Samuel Cooper,

15 November 1853, "Hitchcock" ACP 1893, LR ACPB (M1395), RG 94, fiche ACP 70; Townsend to Capt. Henry S. Burton (confidential), 9 December 1853; and Townsend to Capt. Sameul P. Heintzelman (confidential), 9 December 1853, vol. 3/7*, LS DPac (no. 3578), pt. 1, RG 393, pp. 22–23, 23–24.

23. Adj. Gen. Samuel Cooper to Hitchcock, 15 November 1853, Box 6, 1853, LR DPac (no. 3584), pt. 1, RG 393; Hitchcock, *Diary*, 405; Cooper to Maj. Gen. Winfield Scott, 7 January 1854; Head Quarters of the Army, General Orders No. 1, 9 January 1854; Wool to Davis, 7 January 1854; Wool to Davis, 10 January 1854; Wool to Cooper, 14 January 1854; and Wool to Adj. Gen. Samuel Cooper, 19 January 1854, *Correspondence*, HED 88, serial 956, 3, 5, 4, 7, 8.

24. Davis to Wool, 12 January 1854; and Adj. Gen. Samuel Cooper to Wool, 16 January 1854, *Correspondence*, HED 88, serial 956, 6, 7; Bolaños-Geyer, *Walker*, 2:255; Hinton, "Wool," 232–33.

25. "Democratic Candidates for the Presidency," *American Whig Review* 15 (April 1852), 311–16; Hinton, "Wool," 45, 65, 114, 233.

26. Wool to Maj. Gen. Winfield Scott, 14 February 1854, *Correspondence*, HED 88, serial 956, 8; Crist and Dix, *Davis*, 5:88–89, 89, n. 2; Williams, *Broderick*, 52; "Latest Intelligence," *New York Daily Times*, 8 January 1855; John Edmond Gonzales, "Henry Stuart Foote," Lamar, *Reader's*, 386–87. Wool and Foote are quoted in Hinton, "Wool," 240–41.

27. Quinn, *Rivals*, 149–50; Hinton, "Wool," 241.

28. Wool to Secretary of War Jefferson Davis, 1 March 1854; Wool to Lt. Col. Lorenzo Thomas, 28 February 1854; Wool to Adj. Gen. Samuel Cooper, 15 March 1854; and Wool to Capt. Thomas A. Dornin, 15 March 1854, San Francisco, *Correspondence*, HED 88, serial 956, 10–11, 9–10, 19, 36; Wool to Cripps, 28 February 1854, vol. 3/7*, LS DPac (no. 3578), pt. 1, RG 393, pp. 67–68.

29. Brown, *Agents*, 168; Metcalf, "French," 16–17; Nasatir, "Dillon," 316–18, 319, 320, 321; Wyllys, "French," 340, 343, 344–45, 353–54; Del Valle to Consul [Dillon], [n.d.]; Cavailler to McKinstry, 27 March 1854; Manuel Diez de Bonilla to Alphonse Dano, 17 January 1854; and "Contract," 4 March 1854, *Correspondence*, HED 88, serial 956, 45, 37, 43–44, 32–33.

30. Wool to Del Valle, 15 March 1854; Del Valle to Wool, 15 March 1854; Del Valle to Wool, [n.d.]; Wool to Collector Richard P. Hammond, 15 March 1854; Wool to Cripps, 29 July 1854, *Correspondence*, HED 88, serial 956, 40, 41, 41–42, 35–36, 94–95; Wool to Capt. Thomas A. Dornin, 10 March 1854; and Wool to Collector Richard P. Hammond, 25 April 1854, vol. 3/7*, LS DPac (no. 3578), pt. 1, RG 393, pp. 71, 105; Nasatir, "Dillon," 319.

31. Wool to Hammond, 13 March 1854; Wool to Hammond, 15 March 1854; and Wool to Major [Hammond], 17 March 1854, *Correspondence*, HED 88, serial 956, 39–40, 35–36, 45.

32. Wool to Capt. William Ball (confidential), 20 March 1854; Wool to Capt. William Ball, 22 March 1854; Wool to Capt. James Alden (confidential), 27 March 1854; "The Ship Challenge Libelled"; Wool to Collector Richard P. Hammond, 31 March 1854, *Correspondence*, HED 88, serial 956, 46, 31–33, 47; Hinton, "Wool," 250.

33. Wool to Inge, 30 March 1854; "Arrest of the Mexican Consul," 31 March [1854]; and Wool to Secretary of War Jefferson Davis, 14 April 1854, *Correspondence*, HED 88, serial 956, 49, 30–31, 53.

34. Wool to Secretary of War Jefferson Davis, 15 May 1854, *Correspondence*, HED 88, serial 956, 57; Nasatir, "Dillon," 321–22.

35. Wool to Davis, 15 May 1854; Dillon to Wool, 18 March 1854; Dillon to [Wool], 20 March 1854; Wool to Dillon, 20 March 1854, *Correspondence*, HED 88, serial 956, 33–34, 42–43, 34–35, 57–58; Nasatir, "Dillon," 321.

36. Nasatir, "Dillon," 321–22; Inge to Davis, 1 June 1854, Dunbar, *Constitutionalist*, 2:361–63; Hinton, "Wool," 261–64.

37. Townsend to Capt. Henry S. Burton, 17 May 1854, vol. 3/7*, LS DPac (no. 3578), pt. 1, RG 393, p. 126; Wool to Davis, 15 May 1854, *Correspondence*, HED 88, serial 956, 58; Bolaños-Geyer, *Walker*, 2:311; Hinton, "Wool," 257–58.

38. Davis to Wool, 14 April 1856, *Correspondence*, HED 88, serial 956, 52.

39. Potter, *Impending*, 157–76, 178, 182–83; William C. Davis, *Jefferson Davis*, 252. Among others, District Attorney Samuel Inge kept Davis abreast of Democratic politics, particularly Foote's activities, in California. See Inge to Davis, 1 June 1855; and Inge to Davis, 10 June 1855, Dunbar, *Constitutionalist*, 2:361–63, 470–71.

40. Wool to Davis, 30 May 1854; Inge to Wool, 30 May 1854; and Richardson to Wool, 22 May 1854, *Correspondence*, HED 88, serial 956, 67–68, 155, 157,

41. Davis to Wool, 13 April 1854; Adj. Gen. Samuel Cooper to Wool, 17 May 1854; Head Quarters of the Army, Special Orders No. 80, 18 May 1854; Wool to Lt. Col. Lorenzo Thomas, 1 June 1854; Wool to Lt. Col. Lorenzo Thomas, 14–15 June 1854; Wool to Lt. Col. Lorenzo Thomas, 1 July 1854; Scott, 25 July 1854, endorsement on Wool to Thomas, 1 July 1854; and Davis, 16 August 1854, endorsement of Wool to Thomas, 1 July 1854, *Correspondence*, HED 88, serial 956, 51, 64, 72–73, 74–75, 83–85, 85. The Scott-Davis acrimony is discussed in Eisenhower, *Agent*, 332–33.

42. Hammond to Wool (confidential), 16 August 1854; Wool to Hammond, 17 August 1854; Gadsden to Wool, 2 August 1854; Wool to Gadsden, 25 September 1854; and Adj. Gen. Samuel Cooper to Wool, 3 February 1855, *Correspondence*, HED 88, serial 956, 101, 102, 107, 109–10, 129.

43. The two antagonists exchanged letters through the summer to fall and winter: Davis to Wool, 18 August 1854; Wool to Davis, 13 October 1854; Davis to Wool, 13 December 1854; and Wool to Davis, January 1855, *Correspondence*, HED 88, serial 956, 99, 111–14, 122–28, 146–48. Hinton details the Wool-Davis battle in "Wool," 265–80. "The Wool Correspondence," *New York Daily Times*, 13 January 1855; "Latest Intelligence," *New York Daily Times*, 8 January 1855.

44. Bolaños-Geyer, *Walker*, 2:310–11, 336–37; Williams, *Broderick*, 74–76, 78; Inge to Davis (private), 16 October 1854, Crist and Dix, *Davis*, 5:87–88.

45. Bolaños-Geyer, *Walker*, 2:320–21, 322–23, 324, 349–50, 358–60; Wyllys, "Republic," 211.

46. Cooper to Wool, 19 September 1855; Secretary of State William Marcy to Secretary of War Jefferson Davis, 7 September 1855; Minister James Y. Mason to Count Walewski, 3 August 1855; and Count Walewski to Minister James Y. Mason, 7 August 1855, Paris, in *Correspondence*, HED 88, serial 956, 133, 134, 136; Hinton, "Wool," 278.

47. Bancroft, *Popular*, 2:29, 39–40, 57–60; Senkewicz, *Vigilantes*, 167–68; Governor Johnson to President [Pierce], 19 June 1856, *Presidential*, SED 101, serial 824, 2–4; Gibson to Capt. Edward O. C. Ord, 23 September 1856, *Correspondence*, HED 88, serial 956, 204.

48. Senkewicz, *Vigilantes*, 168–69, 170, 172; Bean, *California*, 148; Brown, *Strain*, 124, 128, 137, 138; Bancroft, *Popular*, 2:164; Sherman, *Memoirs*, 1:148–49, 152; Johnson to [Pierce], 19 June 1856, *Presidential*, SED 101, serial 824, 2–3.

49. Sherman, *Memoirs*, 1:124; Johnson to [Pierce], 19 June 1856, *Presidential*, SED 101, serial 824, 2–4; Bancroft, *Popular*, 2:269–83; Lotchin, *San Francisco*, 194; Myers, *Terror*, 116. My figure for the number of men enrolled in the vigilante militia splits the difference between Lotchin's three thousand and Myers's fifty-seven hundred.

50. Johnson, Sherman, and Douglass heard Wool promise federal arms on three separate occasions at Benicia. Sherman, *Memoirs*, 1:125–27 (Sherman quotes himself on 127); Johnson to Wool, 25 September 1856; Douglass to Johnson, 26 September 1856; and Sherman to Johnson, 11 June 1856, *RSW*, SED 43, serial 881, 23–25, 26, 26–28.

51. Johnson, Proclamation, 3 June 1856, *Presidential*, SED 101, serial 824, 6; Johnson to Wool, 4 June 1858, *Correspondence*, HED 88, serial 956, 186–87; Sherman, *Memoirs*, 1:156; Buchanan, *Terry*, 26–27; Sherman's order of assembly is quoted in Bancroft, *Popular*, 2:297.

52. Wool to Johnson, 5 June 1856; Johnson to Wool, 7 June 1856, *Correspondence*, HED 88, serial 956, 188, 188–89; Rowe to Johnson, 9 October 1856, *RSW*, SED 43, serial 881, 28–29; Sherman, *Memoirs*, 1:156; Bancroft, *Popular*, 2:306.

53. Sherman, *Memoirs*, 1:156–59; Sherman to Johnson, 11 June 1856, *RSW*, SED 43, serial 881, 26–28; Buchanan, *Terry*, 31 n. 22.

54. Sherman, *Memoirs*, 1:127; Bancroft, *Popular*, 2:307–8; Wool to Johnson, 9 June 1856, *Correspondence*, HED 88, serial 956, 191–92. For Bleeding Kansas and the Democratic party convention, see chapter 7.

55. Wool to Milton Latham, 12 June 1856; and 1st Lt. David Jones to Lt. Col. René E. DeRussy, 10 June 1856, *Correspondence*, HED 88, serial 956, 192, 191; 1st Lt. Richard Arnold to First Lieutenant Gibson, [n.d.]; and 1st Lt. David Jones to First Lieutenant Gibson, 7 June 1856, vol. 4/8*, LS DPac (no. 3578), pt. 1, RG 393, pp. 22, 15; Johnson to President [Pierce], 19 June 1856; and Cushing to President [Pierce], 19 July 1856, *Presidential*, SED 101, serial 824, 2–4, 10–13.

56. Buchanan, *Terry*, 38–41, chap. 3; Bancroft, *Popular*, 2:372–75, 529–33; Senkewicz, *Vigilantes*, 175–77.

57. Senkewicz, *Vigilantes*, 188, 190; Brown, *Strain*, 136–37; Sherman to Brother [John], 7 July 1856, Thorndike, *Letters*, 59; Wool to Davis, 4 October 1856, *Correspondence*, HED 88, serial 956, 200–201.

58. James T. McDuffie to Wool, 5 September 1856; McAllister and Hoffman to Wool, 9 September 1856; and Wool to Davis, 4 October 1856, *Correspondence*, HED 88, serial 956, 195, 196, 201; Davis to Wool, 4 November 1856, *RSW*, SED 43, serial 881, 16.

59. Johnson to Wool, 17 October 1856; Douglass to Johnson, 26 September 1856; Sherman to Johnson, 11 June 1856; and Row to Johnson, 9 October 1856, *RSW*, SED 43, serial 881, 23–25, 26, 26–28, 28–29; Wool to Johnson, 17 September 1856, *Correspondence*, HED 88, serial 956, 197–98.

60. Skelton, *Profession*, 283, 285.

61. Coffman agrees. Coffman, *Army*, 85–86.

62. Warner, *Blue*, 230–31, 573–74; Hitchcock, *Diary*, 411, 418; Hitchcock to Thomas, 6 October 1855, "Hitchcock" ACP 1893, LR ACPB (M1395), RG 94, fiche ACP 70; Thian, *Notes*, 59, 86.

CHAPTER 6

1. See Rippy, "Border," 91–111; Bender, "Texas," 135–48; Tyler, "Callahan," 574–85; Fornell, "Texans," 411–28; Shearer, "Carvajal," 201–30. Two excellent sources on the border are *Mexican Border Commission* and Emory, *Report*. Richard Griswold del Castillo explores the legacy of conflict and violence left by the Mexican-American War and the Treaty of Guadalupe Hidalgo in *Treaty*.

2. Shearer, "Carvajal," 205–8; Rippy, "Border," 94–96. For reports on and complaints against the Mexican tariff policy, see *Claim*, SED 80, serial 620. For a sketch of the tariff problem, see *Mexican Border Commission*, 179–80.

3. Rippy, "Border," 96; Shearer, "Carvajal," 201–4; Ford, *Rip*, 195–96; Vielé, *Following*, 192, 193.

4. Shearer, "Carvajal," 208; Rippy, "Border," 96–97; Col. Persifor F. Smith to Adj. Gen. Roger Jones, 18 July 1852, *RSW*, HED 1, serial 674, pt. 2, 16.

5. Smith, *Presidencies*, 210–14, 226–30; Potter, *Impending*, 121–22; Minister Luis de la Rosa to Acting Secretary of State William S. Derrick, 3 October 1851; and Buckingham Smith to Secretary of State Daniel Webster, 5 October 1851, Manning, *Diplomatic*, 9:412–13. For a discussion of filibusters against Cuba, see Brown, *Agents*, pt. 1.

6. Fillmore's proclamation is in Severence, *Fillmore*, 1:310. The proclamation is quoted in Richardson, *Compilation*, 5:112. Acting Secretary of State William S. Derrick to Minister Robert P. Letcher, 24 September 1851, Manning, *Diplomatic*, 9:96.

7. Smith to Jones, 18 July 1852, *RSW*, HED 1, serial 674, pt. 2, 16–17; Smith to Harney, 21 October 181, Letterbook, HQ, DTex, 1851–54, Persifor Frazer Smith Papers, HSP; Adams, "Harney," 175–77; Frazer, "Ringgold," *West*, 158–59.

8. Shearer, "Carvajal," 213–18; Rippy, "Border," 97; Ford, *Rip*, 198–201; Frazer, "Brown," *West*, 144–45.

9. Webster to De la Rosa, 7 November 1851; Webster to De la Rosa, 4 November 1851; De la Rosa to Webster, 13 November 1851; Webster to Robert P. Letcher, 22 December 1851; and Robert P. Letcher to Webster, 12 November 1851, Manning, *Diplomatic*, 9:100–106, 99–100, 424, 107, 424–25.

10. Minister José Ramirez to Minister Robert P. Letcher, 22 January 1852; Minister Manuel Larrainzar to Secretary of War William Marcy, 21 April 1853; and Minister Robert P. Letcher to Secretary of State Daniel Webster, 18 March 1852, Manning, *Diplomatic*, 9:457–58, 556–50, 467–68; Ford, *Rip*, 203–4; Shearer, "Carvajal," 222–24.

11. Adams, "Harney," 177; Smith to Jones, 18 July 1852, *RSW*, HED 1, serial 674, pt. 2, 17–18; Asst. Adj. Gen. George Deas to Harney, 28 January 1852, Letterbook, HQ, DTex, Persifor Smith Papers.

12. Webster to President [Fillmore], 11 June 1852, *Frontier*, HED 112, serial 648, 1–2.

13. Minister Manuel Larrainzar to Webster, 16 June 1852; Minister Mariano Yáñez to William Rich, 27 November 1852; and Asst. Minister J. Miguel Arroyo to Minister Alfred Conklin, 12 March 1853, Manning, *Diplomatic*, 9:509–11, 521–22, 538–39; Shearer, "Carvajal," 226.

14. Shearer, "Carvajal," 226–27; [Wright], *Recollections*, 71–74; Rippy, "Border," 99; [Emory,] *Boundary*, HED 135, vol. 1, serial 861, 61.

15. Minister Juan N. Almonte to Secretary of War William Marcy, 20 July 1854;

Minister Juan N. Almonte to Secretary of War William Marcy, 12 December 1854; Minister Juan N. Almonte to Secretary of War William Marcy, 22 June 1855; Minister Juan N. Almonte to Secretary of War William Marcy, 14 August 1855; and Smith to Adj. Gen. Samuel Cooper, 8 September 1855, Manning, *Diplomatic*, 9:722–23, 735–36, 778, 781, 193–94; Tyler, "Callahan," 578, 579; Shearer, "Callahan," 431–32.

16. Monographs of the Callahan expedition include Shearer, "Callahan," 430–51, and Tyler, "Callahan," 574–85.

17. Col. Persifor F. Smith to Adj. Gen. Samuel Cooper, 14 July 1856, Manning, *Diplomatic*, 9:191–92n.

18. Bancroft, *Mexican*, 2:417–19; Rippy, "Border," 103–4; Twiggs to Lt. Col. Lorenzo Thomas, 20 September 1857, vol. 1, LS DTex (no. 4775), pt. 1, RG 393, pp. 455–56.

19. For Cortina's background, see Goldfinch, "Re-Appraisal," *Cortina*, chaps. 2–4. Goldfinch examines Cortina as a social rebel. An overdrawn indictment of Cortina is Woodman, *Rogue*. See also Ford, *Rip*, 261–62.

20. Exaggerated accounts of the raid are Collector Francis W. Latham to Brig. Gen. David E. Twiggs, 28 September 1859, *RSW*, SED 2, serial 1024, 378–79; and Webb, et al., to Gov. Hardin R. Runnels, 2 October 1859, *Difficulties*, HED 52, serial 1050, 20–23. A more balanced assessment is W. P. Reyburn to Collector F. W. Hatch, 21 November 1859, *Difficulties*, HED 52, serial 1050, 64–68. An extreme secondary account is Woodman, *Rogue*, 11–12. Goldfinch provides an evenhanded evaluation in "Re-Appraisal," 43–45, as does Thompson, *Cortina*, 11–12.

21. Juan Nepomuceno Cortina to "the inhabitants of the State of Texas, and especially to those of the City of Brownsville," Proclamation, 30 September 1859, *Difficulties*, HED 52, serial 1050, 70–72. For the land battles, see Goldfinch, "Re-Appraisal," 35–39.

22. Maj. Stephen Powers, et al., to Pres. James P. Buchanan, 2 October 1852; Maj. Stephen Powers to Pres. James P. Buchanan, 18 October 1859; 2d Lt. Loomis L. Langdon to Pres. James P. Buchanan, 18 October 1859; Harris, et al., to Buchanan, 25 October 1859; John Slidell to Pres. James P. Buchanan, 25 October 1859; and William G. Hale to Secretary of War John B. Floyd, 7 November 1859, *Difficulties*, HED 52, serial 1050, 70–72, 34–35, 35, 36–37, 37, 41–44. For troop transfers, see Headquarters, Department of Texas, General Orders No. 1, 5 February 1859, *Difficulties*, HED 52, serial 1050, 7–8.

23. For the assault on Rancho del Carmen, see W. B. Thompson to Stephen Powers and I. G. Brown, 26 October 1859; and Hale to Floyd, 7 November 1859 in *Difficulties*, HED 52, serial 1050, 68–69, 41–44. Two sensationalistic reports are [Newspaper clipping] (Corpus Christi [,Texas]), 7 November 1859; and "Urgent Call for Volunteers," *Goliad (Texas) Messenger*, enclosed in Twiggs to Adj. Gen. Samuel Cooper, 14 November 1859 in *Difficulties*, HED 52, serial 1050, 53, 57, ibid. Twiggs's response is Twiggs to [Secretary of War John B. Floyd], 12 November [1859], *Difficulties*, HED 52, serial 1050, 56. Goldfinch, "Re-Appraisal," 47; Thompson, *Cortina*, 21.

24. Adj. Gen. Samuel Cooper to Twiggs, 25 October 1859; Headquarters, Department of Texas, Special Orders No. 96, 1 November 1859; Headquarters, Department of Texas, Special Orders No. 103, 12 November 1859; Headquarters, Department of Texas, Special Orders No. 105, [?] November 1859; and Twiggs to Cooper, 14 November 1859, *Difficulties*, HED 52, serial 1050, 36, 41, 54–55, 55–56, 56. The description of Heintzelman is drawn from Meyers, *Ranks*, 39; and Warner, "Samuel Peter Heintzelman," *Blue*, 227–28. At Fort Yuma, 1st Lt. Thomas Sweeny and other officers quarreled with Heintzelman.

For example, see Sweeny to Ell[en Swain Sweeny], 10 April 1851, Letterbook (SW 850[13]); and Sweeny to Ell[en Swain Sweeny], 12 May 1851, Letterbook (SW 850[14]), Sweeny Papers. Frazer, "Yuma," *West*, 34–35.

25. Floyd to Collector F. W. Hatch, telegram, 18 November 1859; the order to "Commanding Officer of Fort Monroe, Virginia" enclosed in Adj. Gen. Samuel Cooper to Maj. M. M. Clark, 18 November 1859; Adj. Gen. Samuel Cooper to Quartermaster General, Commissary General, Colonel of Ordnance, Surgeon General, and Paymaster General (circular), 19 November 1859; Adj. Gen. Samuel Cooper to Col. Edwin Sumner, telegram, 19 November 1859; Williams to Asst. Quartermaster Meyers, telegram, 19 November 1859; Twiggs to Floyd, telegram, 18 November [1859]; Twiggs to Secretary of War, 21 November 1859, San Antonio, enclosed in Collector F. W. Hatch to Floyd, n.d.; Collector F. W. Hatch to Floyd, 20 November 1859; Reyburn to Hatch, 21 November 1859; [Adj. Gen. Samuel Cooper] to Commanding Officer of Fort Monroe, enclosed in Adj. Gen. Samuel Cooper to Clark, 21 November 1859; Adj. Gen. Samuel Cooper to Asst. Quartermaster Meyers, 21 November 1859; and Adj. Gen. Samuel Cooper to Col. Edwin Sumner, 21 November 1859, *Difficulties*, HED 52, serial 1050, 59, 59–60, 60, 61, 58, 62, 61–62, 64–68, 62, 62–63, 63.

26. Thompson, *Fight*, 31–33; Cortina, *Pronunciemento*, 23 November 1859, Thompson, *Cortina*, 23–28; Reyburn to Hatch, 21 November 1859; and Twiggs to Secretary of War, 21 November 1859, enclosed in Hatch to Floyd, n.d., *Difficulties*, HED 52, serial 1050, 62, 64–68.

27. Capt. James B. Ricketts to Adj. Gen. Samuel Cooper, 1 December 1859, *Difficulties*, HED 52, serial 1050, 76; Heintzelman to Lt. Col. Robert E. Lee, 1 March 1860, *Troubles*, HED 81, serial 1056, 7.

28. Heintzelman, 16 December 1859, Thompson, *Fight*, 138–43; Heintzelman to Lee, 1 March 1860, *Troubles*, HED 81, serial 1056, 7–8; Ford, *Rip*, 267.

29. Heintzelman to Lee, 1 March 1860, 8–9; Thompson, *Fight*, 149–56; Ford, *Rip*, 269–70.

30. Heintzelman to Adjutant General, 27 December 1859, *Difficulties*, HED 52, serial 1050, 97–99; Heintzelman to Lee, 1 March 1860, 9–10; Ford, *Rip*, 271–75.

31. Heintzelman to Adjutant General, 27 December 1859, 97–98; Heintzelman to 1st Lt. John Withers, 29 January 1860, *Difficulties*, HED 52, serial 1050, 106–7; Heintzelman to Lee, 1 March 1860, 9–10.

32. Heintzelman to Angel Navarro and Robert H. Taylor, 2 February 1860; Ford to Heintzelman, 4 February 1860; 2d Lt. Loomis Langdon to Heintzelman, 4 February 1860; and Heintzelman to Adj. Gen. Samuel Cooper, 5 February 1860, *Difficulties*, HED 52, serial 1050, 118–19, 114, 110–11. The rangers fired first on a party of Hispanos driving livestock, stolen according to Ford's men, across the river. The skirmish escalated from that point. Ford, *Rip*, 282–83. For Ford's attack on La Bolsa, see *Rip*, 283–287. Goldfinch doubts that Cortina attacked the *Ranchero*. Goldfinch, "Re-Appraisal," 19.

33. Houston to Secretary of War John B. Floyd, 15 February 1860; Angel Navarro to Houston, 15 February 1860; Houston to Secretary of War John B. Floyd, telegram, 20 February 1860; Houston to Secretary of War John B. Floyd, telegram, 8 March 1860; and Asst. Secretary of War W. R. Drinkard to Houston, telegram, 14 March 1860, *Difficulties*, HED 52, serial 1050, 116, 120–22, 131, 138, 145–46.

34. Secretary of War John B. Floyd to Houston, telegram, 28 February 1860; Head-

quarters of the United States Army, General Orders No. 6 (extract), 12 March 1860; Cooper to Lee, 24 February 1860; Cooper to Lee, 2 March 1860; and Maj. Edward D. Townsend to Lee, 3 March 1860, *Difficulties*, HED 52, serial 1050, 134, 139, 133, 134, 134–35; Thomas, *Lee*, 180–82.

35. Lee to Adj. Gen. Samuel Cooper, 15 March 1860; Lee to Adj. Gen. Samuel Cooper, 20 March 1860; Lee to Adj. Gen. Samuel Cooper, 11 April 1860; Lee to Trevino, 2 April 1860; Lee to Civil and Military Authorities of the city of Reynosa, Mexico, 7 April 1860; Zepeda to Lee (translation), 8 April 1860; and Garcia to Lee (translation), 14 April 1860, *Troubles*, HED 81, serial 1056, 78, 82, 83–84, 84–85, 85, 85–87, 104.

36. Heintzelman to 1st Lt. John Withers, 18 March 1860; and Stoneman and Ford to C. W. Thomas, 18 March 1860, *Troubles*, HED 81, serial 1056, 79–80, 80–81; Ford, *Rip*, 290–93.

37. Stoneman and Ford to C. W. Thomas, 18 March 1860, 80–81; Heintzelman to Cooper, 25 March 1860, *Troubles*, HED 81, serial 1056, 82–83; Ford, *Rip*, 293–95, 296–305.

38. Lee to Cooper, 11 April 1860, 82–83; McKnight to Lee, 11 April 1860; Lee to McKnight, 11 April 1860; Houston to Secretary of War John B. Floyd, 14 April 1860; and Lee to Adj. Gen. Samuel Cooper, 17 April 1860, *Troubles*, HED 81, serial 1056, 88–89, 89, 90–95, 100; Ford, *Rip*, 307–8.

39. Rister, *Lee*, 126–27; Freeman, *Lee*, 1:409; Goldfinch, "Re-Appraisal," 50–51.

CHAPTER 7

1. Long, "Origin," 187; Gough, "British," 60; Tunem, "Dispute," 38–39. For the Oregon Treaty of 1846, see Billington and Ridge, *Westward*, 472–73.

2. Tunem, "Dispute," 136–37; Fish, "Last," 187–88; Long, "Origin," 203–5.

3. Long, "Origin," 205; Tunem, "Dispute," 134–36; Fish, "Last," 187–88. The HBC assessment appears in *Island*, HED 77, serial 1056, 9.

4. Fish, "Last," 191–92; Long, "Origin," 206; Tunem, "Dispute," 136–37.

5. Schlicke, *Wright*, 197. For Harney's commands see chaps. 3, 5, 9.

6. Wright's Spokane Expedition is discussed in chapter 3. See also Schlicke, *Wright*, 153–84; and Utley, *Frontiersmen*, 203–9.

7. Legislative Assembly of the Territory of Oregon, "Resolution," 10–11 December 1858, enclosed in Governor Curry to Harney, 5 January 1859, Salem, O-1, Box 2, 1859, LR DOR (no. 3574), pt. 1, RG 393. Wool's closure of the Oregon interior is discussed in Schlicke, *Wright*, 129, and Utley, *Frontiersmen*.

8. Hubbs, et al., to Harney, 11 July 1859, H-60, Box 2, 1859, LR DOR (no. 3574), pt. 1, RG 393. A graphic alarmist summary is Crosbie to Secretary of State Lewis Cass, 3 April 1860, *Island*, HED 77, serial 1056, 1–8. Harney recalls his San Juan visit in Harney to General-in-Chief Scott, 19 July 1859, *Affairs*, HED 65, serial 1051, 10–11. The problems with unlicensed whiskey dealers are discussed in later letters by Capt. Lewis C. Hunt, who commanded the American unit of the joint-occupation force on San Juan Island. Hunt to Capt. Alfred Pleasonton, 27 March 1860; and Hunt to Capt. Alfred Pleasonton, 30 March 1860, *Correspondence*, HED 98, serial 1057, 16–17, 24–26. See also Newsom to Harney, [30 March 1860?]; and Hewett, et al., to Harney, 30 March 1860, *Correspondence*, HED 98, serial 1057, 26–27, 27.

9. Harney to Lt. Col. Silas Casey, 18 July 1859; and Capt. Alfred Pleasonton to Pickett, 18 July 1859, *Affairs*, HED 65, serial 1051, 7–8, 9–10.

10. Adams, "Harney," 317–19.

11. Harney to Scott, 19 July 1859, *Affairs*, HED 65, serial 1051, 10–11. For the pig-shooting incident, see "Sworn statement of Lyman Cutler," 7 September 1859, *Affairs*, HED 65, serial 1051, 53–55. Written eleven months later, A. G. Dallas's rebuttal of Harney and Cutler is Dallas to Harney, 10 May 1860, D-11, Box 4, 1860, LR DOR (no. 3574), pt. 1, RG 393. Harney registers his indignation to Adj. Gen. Samuel Cooper, 7 August 1859, *Affairs*, HED 65, serial 1051, 13–14. His rabid dislike of the HBC is expressed in Harney to Cooper, 29 August 1859, *Affairs*, HED 65, serial 1051, 13–14.

12. Tunem, "Dispute," 198. For Pickett's early career, see Longacre, *Pickett*, chaps. 1–3; Warner, "George Edward Pickett," *Gray*, 239–40; and Heitman, "George Edward Pickett," *Register*, 1:790. For George McClellan's military record, see Heitman, "George Brinton McClellan," Heitman, *Register*, 1:656.

13. Douglas, Proclamation (enclosure), 2 August 1859, P-16, Box 2, 1859, LR DOR (no. 3574), pt. 1, RG 393; Harney to Douglas, 6 August 1859, *Affairs*, HED 65, serial 1051, 22–23. According to Douglas, Harney never raised the Cutler affair during his visit to Victoria in July 1859. See Douglas to Harney, 13 August 1859, D-18, Box 1, 1858 and 1859, LR DOR (no. 3574), pt. 1, RG 393.

14. Douglas to Harney, 13 August 1859; Harney to Douglas, 24 August 1859, *Affairs*, HED 65, serial 1051, 41–42.

15. Gough, "British," 63; Pickett to Casey, 30 July 1859, *Affairs*, HED 65, serial 1051, 15–16.

16. Gough, "British," 64; Pickett to Capt. Alfred Pleasonton, 3 August 1859 (10:00 P.M.), P-16, Box 2, 1859, LR DOR (no. 3574), pt. 1, RG 393.

17. Pickett to Pleasonton, 3 August 1859. Pickett and Hornby corresponded back and forth several times on August 3: Hornby to Pickett, 3 August 1859, HMS *Tribune*, San Juan Island, enclosure, ibid., in which Hornby invites Pickett aboard; Pickett to [Hornby], 3 August 1859, San Juan Island, enclosure, ibid., in which Pickett invites Hornby to his camp; Hornby to Pickett, 3 August 1859, HMS *Tribune*, San Juan Island, enclosure, ibid., in which Hornby accepts the invitation; Hornby to Pickett, 3 August 1859, HMS *Tribune*, San Juan Island, enclosure, ibid., in which Hornby recapitulates the substance of their exchange; and Pickett to Hornby, 3 August 1859, 11 p. m., San Juan Island, enclosure, ibid., in which Pickett acknowledges Hornby's memorandum of their meeting and contests one point.

18. Harney to Senior Officer of the United States Navy, Pacific Coast Squadron, 7 August 1859; Harney to General-in-Chief Scott, 18 August 1859; Capt. Alfred Pleasonton to Casey, 8 August 1859; and Casey to Capt. Alfred Pleasonton, 12 August 1859, *Affairs*, HED 65, serial 1051, 23–24, 28–29, 29, 30–32.

19. Warner, "Silas Casey," *Blue*, 74–75; Heitman, "Silas Casey," *Register*, 1:289; Casey to Pleasonton, 12 August 1859, 30–32.

20. Casey and Baynes exchanged three notes in Esquimault Harbor on 11 August 1859: see *Affairs*, HED 65, serial 1051, 33. Casey to Pleasonton, 12 August 1859, *Affairs*, HED 65, serial 1051, 30–32.

21. Capt. Alfred Pleasonton to Casey, 16 August 1859; Casey to Capt. Alfred Pleasonton, 22 August 1859; and Governor Gholson to Harney, 11 August 1859, *Affairs*, HED 65, serial 1051, 35–36, 50, 37–38.

22. Fish, "Last," 201–3; Gough, "British," 61, 64–65.

23. "Her Britannic Majesty's Fleet . . ."; and Harney to General-in-Chief Scott, 30 August 1859, *Affairs*, HED 65, serial 1051, 34, 49.

24. Acting Secretary of War Drinkard to Harney, 3 September 1859, W-161, Box 3, 1859, LR DOR, pt. 1, RG 393.

25. Harney to Floyd, 10 October 1859, *Affairs* HED 65, serial 1051, 56–57; Commissioner Campbell to Harney, 14 August 1859, C-108, Box 1, 1858 and 1859, LR DOR (no. 3574), RG 393. Harney replied to Campbell's letter on 16 August 1859. See the War Department endorsement on Campbell to Harney, 14 August 1859, LR DOR (no. 3574), pt. 1, RG 393. Campbell to Harney, 30 August 1859, Camp Semiahoo, *Affairs*, HED 65, serial 1051, 60.

26. Acting Secretary of War Drinkard to Scott, 16 September 1859, *Affairs*, HED 65, serial 1051, 25–27.

27. Lt. Col. Lorenzo Thomas to Adj. Gen. Samuel Cooper, 22 October 1859 and 26 October 1859, *Affairs*, HED 65, serial 1051, 60–61, 61; Scott, *Memoirs*, 2:605.

28. Scott to Douglas, 25 October 1859; Lt. Col. George Lay, Memorandum, 26 October 1859; and Douglas to Scott, 29 October 1859, *Affairs*, HED 65, serial 1051, 64–65, 65, 65–67.

29. Douglas to Scott, 29 October 1859, 65–67.

30. Scott to Douglas, 2 November 1859; [Scott], "Project of a temporary settlement, &c."; and Douglas to Scott, 3 November 1859, *Affairs*, HED 65, serial 1051, 67, 69–70, 70.

31. Scott to Governor Douglas (with endorsement of Lt. Col. Lorenzo Thomas), 5 November 1859; and Headquarters of the Army, 5 November 1859, *Affairs*, HED 65, serial 1051, 71–72, 72; Warner, "Lewis Cass Hunt" and "Henry Jackson Hunt," *Blue*, 243, 242–43.

32. Douglas to Scott, 7 November 1859; and Scott to Douglas, 9 November 1859, *Affairs*, HED 65, serial 1051, 72, 74–75.

33. Lt. Col. Lorenzo Thomas to Harney, 9 November 1859; Scott to Harney, 15 November 1859; and Headquarters of the Army, Special Order, 15 November 1859, *Affairs*, HED 65, serial 1051, 77, 78.

34. Harney to Assistant Adjutant General [Thomas], 17 November 1859; Harney to Adj. Gen. Samuel Cooper, 17 November 1859; and Harney to Adj. Gen. Samuel Cooper, 24 January 1860, *Affairs*, HED 65, serial 1051, 79, 81. The resolution of the Washington Territorial Council is Biles and Moxon, 7 January 1860, *Affairs*, HED 65, serial 1051, 82–83.

35. Scott to Secretary of War [Floyd], 14 May 1860; Darling et al. to General [Harney], 7 March 1860; and Harney to Assistant Adjutant General [Thomas], 11 April 1860, *Correspondence*, HED 98, serial 1057, 21, 23–24, 15.

36. Capt. Alfred Pleasonton to Hunt, 21 March 1860; Hunt to Pleasonton, 30 March 1860; Newsom to Harney, [30 March 1860?]; and Hewett, et al. [Petition Supporting Captain Hunt], 30 March 1860, *Correspondence*, HED 98, serial 1057, 23, 24–26, 26, 27.

37. Capt. Alfred Pleasonton to Pickett, 10 April 1860; and Headquarters, Department of Oregon, Special Orders No. 41, 10 April 1860, *Correspondence*, HED 98, serial 1057, 18–20, 20.

38. Hunt to Lt. Col. Erasmus Keyes, 24 April 1860; Scott, endorsement, 14 June 1860; and Scott to the Secretary of War, 14 May 1860, *Correspondence*, HED 98, serial 1057, 22–23, 23, 21.

39. Floyd, 8 June 1860, endorsement on Scott to Secretary of War, 14 May 1860; and Adjutant General's Office, Special Orders No. 115, 8 June 1860, *Correspondence*, HED 98, serial 1057, 22; Adams, "Harney," 331–32.

40. Schlicke, *Wright*, 205; Thian, *Notes*, 86; Pickett to Capt. Alfred Pleasonton, 1 June 1860, P-16, Box 5, 1860, LR DOR (no. 3574), pt. 1, RG 393.

CHAPTER 8

1. Porter to Adj. Gen. Roger Jones, 18 October 1849, P-5, Box 2, 1850, LR DPac (no. 3584), pt. 1, RG 393; Frazer, "Hall I," *West*, 44–45.

2. For Mormon expulsion and the migration, see Arrington and Bitton, *Experience*, chaps. 5–6; and Arrington, *Moses*, 223–24.

3. A classic account of overland trails is Unruh, *Plains*.

4. A history of the Corps of Topographical Engineers is Goetzmann, *Exploration*. The Mounted Riflemen's journey is recorded in Settle, *March*. Col. John J. Abert to Stansbury, 11 April 1849, Madsen, *Exploring*, 2–6. A sketch of Stansbury's life is in Madsen, *Exploring*, xix–xxii, 154.

5. For Stansbury's reconnaissance to Ogden's Hole, see Madsen, *Exploring*, chaps. 2–3. Stansbury discusses the rumors of threats on his life in Madsen, *Exploring*, 153–54. Two solid biographies of Brigham Young are Arrington, *Moses*, and Bringhurst, *Young*. Stansbury's narrative of his journey from Ogden's Hole to Salt Lake City and of his meeting with Brigham Young is included in Madsen, *Exploring*, 153–55, 155 n. 22.

6. Gunnison's survey activities are covered in Madsen, *Exploring*, chap. 4. Gunnison to Wife, 2 Feb[ruar]y 1850; and Stansbury, fragment from his reports, Madsen, *Exploring*, 262–64, 257–58, 273–75. See also Madsen, *Exploring*, 258–61 n. 10, and chaps. 6–7. Stansbury to Col. John J. Abert, 31 July 1850, Madsen, *Exploring*, 547–48. For the return trip, see Madsen, *Exploring*, chap. 9; and Goetzmann, *Exploration*, 221–23.

7. The winter in Washington is covered in Madsen, *Exploring*, chap. 10; and Goetzmann, *Exploration*, 223–24. Stansbury, *Survey*, 4, 120, 128–30, 131–34, 138, 144; Gunnison, *Mormons*, 23, 24, 31–32, 65, 78; Gunnison to Martha, 7 October 1849, HM 17062, Box 1, Gunnison Papers, HEH.

8. Stansbury, *Survey*, 4–5, 137–38; Gunnison, *Mormons*, 72; Gunnison to Martha, 1 March 1850, HM 17065, Box 1, Gunnison Papers.

9. Morrison, *Slavery*, 124, 132; Potter, *Impending*, 107–12, 121–22; Lamar, *Southwest*, 338; Arrington, *Moses*, 251.

10. Billington and Ridge, *Westward*, 533; Arrington, *Moses*, 227–28; Bringhurst, *Young*, 106, 110; Arrington and Bitton, *Experience*, 164; Creer, *Utah*, 62; Furniss, *Conflict*, 11–20, 32.

11. Arrington, *Moses*, 228–29; Bringhurst, *Young*, 110–11; Arrington and Bitton, *Experience*, 163–64; Furniss, *Conflict*, 32; Hinton, "Fillmore," 112–28; Lamar, *Southwest*, 330.

12. Heitman, "John Williams Gunnison," *Register*, 1:483; Madsen, *Exploring*, xxiv–xxv. An overview of the Great Railroad Survey is Goetzmann, *Exploration*, chap. 7. Weber, *Kern*, 218; Gunnison, *Mormons*, 72; Gunnison to wife [Martha], 16 February 1851, HM 17070, Box 1; and Gunnison to wife, 9 October 1849, HM 17063, Box 1, Gunnison Papers.

13. Andrew Booth, "Notes on the Biography of J. W. Gunnison, formerly 1st Lieutenant of the USA," FAC 706, Box 1, Gunnison Papers; Madsen, *Exploring*, xxii–xxv; Weber, *Kern*, 218–19; Goetzmann, *Exploration*, 266, 273, 274–75, 283–85, 297–98.

14. Gunnison to Mother [Mrs. Delony], 12 June 1853, HM 17049; Gunnison to Love [Martha Delony Gunnison], 19 June 1853, HM 17078; and Gunnison to Wife [Martha], 18 October 1853, HM 17083, Box 1, Gunnison Papers; Goetzmann, *Exploration*, 285.

15. Gibbs, "Gunnison," 69–72; Gunnison to Wife [Martha], 18 October 1853; Beckwith to Martha Delony Gunnison, 29 October 1853, HM 17036(1), Box 1, Gunnison Papers.

16. Beckwith to Martha Delony Gunnison, 29 October 1853; Gibbs, "Gunnison," 72–73; Weber, *Kern*, 237.

17. Beckwith to Martha Delony Gunnison, 29 October 1853; Beckwith to Madam [Martha Delony Gunnison], 1 May 1854, HM 17036(2), Box 1; and extract from [Young] to [Martha Delony Gunnison], [n.d.], quoted in [Martha Delony Gunnison] to Alice [Gunnison] Boothe and Mary [Gunnison] Boothe, 19 February 1854, HM 17089, Box 1, Gunnison Papers.

18. A[ndrew] J[oseph] Gunnison to Sister [Martha Delony Gunnison], 16 March 1854, HM 17093, Box 1, Gunnison Papers.

19. Extract from [Young] to [Martha Delony Gunnison] quoted in [Gunnison] to Boothe and Boothe, 19 February 1854; A[ndrew] Gunnison to Sister, 16 March 1854.

20. Beckwith to Madam, 1 May 1854. Gunnison was "killed 26 October 1853 by a band of Mormons and Ind[ian]s near Sevier Lake[,] Utah." Heitman, *Register*, 1:483.

21. Arrington, *Moses*, 212–22; Morgan, "Administration," 383–409.

22. Steptoe to Pierce, 6 June 1852; Steptoe to Pierce, 30 June 1852; Steptoe to Pierce, 2 July 1852; and Steptoe to Mason, 23 September 1852, series 3, Pierce Papers, reels 4, 5; Arrington, *Moses*, 245–46; Bringhurst, *Young*, 117–18; Bancroft, *Utah*, 492–93.

23. Furniss, *Conflict*, 40–43; Bancroft, *Utah*, 493–94.

24. Bailey, "Report," 329–32; Furniss, *Conflict*, 44; Bancroft, *Utah*, 493n.

25. Arrington, *Moses*, 246–48; Bancroft, *Utah*, 492–93; Bringhurst, *Young*, 117–18; Gara, *Pierce*, 88–96; Potter, *Impending*, 160–71; Lamar, *Southwest*, 330.

26. Arrington, *Moses*, 300, 344–46; Lamar, *Southwest*, 331–38; Bringhurst, *Young*, 127–28; Arrington and Bitton, *Experience*, 212–13.

27. Bringhurst, *Young*, 128–29; Arrington and Bitton, *Experience*, 212–13; Furniss, *Conflict*, 45–50, 56–60, 92–94; Lamar, *Southwest*, 331–38.

28. Lamar, *Southwest*, 331, 338; Arrington, *Moses*, 251.

29. An excellent discussion of the consequences of the Dred Scott decision is Potter, *Impending*, 280–96. Bringhurst, *Young*, 136; Arrington, *Moses*, 248. Furniss provides a good summary of Buchanan's decision in *Conflict*, 45–60, 62–63, 66–67, 74–76.

30. MacKinnon, "Conspiracy," 219–22, 222–27; MacKinnon, "Spoils," 127–50; Scott, *Memoirs*, 2:604; Bringhurst, *Young*, 136–37; Lamar, *Southwest*, 339–40; Furniss, *Conflict*, 68–70; Ball Jr., "'Embroilments,'" chap. 1.

31. Scott to [Buchanan], 26 May 1857, quoted in Cannon, "Scott," 209–10. Cannon suspects that Secretary Floyd held back Scott's letter to President Buchanan (208–9). John W. Phelps, "Diary," Hafen and Woodbury, *Utah*, 90; Warner, "John Wolcott Phelps," *Blue*, 368–69; Capt. Jesse Gove to [Maria Gove], 10 July 1857; and Capt. Jesse Gove to Maria [Gove], 25 July 1857, Gove, *Utah*, 9–12, 20–21.

32. Capt. Jesse Gove to Maria [Gove] and children, 28 June 1857, Gove, *Utah*, 5–8; Harney to Lt. Col. Lorenzo Thomas, 14 June 1857, vol. 145A, DMO, LS DWest (no. 5506), pt. 1, RG 393, pp. 6–7; Maj. Gen. Winfield Scott to Harney, telegram, 14 July 1857; and Major General Scott, circular, 28 May 1857, *Utah*, HED 71, serial 956, 10, 4–5; LeCheminant, "Crisis," 30–31.

33. Capt. Jesse Gove to Maria [Gove] and children, 17 July 1857; Capt. Jesse Gove to Maria [Gove], 20 July 1857; Capt. Jesse Gove to Maria [Gove], 31 July 1857; and Capt. Jesse Gove to Maria [Gove], 2 August 1857, Gove, *Utah*, 12–15, 16–20, 25–27, 26–27. Alexander to Adj. Gen. Samuel Cooper, 3 September 1857, *Utah*, HED 71, serial 956, 19–20.

34. Capt. Jesse Gove to Maria [Gove], 21 September 1857, Gove, *Utah*, 59–61; Capt. Alfred Pleasonton to Van Vliet, 28 July 1857, Hafen and Woodbury, *Utah*, 36–38; Hafen and Woodbury, *Utah*, 35–36, 55; Van Vliet to Capt. Alfred Pleasonton, 16 September 1857, *Utah*, HED 71, serial 956, 24–26. Bringhurst, *Young*, 140–41; Arrington, *Moses*, 254–55.

35. Bancroft, *Utah*, 503–7; Arrington, *Moses*, 252–55; Arrington and Bitton, *Experience*, 166; Bringhurst, *Young*, 138–42; Young, "Proclamation" [15 September 1857], *Utah*, HED 71, serial 956, 34–35; Furniss, *Conflict*, 119, 123–24.

36. Young to "The Officer Commanding the forces now invading Utah Territory," 29 September 1857, *Utah*, HED 71, serial 956, 33; Hamilton, *Reminiscences*, 82; Gove to Maria, 3 October 1857, Gove, *Utah*, 69–70; Col. Edmund B. Alexander to Adj. Gen. Samuel Cooper, 9 October 1857, *Utah*, HED 71, serial 956, 30–32; Charles A. Scott, 5 Oct[ober] [1857], "Diary," 164; Gove to Maria, 6 October 1857, Gove, *Utah*, 71.

37. Alexander to "Any officer of U.S.A. en Route to Utah or to Governor Cumming," 14 October 1857, *Utah*, HED 71, serial 956, 38; Capt. Jesse Gove to Maria [Gove], 6 October 1857, 71; Alexander to "Officers commanding en route to Utah," 8 October 1857; and Alexander to Cooper, 9 October 1857, *Utah*, HED 71, serial 956, 38–40, 30–32; Charles A. Scott, 11, 13, 14, 16, 17, and 20 Oct[ober] [1857], "Diary," 166; Capt. Jesse Gove to Maria [Gove], 15, 16, 17, 18, and 20 October 1857, Gove, *Utah*, 77–81; Alexander to Head Quarters of the Utah Army, 18 October 1857, *Utah*, HED 71, serial 956, 66; Hamilton, *Reminiscences*, 86–87.

38. Asst. Adj. Gen. Irwin McDowell to Johnston, 28 August 1857; 1st Lt. Fitz-John Porter to Alexander, 16 October 1857; Johnston to Asst. Adj. Gen. Irwin McDowell, 24 September 1857; Johnston to Asst. Adj. Gen. Irwin McDowell, 5 November 1857; and Johnston to Asst. Adj. Gen. Irwin McDowell, 5 November 1857, *Utah*, HED 71, serial 956, 13, 40, 22–23, 46–47, 47; Charles A. Scott, 4 Nov[ember] 1857, "Diary," 167; Roland, *Johnston*, 184–85, 188.

39. Canning and Beeton, *Genteel*, xii–xiii; Furniss, *Conflict*, 146, 164–65; Memo, 12 September 1857, Fort Leavenworth, Hafen and Woodbury, *Utah*, 143–44; Hafen and Woodbury, *Utah*, 144 n. 10. Cooke to Assistant Adjutant General of the Utah Army, 12 October 1857; and Cooke to Assistant Adjutant General [of the Utah Army], 21 November 1857, *Utah*, HED 71, serial 956, 82–83, 92–99.

40. Johnston to Asst. Adj. Gen. Irwin McDowell, 30 November 1857; 1st Lt. Fitz-John Porter to Marcy, 26 November 1857; and Johnston to Col. John Garland, 25 November 1857, *Utah*, HED 71, serial 956, 78, 103; Warner, "Randolph Barnes Marcy," *Blue*, 310–11. The narrative of the march is taken from Marcy, *Life* (224–44), and the account of Jim DeForrest from McConnell, *Cavalryman* (150–55).

41. Cumming to Cass, 28 November 1857; Cumming to Cass, 13 December 1857 and 5 January 1858, Hafen and Woodbury, *Utah*, 299–300, 301–2, 302–3; Capt. Jesse Gove to Maria [Gove], 8 November [18]57, Gove, *Utah*, 91.

42. Furniss, *Conflict*, 174–77; Smith, *Buchanan*, 68; Potter, *Impending*, 310–18; Warner, "Thomas Leiper Kane," *Blue*, 256–57; Gove to Maria [Gove], 14 March 1857, Gove, *Utah*, 133–34; Conway, *Expedition*, 27–28; Charles A. Scott, 18 March 1858, "Diary," 169; Furniss, *Conflict*, 178.

43. Furniss, *Conflict*, 179, 181; Johnston to Cumming, 17 March 1858, vol. 1, LS DUtah (no.5029), pt. 1, RG 393, p. 259; Arrington, *Moses*, 262.

44. Gove to Maria [Gove], 17 March 1858, Gove, *Utah*, 135–36; Charles A. Scott, 18 March 1858, "Diary," 169–70.

45. Arrington, *Moses*, 262; Bringhurst, *Young*, 144–46; Lamar, *Southwest*, 348; Capt. Jesse Gove to Maria [Gove], 4–5 April 1859, Gove, *Utah*, 145; Tracy, 7 April 1858, "Journal," 4; [Elizabeth] to [Alfred], 21 April 1858, Canning and Beeton, *Genteel*, 39–42; Hamilton, *Reminiscences*, 98.

46. Cumming to Johnston, 15 April 1858; and Cumming to Secretary of State Lewis Cass, 2 May 1858, Hafen and Woodbury, *Utah*, 286–89, 304–14; Arrington, *Moses*, 264–67; Johnston to Asst. Adj. Gen. Irwin McDowell, 22 April 1858 and 7 May 1858, LS DUtah (no. 5029), pt. 1, RG 393, pp. 279, 287.

47. Lowe, *Dragoon*, 234–38; 1st Lt. Fitz-John Porter to Cumming, 22 March 1858, LS DUtah (no. 5029), pt. 1, RG 393, p. 257; Furniss, *Conflict*, 174.

48. Tracy, 16 May 1858, "Journal," 12; Gove to Maria [Gove], 24–25 March 1858; and Gove to Maria [Gove], 28 April 1858, Gove, *Utah*, 139–41, 160–61; Cumming to Cass, 2 May 1858; Secretary of War John B. Floyd to Powell and McCulloch, 2 April 1858; and Powell and McCulloch to Secretary of War John B. Floyd, 1 June 1858, Hafen and Woodbury, *Utah*, 304–14, 329–32, 339–41; Cutrer, *McCulloch*, 151–53.

49. Powell and McCulloch to Secretary of War John B. Floyd, 26 June 1858; Pres. James Buchanan, "Proclamation," 6 April 1858; minutes of the conference, enclosed in Powell and McCulloch to Floyd; Powell and McCulloch to Secretary of War John B. Floyd, 12 June 1858; and Powell and McCulloch to Col. Albert S. Johnston, 12 June 1858, Hafen and Woodbury, *Utah*, 347–54, 333–37, 355–59, 342–43, 343–44.

50. Johnston to Cumming, 18 June 1858, Hafen and Woodbury, *Utah*, 322–23; Tracy, 1, 8, 10 June 1858, "Journal," 14–15; DuBois, *Campaigns*, ed. Hammond, 51–67; Johnston, "To the People of Utah," 14 June 1858, Hafen and Woodbury, *Utah*, 346.

51. Cumming to Johnston, 15 June 1858, Hafen and Woodbury, *Utah*, 320–21, 320 n. 44; Johnston to Cumming, 18 June 1858, Hafen and Woodbury, *Documentary*, 322–23; Charles A. Scott, 26 June 1858, "Diary," 173.

52. The army's march through the city is from Marcy, *Life*, 264; Tracy, 26 June 1858, "Journal," 26–28; Capt. Jesse Gove to Family, 2 July 1858, Gove, *Utah*, 176–78; DuBois, 28 June 1858, *Campaigns*, ed. Hammond, 70–71; and Young, *Cooke*, 309.

53. Tracy, 28 September 1858, "Journal," 34–37; Hamilton, *Reminiscences*, 109, 110; [Author unknown], 25 September 1858, Langley, *Utah*, 86–87; Turnley, *Reminiscences*, 231–33; Alexander and Arrington, "Sagebrush," 7–17; Frazer, "Crittenden," *Forts*, 166.

54. Johnston, *Life*, 229, 230, 234; Gove to Maria [Gove], 13 August 1858, Gove, *Utah*, 189; and Thian, *Notes*, 100.

55. Cumming to Johnston, 8 October 1858; Johnston to Cumming, 9 October 1858, Camp Floyd; 1st Lt. Fitz-John Porter to Spencer, 5 October 1858; Marshall to Smith, 22 March 1859; [Statement of Sergeant Ralph Pike] in Marshall to 1st Lt. Fitz-John Porter, 25 March 1859; and Cumming to Johnston, 24 March 1859, *RSW*, SED 2, serial 1024, 125, 126, 138, 138–39.

56. [Ralph] Pike [Sworn statement], 11 August 1859, *RSW*, SED 2, serial 1024, 216–17.

57. Hamilton, *Reminiscences*, 112–13; Furniss, *Conflict*, 225.

58. Cradlebaugh to 1st Lt. Fitz-John Porter, 6 March 1859; 1st Lt. Fitz-John Porter to Heth, 9 March 1859; Heth to 1st Lt. Fitz-John Porter, 10 March 1859; Bullock to Cradlebaugh, 11 March 1859; Cradlebaugh to Mayor and City Council of Provo, 12 March 1859; and Berry, Lewis, Major, Wilkins, and fifty-three others to Cradlebaugh, n.d., *RSW*, SED 2, serial 1024, 140, 140–41, 141, 142, 142–48, 146–47; Mayor and City Council of Provo to Cumming, 11 March 1859, *Territory*, HED 78, serial 1056, 6.

59. Brooks, *Massacre*, chap. 5.

60. Cumming to Johnston, 20 March 1859; Heth to 1st Lt. Fitz-John Porter, 21 March 1859; Johnston to Cumming, 22 March 1859; Heth to 1st Lt. Fitz-John Porter, 18 March 1859; 1st Lt. Fitz-John Porter to Capt. Gabriel R. Paul, 19 March 1859; and Heth to Porter, 21 March 1859, *RSW*, SED 2, serial 1024, 149–50, 153–54, 143–44, 151–52, 148–49, 153; Heth, *Memoirs*, 145.

61. Dotson to Cradlebaugh, 24 March 1859; and 1st Lt. Fitz-John Porter to Capt. Gabriel R. Paul, 24 March 1859, *RSW*, SED 2, serial 1024, 155, 156; Scott, 29 March 1859, "Diary," 393; Tracy, 2 April 1859, "Journal," 64.

62. Cumming to Cass, 25 March 1859; and Floyd to Johnston, 6 May 1859, *Territory*, HED 78, serial 1056, 22–23, 31; Black to Cradlebaugh and Sinclair, 17 May 1859, *Message*, SED 32, serial 1031, 2; 1st Lt. Fitz-John Porter to Cradlebaugh, 8 June 1859, *RSW*, SED 2, serial 1024, 197; Tracy, 7 July 1859, "Journal," 71.

63. Capt. Reuben P. Campbell to 1st Lt. Fitz-John Porter, 30 April 1859; and Forney to Johnston, 1 May 1859, *RSW*, SED 2, serial 1024, 172, 172–73.

64. 1st Lt. Fitz-John Porter to Campbell, 17 April 1859; Campbell to Porter, 30 April 1859; Forney to Col. Albert S. Johnston, 1 May 1859; and Campbell to 1st Lt. Fitz-John Porter, 6 July 1859, *RSW*, SED 2, serial 1024, 205–6, 172, 172–73, 207–8.

65. Campbell to Porter, 6 July 1859, 207–8; Asst. Surg. Charles Brewer to Campbell, 6 May 1859, *RSW*, SED 2, serial 1024, 206–7.

66. A biography of Carleton is Hunt, *Carleton*. See Carleton to Asst. Adj. Gen. William W. Mackall, 25 May 1859, *Mountain*, HED 605, serial 4377, 1–10.

67. Carleton to Mackall, 25 May 1859. Regulars at Fort Gibson, Cherokee Nation, captured Pratt. See Wilson to Ass[istan]t Adju[tan]t General, Department of the West, W-38, Box 5, 1857, LR DWest (no. 5486), RG 393.

68. Carleton to Mackall, 25 May 1859.

69. Carleton to Asst. Adj. Gen. William W. Mackall, 24 June 1859, C-39, Box 15, 1859, LR DPac (no. 3584), RG 393.

70. Agent Jacob Forney to Col. Albert S. Johnston, 15 June 1859; 1st Lt. Fitz-John Porter to Agent Jacob Forney, 16 June 1859; and 1st Lt. Fitz-John Porter to Lt. Col. George Crosman, 20 June 1859, *RSW*, SED 2, serial 1024, 190–91, 191–92, 192.

71. Heth, *Memoirs*, 147; Johnston, *Life*, 241, 243; Tracy, 1 March 1860, "Journal," 81–82; Roland, *Johnston*, 236–38.

72. Bandel to Parents, 27 September 1858, Bandel, *Frontier*, 230; Tracy, 12 October 1858, "Journal," 40–42.

73. Scott, 24 July 1861, "Diary," 395; Young, *Cooke*, 325; Arrington, *Kingdom*, 196–99.

CHAPTER 9

1. Shannon to Pres. Franklin Pierce, 1 December 1855; and Pres. Franklin Pierce to Shannon, 3 December 1855, *Papers*, SED 23, serial 820, 26; Sumner to Shannon, 5 December 1855, *Message*, SED 5, serial 875, 59.

2. Shannon to Gen. H. I. Strickler, 27 November 1855; and Shannon to Gen. William P. Richardson, 27 November 1855, *Message*, SED 5, serial 875, 54–55, 53.

3. Sumner to Shannon, 5 December 1855; Shannon to Sumner, 6 December 1855; and Sumner to Shannon, 7 December 1855, *Message*, SED 5, serial 875, 59, 59–60, 61; Nichols, *Bleeding*, 70–71; Corder, *Prelude*, 52–54; [Treaty negotiated between Gov. Wilson Shannon and James H. Lane and Charles Robinson], *KSHC*, 5:246.

4. Background to Bleeding Kansas includes Potter, *Impending*, chap. 9; Goodrich, *War*, chaps. 1–5; McPherson, *Battle*, chap. 5; Morrison, *Slavery*, 160–61; and Gates, *Fifty*, 3–4.

5. "Further Kansas Affairs," *Chicago Daily Tribune*, 16 February 1856; "Kansas Matters—Action of the President," *Chicago Daily Tribune*, 18 February 1856; "New Aspect of Kansas Affairs," *Chicago Daily Tribune*, 18 February 1856; *DAB*, s.v. "Shannon, Wilson"; Campbell, *Catchers*, 104–6.

6. "President's Message," 24 January 1856, *KSHC*, 5:255–56; Pierce, Proclamation, 11 February 1856, *KSHC*, 5:259; Secretary of War Jefferson Davis to Sumner and Lt. Col. Philip St. George Cooke, 15 February 1856, LS Secretary of War Relating to Military Affairs (M6), Records of the Office of the Secretary of War, RG 107, NA, roll 37; Sumner to Cooper, 8 March 1856; and Cooper to Sumner, 26 March 1856, *RSW*, HED 2, pt. 2, serial 894, 1–2, 2.

7. Nichols, *Bleeding*, 89; Monaghan, *Border*, 48–49; Goodrich, *War*, 97–107; Robinson, *Kansas*, 197; Johnson, *Freedom*, 156; Jones to Shannon, 20 April 1856; and Shannon to Sumner, 20 April 1856, *KSHC*, 4:408–9, 409; and Sumner to McIntosh, 22 April 1856, *RSW*, HED 2, pt. 2, serial 894, 3–4.

8. McIntosh to Shannon, 30 April 1856, *KSHC*, 4:418–19; Corder, *Prelude*, 63; Goodrich, *War*, 109–10.

9. Sumner to Shannon, 24 April 1856; Shannon to Sumner, 25 April 1856; and Shannon to Secretary of State William Marcy, 27 April 1856, *KSHC*, 4:410, 411, 407–8; Sumner to Adj. Gen. Samuel Cooper, 24 April 1856, *RSW*, HED 2, pt. 2, serial 894, 6; "Hostilities again Commenced in Kansas," *Atchison (Kans. Terr.) Squatter Sovereign*, 29 April 1856; Corder, *Prelude*, 65–67; Johnson, *Freedom*, 156–58; Monaghan, *Border*, 52–53.

10. Sumner to Adj. Gen. Samuel Cooper, 12 May 1856; Sumner to Shannon, 12 May 1856; C. W. Topliff, W. G. Roberts, and J. Hutchison to Sumner, 11 May 1856; and Rep. William Howard to Sumner, 11 May 1856, *RSW*, HED 2, pt. 2, serial 894, 377, 7–8, 8; Sumner to Mayor of Lawrence, 22 April 1856, *KSHC*, 5:262.

11. 1st Lt. James McIntosh to Col. Edwin Sumner, 21 May 1856; Gov. Wilson Shannon to Pres. Franklin Pierce, 31 May 1856; Gov. Wilson Shannon to Col. Edwin Sumner, 21 May 1856; and Col. Edwin Sumner to Maj. John Sedgwick, 22 May 1856, *KSHC*,

4:435–36, 414–16, 419, 436; Gladstone, *Englishman*, 38; Monaghan, *Border*, 56–59; Corder, *Prelude*, 73; Goodrich, *War*, 114–17.

12. Donald, *Sumner*, 294–97; Pierce, *Sumner*, 1:2; Stanley, *Sumner*, 5.

13. Judge Sterling Cato to Shannon, 27 May 1856; and Pierce to Shannon, 23 May 1856, *KSHC*, 4:419–20, 414; Shannon to Pierce, 31 May 1856, *KSHC* 4:415–18; McPherson, *Battle*, 152–53; Goodrich, *War*, 122–28.

14. Shannon to Sumner, 27 May 1856; Shannon to Sumner, [?] June 1856; Sumner to Cooper, 28 May 1856; Capt. Edward W. B. Newby to Shannon, 31 May 1856; Sumner to Cooper, 2 June 1856; Sumner to Assistant Adjutant General, Department of the West, 2 June 1856; and Shannon, Proclamation, 4 June 1856, *KSHC*, 4:237, 440–41, 437, 390, 438, 437, 442–43; *St. Louis Daily Missouri Democrat*, 31 May 1856, p. 1; Potter, *Impending*, 259–60.

15. Wilson to Sumner, 4 June 1856; and Sumner to Shannon, 4 June 1856, *KSHC*, 4:441; Isely and Richards, *Four*, 139; Corder, *Prelude*, 84–85; Griffith, "Battle," 16:524–25.

16. Sumner to Adj. Gen. Samuel Cooper, 8 June 1856; and James Hughes to Gov. Wilson Shannon, [6] June 1856, *KSHC*, 4:439–40, 390–91; "Letters of John and Sarah Everett," 31–32.

17. Gov. Wilson Shannon to Sumner, 14 June 1856; McIntosh to Woodson, 13 June 1856; and Sumner to Adj. Gen. Samuel Cooper, 23 June 1856, *KSHC*, 4:445, 391, 444–45.

18. Nichols, *Pierce*, 475.

19. Ibid.; Carr, "Reminiscences," 381; Scott, *Memoirs*, 2:598–600; *DAB*, s.v. "Smith, Persifor Frazer"; Smith to Pierce, 23 January 1857, series 3, Pierce Papers, reel 5; Davis to Smith, 27 June 1856, LS Secretary of War (M6), RG 107, roll 38.

20. Shannon to Sumner, 23 June 1856; Sumner to Woodson, 28 June 1856; Sumner to Woodson, 1 July 1856; Sumner to Adj. Gen. Samuel Cooper, 1 July 1856; and Woodson, Governor's Proclamation, [?] July 1856, *KSHC*, 4: 422–23, 446, 447, 446, 449–50.

21. "Topeka Movement," *KSHC*, 13:235; "Fourth of July at Topeka," *Chicago Daily Tribune*, 15 July 1856; Monaghan, *Border*, 66–68.

22. "Bayonet," *New York National Anti-Slavery Standard*, 19 July 1856; "War in Kansas," *New York National Anti-Slavery Standard*, 12 July 1856; Col. Persifor F. Smith to Adj. Gen. Samuel Cooper, 14 July 1856; and Davis, [endorsement of Sumner's report on Topeka dispersal], 24 July 1856, *KSHC*, 4:457–58, 452; Davis to the President, 30 July 1856, *Instructions*, SED 97, serial 823, 1; Sumner to Adj. Gen. Samuel Cooper, 11 August 1856; and Sumner to Adj. Gen. Samuel Cooper, 31 August 1856, *KSHC*, 4:450–51, 452–53.

23. "Matters and Things in Kansas," *Chicago Daily Tribune*, 4 August 1856; "Kansas—Help! Help!" *Chicago Daily Tribune*, 20 August 1856; Monaghan, *Border*, chap. 6; Corder, *Prelude*, 86–87, 90–92, 95–96.

24. Warner, "John Sedgwick," *Blue*, 430–31; Sedgwick to Sister, 11 June 1856, *Correspondence*, 2:8–9; Gleed, "Walker," *KSHC*, 6:270, 271; John Lowrie to Arthur Lowrie, 19 April and 11 May 1857, Gibbens, "Letters," 374, 377; Richards, "Experiences," 547; Sedgwick to Asst. Adj. Gen. George Deas, 17 August 1856, *KSHC*, 4:462–63; King, *War*, 21.

25. Shannon to Col. Persifor F. Smith, 17 August 1856; and Shannon to Pierce, 18 August 1856, *KSHC*, 4:462, 403; *DAB*, s.v. "Wilson, Shannon."

26. *Kansas*, HR 200, Serial 869, 67; Monaghan, *Border*, 80; Victor, "Kansas-Nebraska," 492–94; "Kansas Affairs," *Congressional Globe*, 7 August 1856, 34th Cong., 1st sess., 1089–90, 1098–99, 1107.

27. Woodson, Proclamation, [25 August 1856]; Maj. Gen. William P. Richardson to Smith, 18 August 1856; Smith to officers at Lecompton, 19 August 1856; Smith to Adj. Gen. Samuel Cooper, 22 August 1856; and Smith to Adj. Gen. Samuel Cooper, 29 August 1856, *KSHC*, 4:470–71, 466, 465–66, 461, 468–69; Hatch to Father, 1 September 1856, 4065, Hatch Papers, LC; Corder, *Prelude*, 99–101; Monaghan, *Border*, 80–82.

28. Asst. Adj. Gen. George Deas to Sedgwick, 18 August 1856; Asst. Adj. Gen. George Deas to Cooke, 18 August 1856; Asst. Adj. Gen. George Deas to Cooke, Fort Leavenworth, 28 August 1856; Asst. Adj. Gen. George Deas to Cooke, Fort Leavenworth, 30 August 1856; Cooke to Asst. Adj. Gen. George Deas, 30 August 1856; Cooke to Asst. Adj. Gen. George Deas, 31 August 1856; Cooke to Adj. Gen. Samuel Cooper, 18 June 1856; Woodson to Cooke, 1 September 1856; Cooke to Woodson, 2 September 1856; and Asst. Adj. Gen. George Deas to Cooke, 3 September 1856, Fort Leavenworth, 3 September 1856, *KSHC*, 4:464, 475, 477, 476, 478, 443–44, 479, 478, 482.

29. For Cooke's intervention, see Cooke to Asst. Adj. Gen. George Deas, 5 September 1856, *KSHC*, 4:485–87; Gleed, "Walker," 274; Monaghan, *Border*, 82–84.

30. Geary to Secretary of State William Marcy, 9 September 1856, *KSHC*, 4:522; Tinkcom, *Geary*, 42, 44, 49, 51, 54; Warner, "John White Geary," *Blue*, 169–70.

31. Geary, Proclamation, 11 September 1856, *KSHC*, 4:526–27; Secretary of War Jefferson Davis to Col. Persifor F. Smith, 3 September 1856; Secretary of War Jefferson Davis to Col. Persifor F. Smith, 9 September 1856; and Secretary of War Jefferson Davis to Governors of Kentucky and Illinois, 3 September 1856, LS Secretary of War (M6), RG 107, roll 38; Cooke to 1st Lt. Fitz-John Porter, 13 September 1856; "Executive Minutes of John W. Geary"; Theodore Adams to Geary, 12 September 1856; and Geary to Cooke, 13 September 1856, *KSHC*, 4:497, 530–31, 530, 531; Monaghan, *Border*, 86.

32. Cooke to 1st Lt. Fitz-John Porter, 16 September 1856; Geary to Cooke, 14 September 1856; and "Executive Minutes of John W. Geary," *KSHC*, 4:499–500, 533, 533–34; Monaghan, *Border*, 88–89.

33. Wood to Cooke, 16 September 1856; and "Executive Minutes of John W. Geary," *KSHC*, 4:502–4, 534.

34. Geary to Cooke, 27 September 1856; Cooke to 1st Lt. Fitz-John Porter, 10 October 1856; S. W. Eldridge, et al., to Geary, 14 October 1856; Cooke to Geary, 15 October 1856; Lieutenant Wright to Maj. Henry H. Sibley, 10 October 1856; Maj. Henry H. Sibley to Geary, 14 October 1856; and Geary to Secretary of State William Marcy, 15 October 1856, *KSHC*, 4:569, 516, 609–10, 612, 610, 610–11, 583–86.

35. Geary to Smith, 21 September 1856; Geary to Secretary of State William Marcy, 7 November 1856; Geary to Smith, 11 November 1856; Headquarters, Department of the West, Orders No. 14, 12 November 1856; Geary to Smith, 20 November 1856; and Headquarters, Department of the West, Special Orders No. 171, 27 November 1856, *KSHC*, 4: 547, 587, 633, 636–37, 639, 651.

36. Geary to Pierce, 22 December 1856, series 2, Pierce Papers; Geary to Smith, 9 February 1857; and Smith to Geary, 11 February 1857, *KSHC*, 4:710, 732; Heitman, "Persifor Frazer Smith," *Register*, 1:902.

37. Geary to Buchanan, 20 February 1857, State Department Territorial Papers (M218), General Records of the State Department, RG 59, NA, roll 1; Tinkcom, *Geary*, 94–97; Warner, "John White Geary," *Blue*, 169–70.

38. Klein, *Buchanan*, 269, 290; Smith, *Buchanan*, 15, 27–28, 33; Stampp, *America*, 93–109; Morrison, *Slavery*, 188–89.

39. Smith, *Buchanan*, 33; Klein, *Buchanan*, 290–91; Shenton, *Walker*, 2–3, 41, 70–86, 146–47, 192; Walker to Buchanan, 26 March 1857, *KSHC*, 5:290; Walker to Secretary of State Lewis Cass, 15 July 1857, Territorial Papers (M218), RG 59, roll 1.

40. Reavis, *Life*, 274; Walker to Buchanan, 28 June 1857, "The Covode Investigation . . . ," Walker Papers, LC; Richmond Clow, "Harney," Hutton, *Soldiers*, 43, 45; Robert B. Westbrook and P. Richard Metcalf, "Harney," Lamar, *Reader's*, 485–86; Adj. Gen. Samuel Cooper to Brig. Gen. Persifor F. Smith, 1 April 1857; Adj. Gen. Samuel Cooper to Commanding Officer, Fort Leavenworth, 28 April 1857; and Cooper to Harney, 8 May 1857, *KSHC*, 5:302; Young, *Cooke*, 288.

41. Walker, Inaugural Address, 27 May 1857; and Walker to Cass, 2 June 1857, Territorial Papers (M218), RG 59, roll 1; Klein, *Buchanan*, 291, 295; Shenton, *Walker*, 155–56.

42. Corder, *Prelude*, 117, 120; Potter, *Impending*, 300; Prentis, *History*, 110; J. Blood, et al., "To the People," [n.d.]; and Walker, Proclamation, 15 July 1857, *KSHC*, 5:354–55, 357–58; Harney to Walker, 15 July 1857, Territorial Papers (M218), RG 59, roll 1; Fort Leavenworth PR, July 1857, Returns from Military Posts (M617), RG 94, roll 611.

43. Walker to Secretary of State Lewis Cass, 20 July 1857; Walker to Secretary of State Lewis Cass, 25 July 1857; and Walker to Secretary of State Lewis Cass, 27 July 1857, Territorial Papers (M218), RG 59, roll 1; Walker to Secretary of State Lewis Cass, 2 June 1857, *KSHC*, 5:326–327.

44. Walker to Cass, 15 July 1857; Walker to Cass, 3 August 1857; Walker to Cass, 18 August 1857; and Walker to Cass, 19 August 1857, Territorial Papers (M218), RG 59, roll 1; Cass to Walker, 1 September 1857, *KSHC*, 5:382; Young, *Cooke*, 290; "Evacuation of Lawrence—Threatened Resignation of Gov. Walker," *Chicago Daily Tribune*, 19 September 1857; "Troops Gone—Threatened Resignation of the Governor," *Lawrence (Kans.) Herald of Freedom*, 12 September 1857; Fort Leavenworth PR, September 1857, Returns from Military Posts (M617), RG 94, roll 611; L[awrence] Bacon, Diary, 10 September 1857, Box 1, Miscellany, KSHS.

45. Walker, "To the People of Kansas," 10 September 1857; Walker to Harney, 3 October 1857; Harney, Special Orders No. 85; and Harney, Special Orders No. 78, 28 September 1857, *KSHC*, 5:397–99, 310–11, 311–12, 309; Fort Leavenworth PR, October 1857, Returns from Military Posts (M617), RG 94, roll 611. For the aggregate troop strength of the U.S. Army in 1857, see Secretary of War Floyd, *RSW*, SED 11, serial 943, 1.

46. Walker to Harney, 10 October 1857; and Walker, Proclamation, 19 October 1857; Walker, Proclamation, 22 October 1857; Judge Sterling Cato to Marshal or Sheriff of Douglas County and to Walker and Secretary Frederick Stanton, 23 October 1857; and Walker and Secretary Frederick Stanton to Judge Sterling Cato, 23 October 1857, *KSHC*, 5:314, 403–6, 406–8, 408, 408–10; "The Ballot-Stuffing Governor of Kansas," *Chicago Daily Tribune*, 22 October 1857; "Robert Walker Following in the Footsteps of His Illustrious Predecessor," *Chicago Daily Tribune*, 2 November 1857; Brown, *Reminiscences*, 77, 91–94; Girardi and Hughes, *Carlin*, 22–23.

47. "Progress of Election Frauds," *Chicago Daily Tribune*, 27 October 1857; Fort Leavenworth PR, October 1857; Rawley, *Race*, 232–33; Potter, *Impending*, 307; Shenton, *Walker*, 172–73; Smith, *Buchanan*, 39–40.

48. Shenton, *Walker*, 173–75; Smith, *Buchanan*, 37–38, 40; Col. William S. Harney to Act. Gov. Frederick Stanton, 18 December 1857; Capt. Alfred Pleasonton to 2d Lt. John R. Church, 18 December 1857; Capt. Alfred Pleasonton to Capt. George Anderson, 18 December 1857; Capt. Alfred Pleasonton to Capt. George H. Steuart, 18 December 1857; Capt. Alfred Pleasonton to Capt. Lawrence P. Graham, 19 December 1857; Capt. Alfred Pleasonton to Capt. William Steel, 19 December 1857; Col. William S. Harney to Act. Gov. Frederick Stanton, 19 December 1857; Pleasonton to Lt. Col. George Andrews, 21 December 1857; and Pleasonton to Maj. Martin Burke, 21 December 1857, vol. 145A, LS DMO (no. 5506), pt. 1, RG 393, pp. 127, 127–28, 128, 130, 131, 131–32, 133, 134.

49. Capt. Alfred Pleasonton to Com[man]d[in]g Officer at Oxford, Shawnee Mission, Delaware, Palermo, Doniphan, Atchison, [and] Kickapoo, 1 January 1858; Harney to Denver, 1 January 1858; and Capt. Alfred Pleasonton to Lt. Col. John Munroe, 2 January 1858, vol. 145A, LS DMO (no. 5506), pt.1, RG 393, pp. 147–48, 148; Secretary of State Lewis Cass to Stanton, 8 December 1857; and Stanton, message, 8 December 1857, *KSHC*, 5:413, 415–19; Rawley, *Race*, 232–33; Potter, *Impending*, 318; Warner, "John William Denver," *Blue*, 120.

50. Monaghan, *Border*, 100–101; Corder, *Prelude*, 132–33; Goodrich, *War*, 213–14.

51. Capt. Alfred Pleasonton to Sedgwick, 24 December 1857; and Pleasonton to Capt. Samuel D. Sturgis, 24 December 1857; Harney to Denver, 1 January 1858, vol. 145A, LS DMO (no. 5506), pt.1, RG 393, pp. 130–40, 139, 148; Gov. John Denver to Lt. Col. John Munroe, 15 February 1856; and Special Orders No. 34, 17 February 1858, Territorial Papers (M218), RG 59, roll 2, 1; 1st Lt. O. F. Solomon to Capt. George T. Anderson, 17 February 1858, vol. 145A, LS DMO (no. 5506), pt. 1, RG 393, p. 191; Justice Williams to Gov. John Denver, [?] March 1858, Territorial Papers (M218), RG 59, roll 1.

52. Denver to Cass, 22 March 1858, Territorial Papers (M218), RG 59, roll 1; Sumner to Lt. Col. John Munroe, 22 April 1858, vol. 1, RLS 4Cav. (no. 719), United States Army Mobile Units, RG 391; Warner, "George Thomas 'Tige' Anderson," *Gray*, 6–7.

53. David Cobb to Judd Cobb, 25 April 1858, Cobb, "Letters," 67–68; "A Battle on the Marmaton," *Atchison (Kans. Terr.) Freedom's Champion*, 15 May 1858.

54. 1st Lt. Stephen Lee to Anderson, 26 April 1858; and Munroe to Denver, 26 April 1858, vol. 145A, LS DMO (no. 5506), pt. 1, RG 393, pp. 207, 206; Harney, Special Orders No. 59, 27 April 1858, *KSHC*, 5:523–24.

55. Anderson to Capt. Alfred Pleasonton, 21 May 1858, A-83, Box 3; and Anderson to Buell, 23 May 1858, A-84, Box 3, LR DWest (no. 5486), pt. 1, RG 393; "Fort Scott Difficulties," *Lawrence (Kans. Terr.) Herald of Freedom*, 26 June 1858.

56. Monaghan, *Border*, 103; Goodrich, *War*, 215–18; Corder, *Prelude*, 139–40; Gov. R. M. Stewart to Adj. Gen. G. A. Parsons, 31 May 1858; Statement of Citizens of Bates County, Missouri, June 1858; and Adj. Gen. G. A. Parsons to Gov. R. M. Stewart, 16 June 1858, Viles, "Documents," 200, 201–4, 209; Jones to Denver, 20 May 1858, Territorial Papers (M218), RG 59, roll 1; Monaghan, *Border*, 104.

57. See Jones to Denver, 20 May 1858.

58. Montgomery to Denver, 24 May 1858; and Denver to Cass, 7 June 1858, Territorial Papers (M218), RG 59, roll 1, ibid.; Tomlinson, *Kansas*, 216–17.

59. Monaghan, *Border*, 105; Goodrich, *War*, 214; Denver to Secretary of State Lewis Cass, 23 June 1858, Territorial Papers (M218), RG 59, roll 1.

60. Lyon to Capt. M. Knowlton, 27 July 1854, Miscellany, Lyon Papers, KSHS, 3; "Nathaniel Lyon," *KSHC*, 7:418 n; Adamson, *Rebellion*, 8, 11; Phillips, *Damned*, 14, 105; Meyers, *Ranks*, 143–44; Lyon to Denver, 25 June 1858; Capt. Thomas W. Sherman to Denver, 28 June 1858; Denver to Sherman, 29 June 1858, roll 2; Capt. Thomas W. Sherman to Denver, 15 July 1858; Denver to Secretary of State Lewis Cass, 24 August 1858; Lyon to Denver, 3 August 1858; Denver to Officer Commanding Troops in Kansas, 9 August 1858; Denver to Cass, 24 August 1858; and Denver to Buchanan, 26 August 1858, Territorial Papers (M218), RG 59, rolls 1 and 2; Headquarters, Department of the West, Special Orders No. 65, 23 June 1858, *KSHC*, 5:537.

61. A. J. Weaver to Walsh, 15 November 1858; Justice Williams to Walsh, 20 November 1858; Crawford to Walsh, 22 November 1858; J. E. Jones to Walsh, 4 December 1858; Walsh to Secretary of State Lewis Cass, 9 December 1858; J. E. Jones to Walsh, 3 November 1858; and Citizens of Fort Scott to Medary, [17?] December 1858, Territorial Papers (M218), RG 59, roll 1; J. E. Jones, et al., to Medary, 19 December 1858, *KSHC*, 5:555, 562.

62. Justice Williams to Medary, 30 December 1858; Maj. John Sedgwick to Medary, 31 December 1858; and Medary to Buchanan, 28 December 1858, *KSHC*, 5:567–68, 570, 565–66; 2d Lt. Joseph Jones to Buchanan, 9 January 1859; Citizens of Paola to Medary, 24 December 1858; Medary to Buchanan, 25 January 1859; and Medary to Buchanan, 2 February 1859, Territorial Papers (M218), RG 59, roll 1; Medary to Col. Edwin Sumner, 31 January 1859, *KSHC*, 5:601; Col. Edwin Sumner to 1st Lt. Henry Benson, 1 February 1859, vol. 2, LS DWest (no. 5481), pt. 1, RG 393, p. 327; Goodrich, *War*, 223–25.

63. 1st Lt. David R. Jones to Wessells, 23 November 1860; 1st Lt. David R. Jones to Wessells, 27 November 1860; 1st Lt. David R. Jones to Wessells, 26 November 1860; and Harney to Adj. Gen. Samuel Cooper, 2 December 1860, vol. 3, LS DWest (no. 5481), pt. 1, RG 393, pp. 297, 302, 301, 304–5; Beebe, Proclamation, [?] November 1860; Beebe to Buchanan, 26 November 1860; Beebe, Proclamation, [?] November 1860; and Beebe to President Buchanan, 26 November 1860, Territorial Papers (M218), RG 59, roll 1.

64. 1st Lt. David R. Jones to Wessells, 5 December 1860; and 1st Lt. David R. Jones to Wessells, 5 December 1860, vol. 3, LS DWest (no. 5481), pt. 1, RG 393, pp. 308, 310; Phillips, *Damned*, 123–24, 125–26.

65. Steele to 1st Lt. David R. Jones, 16 December 1860, S-98, Box 9, 1860; Steele to Assistant Adjutant General, 23 December 1860, S-100, Box 9, 1860; Steele to Assistant Adjutant General, 30 December 1860, S-103, Box 9, 1860; and Steele to Williams, 6 January 1860, S-5, Box 11, 1861, LR DWest (no. 5586), pt.1, RG 393; Phillips, *Damned*, 126–27.

CHAPTER 10

1. Smith, *Fuss*, 360–61; Elliott, *Scott*, 676–77.

2. Smith, *Fuss*, 363–64; Elliott, *Scott*, 678, 679, 680–82, 686–87; Potter, *Impending*, 518–19, 521.

3. Elliott, *Scott*, 687, 689, 693–95 (Winfield Scott is quoted on 688).

4. Smith, *Fuss*, 365; Sandburg, *Lincoln*, 1:36; Long, "Sumner," 209–14; Elliott, *Scott*, 694–96; Shutz and Trenery, *Abandoned*, 60; Potter, *Impending*, 275, 566.

5. Townsend, [Notes on the Civil War], HM 41699, Box 2, Townsend Papers; Averell, *Saddle*, 247–48; Symond, *Johnston*, 94, 96; Freeman, *Lee*, 1:429–32, 436–37 (Scott quotation is on 437); Lee to Gen[era]l [Scott], 20 April 1861, Jones, *Lee*, 133.

6. Smith, *Fuss*, 359; Elliott, *Scott*, 672, 675, 688 n. 29, 714, 715.

7. Rister, *Lee*, 149; Brown, "Woman," 57–58, 61; Freeman, *Lee*, 1:416–18; King, *War*, 34; Twiggs to Scott, 13 December 1860, *OR*, ser. 1, vol. 1, 579; Lee to Markie [Martha Custis Williams], 22 January 1861, Craven, "*Markie*," 58.

8. Brown, "Woman," 61; Twiggs to Scott, 13 December 1860, 579; Twiggs to Lt. Col. Lorenzo Thomas, 27 December 1860; Lt. Col. Lorenzo Thomas to Twiggs, 28 December 1860; Twiggs to Lt. Col. Lorenzo Thomas, 2 January 1861; Twiggs to Lt. Col. Lorenzo Thomas, 7 January 1861; and Twiggs to Scott, 15 January 1861, *OR*, ser. 1, vol. 1, 579, 579–80, 580, 588, 581.

9. W[infield] S[cott] endorsement on Twiggs to Scott, 15 January 1861, 581; Gov. Sam Houston to Twiggs, 20 January 1861; Twiggs to Gov. Sam Houston, 22 January 1861; Twiggs to Adj. Gen Samuel Cooper, 23 January 1861; and Lt. Col. Lorenzo Thomas to Twiggs, 31 January 1861, *OR*, ser. 1, vol. 1, 583, 582–83, 584; Fehrenbach, *Lone*, 344–45.

10. An endorsement on Twiggs to Cooper, 23 January 1861, reads, "Received February 2, 1861"; *OR*, ser. 1, vol. 1, 582. Lt. Col. Lorenzo Thomas to Col. Carlos A. Waite, 4 February 1861; Lt. Col. Lorenzo Thomas to Col. Carlos A. Waite, 7 February 1861; Lt. Col. Lorenzo Thomas to Asst. Adj. Gen. Fitz-John Porter, 8 February 1861; and General Orders No. 3, H[ea]dq[uarte]rs, Department of Texas, *OR*, ser. 1, vol. 1, 586, 587, 588, 589; Brown, "Woman," 58. For the commission proceedings, see *OR*, ser. 1, vol. 1, 504–10.

11. Twiggs to Lt. Col. Lorenzo Thomas, 18 February 1861; Twiggs to Lt. Col. Lorenzo Thomas, 19 February 1861; Lt. Col. William Hoffman to Assistant Adjutant-General, Department of Texas, 1 March 1861; and General Orders No. 5, Headquarters, Department of Texas, 18 February 1861, *OR*, ser. 1, vol. 1, 590, 503–4, 517–18, 515; Freeman, *Lee*, 1:427, 429; Hartje, *Van Dorn*, 79; Johnson, *Reminiscences*, 134–35; Parks, *Smith*, 117, 119–20; McMurray, *Hood*, 21; Hood, *Advance*, 15–16.

12. Waite to Lt. Col. Lorenzo Thomas, 26 February 1861; Waite to Lt. Col. Lorenzo Thomas, 26 February 1861; Departmental Return, 26 February 1861; Waite to Lt. Col. Lorenzo Thomas, 3 March 1861; Waite to T. J. Devine, P. N. Luckett, [and] S. A. Maverick, 21 February 1861; T. J. Devine, S. A. Maverick, and P. N. Luckett to Waite, 22 February 1861; Maj. D. H. Vinton to Asst. Adj. Gen. W. A. Nichols, 1 March 1861; Paymaster Daniel McClure to Asst. Adj. Gen. W. A. Nichols, 2 March 1861; Capt. R. K. Whiteley to Asst. Adjutant General Nichols, 3 March 1861; Capt. W. B. Blair to Assistant Adjutant-General [W. A. Nichols], 26 February 1861; 1st Lt. T. G. Williams to Asst. Adj. Gen. W. A. Nichols, 27 February 1861; Waite to Lt. Col. Lorenzo Thomas, 23 March 1861; Waite to Lt. Col. Edward D. Townsend, 25 May 1861; Smith to Assistant Adjutant-General [W. A. Nichols], 1 March 1861; and I. V. D. Reeve to Lt. Col. Lorenzo Thomas, 12 May 1861, *OR*, ser. 1, vol. 1, 521–22, 523, 524, 524–25, 525–26, 526–27, 528–29, 529, 530, 544, 552–53, 559, 567–68.

13. Bell, "Ante Bellum," 439; Brown, "Woman," 60.

14. Secretary of War Joseph Holt, General Orders, No. 5, 1 March 1861, *OR*, ser. 1, vol. 1, 597; Brown, "Woman," 59, 60; Warner, "David Emanuel Twiggs," *Gray*, 312.

15. Lt. Col. Edward D. Townsend to Emory, 18 March 1861; and Lt. Col. Edward D. Townsend to Emory, 21 March 1861, *OR*, ser. 1, vol. 1, 656, 659; Capt. Eugene A. Carr to Emory (enclosure), 3 April 1861, E-6, Box 10, 1861, LR DWest (no. 5486), pt.1, RG 393; Goetzmann, *Exploration*, 129; Stanley, *Memoirs*, 64–65; Catton, *Coming*, 1:34; King, *War*, 34; Norris, et al., *Emory*, 1–2, 199.

16. Emory to Williams, 21 March 1861, E-1, Box 10, 1861, LR DWest (no. 5486), pt.1, RG 393; Emory to Townsend, 2 April 1861, *OR*, ser. 1, vol. 1, 660–61; Emory to Com[man]d[in]g Officer [at] Fort Cobb (enclosure), 6 April 1861, E-5; and Emory to Commanding Officer [at] Fort Arbuckle (enclosure), 21 March 1861, E-1, Box 10, 1861, LR DWest (no. 5486),pt.1, RG 393; Emory to Lt. Col. Edward D. Townsend, 13 April 1861, *OR*, ser. 1, vol. 1, 665–66; Emory to Williams, 18 April 1861, E-8, Box 10, 1861, LR DWest (no. 5486),pt.1, RG 393; Burns to Taylor, 21 April 1861, *OR*, ser. 1, vol. 1, 647; Brown, "Arkansas," Lamar, *Reader's*, 44.

17. Emory to Townsend, 13 April 1861; Sturgis to Williams, 21 May 1861, *OR*, ser. 1., vol. 1, 650–51; Emory to Williams, 18 April 1861; Stanley, *Memoirs*, 63.

18. Brown, "Arkansas," Lamar, *Reader's*, 44; Lt. Col. Edward D. Townsend to Lieutenant Colonel Emory, 17 April 1861, *OR*, ser. 1, vol. 1, 667; Averell, *Ten Years*, 249.

19. Averell, *Saddle*, 249–68.

20. Emory to Lt. Col. Edward D. Townsend, 19 May 1861, *OR*, ser. 1, vol. 1, 648–49; Stanley, *Memoirs*, 63–64, 64–65; Averell, *Saddle*, 270–71.

21. Emory to Williams, 19 May 1861, E-11, Box 10, 1861, LR DWest (no. 5486), pt.1, RG 393; Stanley, *Memoirs*, 65–66.

22. Stanley, *Memoirs*, 66–67; McPherson, *Battle*, 285; Heitman, "William Hemsley Emory," *Register*, 1:405–6; Warner, "William Hemsley Emory," *Blue*, 142–43; Norris, et al., *Emory*, chap. 7.

23. Johnston, *Life*, 177, 247–48, 257, 258; Johnston to Son [William Preston], 12 September 1856; and Johnston to Will[iam], 23 November [1856], quoted in Johnston, *Life*, 189–90, 190; Chandler, "Velvet," 35–42.

24. Johnston to Adj. Gen Samuel Cooper, 17 January 1861; "Returns from the Department of California and Oregon . . . for the month of December, 1860"; Lt. Col. Lorenzo Thomas to Johnston, 19 January 1861; Johnston to Lt. Col. Lorenzo Thomas, 15 February 1861; and Johnston to Lt. Col. Lorenzo Thomas, 20 February 1861, *OR*, ser. 1, vol. 50, 433, 428, 434, 443, 447; Asst. Adj. Gen. William W. Mackall to Capt. J. Stewart, 20 February 1861, vol. 5/10*, LS DPac (no. 3578), pt. 1, RG 393, pp. 234–35; Chandler, "Velvet," 37–38; Gilbert, "Mythical," 166–68; Roland, *Johnston*, 248–49; Johnston, *Life*, 261–62; Schlicke, *Wright*, 214.

25. Stanley, *Sumner*, 236–37; Sumner to Adjutant General, 23 March 1861, Sumner, W140 (CB 1863), LR ACPB (M1064), RG 94, roll 63; Oates, *Malice*, 225–231; Heitman, "Edwin Vose Sumner," *Register*, 1:936.

26. General-in-Chief Scott to Sumner, 22 March 1861; and Sumner to Lt. Col. Edward D. Townsend, 28 April 1861, *OR*, ser. 1, vol. 50, pt. 1, 455, 471–72; Stanley, *Sumner*, 238–39; Johnston, *Life*, 262–63, 266–67; Johnston to Lt. Col. Lorenzo Thomas, 9 April 1861, vol. 5/10*, LS DPac, pt. 1, RG 393, p. 256.

27. Johnston, *Life*, 273–75, 276–91; Roland, *Johnston*, 249–50; Warner, "Albert Sidney Johnston," *Gray*, 159–60; Scott to Commanding Officer of the Department of the West, 3 June 1861, Headquarters, *OR*, ser. 1, vol. 50, pt. 1, 496.

28. Asst. Adj. Gen. William W. Mackall to Captain Haller, 30 April 1861; Asst. Adj. Gen. William W. Mackall to Captain Carleton, 3 May 1861; Asst. Adj. Gen. William W. Mackall to Colonel Seawell, 9 May 1861; 1st Lt. Richard Drum to Maj. Gen. Henry W. Halleck, 14 May 1861; Asst. Adj. Gen. Don Carlos Buell to Colonel Seawell, 8 June 1861; Sumner to Capt. William Gardner, 26 August 1861; Sumner to Capt. William Gardner, 28 August 1861; Sumner to Lt. Col. Lorenzo Thomas, 10 June 1861; Asst. Adj. Gen. Richard Drum to Major Cady, 28 June 1861; Asst. Adj. Gen. Richard Drum to Lt. Col. George Andrews, 16 July 1861; Asst. Adj. Gen. Don Carlos Buell to Major Blake, 30 May 1861; and Drum to Blake, 29 July 1861, vol. 5/10*, LS DPac, RG 393, pp. 261, 260, 269, 283, 361, 366, 286, 441, 328, 276, 338; Captain Gardner to Sumner, 27 August 1861, G-30, Box 18, 1861, LR DPac (no. 3584), pt. 1, RG 393; Chandler, "Velvet Glove," 40–41; Stanley, *Sumner*, 239, 240; Asst. Adj. Gen. Richard Drum to Capt. Henry Carleton, 18 July 1861; and Sumner to Captain Carleton, 6 August 1861, vol. 5/10*, LS DPac (no. 3578), pt. 1, RG 393, pp. 330, 342; Hunt, *Carleton*, 194–95.

29. Hancock to Asst. Adj. Gen. William W. Mackall, 4 May 1861; Hancock to Asst. Adj. Gen. William W. Mackall, 7 May 1861; Hancock to Asst. Adj. Gen. William W. Mackall, 11 May 1861; Hancock to Asst. Adj. Gen. William W. Mackall, 12 May 1861; and Hancock to Asst. Adj. Gen. William W. Mackall, 14 May 1861, *OR*, ser. 1, vol. 50, pt. 1, 477–78, 479–80, 482–83, 483, 486; Jordan, *Hancock*, 27, 29, 31, 33; Tucker, *Superb*, 62–63; Hancock, *Reminiscences*, 58. A description of the Hancock-Armistead friendship and parting appears in Jordan, *Hancock*, 34.

30. Asst. Adj. Gen. Don Carlos Buell to Wright, 10 June 1861; Assistant Adjutant General to Adams, 21 June 1861, vol. 5/10*, LS DPac (no. 3578), pt. 1, RG 393, pp. 285–86, 297; Warner, "John Adams," *Gray*, 2; Heitman, "John Adams," *Register*, 1:152.

31. Pickett to Buell, 20 June 1861, P-22, Box 18, 1861, LR DPac, (no. 3584), pt. 1, RG 393; Pickett to Mason, 26 July 1861, *OR*, ser. 1, vol. 50, pt. 1, 544–45; Pickett to Maury, 13 February 1861, "Letters," 77; Pickett to La Salle Corbell, 17 September 1861, Inman, *Soldier*, 3; Longacre, *Pickett*, 40–41, 52–53, 131–33.

32. Warner, "Armistead Lindsay Long," *Gray*, 191–92; Mackall, *Recollections*, 3–4; Warner, "William Whann Mackall," *Gray*, 203–4; Heitman, *Register*, 1:670.

33. Ambrose, *Halleck*, 9, 10; Warner, "Henry Wager Halleck," *Blue*, 195–97.

34. Sheridan, *Memoirs*, 1:122, 123; Hutton, *Sheridan*, 11; Morris, *Sheridan*, 41–43.

35. Sumner to Wright, 30 September 1861, vol. 5/10*, LS DPac (no. 3578), pt. 1, RG 393, pp. 415–16; H[ea]dq[ua]r[ter]s, Department of the Pacific, General Orders, No. 28, 20 October 1861; and Headquarters of the Army, Special Orders, No. 309, 19 November 1861, *OR*, ser. 1, vol. 50, pt. 1, 666, 730; Schlicke, *Wright*, 214, 218–221; Warner, "George Wright," *Blue*, 574–75. Wright complained about the injustice as late as 1864. On promotion, see Wright to Adj. Gen. Lorenzo Thomas, 3 November 1861; and Wright to Secretary of War Edwin Stanton, 14 November 1864, W1099, George Wright (CB 1864), LR ACPB, RG 94, roll 134.

36. Asst. Adj. Gen. Edward D. Townsend to Sumner, 16 September 1861; Sumner to Asst. Adj. Gen. Edward D. Townsend, 14 October 1861; and Kibbe to Secretary of War Simon Cameron, 6 September 1861, *OR*, ser. 1, vol. 50, pt. 1, 621, 658, 607–8; Warner,

"Edwin Vose Sumner," *Blue*, 489–90; Warner, "Armistead Lindsay Long," *Gray*, 191–92; Heitman, "Eugene Eckel McLean," *Register*, 1:675. Two of Sumner's sons, Samuel and Edwin Jr., served in the regular army during the Civil War and in the frontier army to the end of the century. See Heitman, "Edwin Vose Sumner" and "Samuel Storrow Sumner," *Register*, 1:936.

37. Loring to Adj. Gen. Lorenzo Thomas, 23 March 1861; Major Lynde to Assistant Adjutant-General, 11 March 1861, Loring to Asst. Adj. Gen. Edward D. Townsend, 22 April 1861; and Loring to Asst. Adj. Gen. Edward D. Townsend, 19 May 1861, *OR*, ser. 1, vol. 1, 599–600, 600, 602, 604; Maury, *Recollections*, 129–30; Wessels, *Born*, 51–52; DuBois, 30 March 1861, Fort Union, *Campaigns*, ed. Hammond, 111.

38. Thompson, *Sibley*, 210–11; Wessels, *Born*, 54–55; Sibley to Loring, 12 June 1861, *OR*, ser. 1, vol. 4, 55–56.

39. Canby to Assistant Adjutant-General, Army Headquarters, 11 June 1861, *OR*, ser. 1, vol. 1, 606; Canby to Assistant Adjutant-General, Army Headquarters, *OR*, ser. 1, vol. 4, 54–55; Anderson to Commanding Officer, Fort Buchanan, 30 June 1861, [n.p.], *OR*, ser. 1, vol. 4, 49; Maury, *Recollections*, 132, 138; Asst. Surg. James C. McKee to Surgeon-General, U.S.A., 16 August 1861; "Statement of Capt. C. H. McNally," [n.d.]; Lynde to Acting Assistant Adjutant-General, 26 July 1861; and Baylor to Washington, 21 September 1861, *OR*, ser. 1, vol. 4, 11–12, 13–14, 4–6, 17–18.

40. The account of Lynde's retreat is taken from Lynde to Acting Assistant Adjutant-General, 7 August 1861; Gibbs to Canby, 6 August 1861; Gibbs to Assistant Adjutant-General, U.S.A., 7 November 1861; "Statement of Captain Gibbs," [n.d.]; "Statement of Ass[istan]t Surg[eon] J. C. McKee, U.S. Army"; General Orders, No. 102, 25 November 1861, Headquarters of the Army; Baylor to Washington, 21 September 1861; and "Recapitulation of troops surrendered at San Augustine Springs, N[ew] Mex[ico], July 27, 1861," *OR*, ser. 1, vol. 4, 5–6, 7–8, 9, 9–11, 12–13, 16, 17–19, 15.

41. Polk, 20 February 1847, *Diary*, 2:385; Clow, "Harney," Hutton, *Soldiers*, 42, 45, 53; Phillips, *Damned*, 150.

42. McReynolds, *Missouri*, 213–14; Lyon, "Jackson," 431–41, 441; Phillips, *Damned*, 133–34.

43. Clow, "Harney," Hutton, *Soldiers*, 42, 53; Lyon, "Jackson," 431; Lt. Col. Lorenzo Thomas to Harney, 26 January 1861, A-5; and Lt. Col. Lorenzo Thomas to Harney, 28 January 1861, A-6, Box 10, 1861, LR DWest (no. 5486), pt. 1, RG 393; Sweeny, "Etat de Service," SW 630, Box 1, Sweeny Papers; Sweeny, *Biographical*, 39n; Phillips, *Damned*, 137–38.

44. Phillips, *Damned*, 139–40; Shalhope, *Price*, 147–48; Lyon, "Jackson," 432–33.

45. Smith, *Blair*, 2:31–32, 34–35; Phillips, *Damned*, 129–30.

46. Harney to Lt. Col. Lorenzo Thomas, 19 February 1861; Capt. Peter Hagner to Craig, 21 February 1861; Harney to Adj. Gen. Lorenzo Thomas, 20 March 1861; Adjutant-General's Office, Special Orders, No. 74, 13 March 1861; and Asst. Adjutant General Williams to Lyon, 13 March 1861, *OR*, ser. 1, vol. 1, 654, 655, 658, 658–59; Phillips, *Damned*, 142–43.

47. Phillips, *Damned*, 149, 152–53; Asst. Adjutant General Williams to Hagner, 6 April 1861, *OR*, ser. 1, vol. 1, 661; Sweeny to David [Banks], 6 April 1861, SW 512, Box 1, Sweeny Papers; Lyon to Asst. Adjutant General Williams, 22 March 1861, L-4, Box 10, 1861, LR DWest (no. 5486), pt. 1, RG 393.

48. McElroy, *Struggle*, 60, 61; Phillips, *Damned*, 159–60; Clow, "Harney," Hutton, *Soldiers*, 53; Schofield, *Forty-six*, 30, 33.

49. Lyon to [Yates], 16 April 1861; Blair to Secretary of War Simon Cameron, 19 April 1861; and Adj. Gen. Lorenzo Thomas to Harney, 21 April 1861, *OR*, ser. 1, vol. 1, 667, 668–69, 669; Smith, *Blair*, 2:38–39; Clow, "Harney," Hutton, *Soldiers*, 53.

50. Adj. Gen. Lorenzo Thomas to Lyon, 21 April 1861; [Adjutant General Thomas] to Lyon, 30 April 1861 (Abraham Lincoln, Winfield Scott, and Simon Cameron endorsed this order); and Lyon to Adj. Gen. Lorenzo Thomas, 30 April 1861, *OR*, ser. 1, vol. 1, 670, 675, 675–76; Asst. Adjutant General Williams to Adj. Gen. Lorenzo Thomas, 29 April 1861, vol. 4, LS DWest (no. 5481), pt. 1, RG 393, pp. 86–87; Phillips, *Damned*, 181; Covington, "Camp," 202–3.

51. Sweeny to Bodge, 10 June 1861, SW 517, Box 1, Sweeny Papers; Lyon to Thomas, 11 May 1861, *OR*, ser. 1, vol. 3, 4–5; Covington, "Camp," 204–6; Phillips, *Damned*, 182–83, 187–90; Grant, *Memoirs*, 1:235.

52. Covington, "Camp," 208–10; Phillips, *Damned*, 191–92; Lyon to Thomas, 12 May 1861, *OR*, ser. 1, vol. 3, 9; Sherman to [Thomas Ewing, Jr.], 23 May 1861, Sherman, *Home*, 197–98; Sherman, *Memoirs*, 1:201–3.

53. Harney to Asst. Adj. Gen. Edward D. Townsend, 13 May 1861; Harney, "Proclamation," 12 May 1861; General Orders No. 10, H[ea]dq[uarte]rs, Department of the West, 11 May 1861; Harney, "To the People of Missouri," 14 May 1861; and Harney to Secretary of War Simon Cameron (endorsed by Blair), 15 May 1861, *OR*, ser. 1, vol. 3, 369–70, 370, 369, 371–72, 373; Parrish, *Turbulent*, 24–25.

54. Harney to Asst. Adj. Gen. Edward D. Townsend, 22 May 1861; Price and Harney, [Agreement], 21 May 1861; and Harney to Asst. Adj. Gen. Edward D. Townsend, 17 May 1861, *OR*, ser 1, vol. 3, 375, 374; Castel, *Price*, 15–17. Shalhope argues that Price was sincere and that Jackson was a committed secessionist (*Price*, 160–62, 161 n. 6).

55. Harney to Asst. Adj. Gen. Edward D. Townsend, 29 May 1861; Adj. Gen. Lorenzo Thomas to Harney, 27 May 1861; and Special Orders No. 135, 16 May 1861, Adj[jutan]t Gen[eral]'s Office, *OR*, ser. 1, vol. 3, 377, 376, 374; Phillips, *Damned*, 202–3, 207; Smith, *Blair*, 2:50–51.

56. Harney to Adj. Gen. Lorenzo Thomas, 31 May 1861; and Harney to Adj. Gen. Lorenzo Thomas, 5 June 1861, *OR*, ser. 1, vol. 3, 381, 383; Clow, "Harney," Hutton, *Soldiers*, 54.

57. Phillips, *Damned*, 210–14, 255–56; Smith, *Blair*, 2:51; Shalhope, *Price*, 164–66; Castel, *Price*, 23–24; Lyon, "Jackson," 439.

58. For the western conflicts during the Civil War, see Josephy, *West*. Utley covers the Indian wars in *Frontiersmen*. For Carleton's activities, see D. Ball, "Fort Craig."

CONCLUSION

1. Dawson, *Generals;* Sefton, *Reconstruction;* Cooper, *Disorder;* Jensen, *Surveillance;* Hutton, *Sheridan;* Coakley, *Role;* Ball Sr., "Military Posses"; Ball Sr., *Marshals;* Laurie, "Filling."

Bibliography

PRIMARY SOURCES

Manuscript Archives

Henry E. Huntington Library. San Marino, California.
Couts, Cave Johnson. Papers, 1832–51.
Hardcastle, Aaron Brown. Journal (1858–59) and U.S. Army Papers (1852–60).
Floyd, W[illiam] P. Journal [kept by the surgeon of Edward Fitzgerald Beale's wagon-road expedition describing his trip from Virginia to Fort Smith, and thence to the Colorado River].
Grabhorn Collection.
Gunnison, John Williams. Papers, 1832–96, 1926.
McCall, George Archibald. Papers, 1831–53.
Ritch, William Gillet. Papers, 1539–1890.
Sweeny, Thomas William. Papers, 1830–1944.
Townsend, Edward Davis. Papers, 1761–1928.
Historical Society of Pennsylvania. Philadelphia.
Letterbook. Headquarters, Department of Texas, 1851–54.
Kansas State Historical Society. Topeka.
Bacon, Lawrence. Diary, 25 July–2 December 1857. Miscellany.
Lyon, Nathaniel. Miscellany.
Library of Congress. Washington, D.C.
Davis, Jefferson. Papers.
Hatch, John Porter. Papers.
Heintzelman, Samuel Peter. Papers, 1822–1904.
Hitchcock, E. A. Papers.
Pierce, Franklin. Papers. Microfilm.
Sumner Family Papers.
Walker, Robert J. Papers.
United States National Archives. Washington, D.C.
"General Records of the Department of State." RG 59.
State Department Territorial Papers: Kansas, 1854–61. M218. Microfilm.

"Records of the Adjutant General's Office, 1780s–1917." RG 94.
Letters Received by the Appointment, Commission, and Personal Branch, 1871–94. M1395. Microcopy.
Letters Received by the Commission Branch of the Adjutant General's Office, 1863–70. M1064. Microcopy.
Letters Received by the Office of the Adjutant General, Main Series, 1822–60. M567. Microfilm.
Returns from Military Posts, 1800–1916. M617. Microfilm.
Returns from Regular Army Cavalry Regiments. Cavalry. M744. Microfilm.
"Records of the Office of the Secretary of War." RG 107.
Letters Sent by the Secretary of War Relating to Military Affairs, 1800–89. M6. Microfilm.
"Records of the U.S. Army Continental Commands, 1821–1920." RG 393.
Registers of Letters Received and Letters Received by Headquarters, Department of New Mexico, 1854–65. M1120. Microcopy.
Register of Letters Received and Letters Received by Headquarters, 9th Military Department, 1848–53. M1102. Microcopy.
"United States Army Continental Commands, 1821–1920." Part 1. RG 393.
Department of Oregon, 1858–61. Letters Received, 1858–60. No. 3574.
Division and Department of the Pacific, 1848–66. Letters Sent, January 1849–July 1865. 8 vols. No. 3578.
Division and Department of the Pacific, 1848–66. Letters and Telegrams Received, 1849–65. No. 3584.
Department of Texas. Letters Sent. No. 4775.
Department and Army of Utah, 1857–61. Letters Sent, July 1857–July 1861. 3 vols. No. 5029.
Department of the West and Western Department, 1853–61. Letters Sent, December 1853–November 1861. 4 vols. No. 5481.
Department of the West and Western Department, 1853–61. Letters Received, 1853–61. No. 5486.
Department of the West and Western Department, 1853–61. Letters Sent by the Troops Serving in Kansas, May 1857–May 1858. No. 5506.
United States Army Mobile Units. RG 391.
Cavalry. Fourth Cavalry. Regimental Letters Sent. No. 719.

Government Documents

U.S. House. *Affairs in Oregon.* 36th Cong., 1st sess., 1859–60. HED 65. Serial 1051.
______. *California and New Mexico.* 31st Cong., 1st sess., 1849–50. HED 17. Serial 573.
______. *Correspondence between the Late Secretary of War and General Wool.* 35th Cong., 1st sess., 1857–58. HED 88. Serial 956.
______. *Correspondence with General Harney.* 36th Cong., 1st sess., 1859–60. HED 98. Serial 1057.
______. *Difficulties on Southwestern Frontier.* 36th Cong., 1st sess., 1859–60. HED 52. Serial 1050.

______. *Island of San Juan.* 36th Cong., 1st sess., 1859–60. HED 77. Serial 1056.
______. *Kansas Affairs.* 34th Cong., 1st sess., 1855–56. H. Rept. 200. Serial 869.
______. *Letter from the Secretary of War.* 31st Cong., 1st sess., 1849–50. HED 66. Serial 577.
______. *Mountain Meadows Massacre.* Special report prepared by J. H. Carleton. 57th Cong., 1st sess., 1901–2. HED 605. Serial 4377.
______. *Notes of a Military Reconnaissance.* Special report prepared by William H. Emory. 30th Cong., 1st sess., 1847–48. HED 41. Serial 517.
______. *Pay of Army Officers.* 34th Cong., 1st sess., 1855–56. HED 22. Serial 851.
______. *Report on the United States and Mexican Boundary Survey.* Special report prepared by William H. Emory. 34th Cong., 1st sess., 1855–56. HED 135. Vol. 1. Serial 861.
______. *Rio Grande Frontier.* 32d Cong., 1st sess., 1851–52. HED 112. Serial 648.
______. *Troubles on Texas Frontier.* 36th Cong., 1st sess., 1859–60. HED 81. Serial 1056.
______. *The Utah Expedition.* 35th Cong., 1st sess., 1857–58. HED 71. Serial 956.
______. *Utah Territory.* 36th Cong., 1st sess., 1859–60. HED 78. Serial 1056.
U.S. Senate. *Claim of Samuel A. Belden & Co. against the Government of Mexico.* 32d Cong., 1st sess., 1851–52. SED 80. Serial 620.
______. *Instructions to Officers in Kansas.* 34th Cong., 3d sess., 1856. SED 97. Serial 823.
______. *Message from the President.* 31st Cong., 1st sess., 1849–50. SED 56. Serial 561.
______. *Message from the President.* 31st Cong., 1st sess., 1849–50. SED 60, pt. 2. Serial 561.
______. *Message of the President.* 32d Cong., 1st sess., 1851–52. SED 5. Serial 875.
______. *Message of the President.* 36th Cong., 1st sess., 1859–60. SED 32. Serial 1031.
______. *Papers Relating to Territorial Kansas.* 34th Cong., 1st sess., 1855–56. SED 23. Serial 820.
______. *Presidential Message.* 34th Cong., 1st sess., 1855–56. SED 101. Serial 824.
______. *Report of the Secretary of War.* 34th Cong., 3d sess., 1856. SED 43. Serial 881.
______. *Statistical Report on the Sickness and Mortality in the Army of the United States.* 34th Cong., 1st sess., 1855–56. SED 96. Serial 825.
War Department. *Annual Report of the Secretary of War.* 29th Cong., 1st sess.,1845–46. SED 1. Serial 470.
______. *Annual Report of the Secretary of War.* 31st Cong., 1st sess., 1849–50. SED 1. Serial 549.
______. *Annual Report of the Secretary of War.* 31st Cong., 2d sess., 1850–51. HED 1. Serial 595.
______. *Annual Report of the Secretary of War.* 32d Cong., 1st sess., 1851–52. HED 2. Serial 634.
______. *Annual Report of the Secretary of War.* 32d Cong., 2d sess., 1852–53. HED 1, pt. 2. Serial 674.
______. *Annual Report of the Secretary of War.* 33d Cong., 1st sess., 1853–54. SED 1, pt. 2. Serial 691.
______. *Annual Report of the Secretary of War.* 33d Cong., 2d sess., 1854–55. SED 1, pt. 2. Serial 747.

______. *Annual Report of the Secretary of War.* 34th Cong., 1st sess., 1855–56. SED 1, pt. 2. Serial 811.
______. *Annual Report of the Secretary of War.* 34th Cong., 3d sess., 1856–57. HED 1, pt. 2. Serial 894.
______. *Annual Report of the Secretary of War.* 35th Cong., 1st sess., 1857–58. SED 11. Serial 920.
______. *Annual Report of the Secretary of War.* 35th Cong., 2d sess., 1857–58. HED 11. Serial 943.
______. *Annual Report of the Secretary of War.* 35th Cong., 2d sess., 1858–59. HED 2, pts. 1–2. Serial 998.
______. *Annual Report of the Secretary of War.* 36th Cong., 1st sess., 1859–60. SED 2. Serials 1024–25.
______. *Annual Report of the Secretary of War.* 36th Cong., 2d sess., 1860–61. SED 1. Serial 1079.
______. *Annual Report of the Secretary of War.* 37th Cong., 2d sess., 1861–62. SED 1. Serial 1118.
______. *Regulations for the Army of the United States, 1857.* New York: Harper and Brothers, [1857].
______. *War of the Rebellion: A Compilation of the Official Records of the Union and Confederate Armies.* 71 vols. Washington, D.C.: Government Printing Office, 1880–1901.

Books

Abel, Annie H., ed. *The Correspondence of James S. Calhoun.* Washington, D.C.: Government Printing Office, 1915.
Alexander, E[dward] P. *Fighting for the Confederacy: The Personal Recollections of General Edward Porter Alexander.* Edited by Gary W. Gallagher. Chapel Hill: University of North Carolina Press, 1989.
American Whig Review 15 (April 1852).
Averell, William Woods. *Ten Years in the Saddle: The Memoir of William Woods Averell, 1851–1862.* Edited by Edward K. Eckert and Nicholas J. Amato. San Rafael, Calif.: Presidio Press, 1978.
Ballentine, George. *Autobiography of an English Soldier in the United States Army.* New York: Stringer and Townsend, 1853.
Bandel, Eugene. *Frontier Life in the Army, 1854–1861.* Edited by Ralph P. Bieber. Glendale, Calif.: Arthur H. Clark, 1932.
Barnes, Thurlow Weed. *Memoir of Thurlow Weed.* Boston, n.p., 1884.
Bennet, James A. *Forts and Forays.* Edited by Clinton E. Brooks and Frank D. Reeves. 1948. Reprint, with a foreword by Jerry Thompson, Albuquerque: University of New Mexico Press, 1996.
Bieber, Ralph P., ed., with Averam B. Bender. *Exploring Southwestern Trails, 1846–1854.* Glendale, Calif.: Arthur H. Clark, 1938.
Canning, Ray R., and Beverly Beeton, eds. *The Genteel Gentile: Letters of Elizabeth Cumming, 1857–1858.* Utah, the Mormons, and the West. Edited by Everett L. Cooley, et al. Salt Lake City: Tanner Trust Fund, University of Utah Library, 1977.

Chamberlain, Samuel E. *My Confession: The Recollections of a Rogue.* With an introduction and postscript by Roger Butterfield. 1956. Reprint, with a foreword by John S. D. Eisenhower, Lincoln: University of Nebraska Press, 1987.

Coker, Caleb, ed. *The News from Brownsville: Helen Chapman's Letters from the Texas Military Frontier, 1848–1852.* Austin: Published for the Barker Texas History Center by the Texas State Historical Association, 1992.

Conway, Cornelius. *The Utah Expedition.* Cincinnati, Ohio: "Safety Fund Reporter," Office Print, 1858.

Cooke, P[hilip] St. Geo[rge]. *The Conquest of New Mexico and California in 1846–1848.* 1874. Reprint, Chicago: Rio Grande Press, 1964.

Craven, Avery, ed. *"To Markie": The Letters of Robert E. Lee to Martha Custis Williams.* Cambridge, Mass.: Harvard University Press, 1933.

Crist, Lynda Lasswell, and Mary Seaton Dix, eds. *The Papers of Jefferson Davis.* Vols. 5–6. Baton Rouge: Louisiana State University Press, 1985–89.

Crook, George. *General George Crook: His Autobiography.* Edited by Martin F. Schmitt. 1946. Reprint, with a foreword by Joseph C. Porter, Norman: University of Oklahoma Press, 1986.

Dobyns, Henry F., ed. *Hepah, California! The Journal of Cave Johnson Couts from Monterey, Nuevo Leon, Mexico, to Los Angeles, California, during the Years 1848–1849.* Tucson: Arizona Pioneers' Historical Society, 1961.

Dunbar, Rowland, ed. *Jefferson Davis, Constitutionalist: His Letters, Papers, and Speeches.* 10 vols. Jackson: Mississippi Archives, 1923.

Emory, William H. *Report on the United States and Mexican Boundary Survey.* 1859. Reprint, with an introduction by William H. Goetzmann, Austin: Texas State Historical Association, 1987.

Ford, John Salmon. *Rip Ford's Texas.* Edited by Stephen B. Oates. Personal Narratives of the West. Edited by J. Frank Dobie. Austin: University of Texas Press, 1963.

Frazer, Robert W., ed. *Mansfield on the Condition of Western Forts, 1853–1854.* Norman: University of Oklahoma Press, 1963.

French, Samuel G. *Two Wars: An Autobiography of Gen. Samuel G. French.* Nashville: Confederate Veteran, 1901.

Girardi, Robert I., and Nathaniel Cheairs Hughes Jr., eds. *The Memoirs of Brigadier General William Passmore Carlin, U.S.A.* Lincoln: University of Nebraska Press, 1999.

Gladstone, T. H. *The Englishman in Kansas.* With an introduction by Frederick Law Olmstead and a foreword by James A. Rawley. Lincoln: University of Nebraska Press, 1971.

Glisan, Rodney. *Journal of Army Life.* San Francisco: A. L. Bancroft, 1874.

Gove, Jesse A. *The Utah Expedition, 1857–1858: Letters of Capt. Jesse A. Gove, 10th Inf., U.S.A., of Concord, N.H., to Mrs. Gove, and Special Correspondence of the New York Herald.* Edited by Otis G. Hammond. New Hampshire Historical Collections. Vol. 10. Concord: New Hampshire Historical Society, 1928.

Grant, U. S. *Personal Memoirs of U. S. Grant.* 2 vols. New York: Charles L. Webster, 1885.

Gunnison, Lieut. J. W. *The Mormons, or, Latter Day Saints, in the Valley of the Great Salt Lake: A History of Their Rise and Progress, Peculiar Doctrines, Present Condition, and Prospects, Derived from Personal Observation during a Residence among Them.* Philadelphia: J. B. Lippincott, 1856.

Hafen, Le Roy Reuben, and Ann Woodbury, eds. *The Utah Expedition, 1857–1858: A Documentary Account of the United States Military Movement under Colonel Albert Sidney Johnston, and the Resistance by Brigham Young and the Mormon Nauvoo Legion.* Glendale, Calif.: Arthur H. Clark, 1958.

Hamilton, Henry S. *Reminiscences of a Veteran.* Concord, N.H.: Republican Press Association, 1897.

Hamlin, Capt. Percy Hamlin, ed. *The Making of a Soldier: The Letters of R. S. Ewell.* Richmond, Va.: Whittet and Shepperson, 1935.

Hammond, George P., ed. *Campaigns in the West, 1856–1861: The Journal and Letters of Colonel John Van Deusen Du Bois.* Tucson: Arizona Pioneers' Historical Society, 1949.

Hancock, Almira R. *Reminiscences of Winfield Scott Hancock.* New York: Charles L. Webster, 1887.

Heitman, Francis B. *Historical Register and Dictionary of the United States Army, from Its Organization, September 29, 1789, to March 2, 1903.* 2 vols. Washington: Government Printing Office, 1903.

Heth, Henry. *The Memoirs of Henry Heth.* Edited by James L. Morrison Jr. Contributions in Military History, no. 6. Westport, Conn.: Greenwood Press, 1974.

Hine, Robert V., and Savoie Lottinville, eds. *Soldier in the West: Letters of Theodore Talbot during His Services in California, Mexico, and Oregon, 1845–53.* Norman: University of Oklahoma Press, 1972.

Hitchcock, Ethan Allen. *Fifty Years in Camp and Field: Diary of Major-General Ethan Allen Hitchcock, U.S.A.* Edited by W. A. Croffut. New York: G. P. Putnam's Sons, 1909.

Hood, John Bell. *Advance and Retreat: Personal Experiences in the United States and Confederate State Armies.* New Orleans: Published for the Hood Orphan Memorial Fund, 1880.

Howard, Oliver Otis. *Autobiography of Oliver Otis Howard, Major General United States Army.* 2 vols. New York: Baker and Taylor, 1908.

Hughes, John T. *Doniphan's Expedition.* Cincinnati: J. A. and U. P. James, 1850.

Inman, Arthur Crew, ed. *Soldier of the South: General Pickett's War Letters to His Wife.* 1928. Reprint, Freeport, N.Y.: Books for Libraries Press, 1971.

Johnson, Brig.-Gen. Richard W. *A Soldier's Reminiscences in Peace and War.* Philadelphia: J. B. Lippincott, 1886.

Jones, Rev. J. William. *Life and Letters of Robert Edward Lee: Soldier and Man.* New York: Neale Publishing, 1906.

Kansas State Historical Society. *Collections of the Kansas State Historical Society.* Vols. 1–27. Topeka: Kansas State Historical Society, 1881–1928.

Keyes, Erasmus D. *Fifty Years' Observation of Men and Events: Civil and Military.* New York: Charles Scribner's Sons, 1884.

Kip, Lawrence. *Army Life on the Pacific; a Journal of the Expedition against the Northern Indians, the Tribes of the Couer D'Alenes, Spokans, and Pelouzes, in the Summer of 1858.* Redfield, New York: Edward O. Jenkins, Printer, 1859.

Lane, Lydia Spencer. *I Married a Soldier.* 1893. Reprint, with an introduction by Darlis A. Miller, Albuquerque: University of New Mexico Press, 1987.

Langley, Harold D. *To Utah with the Dragoons and Glimpses of Life in Arizona and California, 1858–1859*. Salt Lake City: University of Utah Press, 1974.

Larkin, Thomas O. *The Larkin Papers: Personal, Business, and Official Correspondence of Thomas Oliver Larkin, Merchant and United States Consul in California.* Edited by George P. Hammond. Berkeley: University of California Press, 1953.

Lowe, Percival G. *Five Years a Dragoon ('49 to '54) and Other Adventures on the Great Plains.* With an introduction by Don Russell. Norman: University of Oklahoma Press, 1965.

Lynch, James. *The New York Volunteers in California: With Stevenson to California.* Glorieta, N.M.: Rio Grande Press, 1970.

Mackall, William W. *A Son's Recollections of His Father.* New York: E. P. Dutton, 1930.

Madsden, Brigham D., ed. *Exploring the Great Salt Lake: The Stansbury Expedition of 1849–50.* Publications in the American West. Vol. 22. Salt Lake City: University of Utah Press and Tanner Trust Fund, University of Utah Library, 1989.

Manning, William Ray, ed. *Diplomatic Correspondence of the United States: Inter-American Affairs, 1831–1860.* 12 vols. Washington, D.C.: Carnegie Endowment for International Peace, 1932–39.

Marcy, Col. R[andolph] B. *Thirty Years of Army Life on the Border.* New York: Harper and Brothers, 1866.

Maury, Dabney H. *Recollections of a Virginian in the Mexican, Indian, and Civil Wars.* 2d ed. New York: Charles Scribner's Sons, 1894.

McCall, George A. *Letters from the Frontiers, Written during a Period of Thirty Years' Service in the Army of the United States.* Philadelphia: J. B. Lippincott, 1868.

______. *New Mexico in 1850: A Military View.* Edited by Robert W. Frazer. Norman: University of Oklahoma Press, 1968.

McConnell, H. H. *Five Years a Cavalryman or, Sketches of Regular Army Life on the Texas Frontier, 1866–1871.* 1889. Reprint, with a foreword by William H. Leckie, Norman: University of Oklahoma Press, 1996.

Meyers, Augustus. *Ten Years in the Ranks, U.S. Army.* New York: Stirling Press, 1914.

Miller, Darlis M., ed. *Above a Common Soldier: The West of Frank and Mary Clarke in the American West and Civil War, 1847–1872.* Rev. ed. Albuquerque: University of New Mexico, 1997.

Pierce, Edward L, ed. *Memoir and Letters of Charles Sumner.* 2 vols. Boston: Roberts Brothers, 1877.

Polk, James K. *The Diary of James K. Polk during His Presidency, 1845 to 1849.* 4 vols. Edited by Milo M. Quaife with an introduction by Andrew Cunningham. Chicago: A. C. McClure, 1910.

Price, George F. *Across the Continent with the Fifth Cavalry.* New York: D. Van Nostrand, 1883.

Report of the Committee of Investigation Sent in 1873 by the Mexican Government to the Frontier of Texas. New York: Baker and Godwin, 1875.

Richardson, James D. *A Compilation of the Messages and Papers of the Presidents, 1789–1908.* 11 vols. Washington, D.C.: Bureau of National Literature and Art, 1909.

Robinson, Sara T. L. *Kansas. Its Interior and Exterior Life.* Boston: Crosby, Nichols, 1857.

Rodenbough, Theophilus Francis, comp. *From Everglade to Cañon with the Second Dragoons: An Authentic Account of Service in Florida, Mexico, Virginia, and the Indian Country.* New York: D. Van Nostrand, 1875.

Ruxton, George F. *Ruxton of the Rockies.* Collected by Clyde and Mae Reed Porter. Edited by Le Roy R. Hafen. Norman: University of Oklahoma Press, 1950.

Schofield, John M. *Forty-Six Years in the Army.* New York: Century, 1897.

Scott, Roland Garth, ed. *Forgotten Valor: The Memoirs, Journals, & Civil War Letters of Orlando B. Willcox.* Kent, Ohio: Kent State University Press, 1999.

Scott, Winfield. *Memoirs of Lieut.-General Winfield Scott, L.L.D., Written by Himself.* 2 vols. New York: Sheldon, 1864.

Sedgwick, John. *Correspondence of John Sedgwick, Major-General.* 2 vols. New York: Printed for Carl and Ellen Battelle Stoeckel by the De Vinne Press, 1902–3.

Settle, Raymond W., ed. *The March of the Mounted Riflemen: First United States Military Expedition to Travel the Full Length of the Oregon Trail from Fort Leavenworth to Fort Vancouver, May to October 1849.* 1940. Reprint, Lincoln: University of Nebraska Press, 1989.

Severance, Frank Hayward, ed. *Millard Fillmore Papers.* 2 vols. Buffalo, N.Y.: Buffalo Historical Society, 1907.

Sheridan, Philip H. *Personal Memoirs of P. H. Sheridan.* 2 vols. New York: Charles L. Webster, 1888.

Sherman, William T. *Home Letters of General Sherman.* Edited by M. A. DeWolfe Howe. New York: Charles Scribner's Sons, 1909.

———. *Memoirs of Gen. W. T. Sherman.* 1875, with a foreword by B. H. Liddell Hart. Reprint, Bloomington: Indiana University Press, 1957.

Simon, John Y., ed. *The Papers of Ulysses S. Grant.* Vol. 1. Carbondale: Southern Illinois University Press, 1967.

Stanley, David S. *Personal Memoirs of Maj. Gen. D. S. Stanley, U.S.A.* Cambridge, Mass.: Harvard University Press, 1917.

Stansbury, Capt. Howard. *Exploration and Survey of the Valley of the Great Salt Lake of Utah, Including a Reconnaissance of a New Route through the Rocky Mountains.* Philadelphia: Lippincott, Grambo, 1852.

Sweeny, Thomas William. *Journal of Lieutenant Thomas W. Sweeny, 1849–1853.* Edited by Arthur Woodward. Los Angeles: Westernlore Press, 1956.

Tevis, James H. *Arizona in the '50's.* Albuquerque: University of New Mexico Press, 1954.

Thompson, Jerry, ed. *Juan N. Cortina and the Texas-Mexico Frontier, 1859–1877.* El Paso: Texas Western Press, 1994.

———. *Fifty Miles and a Fight: Major Samuel Peter Heintzelman's Journal of Texas and the Cortina War.* Austin: Texas State Historical Association, 1998.

Thorndike, Rachel Sherman, ed. *The Sherman Letters: Correspondence between General and Senator Sherman from 1837 to 1891.* New York: Scribner's Sons, 1894.

Tomlinson, William P. *Kansas in Fifty-Eight: Being Chiefly a History of the Recent Troubles in the Territory.* New York: H. Dayton, 1859.

Townsend, E[dward] D. *The California Diary of General E. D. Townsend.* Los Angeles: Ward Ritchie Press, 1970.

Turnley, Parmenas Taylor. *Reminiscences of Parmenas Taylor Turnley: From the Cradle to Three-Score and Ten.* Chicago: Donahue and Henneberry, 1892.

Vielé, Teresa Griffin. *Following the Drum: A Glimpse of Frontier Life*. 1858. Reprint, with a foreword by Sandra L. Meyers, Lincoln: University of Nebraska, 1984.
[Wright, John]. *Recollections of Western Texas: Descriptive and Narrative (Including an Indian Campaign), 1852–55*. London: W. and F. G. Cash, 1857.
Zwinger, Ann, ed. *John Xántus: The Fort Tejon Letters, 1857–1859*. Tucson: University of Arizona Press, 1986.

Articles

Bailey, Lynn R., ed. "Lt. Sylvester Mowry's Report on His March in 1855 from Salt Lake City to Fort Tejon." *Arizona and the West* 7 (winter 1965): 329–46.
Bell, [William H.]. "Ante Bellum." *Journal of the Military Service Institution of the United States* 4 (1883): 439.
Browne, Albert G. "The Utah Expedition: Its Causes and Consequences." *Atlantic Monthly* 3 (1859): 361–75, 474–91, 570–84.
Carr, E. T. "Reminiscences of Ft. Leavenworth, 1855–56." *Collections of the Kansas State Historical Society* 12 (1912): 375–83.
Clary, David A., ed. "'I Am Already Quite a Texan': Albert J. Meyer's Letters from Texas, 1854–1856." *Southwestern Historical Quarterly* 82 (July 1978): 25–76.
Cobb, David Glenn, ed. "Letters of David R. Cobb, 1858–64." *Kansas Historical Quarterly* 11 (1942): 65–72.
Drum, Richard C. "Reminiscences of the Indian Fight at Ash Hollow." *Collections of the Nebraska State Historical Society* 16 (1911): 143–51.
Ellison, William Henry, ed. "Memoirs of Hon. William M. Gwin." *California Historical Society Quarterly* 19 (March, June, September, December 1940): 1–26, 157–84, 256–77, 344–57.
Espinosa, J. Manuel. "Memoir of a Kentuckian in New Mexico, 1848–1884." *New Mexico Historical Review* 13 (January 1983): 1–13.
Gibbens, V. E., ed. "Letters on the War in Kansas in 1856." *Kansas Historical Quarterly* 10 (1941): 369–79.
Gleed, Charles S. "Paper on Col. Samuel Walker." *Collections of the Kansas State Historical Society* 6 (1897–1900): 249–70.
Griffith, G. W. E. "The Battle of Black Jack." *Collections of the Kansas State Historical Society* 16 (1923–25): 524–27.
Hairston, Peter W., ed. "J. E. B. Stuart's Letters to His Hairston Kin, 1850–1855." *North Carolina Historical Review* 51 (summer 1974): 261–333.
"Information against the Rescuers." *Transactions of the Kansas State Historical Society* 5 (1889–96): 244–45.
"Letters." *Oregon Historical Quarterly* 8 (March 1907): 77–78.
"Letters of John and Sarah Everett, 1854–1856: Miami County Pioneers." *Kansas Historical Quarterly* 8 (1939): 3–34, 143–74, 279–310, 350–83.
McCann, Lloyd E. "The Grattan Massacre." *Nebraska History* 37 (1956): 1–25.
Moore, John Hammond, ed. "Letters from a Santa Fe Army Clerk, 1855–1856." *New Mexico Historical Review* 53 (January 1978): 141–64.
Morrison, James L., Jr., ed. "Getting through West Point: The Cadet Memoirs of John C. Tidball, Class of 1848." *Civil War History* 26 (December 1980): 304–25.

Myers, Harry C. "From 'The Crack Post of the Frontier': Letters of Thomas and Charlotte Swords." *Kansas History* 5 (autumn 1982): 184–213.

Peck, Robert M. "Recollections of Early Times in Kansas Territory from the Standpoint of a Regular Cavalryman." *Transactions of the Kansas State Historical Society* 8 (1904): 484–507.

Reeve, Frank D., ed. "Puritan and Apache: A Diary of Lt. H. M. Lazelle." *New Mexico Historical Review* 23 (October 1948): 269–301; 24 (January 1949): 12–53.

Richards, Oscar G. "Experiences of Oscar G. Richards in 1856–1865." *Transactions of the Kansas State Historical Society* 9 (1905–6): 545–48.

Roland, Charles P., and Richard C. Robbins, eds. "The Diary of Eliza (Mrs. Albert Sidney) Johnston: The Second Cavalry Comes to Texas." *Southwestern Historical Quarterly* 60 (1956–57): 463–500.

Scott, Charles A. "Charles A. Scott's Diary of the Utah Expedition, 1857–1861." Edited by Robert E. Stower and John M. Ellis. *Utah Historical Quarterly* 28 (April 1960): 155–76; 28 (October 1960): 389–402.

Sibley, Marilyn McAdams, ed. "Robert E. Lee to Albert Sydney Johnston, 1857." *Journal of Southern History* 29 (February 1963): 100–107.

Todd, John B. S. "The Harney Expedition against the Sioux: The Journal of Capt. John B. S. Todd." Edited by Ray H. Mattison. *Nebraska History* 43 (1962): 89–130.

"The Topeka Movement." *Collections of the Kansas State Historical Society* 8 (1913–14): 125–249.

Tracy, Capt. Albert. "Journal of Captain Albert Tracy." *Utah Historical Quarterly* 13 (January 1945): 1–119.

Viles, Jonas, ed. "Documents Illustrating the Troubles on the Border, 1858." *Missouri Historical Review* 1 (1906–7): 198–215, 293–306.

Newspapers

Chicago Daily Tribune, 1856–57.

Congressional Globe, 1856.

St. Louis Daily Missouri Democrat, 1856.

Atchison (Kans. Terr.) Freedom's Champion, 1856, 1858.

Lawrence (Kans. Terr.) Herald of Freedom, 1855–58.

New York Daily Times, 1852, 1854–55.

New York National Anti-Slavery Standard

San Francisco Daily Herald, 1851.

Santa Fe (N.M. Terr.) Weekly Gazette, 1853.

Atchison (Kans. Terr.) Squatter Sovereign, 1856.

SECONDARY SOURCES

Books

Adamson, Hans Christian. *Rebellion in Missouri: Nathaniel Lyon and His Army of the West.* New York: Chilton, 1961.

Ambrose, Stephen E. *Duty, Honor, Country: A History of West Point.* Baltimore, Md.: Johns Hopkins Press, 1966.

______. *Halleck: Lincoln's Chief of Staff.* Baton Rouge: Louisiana State University Press, 1962.

Appleton's Cyclopaedia of American Biography. Edited by James Grant Wilson and John Fiske. 7 vols. New York: D. Appleton, 1888.

Appleton's Cyclopaedia of American Biography. Rev. ed. Vol. 2. New York: Press Association Compilers, 1915.

Arrington, Leonard J. *Brigham Young: American Moses.* New York: Alfred A. Knopf, 1985.

______. *Great Basin Kingdom: An Economic History of the Latter-day Saints.* Cambridge, Mass.: Harvard University Press, 1958.

Arrington, Leonard J., and Davis Bitton. *The Mormon Experience: A History of the Latter-day Saints.* 1979. Reprint, New York: Vintage Books, 1980.

Bailey, Thomas A. *A Diplomatic History of the American People.* 10th ed. Englewood Cliffs, N.J.: Prentice-Hall, 1980.

Ball, Larry D., [Sr.]. *The United States Marshals of New Mexico and Arizona Territories, 1846–1912.* Albuquerque: University of New Mexico Press, 1978.

Banaway, Louis Morton. *New Mexico and the Sectional Controversy, 1846–1861.* New Mexico Historical Society Publications in History, vol. 12. Albuquerque: University of New Mexico Press, 1944.

Bancroft, Hubert Howe. *The History of California.* 7 vols. The Works of Hubert Howe Bancroft, vols. 18–24. San Francisco: History Company, 1884–90.

______. *History of the North Mexican States and Texas.* 2 vols. The Works of Hubert Howe Bancroft, vols. 15–16. San Francisco: History Company, 1889.

______. *History of Utah.* The Works of Hubert Howe Bancroft, vol. 26. San Francisco: History Company, 1889.

______. *Popular Tribunals.* 2 vols. The Works of Hubert Howe Bancroft, vols. 36–37. San Francisco: History Company, 1887.

Bauer, K. Jack. *The Mexican War, 1846–1848.* 1974. Reprint, Lincoln: University of Nebraska Press, 1992.

______. *Zachary Taylor: Soldier, Planter, Statesman of the Old Southwest.* Baton Rouge: Louisiana State University Press, 1985.

Bean, Walton. *California: An Interpretive History.* 2d ed. New York: McGraw-Hill, 1973.

Bender, Averam B. *The March of Empire: Frontier Defense in the Southwest, 1848–1860.* Lawrence: University of Kansas Press, 1952.

Billington, Ray Allen, and Martin Ridge. *Westward Expansion: A History of the American Frontier.* 5th ed. New York: Macmillan Publishing, 1982.

Bolaños-Geyer, Alejandro. *William Walker: The Gray-Eyed Man of Destiny.* 2 vols. Lake Saint Louis, Mo.: Privately Printed, 1989.

Bringhurst, Newell G. *Brigham Young and the Expanding American Frontier.* Edited by Oscar Handlin. Boston: Little, Brown, 1986.

Brooks, Juanita. *The Mountain Meadows Massacre.* 1950. Reprint, with a foreword and afterword by Jan Shipps, Norman: University of Oklahoma Press, 1991.

Brown, Charles Henry. *Agents of Manifest Destiny: The Lives and Times of the Filibusters.* Chapel Hill: University of North Carolina Press, 1979.

Brown, George W. *Reminiscences of Gov. R. J. Walker with the True Story of the Rescue of Kansas from Slavery.* Rockford, Ill.: Published by the author, 1902.

Brown, Richard Maxwell. *Strain of Violence: Historical Studies of American Violence and Vigilantism.* New York: Oxford University Press, 1975.

Buchanan, A. Russell. *David S. Terry of California: Dueling Judge.* San Marino, Calif.: Huntington Library, 1956.

Campbell, Stanley W. *The Slave Catchers: Enforcement of the Fugitive Slave Law, 1850–1860.* Chapel Hill: University of North Carolina Press, 1968.

Carpenter, John A. *Sword and Olive Branch: Oliver Otis Howard.* Pittsburgh: University of Pittsburgh Press, 1964.

Carter, Arthur B. *The Tarnished Cavalier: Major General Earl Van Dorn, C.S.A.* Knoxville: University of Tennessee Press, 1999.

Casdorph, Paul D. *Prince John Magruder: His Life and Campaigns.* New York: John D. Wiley and Sons, 1996.

Castel, Albert E. *General Sterling Price and the Civil War in the West.* Baton Rouge: Louisiana State University, 1968.

Catton, Bruce. *The Coming Fury.* The Centennial History of the Civil War. Vol. 1. Garden City, N.Y.: Doubleday, 1961.

Chalfant, William Y. *Cheyennes and Horse Soldiers: The 1857 Expedition and the Battle of Solomon's Fork.* With a foreword by Robert M. Utley. Norman: University of Oklahoma Press, 1989.

______. *Dangerous Passage: The Santa Fe Trail and the Mexican War.* With a foreword by Marc Simmons. Norman: University of Oklahoma Press, 1994.

______. *Without Quarter: The Wichita Expedition and the Fight on Crooked Creek.* With a foreword by Paul Andrew Hutton and illustrations by Roy Grinnell. Norman: University of Oklahoma Press, 1991.

Clarke, Dwight L. *Stephen Watts Kearny: Soldier of the West.* Norman: University of Oklahoma Press, 1961.

Coakley, Robert W. *The Role of Federal Military Forces in Domestic Disorders, 1789–1878.* Army Historical Series. Washington, D.C.: Center of Military History, United States Army, 1988.

Coffman, Edward F. *The Old Army: A Portrait of the Army in Peacetime, 1784–1898.* New York: Oxford University Press, 1986.

Cooper, Jerry M. *The Army and Civil Disorder: Federal Military Intervention in Labor Disputes, 1877–1900.* Contributions in Military History, no. 19. Westport, Conn.: Greenwood Press, 1980.

Corder, Eric. *Prelude to Civil War: Kansas-Missouri, 1854–61.* London: Collier-Macmillan, 1970.

Crackel, Theodore J. *Mr. Jefferson's Army: Political and Social Reform of the Military Establishment, 1801–1809.* New York: New York University Press, 1987.

Cramton, Louis C. *The Department of the Interior: Its History and Proper Function.* Washington, D.C., [1931?].

Creer, Leland Hargarve. *Utah and the Nation.* University of Washington Publications in the Social Sciences, vol. 7. Seattle: University of Washington Press, 1929.

Cunliffe, Marcus. *Soldiers and Civilians: The Martial Spirit in America, 1775–1865.* Boston: Little, Brown, 1968.

Cutrer, Thomas W. *Ben McCulloch and the Frontier Military Tradition.* Civil War America. Edited by Gary W. Gallagher. Chapel Hill: University of North Carolina, 1993.

Cutts, James M. *The Conquest of California and New Mexico by the Forces of the United States in the Years 1846 and 1847*. Philadelphia: Carey and Hart, 1847.

Cyclopaedia of American Biography. 10 vols. New York: Press Association Compilers, 1915.

Davis, William C. *Jefferson Davis: The Man and His Hour*. New York: Harper Collins, 1991.

Dawson, Joseph G. *Army Generals and Reconstruction: Louisiana, 1862–1877*. Baton Rouge: Louisiana State University Press, 1982.

DeVoto, Bernard. *The Year of Decision, 1846*. Boston: Little, Brown, 1943.

Donald, David. *Charles Sumner and the Coming of the Civil War*. New York: Alfred A. Knopf, 1960.

______. *Lincoln*. New York: Touchstone, 1995.

Duffus, R. L. *The Santa Fe Trail*. 1930. Reprint, Albuquerque: University of New Mexico Press, 1972.

Dupuy, R. Ernest. *The Compact History of the United States Army*. Rev. ed. New York: Hawthorn Books, 1961.

Eisenhower, John S. D. *Agent of Destiny: The Life and Times of Winfield Scott*. New York: Free Press, 1997.

Elliott, Charles Winslow. *Winfield Scott: The Soldier and the Man*. New York: Macmillan, 1937.

Fehrenbach, T. R. *Lone Star: A History of Texas and the Texans*. New York: Collier Books, 1968.

Frazer, Robert W. *Forts and Supplies: The Role of the Army in the Economy of the Southwest, 1846–1861*. Albuquerque: University of New Mexico Press, 1983.

______. *Forts of the West: Military Forts and Presidios and Posts Commonly Called Forts West of the Mississippi River to 1898*. Norman: University of Oklahoma Press, 1965.

Freeman, Douglas Southall. *R. E. Lee: A Biography*. 4 vols. New York: Scribner's, 1942–44.

Furniss, Norman F. *The Mormon Conflict, 1850–1859*. New Haven, Conn.: Yale University Press, 1960.

Ganaway, Loomis Morton. *New Mexico and the Sectional Controversy, 1846–1861*. Publications in History by the New Mexico Historical Society, vol. 12. Albuquerque: University of New Mexico Press, 1944.

Ganoe, William Addleman. *The History of the United States Army*. New York: D. Appleton-Century, 1942.

Gara, Larry. *The Presidency of Franklin Pierce*. Lawrence: University Press of Kansas, 1991.

Gates, Paul Wallace. *Fifty Million Acres: Conflicts over Kansas Land Policy, 1854–1890*. Ithaca, N.Y.: Cornell University Press, 1954.

Goetzmann, William H. *Army Exploration in the American West, 1803–1863*. 1959. Reprint, Lincoln: University of Nebraska Press, 1979.

Goodrich, Thomas. *War to the Knife: Bleeding Kansas, 1854–1861*. Mechanicsburg, Pa.: Stackpole Books, 1998.

Gordon, Leslie. *General George E. Pickett in Life and Legend*. Chapel Hill: University of North Carolina Press, 1998.

Govan, Gilbert Eaton, and James Weston Livingood. *A Different Valor: The Story of General Joseph E. Johnston, C.S.A.* New York: Bobbs-Merrill, 1956.

Griswold del Castillo, Richard. *The Treaty of Guadalupe Hidalgo: A Legacy of Conflict.* Norman: University of Oklahoma Press, 1990.

Grivas, Theodore. *Military Governments in California, 1846–1850 with a Chapter on Their Prior Use in Louisiana, Florida and New Mexico.* Glendale, Calif.: Arthur H. Clark, 1963.

Grossman, Lt. Col. Dave. *On Killing: The Psychological Costs of Learning to Kill in War and Society.* Boston: Little, Brown, 1995.

Hamilton, Holmon. *Zachary Taylor.* 2 vols. Indianapolis: Bobbs-Merrill, 1951.

Harlow, Neal. *California Conquered: War and Peace on the Pacific, 1846–1850.* Berkeley: University of California, 1982.

Hartje, Robert G. *Van Dorn: The Life and Times of a Confederate General.* Nashville: Vanderbilt University Press, 1967.

Hassler, William Woods. *A. P. Hill: Lee's Forgotten General.* Richmond, Va.: Garrett and Massie, 1962.

Higginbotham, Don. *The War of American Independence: Military Attitudes, Policies, and Practices.* Wars of the United States Series. New York: Macmillan Publishing, 1971.

Hollon, W. Eugene. *Beyond the Cross Timbers: The Travels of Randolph B. Marcy, 1812–1887.* Norman: University of Oklahoma Press, 1955.

Hoopes, Alban W. *Indian Affairs and Their Administration with Special Reference to the Far West, 1849–60.* Philadelphia: University of Pennsylvania Press, 1932.

Hunt, Aurora. *Major General James Henry Carleton, 1814–1873: Western Frontier Dragoon.* Glendale, Calif.: Arthur H. Clark, 1958.

Hutton, Paul Andrew. *Phil Sheridan and His Army.* Lincoln: University of Nebraska Press, 1985.

Hutton, Paul Andrew, ed. *Soldiers West: Biographies from the Military Frontier.* With an introduction by Robert M. Utley. Lincoln: University of Nebraska Press, 1987.

Isley, Bliss, and W. M. Richards. *Four Centuries in Kansas: Unit Studies.* Wichita, Kans.: McCormick-Mathers, 1936.

Jensen, Joan M. *Army Surveillance in America, 1775–1980.* New Haven, Conn.: Yale University Press, 1991.

Johannsen, Robert W. *Frontier Politics on the Eve of the Civil War.* Seattle: University of Washington Press, 1955.

Johnson, Samuel A. *The Battle Cry of Freedom: The New England Emigrant Aid Company in the Kansas Crusade.* Lawrence: University Press of Kansas, 1954.

Johnson, Timothy D. *Winfield Scott: The Quest for Military Glory.* Lawrence: University Press of Kansas, 1998.

Johnston, William Preston. *The Life of Albert Sidney Johnston.* New York: Appleton, 1878.

Jordan, David M. *Winfield Scott Hancock: A Soldier's Life.* Bloomington: Indiana University Press, 1988.

Josephy, Alvin M., Jr. *The Civil War in the American West.* New York: Alfred A. Knopf, 1991.

Keleher, William A. *Turmoil in New Mexico, 1846–1868.* 1951. Reprint, with an introduction by Lawrence R. Murphy, Albuquerque: University of New Mexico Press, 1982.

King, James T. *War Eagle: A Life of General Eugene A. Carr.* Lincoln: University of Nebraska Press, 1963.

Klein, Maury. *Edward Porter Alexander.* Athens: University of Georgia Press, 1971.

Klein, Philip Shriver. *President James Buchanan: A Biography.* University Park: Pennsylvania State University Press, 1962.

Kohn, Richard H. *Eagle and Sword: The Beginnings of the Military Establishment in America.* New York: Free Press, 1975.

Lamar, Howard R. *The Far Southwest, 1846–1912: A Territorial History.* New York: W. W. Norton, 1970.

Lamar, Howard R., ed. *The Reader's Encyclopedia of the American West.* New York: Harper and Row Publishers, 1977.

Larson, Robert L. *New Mexico's Quest for Statehood, 1846–1912.* Albuquerque: University of New Mexico Press, 1968.

Lavender, David. *Bent's Fort.* 1954. Reprint, Lincoln: University of Nebraska Press, 1972.

Leach, Douglas E. *Arms for Empire: A Military History of the British Colonies in North America, 1607–1763.* The Wars of the United States. New York: Macmillan Publishing, 1973.

Lewis, Lloyd. *Captain Sam Grant.* Boston: Little, Brown, 1950.

Longacre, Edward G. *Pickett, Leader of the Charge: A Biography of General George E. Pickett.* Shippensburg, Pa.: White Mane Publishing, 1995.

Lotchin, Roger W. *San Francisco, 1846–1856: From Hamlet to City.* New York: Oxford University Press, 1974.

Martin, James Kirby, and Mark Edward Lender. *A Respectable Army: The Military Origins of the Republic, 1763–1789.* American History Series. Arlington Heights, Ill.: Harlan Davidson, 1982.

McElroy, John. *The Struggle for Missouri.* Washington, D.C.: National Tribune, 1909.

McFeely, William S. *Yankee Stepfather: General O. O. Howard and the Freedmen.* New York: W. W. Norton, 1968.

McMurray, Richard M. *John Bell Hood and the War for Southern Independence.* Lexington: University of Kentucky Press, 1982.

McNitt, Frank. *Navajo Wars: Military Campaigns, Slave Raids, and Reprisals.* 1972. Reprint, with an introduction by Robert M. Utley, Albuquerque: University of New Mexico, 1990.

McPherson, James B. *Battle Cry of Freedom: The Civil War Era.* The Oxford History of the United States. Edited by C. Vann Woodward. New York: Oxford University Press, 1988.

McReynolds, Edwin C. *Missouri: The History of a Crossroads State.* Norman: University of Oklahoma, 1962.

Merk, Frederick. *Manifest Destiny and Mission in American History: A Reinterpretation.* New York: Vintage Books, 1963.

Miller, Darlis A. *Soldiers and Settlers: Military Supply in the Southwest, 1861–1885.* Albuquerque: University of New Mexico, 1989.

Millett, Allan R., and Peter Maslowski. *For the Common Defense: A Military History of the United States of America.* New York: Free Press, 1984.

Millis, Walter. *Arms and Men: A Study of American Military History.* New York: G. P. Putnam's Sons, 1956.

Monaghan, Jay. *Civil War on the Western Border, 1854–1865.* Boston: Little, Brown, 1955.

Moorman, Donald R. *Camp Floyd and the Mormons: The Utah War.* Completed and edited by Gene A. Sessions. Salt Lake City: University of Utah Press, 1992.

Morris, Roy, Jr. *Sheridan: The Life and Wars of General Phil Sheridan.* 1992. Reprint, New York: Vintage Books, 1993.

Morrison, James L. *"The Best School in the World": West Point, the Pre-Civil War Years, 1833–1866.* Kent, Ohio: Kent State University Press, 1986.

Morrison, Michael A. *Slavery and the American West: The Eclipse of Manifest Destiny and the Civil War.* Chapel Hill: University of North Carolina Press, 1997.

Myers, John Myers. *San Francisco's Reign of Terror.* Garden City, N.J.: Doubleday, 1966.

National Park Service. *Soldier and Brave: Historical Places Associated with Indian Affairs and Indian Wars in the Trans-Mississippi West.* New Edition. National Survey of Historic Sites and Buildings, vol. 12. Edited by Robert G. Ferris. Washington, D.C.: United States Department of the Interior, National Park Service, 1971.

Nevins, Alan. *Frémont: Pathmarker of the West.* New York: D. Appleton-Century, 1939.

Nichols, Alice. *Bleeding Kansas.* New York: Oxford University Press, 1954.

Nichols, Roy Franklin. *Franklin Pierce: Young Hickory of the Granite Hills.* Philadelphia: University of Pennsylvania Press, 1931.

Norris, L. David, James C. Milligan, and Odie B. Faulk. *William H. Emory, Soldier-Scientist.* Tucson: University of Arizona Press, 1998.

Oates, Stephen B. *With Malice toward None: The Life of Abraham Lincoln.* New York: New American Library, 1977.

Oliva, Leo E. *Soldiers on the Santa Fe Trail.* Norman: University of Oklahoma Press, 1967.

Parks, Joseph Howard. *General Edmund Kirby Smith, C.S.A.* Baton Rouge: Louisiana State University Press, 1954.

Parrish, William E. *Turbulent Partnership: Missouri and the Union, 1861–1865.* Columbia: University of Missouri Press, 1965.

Pfanz, Donald C. *Richard S. Ewell: A Soldier's Life.* Civil War America. Edited by Gary W. Gallagher. Chapel Hill: University of North Carolina Press, 1998.

Phillips, Christopher. *Damned Yankee: The Life of General Nathaniel Lyon.* Columbia: University of Missouri Press, 1990.

Potter, David M. *The Impending Crisis, 1848–1861.* Completed and edited by Don E. Fehrenbacher. The New American Nation Series. Edited by Henry Steele Commager and Richard B. Morris. New York: Harper and Row, 1976.

Prentis, Noel. *History of Kansas.* Edited by Henrietta V. Race. Topeka, Kans.: Caroline Prentis, 1909.

Prucha, Francis Paul. *Broadax and Bayonet: The Role of the United States Army in the Development of the Northwest, 1815–1860.* 1953. Reprint, Lincoln: University of Nebraska Press, 1967.

______. *The Great Father: The United States and the American Indians.* 2 vols. Lincoln: University of Nebraska Press, 1984.

______. *The Sword of the Republic: The United States Army on the Frontier, 1783–1846.* Wars of the United States Series. 1969. Reprint, Bloomington: Indiana University Press, 1977.

Quinn, Arthur. *The Rivals: William Gwin, David Broderick, and the Birth of California.* New York: Crown Publishers, 1994.

Rawley, James A. *Race and Politics: "Bleeding Kansas" and the Coming of the Civil War.* Philadelphia: J. B. Lippincott, 1969.

Reavis, L. U. *The Life and Military Services of Gen. William Selby Harney.* Saint Louis, Mo.: Bryan, Brand Publishers, 1878.

Rickey, Don, Jr. *Forty Miles a Day on Beans and Hay: The Enlisted Soldier Fighting the Indian Wars.* Norman: University of Oklahoma Press, 1963.

Rister, Carl Coke. *Robert E. Lee in Texas.* Norman: University of Oklahoma Press, 1946.

Roberts, Brigham H. *The Mormon Battalion: Its History and Achievements.* Salt Lake City: n.p., 1919.

Roland, Charles P. *Albert Sidney Johnston: Soldier of Three Republics.* Austin: University of Texas Press, 1964.

Royster, Charles. *A Revolutionary People at War: The Continental Army and American Character, 1775–1783.* Chapel Hill: University of North Carolina Press, 1979.

Sandburg, Carl. *Abraham Lincoln: The War Years.* 4 vols. New York: Harcourt, Brace, 1939.

Sanger, Donald Bridgman, and Thomas Robson Hay. *James Longstreet.* Baton Rouge: Louisiana State University Press, 1952.

Satz, Ronald. *American Indian Policy in the Jacksonian Era.* Lincoln: University of Nebraska Press, 1975.

Schlicke, Carl P. *General George Wright: Guardian of the Pacific Coast.* Norman: University of Oklahoma Press, 1988.

Schutz, Wallace J., and Walter N. Trenerry. *Abandoned by Lincoln: A Military Biography of General John Pope.* Urbana: University of Illinois Press, 1990.

Sears, Stephen W. *George B. McClellan: The Young Napoleon.* New York: Ticknor and Fields, 1988.

Sefton, James E. *United States Army and Reconstruction, 1865–1877.* Baton Rouge: Louisiana State University Press, 1967.

Senkewicz, Robert M. *Vigilantes in Gold Rush San Francisco.* Stanford, Calif.: Stanford University Press, 1985.

Shalhope, Robert E. *Sterling Price: Portrait of a Southerner.* Columbia: University of Missouri Press, 1971.

Shenton, James P. *Robert John Walker: A Politician from Jackson to Lincoln.* New York: Columbia University Press, 1961.

Sifikas, Stewart. *Who Was Who in the Civil War.* New York: Facts on File Publications, 1988.

Skelton, William B. *An American Profession of Arms: The Army Officer Corps, 1784–1861.* Lawrence: University Press of Kansas, 1992.

Smith, Arthur D. Howden. *Old Fuss and Feathers: Life and Exploits of Lieutenant General Winfield Scott.* New York: Greystone Press, 1937.

Smith, Elbert B. *The Presidencies of Zachary Taylor & Millard Fillmore.* Lawrence: University Press of Kansas, 1988.

______. *The Presidency of James Buchanan.* Lawrence: University Press of Kansas, 1975.

Smith, Justin F. *The War with Mexico.* 2 vols. New York: Macmillan, 1919.

Smith, William Ernest. *The Francis Preston Blair Family in Politics.* 2 vols. New York: Macmillan, 1933.

Socolofsky, Homer E. *Kansas Governors.* Lawrence: University Press of Kansas, 1990.

Stampp, Kenneth M. *America in 1857: A Nation on the Brink.* New York: Oxford University Press, 1990.

Stanley, F. [Crocchiola, Stanley Francis]. *E. V. Sumner, Major General, United States Army (1797–1863).* Borger, Tex.: Jim Hess Printers, 1969.

Steffen, Randy. *The Horse Soldier, 1776–1943: The United States Cavalryman: His Uniforms, Arms, Accoutrements, and Equipments.* 3 vols. Norman: University Oklahoma Press, 1978.

Stegmaier, Mark Joseph. *Texas, New Mexico, and the Compromise of 1850: Boundary Dispute and Sectional Crisis.* Kent, Ohio: Kent State University Press, 1996.

Stout, Joseph A. *The Liberators: Filibustering Expeditions into Mexico, 1848–1862.* Los Angeles: Westernlore Press, 1973.

Strobridge, William F. *Regulars in the Redwoods: The U.S. Army in Northern California, 1852–1861.* Frontier Military Series, no. 17. Spokane, Wash.: Arthur H. Clark, 1994.

Strode, Hudson. *Jefferson Davis: American Patriot, 1808–1861.* 3 vols. New York: Harcourt, Brace, 1955.

Sweeny, William M. *A Biographical Memoir of Thomas William Sweeny, Brigadier-General, United States Army.* N.p., 1907.

Symonds, Craig L. *Joseph E. Johnston: A Civil War Biography.* New York: W. W. Norton, 1992.

Tate, Michael L. *The Frontier Army in the Settlement of the West.* Norman: University of Oklahoma Press, 1999.

Thian, Raphael P. *Legislative History of the General Staff of the Army of the United States from 1775 to 1901.* Washington, [D.C.]: Government Printing Office, 1901.

______. *Notes Illustrating the Military Geography of the United States, 1813–1880.* 1911. Reprint, edited by John M. Carroll with a foreword by Robert M. Utley, Austin: University of Texas, 1979.

Thomas, Emory M. *Bold Dragoon: The Life of J. E. B. Stuart.* New York: Harper and Row, 1986.

______. *Robert E. Lee: A Biography.* New York: W. W. Norton, 1995.

Thomas, Lately. *Between Two Empires: The Life Story of California's First Senator, William McKendree Gwin.* Boston: Houghton Mifflin, 1969.

Thompson, Gerald. *Edward F. Beale and the American West.* Albuquerque: University of New Mexico Press, 1983.

Thompson, Jerry. *Henry Hopkins Sibley: Confederate General of the West.* With a foreword by Frank E. Vandiver. Natchitoches, La.: Northwestern State University Press, 1987.

Thrapp, Dan L. *Encyclopedia of Frontier Biography.* 3 vols. Glendale, Calif.: Arthur H. Clark, 1988.

Tinkcom, Harry Marlin. *John White Geary: Soldier-Statesman, 1819–1873.* Philadelphia: University of Pennsylvania Press, 1940.

Trennert, Robert A., Jr. *Alternative to Extinction: Federal Indian Policy and the*

Beginnings of the Reservation System, 1846–51. Philadelphia: Temple University Press, 1975.

Tucker, Glenn. *Hancock the Superb.* Indianapolis: Bobbs-Merrill Company, 1960.

Twitchell, Ralph Emerson. *The History of the Military Occupation of the Territory of New Mexico from 1846 to 1851 by the Government of the United States, Together with Biographical Sketches of Men Prominent in the Conduct of the Government during that Period.* Denver, Colo.: Smith-Brooks, 1909.

Unruh, John D., Jr. *The Plains Across: The Overland Emigrants and the Trans-Mississippi West, 1840–60.* Urbana: University of Illinois Press, 1979.

Utley, Robert M. *Frontier Regulars: The United States Army and the Indian, 1866–1891.* Wars of the United States Series. 1973. Reprint, Bloomington: Indiana University Press, 1977.

______. *Frontiersmen in Blue: The United States Army and the Indian, 1848–1865.* Wars of the United States Series. New York: Macmillan Publishing, 1967.

______. *The Indian Frontier of the American West, 1848–1890.* Histories of the American Frontier. Edited by Ray Allen Billington, et al. Albuquerque: University of New Mexico Press, 1984.

Victor, Orville J. *History of American Conspiracies.* N.p., 1863.

Wakelyn, Jon L. *Biographical Dictionary of the Confederacy.* Frank E. Vandiver, advisory editor. Westport, Conn.: Greenwood Press, 1977.

Warner, Ezra J. *Generals in Blue: Lives of the Union Commanders.* Baton Rouge: Louisiana State University Press, 1964.

______. *Generals in Gray: Lives of the Confederate Commanders.* Baton Rouge: Louisiana State University Press, 1959.

Weber, David J. *Richard H. Kern: Expeditionary Artist in the Far Southwest, 1848–1853.* Albuquerque: Published for the Amon Carter Museum by the University of New Mexico Press, 1985.

Weems, John Edward. *To Conquer a Peace: The War between the United States and Mexico.* College Station: Texas A&M University Press, 1974.

Weigley, Russell F. *The American Way of War: A History of United States Military Strategy and Policy.* Wars of the United States Series. Bloomington: Indiana University Press, 1973.

______. *History of the United States Army.* New York: Macmillan, 1967.

Wessels, William L. *Born to Be a Soldier: The Military Career of William Wing Loring of St. Augustine, Florida.* Fort Worth: Texas Christian University Press, 1971.

Williams, David R. *David C. Broderick: A Political Portrait.* San Marino, Calif.: Huntington Library, 1969.

Williams, T. Harry. *Lincoln and His Generals.* New York: Alfred A. Knopf, 1952.

Winders, Richard Bruce. *Mr. Polk's Army: The American Military Experience in the Mexican War.* College Station: Texas A&M Press, 1997.

Woodman, Lyman L. *Cortina: Rogue of the Rio Grande.* San Antonio, Tex.: Naylor, 1950.

Wooster, Robert. *The Military and United States Indian Policy, 1865–1903.* Yale Western Americana Series, no. 34. Edited by Archibald Hanna Jr., Howard Roberts Lamar, and Robert M. Utley. New Haven, Conn.: Yale University Press, 1988.

______. *Soldiers, Sutlers, and Settlers: Garrison Life on the Texas Frontier.* The Clayton Wheat William Texas Life Series, no. 2. College Station: Texas A&M University Press, 1987.

Young, Otis E. *The West of Philip St. George Cooke.* Glendale, Calif.: Arthur H. Clark, 1955.

Articles

Alexander, Thomas G., and Lenoard J. Arrington. "Camp in the Sagebrush: Camp Floyd, Utah, 1858–1861." *Utah Historical Quarterly* 34 (winter 1966): 3–21.

Ball, [Larry] Durwood, Jr. "Fort Craig, New Mexico, and the Southwest Indian Wars, 1854–1884." *New Mexico Historical Review* 73 (April 1998): 153–73.

Bender, A. B. "Frontier Defense in the Territory of New Mexico, 1846–1853." *New Mexico Historical Review* 9 (July/October 1934): 249–72, 345–74.

______. "Military Posts in the Southwest, 1848–1860." *New Mexico Historical Review* 16 (April 1941): 125–47.

______. "The Texas Frontier, 1848–1861, II." *Southwestern Historical Quarterly* 38 (October 1934): 135–48.

Brown, Russell K. "An Old Woman with a Broomstick: General David E. Twiggs and the U.S. Surrender in Texas." *Military Affairs* 48 (April 1984): 57–61.

Cannon, M. Hamlin. "Winfield Scott and the Utah Expedition." *Military Affairs* 5 (1941): 208–11.

Chandler, Robert J. "The Velvet Glove: The Army during the Secession Crisis in the California, 1860–1861." *Journal of the West* 20 (October 1981): 35–42.

Clow, Richmond L. "Mad Bear: William S. Harney and the Sioux Expedition of 1855–1856." *Nebraska History* 6 (1980): 133–53.

Covington, James W. "The Camp Jackson Affair." *Missouri Historical Review* 55 (April 1961): 197–212.

Edrington, Thomas S. "Military Influence on the Texas-New Mexico Boundary Settlement." *New Mexico Historical Review* 59 (October 1984): 371–93.

Fish, Andrew. "The Last Phase of the Oregon Boundary Question: The Struggle for San Juan Island." *Quarterly of the Oregon Historical Society* 22 (September 1921): 161–224.

Fornell, E. W. "Texans and Filibusters in the 1850s." *Southwestern Historical Quarterly* 59 (April 1956): 411–28.

Gibbs, Josiah F. "Gunnison Massacre—1853." *Utah Historical Quarterly* 1 (July 1928): 67–75.

Gilbert, Benjamin F. "The Mythical Johnston Conspiracy." *California Historical Society Quarterly* 28 (June 1949): 165–73.

Goldfinch, Charles W. "Juan N. Cortina, 1824–1892: A Re-Appraisal." In *Juan N. Cortina: Two Interpretations,* by Charles W. Goldfinch and Jose Tomas Canales. The Mexican American. New York: Arno Press, 1974.

Gough, Barry M. "British Policy in the San Juan Boundary Dispute, 1854–72." *Pacific Northwest Quarterly* 62 (April 1971): 59–68.

Hinton, Wayne K. "Millard Fillmore, Utah's Friend in the White House." *Utah Historical Quarterly* 48 (spring 1980): 112–28.

Kajencki, Francis C. "Charles Radziminski and the United States Boundary Survey." *New Mexico Historical Review* 63 (July 1988): 211–40.
Laurie, Clayton D. "Filling the Breach: Military Aid to the Civil Power in the Trans-Mississippi West." *Western Historical Quarterly* 25 (summer 1994): 149–62.
LeCheminant, Wilford Hill. "A Crisis Averted? General Harney and the Change in Command of the Utah Expedition." *Utah Historical Quarterly* 51 (winter 1983): 30–45.
Long, John W., Jr. "The Origin and Development of the San Juan Island Water Boundary Controversy." *Pacific Northwest Quarterly* 43 (July 1952): 187–213.
Lyon, William H. "Claiborne Fox Jackson and the Secession Crisis in Missouri." *Missouri Historical Review* 58 (July 1964): 422–41.
MacKinnon, William P. "125 Years of Conspiracy Theories: Origins of the Utah Expedition of 1857–58." *Utah Historical Quarterly* 52 (summer 1984): 212–30.
______. "The Buchanan Spoils System and the Utah Expedition: Careers of W. M. F. Magraw and John M. Hockaday." *Utah Historical Quarterly* 31 (spring 1963): 127–50.
May, Robert E. "Young American Males and Filibustering in the Age of Manifest Destiny: The United States Army as a Cultural Mirror." *Journal of American History* 78 (December 1991): 857–86.
Metcalf, Helen B. "The California French Filibusters in Sonora." *California Historical Society Quarterly* 18 (March 1939): 3–21.
Morgan, Dale L. "The Administration of Indian Affairs in Utah, 1851–1858." *Pacific Historical Review* 17 (November 1948): 383–409.
Morrison, James L., Jr. "Educating the Civil War Generals: West Point, 1833–1861." *Military Affairs* 38 (October 1974): 108–11.
______. "The Struggle between Sectionalism and Nationalism at Ante-Bellum West Point, 1830–1861." *Civil War History* 19 (1973): 138–48.
Nasatir, A. P. "Gillaume Patrice Dillon." *California Historical Society Quarterly* 35 (December 1956): 309–24.
"Nathaniel Lyon." *Transactions of the Kansas State Historical Society* 7 (1901–2): 418–19.
Rippy, J. Fred. "Border Troubles along the Rio Grande, 1848–1860." *Southwest Historical Quarterly* 23 (October 1919): 91–111.
Rodenbough, Theophilus Francis. "The Fourth Cavalry." *Journal of the Military Science Institute* (July 1895): 202.
Rolle, Andrew F. "California Filibustering and the Hawaiian Kingdom." *Pacific Historical Review* 19 (August 1950): 251–63.
Shearer, Ernest C. "The Callahan Expedition, 1855." *Southwestern Historical Quarterly* 54 (April 1951): 430–51.
______. "The Carvajal Disturbances." *Southwest Historical Quarterly* 55 (October 1951): 201–30.
Skelton, William B. "Officers and Politicians: The Origin of Army Politics Before the Civil War." *Armed Forces and Society* 6 (fall 1979): 22–48.
Tunem, Alfred. "The Dispute over the San Juan Water Boundary." *Washington Historical Quarterly* 23 (January/April/July/October 1932): 38–46, 133–37, 196–204, 286–300.
Tyler, Ronnie C. "The Callahan Expedition of 1855: Indians or Negroes?" *Southwest Historical Quarterly* 70 (April 1967): 574–85.

Wooster, Robert. "Military Strategy in the Southwest, 1848–1860." *Military History of Texas and the Southwest* 15, no. 2 (1979): 5–15.

Wyllys, Rufus K. "The French in California and Sonora." *Pacific Historical Review* 1 (1932): 337–59.

———. "Henry A. Crabb—a Tragedy of the Sonora Frontier." *Pacific Historical Review* 9 (June 1940): 183–94.

———. "The Republic of Lower California, 1853–1854." *Pacific Historical Review* 2, no. 2 (1933): 194–213.

Theses, Dissertations, and Unpublished Papers

Adams, George Rollie. "General William Selby Harney: Frontier Soldier, 1800–1889." Ph.D. diss., University of Arizona, 1983.

Ball, Larry D[urwood], Jr. "'Petty Embroilments of Armed Constabulary Duty: The United States Army in Law Enforcement during the Kansas-Missouri Border Wars, 1856–1860." Master's thesis, University of New Mexico, 1984.

———. "The United States Army on the Interwar Frontier, 1848–1861." Ph.D. diss., University of New Mexico, 1994.

Ball, Larry D., [Sr]. "Military Posses: The United States Army in Civil Law Enforcement on the Frontier." Unpublished paper in possession of the author, Arkansas State University, Jonesboro.

Hinton, Harwood Perry. "The Military Career of John Ellis Wool, 1812–1863." Ph.D. diss., University of Wisconsin, 1960.

Long, William Wallace. "A Biography of Major General Edwin Vose Sumner, U.S.A, 1797–1863." Ph.D. diss., University of New Mexico, 1971.

INDEX

Page numbers in italics refer to photographs